Comrade Criminal

Also by the Author

Uncommon Kingdom: The British in the 80s

Comrade Criminal

Russia's New Mafiya

Stephen Handelman

Yale University Press   New Haven and London

Designed by Sonia L. Scanlon.
Set in Times Roman type by Tseng Information
Systems, Inc., Durham, North Carolina.
Printed in the United States of America by
Vail-Ballon Press, Binghamton, New York.

A catalogue record for this book is available from the
British Library.

The paper in this book meets the guidelines for
permanence and durability of the Committee on
Production Guidelines for Book Longevity of the
Council on Library Resources.

10 9 8 7 6 5 4 3 2

Library of Congress Cataloging-in-Publication Data
Handelman, Stephen,
Comrade criminal : Russia's new mafiya /
Stephen Handelman.
p. cm.
Includes bibliographical references and index.
ISBN 0-300-06352-0 (alk. paper)
1. Organized crime—Russia (Federation)
2. Political corruption—Russia (Federation)
3. Russia (Federation)—Social conditions.
4. Post-communism—Russia (Federation)
5. Russia (Federation)—Politics and
government—1991–   I. Title.
HV6453.R8H36   1995
364.1'06'0947—dc20   95-2378
                                   CIP

In loving memory of my parents,
Phyllis Handelman and Theodore Handelman

Contents

III Crime Fighting in Utopia

Acknowledgments

This book could never have been written without the help of Toby Latta, who served as my principal researcher and collaborator in Moscow. His judgments on the murky worlds of Russian politics, business, and crime, and his keen eye for detail, provided the best foundations an author could hope for. I am doubly proud to call him a friend.

No work on post-Communist Russia—and particularly no examination of a subject as mutable as the Russian mafiya—can hope to be definitive. But whatever lasting value this book may have I owe to the people across the former Soviet Union who shared with me their fears and hopes. Many cannot be named. Among those who can, I want to single out for gratitude Boris Aliabyev, Igor Baranovsky, Yuri Lebedev, Sergei Molodtsov, Varvara Shavrova, Allan Martinson of Tallinn, and Andrejs Veisbergs of Riga. I also owe a debt of thanks to those members of Russian law enforcement agencies whose dedication to their jobs and confidence in their country's future inspired me to write and to complete this work. They are Gen. Aleksandr Gurov and Col. Anatoli Zhoglo, of the Russian Ministry of Internal Affairs; Col. Vladimir Koltsov, of the Yekaterinburg militia; Capt. Yuri Nikishin, of the Moscow police's organized-crime squad; and Vladimir Kalinichenko, formerly of the Russian Investigative Commission. Throughout my years in the Soviet Union, Natasha Kazina and Nikolai Milchikov were priceless guides and assistants.

A number of people performed service beyond the call of duty in reading and commenting on all or portions of the manuscript. Any virtues of this work belong to them: Rupert Cornwell, Carol Goar, Alexander Motyl, Paul Quinn-Judge, Jack Simpson, and Janet and Mitchell Weingarden. Juan Gonzalez provided invaluable help on the connection between Russian and Colombian cartels. I owe a special debt to Sergei Grigoriev for his cheerful and microscopic examination of Russian phrases and political themes. I would also like to thank the staff of the Harriman Institute at Columbia University, New York; and, at *The Toronto Star,* John Honderich, editor-in-chief and publisher, and

Paul Warnick, foreign editor, for granting—and then extending—my leave to complete the book. My father, Theodore Handelman, who did not live to see the final product, devoted to its early stages a writer's attention and a father's love, which I can never repay.

I have appreciated the enthusiasm and support provided by Ted Macri, my New York agent. And, at Yale University Press, I am especially grateful to John Ryden, director, and John Covell, senior editor, for their conviction that this story needed to be brought to an American audience. Richard Miller provided expert and invaluable editing.

Finally, without the wisdom, sharp editor's eye, and companionship provided by my wife, Susan—not only during the writing of this book but over five-and-a-half long years in Moscow—the author, as he knows better than anyone else, would never have reached the final paragraph.

Introduction
Horse without a Bridle

We are the heirs of a great civilization, and its rebirth into a new, modern and dignified life now depends on one and all.
—Soviet president Mikhail Gorbachev, in his resignation speech, December 25, 1991

Inspector Vladimir Kalinichenko, legendary crime fighter of the old Soviet Union, stood on a sidewalk in midtown Manhattan and stared. He stared at the men and women hurrying by him as if he weren't there. He stared at the elegant glass doors of the building in front of him. And then he stared at his American hosts, who had just told him that the building had been purchased by a senior politician in the government of the Russian Federation. The Americans waited for his reaction.

"You might call this," one said, with deadpan gravity, "the start of the Communist takeover of New York."

Kalinichenko didn't laugh. He looked again at the building. There was an opulent restaurant and a trade exhibition center on the ground level. The image of his own peeling quarters in Moscow flashed before his eyes. Deciding that the Americans would never understand the irony, he finally turned away.

It was early autumn, 1991, a few weeks after the collapse of the Moscow coup and the destruction of the Soviet Communist Party—and less than four months before the Soviet Union crumbled. Kalinichenko was on a mission for the Russian government to solve what would become one of the greatest mysteries surrounding the end of the Cold War: the location of the Communist fortune—millions, possibly billions, of dollars squirreled away in Europe and the United States by the Soviet leadership. The government was serious enough about the enterprise to hire a respected New York security agency to assist Kalinichenko in his inquiries. He was beginning to wonder, however, whether Americans really understood what they were dealing with.

Diminutive and pot-bellied, with a smiling pink face set off by wisps of white hair, Kalinichenko gave the impression of being someone's kindly uncle. But his exploits made him one of the Soviet Union's most famous detectives. As a senior inspector in the Office of the USSR Chief Prosecutor, he led the team that smashed the influence-peddling rings operated by the Party barons of southern Russia and Central Asia in the 1970s and 1980s. He accumulated a chestful of socialist medals while managing to elude the corrupt machine that operated at the heart of the Soviet state—a machine so wary of his skills that having failed to bribe him, it once tried to murder him.

Yet even for a man of talent, the mission to New York was a challenge. It was as if Arkady Renko, the fictional Soviet detective hero of *Gorky Park,* were suddenly thrust into the West with an expense account and an interpreter, and then asked to establish the crime rather than catch the criminal.[1]

He made a cursory check with the Soviet consulate in New York, but as he expected, they could not confirm what the Americans had told him. Kept busy following up other leads to the Communist money, he let the matter slide until he returned to Moscow, where he found evidence that several million dollars were transferred earlier that year from the Soviet State Bank to New York. But that was as far as he was able to get. Why probe further? he was told by his government superiors. You can't bring back a building. And there was no law in the Soviet Union against buying New York real estate. Kalinichenko's other investigations began to receive a similar brushoff. Within six months, the epic search for the Communist millions seemed to be running out of steam.[2]

It wasn't long before Kalinichenko left government service to take a job as a legal adviser to a private Moscow bank. He has since been promoted to vice-president.

"I was no fool," he told me in his spacious new office in Moscow in November, 1992, as he finished recounting the story of his trip to New York. "There were plenty of cases in which I could trace the money: I had names, bank account numbers. But not a single criminal proceeding was started as a result of my investigations. I decided fighting corruption in our country is like fighting windmills."

By then, most of Kalinichenko's compatriots had come to the same conclusion.

Less than three years after it began, the second great Russian revolution of this century is awash in corruption, opportunism, and crime. The government not only has failed to pursue the evidence of its predecessors' venality; it has been unable to hold in check the greed of its own ministers. Scandal has became ordinary in the New Russia.

Newspaper headlines chart Russia's descent from superpower pride to third-world embarrassment. Ministry offices sell contracts. Stolen-weapons rings are discovered in army barracks, and uranium thieves are caught in the military-industrial complex. Millions of dollars' worth of timber, oil, gold, and drugs are smuggled out of Russia and the Commonwealth of Independent States every month. Since Russia is now a comparatively free economy, government does not have a monopoly on crime. In a murderous parody of free-market competition, mobsters fight open battles over territory in the streets of Russian cities, leaving their victims riddled with bullets in Chicago-style gangland assassinations. Criminal cartels, believed by police to control as much as 40 percent of Russia's wealth, infiltrate stock exchanges and the real estate market. Gangsters not only open bank accounts; they open banks.

By 1992, crime had become the first post-Soviet growth industry. The Russian public prosecutor reported a 33 percent increase in crime between 1991 and 1992. Murder and aggravated assault accounted for more than half of the 2.7 million crimes recorded. The Soviet police state had come to a nightmarish end in the emergency rooms of some Moscow hospitals, which filled every weekend with victims of bullet and knife wounds. In 1993, the murder rate rose 27 percent, and crimes committed with firearms climbed by 250 percent. In a country where the confiscation of a revolver from a private citizen had once been a singular event, these figures were unnerving.[3]

As the hopes engendered by the dismantling of Communism turned sour, *demokratiya* practically disappeared from everyday Russian usage. Instead of democracy, the new word sprinkled through conversations was *bespredel*—literally, "without limits"—which captured Russians' sense of living in a frontier where all the comforting signposts were missing.

"Some of our people seem to understand democracy as being able to do whatever they want," Aslambek Aslakhanov, the head of what was then the Supreme Soviet Parliamentary Committee on Law and Order, complained to me in the summer of 1992, before my meeting with Kalinichenko. "As a result, *bespredel* has completely overtaken us. Now, we have wild democracy, an epidemic of seizing everything in sight, of getting rich at any cost."[4]

When Mikhail Gorbachev appeared on television on Christmas Day, 1991, to announce his resignation as president of the Soviet Union, no one expected change to happen easily or quickly. But the weight of international opinion rallied behind Gorbachev's conviction that Russia's strengths would overcome its weaknesses, and supported his belief that a "modern and dignified life" could be realized with the shared sacrifices of a new leadership and its people.

That has not happened. The purpose of this book is to explain why— and to map the paths Russia and the West can take to recover the hope that bloomed so briefly in 1991.

When I arrived in Moscow as a newspaper journalist in May, 1987, Russia's post-Communist traumas were as inconceivable as the concept of post-Communism itself. Mikhail Gorbachev was then a vigorous young leader, who promised to modernize a failing economy, end his country's bloody entanglement in Afghanistan, and expose what had become an insular, militarized state to the currents of the contemporary world. *Perestroika,* the "restructuring" campaign he launched in 1986, was as much a crusade for moral regeneration as an exercise in economic reform. It seemed to be working. The soldiers returned from Afghanistan to join an ongoing debate that at times made the Soviet Union resemble an enormous family argument. There were few more intellectually exhilarating places to be in the world, as dissidents, artists, filmmakers, bureaucrats, miners, factory workers, and politicians fought over competing visions of the new Soviet society.

There were dark patches along the way, but after August, 1991, and the botched military coup, the argument finally seemed to be coming to an end. The family was splitting up, but there was an air of shaky optimism and goodwill. Along with millions of Soviet viewers, I watched Gorbachev's December 25, 1991, telecast with mixed feelings of shock and excitement. One of history's most awesome experiments had ended, and an equally awesome one was beginning. No former empire had ever set out on the journey that now lay before Russia and the ex-Soviet republics—a journey, in effect, back from utopia—but the energy and optimism of the previous five years offered reason for hope.

Perhaps we should have known better, or at least paid attention to history. In the heady atmosphere of the 1990s, it had been easy to ignore the extent to which Russians' immediate political options were shaped by their past. The fear of chaos and disorder was deeply ingrained in Russian political culture.

Between 1905 and 1920, the years of the first great revolution and civil war, the nation experienced a prolonged period of *bespredel*. The 1917 victory of the Bolsheviks triggered a social and economic convulsion across the country. Armed gangs roamed the countryside, plundering farmers and attacking police. Law and order broke down in the cities. As Vladimir Lenin, the founder of the Soviet state, was driven through the outskirts of Moscow in 1919, he was robbed by a gang of highwaymen. His reaction to becoming a victim of crime was predictably swift. Lenin declared a war on crime as brutal as the one being conducted against counterrevolutionaries. Bandits were shot on sight, and the NKVD, the security service that was one of the precursors of the KGB, took over most of the functions of police. From then on, the state was judge, policeman, and executioner. Soviet apologists later explained the authoritarianism of the Bolshevik state as a necessary reaction to the persistent threat from enemies abroad. But Lenin's use of repressive measures to halt internal chaos was firmly in the Russian tradition.[5]

Historically, the club and the whip were regarded not only as dependable instruments of administration, but also as good therapy. Ivan Peresvetov, who lived in the time of Ivan the Terrible, observed that a healthy sense of government-inspired "dread" was all that stood between order and anarchy. "If the people are not kept in great dread they will never obey the laws," he wrote. "As a horse without a bridle is under its rider, so is a kingdom without dread under its king."[6]

Ivan the Terrible's death, as every Russian knows, ushered in the murderous, chaotic period known as the "Time of Troubles." Not surprisingly, many Russians concluded a new Time of Troubles had fallen upon their country after August, 1991. As the reins of Soviet dictatorship fell away, the horse once again had slipped its bridle. And once again, there were calls for a strong hand on the reins.

The crime and corruption of post-Communist Russia have triggered a wide-ranging debate. Is "wild democracy" proof of the moral bankruptcy of capitalism? Or is it an inevitable feature of transition? If so, what is it a transition to? These questions form the underlying themes of post-Soviet politics. They need to be answered before Russia's ambitious experiment in reform can go any further.

The answers for the most part will come from Russians themselves. What is required of the rest of us is a realistic perspective on a world that has been fogged with too much wishful thinking.

Realism must begin with an acknowledgment that many of the cheerful conclusions drawn in the West following the fall of the Soviet Union were premature. We believed that Communism was dead. We told ourselves that Russians, given a genuine choice, would grab democracy with eager hands. And we were convinced that capitalism and a free-market economy would provide the motor for Russia's transformation.

Those conclusions were premature, not because the Soviet Union threatens to be resurrected, but because parts of it haven't quite died. This was not a surprise to Russians themselves. But to the outside world it first became brutally obvious in October, 1993, when a group of parliamentary deputies occupied the "White House," the legislative and administrative center of the Russian Federation, after months of quarreling with President Boris Yeltsin's government. Backed by thousands of supporters in the streets, they triggered the worst violence in Moscow since 1917. Army tanks shelled the White House, symbol of democratic resistance to the 1991 coup, and over the course of the two-day confrontation at least 144 people died and 878 were wounded.

The violence shocked and divided international opinion. Yeltsin's defenders at home and abroad said that the assault on parliament was the only way to crush a bizarre coalition of Communists, ultranationalists, and fascists who were determined to turn back the clock on democratic reforms. More skeptical observers argued that the parliamentary revolt was part of a wider backlash against the increasingly corrupt and authoritarian government of the reformers. Neither interpretation was wrong. The October uprising revealed a new fault in Russian society, a line dividing two ways of seeing Russia.

The revolt's nominal leaders, Vice-President Aleksandr Rutskoi and

Parliamentary Speaker Ruslan Khasbulatov, had stood with Yeltsin at the White House barricades two years earlier. They were part of the awkward coalition of Communist reformers, democratic activists, dissident bureaucrats, and industrial managers who shared a common determination to prevent the most discredited forces of the old Soviet Communist Party leadership from returning to power. Once the common enemy disappeared, there was little to keep the coalition together. There were many for whom the final breakup of the Soviet Union represented a tragic and unexpected consequence of the revolution. Others saw in the ascension to influence of the young economic reformers and activists around Yeltsin a plot to weaken Russia still further and leave her vulnerable to Western bankers. Behind these self-styled patriots and nationalists was a corporate and political establishment in the process of exploiting the disarray left by the old Soviet regime, and whose power was endangered by rapid privatization. As this book will show, that establishment had already begun to work secretly with the former state security apparatus and organized criminal groups to undermine Russian hopes for a competitive open market.

The only thing "new" about that establishment was the fact that its members no longer carried a Communist Party card. The former Soviet bureaucracy had spent the previous two years reconstituting itself as the country's industrial and managerial elite. The fall of the Soviet regime left senior members of the former Party apparatus—the so-called *nomenklatura*—in administrative control of most of the assets of Soviet power. They ran the large state enterprises and farms, operated the factories of the military-industrial complex, and continued to determine the policies of most central ministries and local governments. Many had grown rich thanks to the judicious investment of Party funds.

In the final years of the system, enormous amounts of Party wealth and property were transferred to the control of commercial trading houses and banks that had been established during perestroika. A fortune was transferred to bank accounts abroad. The Russian government's interest in recovering the funds and in making scapegoats out of its predecessors faded as its hold on power strengthened. Government spokesmen argued that most of the money was either unrecoverable or had long since become such an integral part of the boom in Russian business activity that it no longer was possible to separate it from "legitimate" earnings. There was another reason, however. As Kalini-

chenko and other investigators discovered, the government itself benefited from the hidden flows of wealth. Since many former nomenklatura
now occupied senior ministry positions—often while acting as directors
of private companies—further investigation could be embarrassing.

This is not the place to review the debate over the so-called "shock
therapy" program, but it should be noted that the architects of fast-
track economic reform declared that they wanted to loosen the old bureaucracy's feudal grip on state enterprises. Most of the architects are
now gone, but success in that goal still remains the test of the Russian government's seriousness about overturning the economic legacy
of Communism. The criminality and corruption of the former regime
has already become standard operating procedure in the new.

Two months after the events of October, the elections called to fill a
new, remodeled Russian legislature made the fault line in post-Soviet
Russian society even sharper. Nationalist and populist candidates, including the neo-fascist Vladimir Zhirinovsky, won huge followings on
the strength of the connection they made between falling living standards and the reformers who were "selling out" Russia to Western
multinational corporations. Voters were attracted to the nationalists'
vision of a strong, powerful, self-reliant state—which bore an eerie
resemblance to the kind of corporatist economy favored by the managers and industrialists. By February, 1994, the reformers who piloted
the revolution three years earlier were, mostly, a memory. In a pattern
repeated elsewhere across the former Soviet republics, the old Soviet
establishment was once again in control of the levers of political and
economic power.

Both the nationalists and the "nomenklatura capitalists" argued that
they spoke for the average Russian worker, whose experience with
Russian-style democracy up to that point had left much to be desired. By
the 1993 elections, the breakdown of law and order was at least as much
of a factor in the rightward swing of Russian society as the worsening
economy. Even the victors of the August, 1991, barricades echoed the
hardline rhetoric of the Kremlin hawks they had defeated. "Crime has
become problem number one for us," President Boris Yeltsin acknowledged at a special conference of law enforcement officials in February,
1993. "[It] has acquired such scale and character that it poses great danger for . . . the whole Russian state. Crime is destroying the economy,
interfering with politics and undermining public morale." [7]

As law and order becomes one of the principal battlegrounds—perhaps the principal battleground—for Russian politics, it is even more important to understand the nature of post-Soviet crime. The opponents of reform enjoyed much public support for their argument that lawlessness was a direct consequence of the introduction of "capitalism" into Russian society. But there was plenty of evidence to suggest that the roots of crime were firmly planted in the old Soviet system.

That is why I have begun this guide to the post-Soviet landscape with a look at a part of Soviet culture which few Russians and even fewer foreigners have ever bothered to examine. The criminal underworld, known to its members as the *vorovskoi mir* (Thieves Society or Thieves World), has existed on the margins of Russian life for centuries. A complex paramilitary culture whose exclusive rituals and codes of honor were often copied by the early Bolshevik conspirators, it was awarded the ultimate honor of invisibility during the Communist era. Soviet criminologists assured their people that despite the evidence, organized crime did not and could not exist in a socialist society. Criminals by definition were anti-socialist and could be dealt with individually. The *vorovskoi mir* flourished, like so much of the crime and corruption of Soviet life, in the shadows. Although it was officially unrecognized, the *vorovskoi mir* played a role in the life of the world's most powerful Communist state which its counterparts in the West might have envied.

Over the last twenty years of Soviet power, organized crime had become a silent partner in the black-market economy. The Russian mob, working with corrupt officials, developed the underground channels of trade which helped that economy prosper. When Mikhail Gorbachev came to power in 1985, most major Russian cities already had powerful organized gangs. Their cohesiveness and wealth enabled them to survive the collapse of the old regime, and to profit from the disarray of the new one.

While preparing this book, I spent many hours in conversation with Russia's gangsters. It felt, occasionally, like talking to officials of the old Communist bureaucracy. They were men of tradition, who put a premium on the values of loyalty to the group and on the preservation of order. Many, of course, were violent people, and they would have had no hesitation about ordering my death if I displayed a lack of "respect." Yet it was often they who volunteered the comparison between their own associations and the Communist Party.

They certainly shared with the former Communist establishment a distaste for "wild democracy." This seemed strange, considering how much they had contributed to the high crime rates. But they insisted that the chaos of post-Communism had been produced by the entry of "new" professional competitors into the field: narcotics traders from the southern Caucasus, former black-market entrepreneurs, and some of the greedy new ministers and officials of the Russian government. Those who had once supported democratic reform now turned against it. In the saunas and steamrooms where the mobsters gathered, the "democrats" had become an object of derision.

They found an understanding ally in the ex-Communist bureaucracy. The unofficial working arrangements between Communist functionaries and black-market crime bosses turned into political alliances. Some underground leaders supported officials in the Yeltsin government; others sent weapons and soldiers to the aid of the parliamentary rebels of October, 1993. It became harder and harder to tell gangsters apart from bureaucrats, as Russia fell under the grip of a gangster economy.

It is not possible to write the story of this development, and to discuss the threat it poses to the post–Cold War world, without a sense of sadness and anger. But this book is not an excuse for gloom. I believe the second Russian revolution is not over; it has only been stolen. Whether it will be restored to its owners, and in what shape, is mostly up to Russians themselves. Many of the Russians I interviewed in the course of researching this book have been victims of the chaos. But others, plainly, have been inspired by it. They appear in these pages as a testimony to the survival skills of a people who have already suffered a disproportionate share of this century's agonies.

Contemporary Russia has been compared to the raucous and turbulent frontier of nineteenth-century America. The analogy works, but only to a point. American pioneer capitalists were staking out claims in a largely undeveloped economy. In Russia and other successor states to the former Soviet Union, the prize is the wealth and property of the old regime. The fierce and often violent competition for the spoils of Communism has forged a special kind of frontier character, a unique post-Communist variety of felon. He (so far, it is always a "he") is a curious blend of the Soviet establishment and the classic Russian underworld. I believe he will be a force in Russia and its neighbors for years to come. I have called him comrade criminal.

I Godfathers of Russia

**We have no mafiya in the Soviet Union,
get that into your head.**

—Aleksandr Chakovsky, editor of *Literaturnaya Gazeta*,
to a member of his staff in 1980

1 Thieves World

The instructions I was given left no room for questions. I was to go to a former state-owned Intourist Hotel in southern Moscow and then make my way to the restaurant on the second floor. I was not to give my name, or say whom I was looking for. The man called the Armenian would be waiting.

It was a treeless neighborhood of potholed streets and tall apartment blocks built in the shoebox style favored by Soviet planners in the 1960s and 1970s. The buildings were already disfigured by cracks, but post-Communism had clearly been profitable for the hotel, a squat concrete-and-glass building occupying most of a city block. Its parking lot was filled with Peugeot and Mercedes Benz automobiles. Several young men in track suits stood in attitudes of studied vigilance near the entrance, and the hotel was encircled by a wire fence, which gave it the air of a fortress. I could feel the hostile looks of the young track suits as I walked up to the door.

Inside, a matronly woman sitting at the checkroom desk was reading *Izvestiya*. She looked up angrily when I approached, and went back to her newspaper.

I walked down a narrow corridor to a lift, and at the second floor I emerged into a large ballroom with a raised platform draped by cloth of an indeterminate color and fastened with sequins at one end. Two giant amplifiers, beloved of Russian rock bands, stood like bodyguards on either side of the platform. The surroundings were vaguely familiar. I had been in dozens of similar Intourist restaurants, stamped from the same design, across the Soviet Union. But there were subtle changes. The white tablecloths were spotless. There was a sense of brisk efficiency about the place. Even though it was the middle of the afternoon, the restaurant had customers, and all of them were men, drinking quietly at tables on the edge of the dance floor. As I stood in the entranceway, I tried to look inconspicuous and purposeful at the same time. At one table close to the wall, five young men wearing track suits identical to those worn by the guards outside were eating popsicles and American-made chocolate cookies—and looking at me.

A sixth man sitting with them rose. He was not wearing a track suit. Short and hefty, in his mid-thirties, he wore an expensive leather jacket. After bending to whisper to his companions, he beckoned me to follow him to another table.

We sat facing each across the tablecloth. A waitress materialized from one of the back rooms and brought us coffee without a word.

I pulled out my notebook, but he made an angry gesture.

"No notes," he said, nodding his head in the direction of his companions. "If those boys thought you were interviewing me, they would get very annoyed." [1]

I noticed they were still staring at us, and I put away my notebook.

"We will have a conversation, just a conversation," said the man.

I had been told not to ask his real name. The mutual friends who arranged the meeting referred to him only as the Armenian. Indeed, he had the dark complexion of a man of the south, but he was a Moscow native, born of Armenian parents. Despite his relative youth, he was a senior underboss in one of Moscow's most powerful crime syndicates.

The Armenian did not bother to disguise his hostility toward me. Russian crime-lords, unlike their Western counterparts, were not accustomed to dealing with inquiring reporters. As our initial conversation dragged, I became aware of the young gangsters sucking popsicles behind me. The sound drained some of my tension. It was so incongruous that I had to stop myself from smiling.

I complimented the restaurant's coffee, and that seemed to evoke in the Armenian a proprietary warmth. The hotel turned out to be the property of his syndicate.

"We bought it from the state," he said. "Very legitimate. But we don't make as much money as we should from this place. No one really knows anything about business in this country."

I asked him if he would describe himself as a businessman.

"I don't have a job," he said. "I don't need to work, but I make very good money. This is a country where you can make a lot of money without doing anything."

There was nothing in his expression to suggest that he was being even mildly sarcastic. On the contrary, he seemed proud of himself.

He said he was paid by "three or four businesses," who supplied regular "commissions."

"You protect them?" I said.

"Somebody's going to have to protect their business anyway," he explained. "They chose me."

"Which syndicate do you belong to?"

"I told you," he said, wagging his finger. "No names."

Whichever organization he belonged to, there was no doubt of his high standing in it. As he proceeded to demonstrate with a story, people crossed him at their own risk.

The day before, a group of hoodlums visited one of "his" businesses in the center of Moscow and demanded money. The frightened shop-owner mentioned the Armenian's name, stammering that he had already paid the proper tribute.

The hoodlums didn't believe him. They gave him two days to come up with the cash. The shopowner called his protector, and the Armenian swung into action.

"We set up a *strelka* (a meeting or appointment) that they couldn't refuse," he said contemptuously.

The gang leader went to the meeting in a black limousine, accompanied by his bodyguards, as if he were a government official. The head of the rival band of hoods arrived in the same style. Everyone was well dressed and extremely polite.

They discussed matters "firmly," the Armenian said, with a hint of a smile. Finally, the opposing gangsters allowed that they might have made a mistake. "Shopkeepers will say anything to save their skins, but who believes them?" they joked. "Don't worry; the place is yours." The meeting ended with handshakes all around.

The Armenian was unabashedly proud of his diplomacy.

"This was how armed conflicts usually developed in the past," he told me. "But we don't need that sort of thing anymore. We're beyond that. What we need is order. Before, we had war."

War, in fact, was one of the reasons I found myself sitting in that restaurant in the spring of 1993. I wanted to know why, in the previous two years since the collapse of the Soviet Union, gang violence had turned the streets of dozens of Russian cities into public battlegrounds. Moscow had been one of the cities worst hit. "Almost every day, corpses are found in Moscow with bound hands and feet, sometimes even parts of bodies," reported *Moskovsky Komsomolets* in July, 1992. "Police are strained to the breaking point."[2] For a time, the reports of criminal violence resembled news from a war front. There seemed to be more gangsters in the country than policemen. One out of every four crimes in 1992 was committed by criminal gangs, and in 1993 the number of crimes committed by organized groups rose a staggering 28 percent.[3]

The statistics did not provide an adequate portrait of the armed terror on the streets. In one celebrated incident in 1992, unidentified gang members fired an anti-tank grenade launcher into the offices of a medical clinic located on Kutuzovsky Prospekt, the busy Moscow boulevard that housed the state apartments once used by Politburo members. Police said later that the attack was part of a struggle between two large gangs for control of the area. But since their forces were already stretched to the limit by similar assaults, they couldn't investigate further.

The violence was not confined to large cities. The twenty-eight-year-old head of a small enterprise in Novokuznetsk, a mining town in Siberia, unlocked his car one morning before he went to work and brushed his leg against a lump of clay stuck on the car door. A powerful explosion went off instantly. He survived, but Vadim Kustikov, director of a firm in the town of Tver, was not as lucky. Kustikov was found dead on a riverbank near the town, with a bullet in his head. Robbery was rejected as a motive after police found one million rubles in cash inside his leather coat.

The Armenian stoically recounted his own experiences on the frontlines of the conflict he admitted had engulfed the entire Russian underworld following the fall of Communism.

"During one of our gang fights, I lost four of my men. One was blown up in his car, but others had even worse luck," he said.

One bloody struggle he described was over control of a "chain" of automotive service centers in Moscow. The struggle involved the Podolski and the Balashikhinski, competing bands in northern Moscow, but I suspected that he had played a role in it.

The fight was started by two ambitious Balashikhinski leaders, nicknamed Gera and Sukhoi, who were offended by their rivals' failure to accord them the proper respect. A series of skirmishes between the groups led to a pitched battle on a housing estate in the Moscow suburb of Butovo. While neighbors ducked for cover, forty gunmen from the Podolsk band attacked a smaller force of Balashikhinski.

When the firing stopped, three Balashikhinski and two Podolski gangsters were corpses. Police later found 250 spent cartridges on the ground. Both Gera and Sukhoi managed to escape, but a week later Gera was gunned down in the Hotel Druzhba (Friendship) a noted hangout for Georgian mobsters on Vernadsky Prospekt. Soon afterward, Sukhoi was fatally stabbed while he and his bodyguards relaxed on a beach near the riverside Istrinski district.

"These things can be talked about now because the men who were responsible for the quarrel, Gera and Sukhoi, are dead," the Armenian told me. "Ordinarily, one doesn't speak about such matters if one wants to be safe and sound."

As we continued talking, something in his manner intrigued me. He had addressed me with the familiar form of the Russian word for "you" —*ty*—a form usually reserved for one's closest friends and family, or for those one wanted to patronize.

Afterward, a friend whose knowledge of Russian criminal culture I respected explained that it was no oversight. Russian gangsters treated everyone outside their culture as being from a different, and lesser, world, he said. We could not be regarded as equals. They felt no obligation to respect outsiders, or even tell them the truth.

Nevertheless, I believed the Armenian was being honest with me, in his own fashion, even if he couldn't avoid the Russian temptation to dazzle a foreigner.

"Order" was what mattered most in his philosophy. As far as the Armenian was concerned, the gang wars were an embarrassing lapse of manners. The criminal world had not lived up to its self-appointed mission of preserving order.

"After the breakup [of the USSR], there were too many thugs running around this city on their own, and the police couldn't do a thing," he said. "We had to clean up this situation."

"It's not that we need one organization," he went on. "But we have come to the point of trying to consolidate and coordinate our activities better.

"We have a certain responsibility. Our leaders have the task of preventing total *bespredel*. I would say things are better now. You can ask anyone. They have kept the peace. They have prevented a lot of groups from sorting their relations out in a bloody way. Without our leaders, it would have been even worse. And that would have led to a weakening of the entire criminal world.

"Just two weeks ago, we held a major council to discuss these problems. We decided our strategy, our tactics, how to behave in the changing economic situation. I think you will see some changes. All the restaurants, all the hotels, are under the control of different groups now. We were never so organized before, and our control is much stricter even than it was a few months ago.

"We need to be strong, and not weakened from within. Our code keeps criminal structures with orderly limits. It's in all our interests. We are like the Communists, you know, but more successful."

The Armenian couldn't hide the triumph in his voice as he explained the ethos of Russia's crime-lords.

"We still have plenty of problems, but the important thing is that we outlasted Soviet power," he told me. "The Communists succeeded in grinding into powder the intelligentsia, the White Guards, the Baptists. They destroyed everything for the sake of their ideology, but they always failed to destroy us.

"And I will tell you why we are so strong, why we even outlasted Stalin. It is because our system remained crystal pure. For a long time, things were frozen even for us; we were in a state of neither death nor development. But thanks to our purity, our structure, our ideology, we survived. And now, we have received a new lease on life."

Then he stood up, abruptly concluding our chat. "Thanks for meeting me," I called out, but his back was already turned. He sat down again, with evident relief, at the popsicle-eaters' table. As I passed them on my way back to the lift, I noticed that they had opened several new packages of chocolate cookies.

A few days later, I sat in the cramped Moscow offices of the organized-crime division of the Russian Ministry of Internal Affairs (MVD). The offices overlooked Oktyabrskaya Square, where a large, imposing statue of Vladimir Lenin appeared to be directing traffic. There was, of course, nothing else for him to direct anymore. Even the MVD building, once one of the nerve centers of the Soviet police state, had traded its Leninist theories for the virtues of non-ideological police work.

One example of that work was spread out on the desk in front of me.

It was a remarkable letter, intercepted by police in the middle of 1993 on its way from a prison in Russia's Far East to a nearby penitentiary on the island of Sakhalin.

"GOOD DAY VAGABONDS AND ALL PRISONERS!" the message began— in large, painstakingly printed Cyrillic letters.

"Success to you! You are being addressed by the prisoners of Khabarovsk Central Penitentiary. Consider everything written below as having been coordinated with the highest authorities of the Thieves World and the entire vagabond brotherhood."

The letter went on to discuss what it called the "grave problems" affecting prisoners across Russia, and it announced a hunger strike in protest over human-rights abuses. Every labor camp, penitentiary, and prison facility—the grim islands that made up the old Soviet Gulag archipelago—was expected to join in.

"Forty-seven demands have been prepared," the letter said. "Our main demand is to stop the police terror in prison colonies. Unless the terror is stopped, various houses will be blown up not only in Moscow but in other cities as well. We urge you to support our common cause. You will receive a copy of our ultimatum for familiarization in the near future.

"Arrested ones! For the time being, for the sake of our common cause, refrain from escapes from your places of imprisonment and from hostage taking. Women, minors, and the sick will not take part in the strike. Let success and a favorable outcome greet our common cause. Luck to you, and to us!"

At the time the manifesto of the "arrested ones" was written, Russia's penitentiary system was boiling with unrest over reductions in food rations and in visiting hours. Nevertheless, the bomb threats were not carried out. Eleventh-hour negotiations between authorities and the prison criminal leadership calmed the situation in time.

This should have been a happy outcome, but it left a sour taste among police. "I don't mind telling you it's embarrassing to negotiate with these people," confessed Col. Anatoli Zhoglo, an investigator with the Ministry of Internal Affairs, who showed the letter to me. "In the old days, such negotiations would have been unthinkable, but those are the times we live in now."[4]

Zhoglo, a lean, fast-talking man who bore a resemblance to Clint Eastwood's film character Dirty Harry, had spent his entire career in

Soviet law enforcement. He was one of Russia's foremost experts on organized crime—and a witness to the strange upset in the power balance that forced authorities into what they considered a humiliating accommodation with convicts.

What mysterious organization could threaten bombs and violence from one end of the Eurasian continent to the other with such brazen impunity? What was the Thieves World?

The answers to those questions went to the heart of explaining Russia's troubled passage towards democracy. For decades, the prisons of the Soviet Union had been home to the world's most extraordinary criminal society. For almost a century, it had been known as *vorovskoi mir*, the Thieves World. From their cells, crime bosses planned and organized their operations across the country. No self-respecting gang leader ever needed to soil his hands by contact with the "civilian" world. Lieutenants, often called *brodyagi* (vagabonds), conducted formal dealings with the outside. The so-called vagabond brotherhood provided the network for transmitting orders and collecting profits. In the Soviet era, the gangs operating from their prison bases were no threat to ordinary civilians. Their enemy and rival was the Communist Party, for which they bore an old and long-standing grudge.

Once the Soviet Union had collapsed, however, criminal organizations emerged from their lofty isolation. It was no longer necessary to guard against Communist infection. A modern gang leader could manage his empire from outside prison walls without shame; in fact, the new opportunities available for profit made this nearly a requirement. And even for those who remained inside, there was no risk of embarrassment or censure in bargaining with straight society. Like caged lions who suddenly realized their strength, the leaders of the Thieves World were ready to take what they considered their rightful place in the pecking order of the New Russia. And, as the Armenian demonstrated, they took their new social responsibilities seriously.

Yet it was hard to regard the hoodlum-diplomats who emerged from the shadows of the Soviet underworld with the same seriousness with which they regarded themselves. To Westerners versed in the subtle arts of Sovietology, the mobster with his leather coat and his theories of order seemed like a droll figure from a turn-of-the-century Russian novel.

It took an effort to recognize that such men not only had become behind-the-scenes arbiters of Russian society, but had altered the direction of their country's political development. By late 1992, police believed, the most powerful gangs had carved Russia into twelve regions that cut across Soviet administrative boundaries. Politicians, bureaucrats, and industrial managers accepted the secret divisions with the alacrity they once reserved for Party decrees. Profits from the regions poured into Moscow banks and investment houses in Moscow operated by the collective leadership of the criminal world and were then recirculated around the country.

In the months following the August coup, a word even more ominous than *bespredel* began to dominate Russian public debate. At a press briefing in June, 1992, Deputy Russian Internal Affairs Minister Andrei Dunayev blamed the explosion of criminal violence on the *mafiya*.[5]

It was not the first time the word had been used in Russia. *Mafiya* had been a part of the Russian political vocabulary for more than twenty years, covering such a variety of sins in Soviet life as to be almost undefinable. Soviet prosecutors and journalists used it to describe corrupt Communist bureaucrats; dissidents used it to describe the KGB. By the late 1980s, it included con men, smugglers, and owners of cooperatives—anyone, in fact, who had made the mistake of getting rich and flaunting it.

In the post-Communist era it took on a fourth, more sinister, meaning, which reflected the helplessness most Russians felt in response to the new forces that ruled their lives. This "new" mafiya reflected the political and economic power of a criminal class more sophisticated than anything Russia had ever experienced before. After August, 1991, police found evidence that organized crime had expanded into nearly all areas of the new Russian economy. Shadowy syndicates were said to be in control of banks, stock exchanges, hotels, and commercial enterprises in most Russian cities. Moscow gangsterdom appeared to have lost all fear of the authorities. Armed mafiosi strutted through the center of town. They drove their flashy cars to the new hotels, discos, and casinos. And they openly ate lunch with government officials.

The mafiya's power was recognized by public opinion as well. A poll in the summer of 1992 indicated that one-third of residents in the Russian Far East believed that criminal structures "determined the course of events in their region." Such things were impossible to prove, of course, but perceptions were as important as facts. A year after the Far

East survey, another poll taken in the city of Yekaterinburg, in the Ural Mountains, suggested that three-quarters of the residents believed their city was ruled by the mafiya. Interestingly, so did 14 percent of the city's police.[6]

The mafiya had a measurable effect on the larger political world. Boris Yeltsin's government was forced to compromise some of its most liberal policies, and to withdraw others, in order to prevent their further exploitation by the country's criminal clans.

To dampen the growing smuggling trade, for instance, Moscow reversed its efforts to relax control over foreign exports in July, 1993. Originally, commercial firms were allowed major concessions in long-standing Soviet policies that prevented them from selling products directly abroad and from retaining a significant percentage of their foreign-currency earnings. The reformers hoped that this would spur competition in the regions and provide tax revenues for the central treasury from expanding foreign trade. But they had not counted on the power of criminal groups that had invested heavily in many of those companies and now exploited the liberalized rules to smuggle enormous amounts of goods abroad. Thirty percent of the gold produced in the remote northern city of Magadan, for example, evaded federal tax inspectors to turn up in foreign markets. But even the July, 1993, clampdown proved counterproductive, since it stimulated a closer alliance between crime groups and local authorities who were profiting from the smuggling trade. Many of these authorities joined the political opposition to the Yeltsin government, to protest attempts by the central government to restrict their autonomy and their control over local resources.[7]

The converging interests of criminals, bureaucrats, and local politicians similarly undermined efforts to extend the rights of private ownership. Individual farmers had been permitted their own plots of land, but they found it nearly impossible to obtain credits, machinery, or fertilizer from regional banks and agricultural enterprises, which were controlled by corrupt local officials determined to protect the interests of the large state collective farms. Real estate development in Moscow, St. Petersburg, and other major cities was monopolized by the coalition of the mafiya and the new urban bureaucracy. Many of the state-owned shops and restaurants fell under racketeers' control, if not outright ownership, as soon as they were privatized. Some syndicates took the extra precaution of buying interests in the media—and those parts of the media which they did not own they tried to terrorize. The press fell victim to a more violent form of censorship than it had experienced under the Soviet regime.

In April, 1993, gangland representatives visited the offices of a privately owned newspaper in the Crimean city of Simferopol, demanding a monetary "arrangement." When they were turned down, the newspaper was assaulted the next day by gun-wielding thugs. Although the paper's directors had the foresight to alert police, who arrested the stunned intruders before they could do much damage, it did them little good. Thanks to friends in the militia and the city government, the hoodlums were swiftly released from jail, and they took swift revenge. A few days after the foiled assault, the newspaper was closed by officials, without explanation.[8]

It was not an isolated case. In 1992, a Yekaterinburg newspaper editor named Tamara Lomakina was severely beaten after she published articles on organized crime. There had been some unmistakable warnings. Strangers were seen watching her apartment around the clock. And managers of some commercial firms in the city telephoned her to "suggest" that she cease publishing articles. "When we asked these businessmen for details, all they said was they had been told to pass along the warning and nothing more," she told me.[9]

The gangs apparently had no quarrel with the facts reported by Lomakina's newspaper, *Na Smenu*. What they did not appreciate was the sardonic tone of the coverage.

"They thought we weren't treating them with the respect they deserved," said Lomakina. She confessed that she would think twice before running another story on organized crime. "The mafiya is the only real power in this city," she said testily. "No court can protect us against them."

Russians were not suffering alone. By 1993, mobsters strengthened by growing ranks and swelling coffers had become parallel authorities in virtually all the former Soviet republics. From Ukraine, where Prime Minister Leonid Kuchma warned that his country faced a "secret syndicate of Ukrainian gangsters . . . much more dangerous than the Sicilian mafia," to tiny, mountainous Kyrgyzstan, the self-styled Switzerland of the new Commonwealth of Independent States, organized crime dramatically transformed post-Soviet politics.

"They have paralyzed state authority, and slowed down our reforms," Kyrgyz president Askar Akayev complained in February, 1993. In Tajikistan, Gennadi Blinov, deputy minister of internal affairs, said that at least thirty armed bands operated in Dushanbe, the capital, including several run by ex-convicts linked to members of the political opposition in the republic. Bribery, smuggling, and bank fraud conducted by criminal cartels cost the state of Kazakhstan an estimated twenty billion rubles by July, 1993. "The situation places in doubt the possibility of transferring to market relations in a civilized way," said Kazakh president Nursultan Nazarbayev.[10]

Mobsters terrorized courts and intimidated judges with casual insolence. The leaders of three of the largest Moscow-area gangs were arrested during one investigative round-up—only to be released from custody with little more than a warning. Gangsters broke into the Supreme Court building of Dagestan and opened fire as judges began hearing a case against mafiosi from the nearby autonomous republic of Chechnya. Several persons were injured. After the court reopened for business, the Dagestani prosecutor lost no time in filing a reduction in the charges.[11] "Incidents of pressure on judges, and their persecution by mafiya structures, including physical reprisals, have become more frequent," admitted Sergei Kiyakin, deputy chairman of Yekaterinburg's district court.[12]

Basic security measures were to be installed in courts around the country by the end of 1993, including the removal of judges' addresses and phone numbers from official directories, the installation of private alarms in their homes and courtrooms, and the granting of permission to carry firearms. But little could be done about the gangsters' overweening contempt for legal authority.

"It's difficult to get respect in there," said Zoya Korneyeva, the chief judge of the Moscow appeals court, told me one afternoon, gesturing in the directions of the courtrooms down the hall from her offices. "The whole attitude of society towards judges has changed." [13]

Korneyeva was a pleasant, well-dressed woman of sixty-two. In the twilight of a long, respectable career in the Soviet judiciary, she had to endure the daily humiliation of passing through a checkpoint of soldiers guarding the entrance to her building as she came to work. At least she could be proud of having stayed on the job. Fear had taken a toll on her colleagues. There were ninety vacancies for court justices in Moscow, but only fifty people had applied.

Meanwhile, the courts' backlog grew. More than four thousand cases were still waiting to go to trial across the city in 1993. "Often, we can't do anything because the witnesses are afraid to come forward," sighed Judge Korneyeva. "I am amazed at how bold these criminals have become."

It was boldness born from a vacuum. The failure—often deliberate—of the state to impose its authority left mobsters free to sabotage what had been the most inspiring promise of the second Russian revolution: to create a new society based on the rule of law.

The demise of the Soviet Union offered an opportunity to shed the legacy of totalitarianism and create a "civil society." During perestroika, the foundations had been laid. Work had begun on a new constitution, on the creation of an independent judiciary, and on the reform of criminal procedure. But during the first years of Russia's post-Soviet government, the effort disintegrated. While plans were drafted for a new criminal code, existing law was modified, amended, or repaired, until the system resembled a patient covered with so many bandages as to be nearly unrecognizable. Beneath the bandages, the patient was growing sicker. Russia's dream of moving to a just society was suffocated by rhetoric and red tape.

"Every day I get a folder with new laws, new resolutions, new regulations, and new resolutions on old regulations," said Yevgeni Maksimov, deputy head of the Main Department for Economic Crimes of the Ministry of Internal Affairs. "In the old days, there were rules for everything, and you knew whether someone had violated them. Now, with our so-called freedom, it's not clear what is legal and what isn't." [14]

It was hard to avoid the conclusion that the second great Russian revolution of the twentieth century had been stolen before it really had had a chance to fulfill its promise of democratic reform. As evidence began to pile up of the expanding activities of Russian mobsters abroad, Yeltsin bitterly announced in January, 1993, that Russia had joined Western countries in the dubious distinction of being both a victim and a progenitor of organized crime. "We have become a mafiya power on a world scale," he said. [15]

It was a poignant irony: Russians had survived one form of criminal dictatorship only to be threatened by another. But the new tyranny of the crime syndicate was also an inescapable consequence of Russia's historical quest for order. The authors of the manifesto from Khabarovsk Penitentiary shared with the Armenian and his comrades and former bureaucrats the fear of unbridled change.

Many ordinary Russians found no difficulty in drawing a distinction between street crime and the activities of crime professionals, who came to be regarded, with a perverse respect, as upholders of law and order. It was a line originally drawn by mobsters themselves. "The (gangsters), if they can help it, break only one of the ten commandments: the one that says don't steal," said Colonel Zhoglo. "Of course, they kill each other; but they don't kill civilians. They certainly have no quarrel with the *muzhik,* the ordinary guy. That's why a lot of people see them as their protectors from the hoodlums on the street."

This perhaps accounted for the *vorovskoi mir*'s curious rise to cult status in post-Communist society. In what seemed at first a refreshing change from drab decades of socialist realism, radio stations broadcast songs from the criminal world and prison camps, and popular films made rogues into heroes. Many Russians were appalled. "Even the avant-garde sector of literature is penetrated by criminal jargon," the filmmaker Stanislav Govorukhin noted with disapproval.

Not surprisingly, Russia's youth were among those most readily seduced by gangworld glamor. The mafiya became a metaphor for rebellion against the puritanism of their elders. One young Muscovite told an American journalist that it used to be "fashionable" to have an artist, a rock singer, or even a journalist for a boyfriend. "Now the attractive girls want mafiya boys," she said.[16]

Sometimes, it was more than a metaphor. One of the most ominous trends of post-Soviet life was the spread of criminal behavior among those under thirty. The Moscow newspaper *Megapolis Express* warned its readers that young people were the "prime movers" of violence in Russian society. "Education is no longer a prestigious occupation," it complained.

To the young, crime offered an easy route to riches in the New Russia. A twenty-five-year-old Muscovite named Mikhail boasted to a British journalist that he had committed fifteen murders in order to solve his "financial problems." The youth said that his "work" for a cooperative had already provided enough money to buy a car. He was paid forty thousand rubles (230 dollars, at the time) for each "job." If he arranged it so that the body would never be found, he could expect more. "I know people who can take care of [destroying a corpse] with acid and stuff," he confided knowledgeably.[17]

Even teenagers began to act out the crime dramas they saw in newspapers, films, and magazines. In January, 1993, six teenagers kidnapped a nine-year-old boy and demanded a twelve-million-ruble ransom from his father, a businessman in the Siberian city of Surgut. In Tyumen, a band of fifteen-year-old students ran a successful counterfeiting ring, until police confiscated the copying machine on which they had been cheerfully manufacturing fake five-thousand-ruble notes. In 1992, youths under the age of twenty-one committed or were involved in every third theft and robbery, every fourth theft of weapons and ammunition, and every fifth rape.[18]

Most painful of all to the authorities was the knowledge that the young were becoming an attractive labor pool for Russia's criminal organizations. In their distinctive Western track suits they soon became a common—and ominous—sight in Moscow and other Russian cities. "Unemployed young people are increasingly being recruited by crime syndicates," worried Alexander Lulikov, a deputy internal-affairs minister.[19]

The appeal of organized crime was not just mercenary. "The criminal world offers a kind of spiritual satisfaction to the younger generation," Colonel Zhoglo acknowledged. "It's a spirituality based on immoral behavior, but that doesn't make it less attractive. For that unfortunate state of affairs, we have to blame ourselves. The old system had nothing to offer except hypocrisy."

With such an impressive list of "endorsements" from popular culture and public opinion, Russian mafiya groups could be forgiven for believing that they had inherited the mantle of authority from their former Communist enemies. Colonel Zhoglo once asked a gang leader why he felt free to become involved with "politics." Wasn't he concerned about being forced into an unseemly alliance with the state?

"At this time," came the cool reply. "There is nothing higher than the mafiya."

2 Vor

The thirty men who gathered secretly at a dacha in the rolling hills of the Vedentsovo region near Moscow, late in December, 1991, were a cross-section of an empire that was soon to implode. There were Georgians and Armenians from the lands beyond the Caucasus Mountains, Russians from Moscow and St. Petersburg, and Ukrainians from Kiev and Odessa. For some of them, the trip to Vedentsovo had not been easy. Several had to slip out of the closed cities of the military-industrial complex beyond the Urals. One crossed seven time zones to get there, flying from Vladivostok on the Pacific coast.

There was unintended irony in this mixture of geographical and racial origins. Although the country was already beginning to splinter into its national components, the Vedentsovo meeting was living proof of the "internationalism" claimed, but rarely achieved, by the Soviet state. There was one crucial difference: the participants had obliterated national differences in the name of crime, not Marx. They were senior leaders of the Thieves World.

Each of those present carried a title that proclaimed his unique authority to criminals throughout Russia. He was called a *vor v zakonye,* a "Thief-in-Law," usually shortened to the simple word *vor,* after being anointed or "crowned" by his peers inside Soviet prisons. Most Russians would not have recognized any of the faces, but the Honorable Thieves or *vory* who gathered at Vedentsovo were among the nation's most powerful men.[1]

At the time of the Vedentsovo meeting, police knew of at least six hundred *vory* across the length and breadth of the country. Although, officially, organized crime did not exist during the Soviet era, the *vorovskoi mir* had been hard to ignore. The Thieves World controlled a large part of the underground trade in spare parts, automobiles, timber, caviar, and gems between the nation's most remote towns and its largest industrial centers. In the final year of the Soviet Union's existence, the wealth of this black economy was estimated at 110 billion rubles (60.5 billion dollars at 1992 rates).[2]

Money was the urgent question that brought senior *vory* together from the far corners of the Soviet Union that December day. The imminent collapse of Communism meant a dramatic change in their business fortunes. The bosses of the Soviet underworld had enjoyed a unique relationship with the mandarins of Communist society. No one in the government could openly admit it, but the clandestine smuggling networks saved the state's industrial machine from choking on red tape. Circulating goods and services freely around the country, they were the Soviet Union's closest equivalent to a service industry. The paralysis of the command-administrative economy after the 1970s made their role as free economic agents increasingly important.

Optimists among the *vory* saw opportunities ahead. With the breakdown of the federal system, each republic exercised legal jurisdiction only inside its borders. This meant goods stolen from Russian factories could be sold or traded legally anywhere outside Russia—thus opening the way to a windfall in smuggling income. The disintegration of the central banking system created unlimited opportunities for currency speculation; and the looming disappearance of the nationwide law enforcement structure offered criminals a freedom of movement that had been denied them under the police-state system. Moreover, they could open operations abroad without fearing intervention from the KGB. Russian police attached special importance to the presence at Vedentsovo of a *vor* named Vyacheslav Ivankov, nicknamed Yaponets, "Japanese," from Vladivostok. One of the most senior crime bosses in the country, Ivankov was to turn up later in America with instructions from his peers to explore "business opportunities" there.

The godfathers at Vedentsovo, however, were also disconcerted by the chaos of democracy. Under the old system, at least, there had been a kind of order. The *vory* had been able to count on setting up mutual arrangements with police and government officials. Criminal life was predictable. But the erosion of central authority also allowed new criminal groups from bases outside Russia—in particular from the Caucasus region—to move into territories once considered exclusive by the *vorovskoi mir*. Chechens, Azeris, and other armed gangs from the south challenged the cozy black-market monopolies held by the *vory* in Moscow and other large cities. They opened new fields of lucrative criminal activity, such as drug trafficking and gun-running. There had already been alarming quarrels between the traditional Slav gangs and the newcomers. And every small-time hoodlum thought he could run his own protection racket.

The most pressing business at Vedentsovo was to return a sense of order to the crime world. The assembled *vory* agreed to combine their forces in a war against the Caucasian intruders. In the coming months, there were to be many more meetings, involving other *vory* from around the country, and the bloodshed in Russia's cities would grow. Vedentsovo established the climate for post-Communist Russia as much as any government policy worked out by the new leaders in the Kremlin, but the timing of the meeting was even more revealing than its agenda. A few days after the Russian godfathers met in the dacha, the hammer-and-sickle flag came down for the last time from the Kremlin walls. Vedentsovo registered the indisputable fact that the *vorovskoi mir* had survived Communism.

No one, on reflection, should have been surprised. The Russian under-world's capacity for self-renewal has frustrated, even awed, several generations of Russian law enforcement officials. It is as impossible to imagine the post-Communist state without the presence of the *vorovskoi mir* as it is to conceive of Russia without winter. The gangster reigning over the former state hotel he had "privatized" is a symbol of a culture that matches only the Russian Orthodox Church in durability and in the determined faith of its adherents.

"The *vory* are a unique criminal group which has no analogies any-where else in the world," said Colonel Zhoglo, almost against his will making this sound like a patriotic boast. "In the world history of crime, there has never been a criminal group like our *vory*," Zhoglo went on, "and I hope there will not be. That is, if they don't transfer themselves to the U.S., which I can't believe the Americans will allow. The Italian, Sicilian, or American mafia are completely different types of criminals. The *vory* are a product of Soviet reality." [3]

Zhoglo was not the first of his countrymen to notice how criminal and Communist structures intertwined in Russia. Sixty years before Vedentsovo, a Leningrad academician named Dmitri S. Likhachev ob-served that convicts in construction squads building Stalin's infamous Baltic–White Sea Canal formed a cohesive unit mirroring the rigid orga-nization of the Communist Party. "Despite thieves' apparent lack of discipline, their lives are governed by a network of strict regulations that extend to the most minute matters," he wrote. "And ultimately [they are governed] by a system of collective beliefs that is remarkably uniform among criminals with different ethnic roots." Likhachev noted that a so-called "Thieves Court" regularly punished anyone who broke the rules: "[The convicts' lives are] regulated and circumscribed by innumerable rules, standards, and notions of property and good manners." [4]

They had been so regulated, in fact, for centuries. Russia's underworld emerged out of a dysfunctional political culture that stretched back several hundred years. The faint beginnings of organized crime in modern Russia can be seen in the outlaw peasant bands of the early seventeenth century. In a society where land and all who labored on it were the property of the czar, political resistance and criminal activity were nearly indistinguishable. Highwaymen who robbed government functionaries were admired for striking a blow against state authority. Systematic plunder often turned into organized rebellion.

The early gangs adopted the organizational structure of the communal peasant society out of which they emerged. Profits were divided equally among their members, and the leader, regarded as the first among equals, was usually an older, more experienced member of the band who tested the newest recruits. [5]

During its subsequent history, the Russian underworld elaborated a remarkably complex body of rules and traditions to distinguish itself from outsiders and to protect itself from infiltration. Beggars' guilds and thieves societies in the nineteenth century were among the forerunners of modern Russian gangs, and they put prospective members through a six-year period of probation during which they learned the expected code of behavior and were weaned from the "corrupt" habits of normal society. Desertion was considered one of the worst transgressions. The beggars' guilds punished turncoats by slitting their wallets, symbolically casting them back into the detested outside world by destroying their means of earning a living.

Criminal fraternities in early Russia sometimes went to more extreme lengths to achieve group solidarity. During the seventeenth century, some Cossack highwaymen killed their wives and children before going off on a raid to prevent them from falling into the hands of enemies. Russian gang leaders in the nineteenth century, however, developed a somewhat more humane way of ensuring that family ties did not supersede the criminal bond: they encouraged followers to marry women already in the criminal milieu, such as the daughters of other thieves or prostitutes. The offspring of those unions provided a natural replenishment of criminal ranks, as well as assurance that traditions would carry on.

No tradition was more compelling than the underworld code. It was that code, formed over centuries of adaptation to the Russian political environment, which impressed Likhachev and continued to impress everyone who came in contact with the *vorovskoi mir*. The most important commandment was to abstain from any activity that suggested the state had any power over a gang member's life, whether it involved serving in the army or paying taxes. In the Soviet era, the one unfailing test of a bandit's suitability was his willingness to defy the socialist system. He was not only prohibited from joining the Communist Party but was barred from holding a regular job—which made him someone with outlaw status in the eyes of a state that required every able-bodied person to have a permanent place of employment. To rise in the old criminal hierarchy, he was expected to have avoided membership in the Young Pioneers, Komsomol (Young Communist League), and all the other organizations that were part of the Soviet Union's socialization process. This was often easier to achieve in theory than in practice.

The Armenian admitted to me that he had once worn a "red cravat," as a member of the Young Pioneers. Although he managed to overcome the stigma, it permanently disqualified him from a senior place in the underworld hierarchy. "Even if you were only seven years old and had to join the Young Pioneers," as nearly every Soviet schoolchild was obliged to do, "that was just too bad," he said. "Putting on a red scarf, wearing a [Communist] pin, or a badge with Lenin's portrait even once in your life meant you would never become a *vor v zakonye*."

A gang member was folded into the bosom of criminal culture by intricate bonding mechanisms. Prospective members of a gang in Cherkessk, in the Stavropol region, where Mikhail Gorbachev first rose to become a Party official, kissed a *kinjal*—the traditional dagger of the Caucasus—and swore allegiance before a huge portrait of the crime boss, just as Soviet citizens regularly paid obeisance to the cult of Lenin and Stalin. Thieves in another band signaled each other by flicking their right thumb against the teeth and then moving it in a circle around the chin. Members of a Yekaterinburg gang piously described to me in 1992 how they visited the graves of their "elders" in a local cemetery every

week as "a sign of respect for those who taught us." In the twentieth century, it was easier to join the Communist Party than a criminal
gang. Party membership required only two individual sponsors; gangs
required three.[6]

In 1992, a leading *vor* in the Russian Far East, whose underworld
nickname is Dzhem (Jam), appeared at the wedding of one of his
younger gang members to deliver a toast intended to inculcate the guiding ethic of the band. Standing with his feet spread apart, he raised a
brimming glass of vodka before the rapt faces of his followers, most of
them in their teens and twenties and hanging on his every word. "We
must remember that what is more important than anything else to us is
not money, but friendship," he intoned. "The more friends a person
has, the better he is, and that's what gives us our strength."[7]

"*Pravilno, batya!* That's right, father," the young people murmured.

"There will always be problems," the avuncular leader went on.
"Somebody may stumble and find himself in the clutches of police,
maybe he will start providing them information and violate thieves'
ethics." He paused and frowned at his audience. "But if he does that,
he should come to us, to his brothers, and confess honestly. He must
not keep it inside his soul. And I promise we'll help him get back on the
straight line again. We'll sort it all out ourselves. We'll pass judgment."

"*Pravilno, batya!*"

The leader raised his glass. "So let us drink to our cause, which is
always to help each other, to stay close to each other, and to be together
all the time. This is our dignity as *blatnye* [members of the criminal
world]. And then everyone will fear us. Cops will never break us. If a
person is alone, he doesn't count for anything. But if we are together,
and support each other, then we are strong. Let's drink, brothers!"

"To friendship! To Russia, father!" the solemn chorus repeated.

The ultimate proof of gang loyalty was a member's willingness to
endure the long, hazardous process of separating himself from conventional society. In the pre-Communist era, gang members demonstrated
their defiance of convention by cutting off a finger, slicing a wrist, or,
almost as painfully, covering their bodies with tattoos. The most distin-
guishing mark of a professional criminal in Russia, however, was prison
time. Unlike in other modern cultures, jail meant permanent ostracism.
Like the brand applied to the foreheads of runaway serfs in Old Russia, a prison record in the Soviet era meant automatic exclusion from

the guarantees that came with citizenship, such as the right to a job or residence permit in most major cities. The prison experience accounted for the striking continuity of gangland traditions. Whether they were in the czarist prison camps on Sakhalin Island in the Far East, or in Stalin's gulag, gang members entered a society that stood proudly aloof from the normal world. Like the Thieves Court on the White Sea Canal, prison provided the discipline and the planning apparatus for everything that happened outside. It was both university and parliament for gang members. One famous Russian crime boss, nicknamed Uncle Vasya, spent more than forty years behind bars, but when he died in 1933 he was universally credited by both police and mobsters as one of the most powerful denizens of the underworld.

The code's other striking tenet, as outlined by Jam, was a rejection of the materialism that criminals considered the most demeaning aspect of conventional society. Paradoxically, no Russian thief of the old school was interested in getting rich. He would never haggle over the price of goods he had obtained, even if he knew he could get more than the asking price. Valery Chalidze, an emigre anti-Communist who wrote a study of Soviet crime, observed that "thieves in the Soviet Union are generally indifferent to the accumulation of wealth." [8] Like their peasant forebears, criminal bands pooled their earnings in a communal fund, called an *obshchak,* for later distribution. The Yekaterinburg gangsters I met in 1992 said they only took as much "salary" from the *obshchak* as they needed. The rest went to support wives and families of the "collective" who were in prison. "We're more decent and democratic than the Communists," one of them bragged.

The underworld's austere code of ethics and its antimaterialistic behavior lent it a special cachet. Like the Cossacks who fought the czar's functionaries, Russian bandits often saw themselves as defenders of the poor and oppressed. This Robin Hood quality made them particularly attractive during periods of political upheaval. In the declining years of czarist rule, organized criminal groups were idealized as symbols of political resistance.

"In Russia, the brigand is the only true revolutionary," wrote the nineteenth-century anarchist Mikhail Bakunin. "[He is] a revolutionary without phrases, without bookish rhetoric. . . . The brigands of the forests, towns and villages, scattered throughout Russia, together with the brigands confined in the innumerable prisons of the empire—these constitute a single indivisible, tight-knit world, the world of the Russian revolution. In this world, and in it alone, there has always been revolutionary conspiracy. Anyone in Russia who seriously wants to conspire, anyone who wants a people's revolution, must go into this world." [9]

Some of the future leaders of the Soviet state took this advice literally. Stalin was so captivated as a child by stories of a Caucasian brigand who protected peasants from their enemies that he borrowed the bandit's name for his first revolutionary nom de plume: Koba. In unguarded moments during his later career, Stalin wistfully described the professional bandits he met during his years in prison and exile as the "salt of the earth." He was not the only revolutionary dazzled by the underworld. [10]

The early Bolsheviks made a point of recruiting criminals to their cause. Several bands lent their skills to what were euphemistically called "expropriations"—bank robberies and the kidnapping of czarist officials for ransom—and their activities added substantially to the Bolshevik war chest. Although he eventually tried to expunge from the record his gangland associations, Stalin, the future "Great Father" of the Soviet state, was implicated in several heists, including a celebrated 1907 bank robbery in Tbilisi, the capital of Georgia.

Stalin and his colleagues received more than sentimental inspiration from their criminal friends. The gangs' harsh discipline and secrecy, and their defiance of conventional culture, came to characterize the Bolshevik cells and, eventually, the Communist Party itself. Some leading bandits even found congenial positions as police officials in the new regime. [11]

The remarkable affinity between the two groups raises the interesting question of whether the development of the Soviet Communist Party owes at least as much to the ethos of the gang world as to the tenets of Marxism. Although the *vorovskoi mir,* as the weaker force, appeared to borrow much of its rhetoric and organizational tactics from the Party, the evolution of the Communist leadership—as we will see in later chapters—resembled nothing so much as the growth of a large criminal syndicate.

That was perhaps why the Party came to see the Thieves World as one of the more potent threats to its own authority. The mutual admiration between the two barely survived the revolution. To Moscow's lasting irritation, most of the gang leaders refused to submit to the proletarian utopia, proving as resolute in their resistance to Soviet commissars as they had been to czarist police. To make matters worse, some of the Bolsheviks' worst enemies joined their ranks. "Whites," "Greens," and other opponents of the new regime swelled the bandit ranks in the 1920s, highlighting once again the curious political subtext of Russia's crime world.[12]

According to Colonel Zhoglo, the first *vory v zakonye* formally appeared in the earliest years of Soviet power, to forge the modern version of the *vorovskoi mir* as the antithesis to Communism. "No one really knows how they got their name," he said. "But someone must have stood up at one of their early gatherings and said, 'We are thieves all right, but we have our own law opposed to the authorities; therefore, we are thieves within our law: *vory v zakonye*.' "

Since at least the 1920s, the *vory* exerted a special, hidden power in Soviet life. Like their predecessors in the Russian criminal underworld, they ensured the continuation of traditions, judged violators of the thieves' code, and administered the *obshchak*, the collective treasury. In the Soviet era, the *vor* was a gangland bureaucrat. Zhoglo describes the *vory* as "semi-legal" figures—"I would even call them semi-Masons"—who act as judges, politicians, and diplomats.

"They are expected to promote the spiritual welfare of the underworld, the *vorovskoye blago*," Zhoglo said. "For us, perhaps, that welfare is based on a kind of immorality, but it's strong enough so that thousands of young criminals want to follow it."

The traditional *vory* evoke a grudging respect from police. "Many of the old Thieves-in-Law were philosophers, and well read," Zhoglo said. "You can have a genuine conversation with them. They have deep authority in the same way as top military people, scientists, state leaders."

Although commanding illicit wealth, they were expected to be privately incorruptible, paragons of virtue. "The *vory* I knew weren't demoralized or sunk into depravity like many two-bit hooligans or even some ordinary citizens," said Capt. Yuri Nikishin of the Moscow Police's Organized Crime Squad. "They were clear about their place in life. They could order a robbery or run a racket, but they weren't personally dishonest, and they weren't show-offs. You sometimes might find a *vor* who bought himself a dacha, but most were modest men." [13]

The gangland code once prohibited a *vor* from marrying or holding down a normal job. His monastic purity accorded him, in many places throughout the Soviet Union, a higher status than the local Communist Party boss. A forty-five-year-old Moscow shopkeeper named Seran Akopyan, an Armenian who grew up in Karabakh, in the southern Caucasus Mountains, remembers with a mixture of awe and fascination one *vor* from his youth. "We only knew his last name—Uganov—but we knew there was something special about him," Akopyan said. Uganov was a grizzled, powerfully built man in his seventies. He dressed in nondescript clothes, but the children sensed his quiet authority. He spoke several languages, and he was unmarried. "That was the custom of the *vory* then," said Akopyan. "But he had children, and he got them all good government positions."

One day, the old *vor* ordered his followers to erect a barrier on the road that passed by his house to collect tolls from travelers. A few weeks later, learning that the commandant of the regional police was coming to get him, Uganov went outside and waited, with a machine gun cradled in his arms.

"The commandant got out of his car and everyone was tense, as we watched to see what would happen," Akopyan remembered. "But the policeman just came up to Uganov and shook him by the hand. The commandant told people later that anyone who had the courage to meet him with a machine gun in his hands could not be trifled with. Now that I'm older I think maybe he was being paid by Uganov. But you had to admire the man. He was a real boss."

Another day, Uganov simply disappeared from the village. Adults whispered that he had been arrested. According to rumor, he had been tried and sentenced to seventy years in prison for murder. But a few months later, he was back as if nothing had happened. After that, the children were in awe of him.

Once, Akopyan followed him so closely that the old man grew annoyed. "He stopped and looked me over for a long time," he said. "Then he reached into his pocket and brought out money, wads of it, and stuffed it inside my shirt. Before I could say anything, he was gone. Men like that lived by their own special laws." [14]

A modern example of the best of the old *vor* tradition was a man known in the underworld as Sylvester. His real name was Antonov, and until his arrest in 1991, he led the Solntsevskaya gang in Moscow. He was considered by police to be a gangland Robin Hood. Refusing to rob anyone he considered poor, Sylvester was a kind of tax inspector in the capital's underworld. He sometimes relieved minor racketeers in his territory of their earnings, if he felt they had overstepped the bounds, and deposited the money into his gang's *obshchak*.

Occasionally, as even police were forced to concede, the old *vory* acted as barriers to criminal chaos. Peso, a Georgian crime boss whose real name was Kuchigoriya, was exiled from Moscow by government decree in the early 1980s. But before he left, he warned authorities that without his restraining hand several of the neighborhoods under his control would erupt in fighting. Police reluctantly acknowledged that he was right. Only when Peso was allowed to return to practice his special brand of gangland diplomacy did the territories under his control settle down again. Peso's diplomatic skills failed him in death. His family arranged a plot for him in a local cemetery, but someone discovered that his tomb stood next to that of a soldier killed in the Afghan war and wrote a letter of complaint to the newspapers. Peso's humiliated comrades were forced to dig up his remains and find another resting place.

With the exception of such embarrassing examples, the rituals marking the passing of an old *vor* rivaled the last rites of a party boss for splendor and pomp. One afternoon in September, 1992, a cavalcade of black limousines, each fitted out with a private telephone—top Communists and senior state police officials were the only other Soviet citizens to boast such conveniences—rolled up to Vostryakovo Cemetery in Moscow. Accompanied by their bodyguards, the leaders of criminal groups from all over the Soviet Union were coming to pay their respects to Viktor Maksimov, a veteran Thief-in-Law who was known by the nickname Malina, which means "safe house" in gangster slang, as well as "raspberry."

Maksimov died of natural causes at the age of sixty-three in Valentinovka, outside Moscow, where he had lived with his mistress after his release from prison. He had been a power in the underworld for as long as anyone could remember. A protégé of Uncle Vasya, Malina had been taken to trial eleven times. This experience, apparently, had helped him become the main arbiter of disputes between gangs. In a fitting image, his peers from the unofficial kingdom of Russian organized crime strode toward Raspberry's final resting place on a path covered with half a million rubles' worth of rose petals.[15]

A thirty-three-year-old convict tried to convey the solemn weight of the *vor* tradition during a prison chat with Zhoglo in 1993. The prisoner said that he hoped to be a Thief-in-Law some day; he had already received a recommendation. But he did not feel quite ready. "I have not yet matured psychologically for the crown," he said, with quiet emphasis. Zhoglo, intrigued, asked him where he had worked before he went to prison. "*Grazhdanin nachalnik!* Citizen Chief!" he responded, in a tone of injured pride. "I have spent my whole conscious life in crime. This is my work. At fifteen, I committed my first crime. All this time, I have never taken a hammer in my hands, and I never will."

"The continuity of traditions is very strict," Zhoglo said. "The younger *vory* have to be subordinate to the older ones in every respect, until they gain their own authority. And some of these older men cannot make sense of the modern pace of life. Look at Uncle Vasya, who spent his whole life in prison. He couldn't possibly understand a Georgian hoodlum of twenty who already makes millions and millions of rubles."

A *vor* was chosen by his peers at a gangland assembly or in prison. At least two recommendations from other criminal bosses were required before a future ganglord was anointed at a *podkhod,* or "approach." The more recommendations he received, the more authority a *vor* would have. One powerful ally of Yaponets, the Vladivostok crime lord, received eleven separate recommendations. But even among the six hundred–odd Soviet mobster bosses, there was a definable hierarchy. Formally, they were equal, like members of the Communist Party Central Committee; but some thirty senior leaders set general policy for the country's entire criminal class at private councils, like the one held at Vedentsovo. Within this group, there was an even smaller leadership core. The so-called Bratsky Krug, or Circle of Brothers, contained about seven of the leading Thieves-in-Law in the late 1980s and early 1990s. Many of them have since met violent ends or have left the country. Rafik, a sixty-one-year-old gentlemanly criminal from central Russia, was murdered in prison. Globus, a formidable Moscow boss, was cut down on a Moscow street in 1993. Yaponets, the fifty-two-year-old kingpin of Vladivostok, is somewhere in the United States.

Despite the *vory*'s careful plans at Vedentsovo, keeping order in the post-Soviet criminal world has not been easy. Since the Vedentsovo meeting, the MVD has enlarged the number of *vory* on its books from 600 to 740 men, including 100 who were serving time in prison. In Russia alone, according to 1994 figures, there were 387 active godfathers. Since the Russian crime lord traditionally used prison as his strategic headquarters, the fact that many were behind bars was irrelevant to any measure of the strength of the *vorovskoi mir*. Nevertheless, the increase in the ranks of senior crime lords was also a sign of potential trouble.

Like partisans of any clandestine organization that discovers it has to share responsibility and power once it emerges into the open, veterans of the "frozen era" have not reacted well to younger leaders on the make. The enormous wealth pumped into criminal coffers since 1991 has created unfamiliar pressure on the old criminal structure. Success is clearly generating strains for the Russian underworld, and the inner circles of the criminal leadership have been torn apart by betrayal and jealousy.

One young leader, named Kalina, was murdered on January 19, 1992, after what was believed to be a formal sentence of death by the Circle of Brothers. The twenty-eight-year-old Kalina had received authority beyond his years, because of family connections. His grandfather had been a leading Bolshevik official. Police believe that he was killed because he wanted to diversify into drug trafficking. The *torpedo,* or contract killer, was also executed, a distinctive sign of high-level *vory* involvement.

Even as they triumphed over their Communist opponents, the leaders of the *vorovskoi mir* were challenged by new criminal forces unleashed in the post-Communist world. Several older crime bosses complained to police that high-living "capitalist" thieves were giving them a bad name. "According to *vor* tradition, thieves are not meant to live in luxury, but now that many of them are no longer following the tradition, there is constant conflict," said Colonel Zhoglo.

The present conflict also has roots in the murky history of Russia's underworld. Just as the Soviet Communist Party broke apart under the weight of its historical contradictions, the *vorovskoi mir* was vulnerable because of a schism in its ranks that occurred many decades before, at the time of the outbreak of the Great Patriotic War—the Soviet name for World War II. The consequences of that schism did not become apparent until the Soviet Union collapsed.

After the 1941 Nazi invasion of Russia, thousands of Russian gangsters joined their fellow citizens in the army or in munitions plants. The tug of patriotism outweighed the traditional *vory* ban on association with government. The leaders of the *vorovskoi mir* were appalled by what they considered a betrayal of the gang code of honor. The only concession made by crime elders to the war raging in their front yard was an order prohibiting gang members from robbing or attacking anyone in uniform.

When the gangster heroes returned from the front, they were met with sneers instead of applause from their former comrades. Mobster veterans were labeled with the same pejorative slang word applied to turncoats and informers in prison: *suki,* which means "bitches" or, less profanely, "scabs." Nonplussed, the former criminals resumed their profession after the war, but the final reckoning lay ahead of them: they would inevitably run afoul of the Soviet justice system and find themselves once again behind bars.

In prison, the "turncoats" were judged and sentenced as traitors by the *vory*. Punishment was brutal and swift. During the 1950s, hundreds—perhaps thousands—of convicts were beaten or killed in a so-called Scabs War that engulfed the gulag. The violence had far-reaching consequences both for Soviet society and for the criminal culture.[16]

"The Scabs War allowed the authorities to announce in the mid-1950s that the *vorovskoi mir* had been finished off," Zhoglo said. "They claimed they had extinguished crime in the Soviet Union. And of course that meant police were not supposed to be chasing professional criminals anymore, because they no longer existed. But all that really happened was that the *vory* went further underground. And for the next three decades, while police had their hands tied, the gangs had fertile ground to flourish in."

Inside the *vorovskoi mir,* the wounds of the Scabs War never quite healed. The "bitches" who survived broke their ties with the old crime establishment when they emerged from prison. Having already been punished for violating one tenet of the code, they felt little compunction about ignoring its other commandments, particularly the prohibitions against going into business and trade. The *suki* in effect became the financiers of the black market.

By the late 1980s, some of the most successful wheelers and dealers of the perestroika era were former thieves who had repudiated their origins, and *tsekhoviki,* owners of underground factories. They established working alliances across the black economy with businessmen and government officials—alliances that would have been repugnant to any right-thinking *vor*.

A new type of Russian godfather now challenged the czars of the underworld. Having less regard for gang traditions, he was therefore less susceptible to the cautious morality of the *vor*. The new-style crime boss, called *avtoritet* (authority), transformed the cozy environment of the Soviet underworld. He moved into more risky spheres of criminal behavior, such as bank fraud and drug trafficking, and he commanded wealth beyond the dreams and ambitions of the old *vory*.

"Some of these *avtoritety* can actually rank higher than a *vor* in personal significance," Zhoglo said. "Representatives of the new type of criminal world pay no attention to the *vory*. In prison, of course, everyone has to bow his head to the traditions. But outside, if a criminal has money and his own fighters, he can act independently.

"Every big town in Russia and the former Soviet Union has dozens of powerful groups run by *avtoritety,* some are divided along ethnic lines, and others just by their crime specialties. In cities like St. Petersburg and Yekaterinburg, for instance, the *vory* have lost all their strength to the local groups. In St. Petersburg, when the Authorities sit down to talk with the Thieves-in-Law, they are on equal terms. It's like two generals. And the one who wins is the one who is more intelligent, shrewder. And richer."

By the time of Raspberry's funeral, the tensions between the traditional organized criminal clans and a variety of new "free-lancers" on Russia's crime scene—not to mention the increasingly assertive groups from the Caucasus—were leading to sharply escalated levels of violence. But few people recognized the implications of this gangland competition for post-Communist Russia or how, in particular, it would come to shape the country's transition to the marketplace.

Two years after Raspberry was laid to rest, a very different gangland funeral took place in Moscow. More than a thousand people, including well-known figures from entertainment, politics, and sports, came to

Vagankovskoye Cemetery to pay their respects to Otari Kvantrishvili, a forty-six-year-old former wrestler, who was murdered by a sniper as he emerged from a Moscow bath house. Kvantrishvili was a colorful product of Russian gangster capitalism. Several weeks before his death, one of his business organizations, which exported titanium, aluminum, oil, and cement, was granted a two-year tax holiday in a signed decree from President Yeltsin. It was the most recent sign of Kvantrishvili's complex double life. At the time of his death, he was coach of a popular wrestling team, founder of a new political party (Athletes of Russia), and a benefactor of orphanages. He also owned lucrative gambling interests and was known as an underworld "arbitrator" between mobsters and Russia's elite. Kvantrishvili, in short, was an *avtoritet* of the first order. There were several theories about the motives behind his killing. Some believed that he was murdered by *vory* anxious to cut him down to size. Others wondered whether his liquidation was ordered by senior government officials who decided that he knew too much about their elaborate schemes of kickbacks and insider trading. The range of possibilities spoke volumes about the thickening intrigue of post-Communist Russia.[17]

In the brief period separating the summit at Vedentsovo and the funeral at Vagankovskoye, many of the old *vory*'s worst fears had come to pass. Even as they replaced their Communist enemies as the primary manipulators of the Russian economy, their own authority was under assault. For the first time in more than seven decades, power in the criminal world—just as in politics—was up for grabs to those with the will, weapons, or money to take it. There was no shortage of all three in the New Russia, and those charged with keeping order in the ruins of Communism knew this better than anyone else.

3 Mozhaisky Embankment

Captain Yuri Nikishin, of the Moscow police department's organized-crime squad, was not having a good day. He paced back and forth along the sidewalk in front of 38 Petrovka Street, the faded yellow mansion that serves as the city's central police headquarters. A few pedestrians stopped to watch as members of his squad loaded guns and equipment into unmarked cars double-parked at the curb, but a look from Nikishin sent them on their way. "I have a bad feeling about this," he confided to me.

For nearly a week, Moscow police had been frantically searching for an escaped convict, the leader of a gang that smuggled gold and weapons from the Caucasus. That morning, an informer phoned to report that the man had been seen entering a warehouse owned by his brother on Sevastopol Street. Nikishin immediately pulled his staff away from their other assignments and went to work. But bureaucracy, as usual, was getting in the way.

The chief of the Moscow police department's criminal-investigation division, Nikishin's boss, had to call the Moscow city procurator for approval of the raid. Regulations also required that troops of OMON—the elite counterterrorist unit of the Ministry of Internal Affairs and one of the feared paramilitary arms of the old regime—provide armed backup. It was nearly noon by the time the detectives, buttoning the leather jackets that were the working uniforms of every Moscow plainclothesman, were told they could proceed. Nikishin patted his shoulder holster and stepped into his car. Across the street, an elderly bus with the security agents inside sputtered into motion, and the convoy headed into the midday Moscow traffic.

Twenty minutes later, Nikishin was in despair. The convoy had become thoroughly lost in the city's concrete suburbs. Nikishin called headquarters for new directions, after first borrowing a two-kopek piece from one of his men to use a sidewalk phone box. "I can never find the damn coins any more," he complained. By the time he reached the shabby neighborhood around Sevastopol Street, Nikishin was sure he was too late.

Inside the warehouse, the detectives found only the escaped convict's brother and another employee. Neither of them seemed surprised at the abrupt interruption of their day. Calmly, the brother led police on a tour of the building, through a maze of tiny rooms, each one leading like a child's puzzle to another, and each filled with unopened computer boxes and soiled newspapers.

Nikishin noticed a locked iron door leading to another storeroom, and he allowed himself a faint glimmer of hope. He ordered his men to break the door down. They pounded on it with hammers and then, cursing furiously, tried to pry the hinges apart with a crowbar. Nikishin fought to control his frustration. He glared at the brother, a thin, mustachioed man in a red sweater who was sitting quietly on a bench under the watchful eyes of two sturdy young OMON officers.

"I told you I don't have a key," the man said in a mild, even voice. "You think I'd let you destroy my door if I had a key?"

Nikishin sighed. The iron door seemed to have been bolted shut a century ago. Someone brought a drill, and the room filled with dust and sound.

"We can stop this right now," Nikishin said. "Just tell us where he is."

The noise of the drill made it hard to hear the answer.

"What did you say, idiot?"

"I said I don't know."

Nikishin looked genuinely hurt. He smoothed an invisible wrinkle from his black leather jacket. He sighed again.

"Yob tvoyu mat! Fuck your mother!"

The explosion seemed to come from nowhere. A giant detective with huge hands and a long scar on his cheek brought his wooden billy club down on the bench beside the man with a crack that should have broken it in two. The man flinched.

"You're nothing but shit!" shouted the giant.

Nikishin went on speaking in a pleasant voice, as if there had been no interruption. "Tell us where your brother is, and we'll leave you alone."

The special agents from the OMON watched from the hallway, cradling their Kalashnikovs. Several were smiling. "Good old Yura," one whispered to me. "If anyone can crack this guy, he can."

"I haven't seen my brother in months; he doesn't talk to me," the man insisted.

The giant whistled. He gripped his club again. But Nikishin glanced at him. "No, Sergei," he said.

The man smiled. There was defiance as well as relief in his eyes. "I really don't know what you guys want. But look around. Go ahead. There's nothing to find here."

"Shut up," said the giant, and then he went quietly, after another glance from Nikishin.

The captain touched the man's shoulder. "You think we don't know what you're running here? What all these boxes are for?" Nikishin paused. "It would be easier if you just told us."

"There's no law against having computers," the man said. "The Communists don't run things any more."

"You think smugglers do?" Nikishin flared, and then forced himself to relax. With a great crash, the door fell open. The detectives stormed inside. They pulled down crates from the shelves and ripped open packages. They sniffed at the stale air. A pair of cracked black shoes lay on the floor beside a wrinkled Turkish lira note. A detective held up the note to the light. "What's this worth in dollars?" he joked. Nikishin waited.

Finally, they emerged, perspiring. "Nothing," one of them said. "Not a damn thing."

"I told you," said the man in the red sweater.

He smiled at the officers.

Sergei entered Nikishin's car for the ride back to 38 Petrovka. Without his club the giant seemed subdued, almost gentle. He passed a Marlboro cigarette to Nikishin and shook his head. "These guys," he grunted, "they know what we're doing before we do."

Nikishin was too depressed to reply at first. "It was easier in the old days," he said finally.

The old days were not very long ago. Yuri Nikishin joined the organized crime unit of the Moscow Police Department in 1989, a few weeks after it was created. He was then just twenty-seven years old. The years since have added a touch of brutality to his boyish features. When I first met him through a mutual friend, in the summer of 1992, and asked if I could watch him at work, he was suspicious.

"You won't like it," he said.

"Why?" I said.

"It gets ugly out there," he said with a grin. "Every time we arrest one of these fucking bandits, they warn us they're going to cut up members of our family. So we beat them. It makes them shut up." He laughed. "I sleep with a gun under my pillow every night," he said.

But beneath his macho swagger, there was something intensely likable about Nikishin. As he began to trust me, he felt freer. He was a hockey fanatic, and he would sometimes interrupt a serious conversation with an eager discussion of the game. Or he would suddenly break into a joke. At those moments, he seemed to self-consciously assume the wisecracking sadness of a detective in one of the grade-B Hollywood movies that were then being imported into Russia.

"You no longer feel anything in this job after a while," he said, inhaling deeply on a cigarette. "That's both good and bad. It's good not to feel because of all the ways they can screw your mind up. But you also get blasé, and you lose something, I think."

It struck me that if Nikishin enjoyed playing the tough-guy Hollywood role, it was because there were few other available models for a Russian policeman in his specialty. Ordinary Soviet cops caught thieves and murderers, but Nikishin admitted that they had never been trained in the kind of lateral thinking needed to go after organized crime. Official Soviet law enforcement behavior was carefully programmed. The state was always watching to make sure you never crossed the line. In fact, the forty officers in Nikishin's unit had as much to fear from their bosses as from the criminals. They were assigned to battle a criminal threat which neither their superiors nor their country's leaders acknowledged as real.

Everyone knew that there were gangs, but they were considered isolated pockets of "anti-social" activity. Professional organized crime occurred only in degraded capitalist societies, not in enlightened socialist ones, and the wise cop did not make a point of contradicting official ideology. The Soviet dictionary even defined "racket" as an American concept.[1]

The wall of silence surrounding the Soviet underworld was broken in the late 1980s by a police official-turned-criminologist named Aleksandr Gurov, who warned in a research paper that new and more threatening varieties of organized crime were exploiting perestroika's economic reforms. It was the first time that any senior law enforcement operative had challenged the official view that criminal gangs were anachronistic holdovers of the prerevolutionary area, most of whom had long since been obliterated by Stalin. The notion that organized crime could revive and even take new forms in modern Soviet society was not only unsettling, but subversive. Gurov's paper was never made public, but it was widely circulated inside the interior ministry. He found a valuable ally in Vadim Bakatin, a reform-minded technocrat appointed minister of internal affairs by Gorbachev in 1988, and to the discomfort of the senior bureaucracy Gurov was promoted to general and given the directorship of a new department concerned with fighting crime.

His enemies didn't give up: after only a few years on the job, Gurov was suspended and then fired. But he left one tangible legacy behind him. Thanks to Gurov's efforts, the federal MVD set up an organized crime squad. The Moscow city government followed suit. Like their Kremlin counterparts, however, the city Party authorities at first demonstrated little faith in Western-style law enforcement concepts and tactics.[2]

Moscow's organized crime detectives were given a tiny budget, and they had to struggle for office space. Ironically, they found that their forced invisibility gave them an early edge in the battle with the Moscow underworld. "Few people knew about our unit—and that included criminals as well as police," Nikishin recalled with a grin.

The squad lost no time in proving Gurov right about the threat facing Soviet society. Moscow, the richest city in the country and the hub of political power, was the most glittering prize of all for organized criminals. Gangs of Russian hoodlums, known collectively as *shpana,* began moving into the capital to take advantage of the new "business" opportunities created by perestroika. The Lyubertsy, the Dolgoprudniki, the Solntsevskiye, and the Balashikhinskiye (all named after the Moscow suburbs where they were based) were among the groups that established control over key areas of the city. At the same time, several non-Russian bands from the Caucasus moved into the city and became powerful forces in their own right. The investigation of a racket run by one of the Caucasus gangs gave the Moscow mob squad its first taste of the changing nature of professional crime in Russia.

In the late 1980s, a group of gangsters from what was then the Chechen-Ingush Autonomous Republic of the Russian Federation took over a car dealership run by small-time Georgian criminals at Yuzhny Port (South Port) on the Moscow river. Automobile production was just then beginning to expand in the Soviet Union, as the government tried to meet the rising hunger for consumer goods. But the car business was a state monopoly. A would-be motorist often waited years after putting his name down on a list at his enterprise or factory for his car. He had no choice of models, and if the car happened to arrive unusable, or missing key parts, there was no recourse.

At Yuzhny Port, the enterprising Georgians took control of a Moscow version of a used-car lot. Muscovites who wanted to trade or resell brought their cars to the lot, circumventing the state's red tape. It was formally against the rules of course, but the Georgians bought the co-operation of local officials and police with bribes. The business prospered so well that it soon attracted the Chechens. They offered to buy the Georgians out. When they refused, the Chechens merely turned to the police and offered a larger piece of the action in return for their help in evicting the Georgians.

The Chechens quickly improved on the Georgian operation. They increased the volume of sales on the lot by the simple expedient of stealing cars wherever they could find them. Soon, Yuzhny Port was a central trading house for hot cars around the Soviet Union, and the profits financed other illicit businesses.

When the Moscow organized-crime squad was formed, the Chechen gangs were already among the wealthiest criminal groups in the city. No ordinary group of hoodlums, they were a paramilitary organization— well-armed and disciplined, with links to cities across southern Russia and the Caucasus. The private car markets of Moscow were just one of their springboards to influence. They were exactly the kind of sophis- ticated criminal group that Gurov had identified as beneficiaries and exploiters of perestroika. With no clearly defined boundaries between legal and illegal economic behavior, the shrewdest criminal bosses were hard to distinguish from entrepreneurs. But this was not the only aspect of the Chechens' special challenge to Soviet police.

The Chechens belonged to a chapter of Russian history shrouded in romantic legend. In the nineteenth century, they had been one of the fiercest of the Muslim Caucasian tribesmen standing in the way of czarist expansion to the south, and they were subdued only after more than a hundred years of bitter guerrilla warfare. Few twentieth-century Russians considered that the mountain peoples might ever again be a threat. Soviet history books, after all, went to great pains to point out how those nations once victimized by czarist imperialism had happily joined the union of Soviet peoples under the banner of internationalism.

Nikishin's small band of crime fighters only began to make headway against the Chechens when they ignored the official Party line and studied the Chechens' genuine historical grievances. "They came from a poor land, which they couldn't farm, and after all those years they still considered themselves the victims of Russian imperialism," he observed.

Even in 1989, this was risky intellectual territory for a Soviet police officer. Despite Gorbachev's decision in 1987 to raise the curtain on Stalinist crimes, most Soviet citizens were well aware that many of the "dark spots" in their country's past continued to remain off-limits to public examination. But for the organized-crime squad's understanding of their opponents, it was crucial to learn that during World War II, thousands of Chechens had been uprooted from their homes and deported to Central Asia as a result of Josef Stalin's fear that the Caucasian peoples would collaborate with the German troops driving up from the Caspian Sea. In conversations with the Chechen gangsters, Nikishin discovered that the deportations had strengthened the very characteristics that made them such a cohesive and dangerous criminal threat.

"They had a strong clan system, based on family ties," he said. "Every Chechen youth was taught to respect and obey his elders and distrust outsiders." They were also addicted to firearms as a way of settling disputes or merely demonstrating prowess. "They seemed to me very similar to the Sicilian mafia," Nikishin said.

When the Chechens were finally permitted to return after the war, they found that their best land had been occupied by strangers. "What else could many of them do but turn to crime?" said Nikishin. "The land left to them wasn't fertile, and they had big families. It was a logical step to turn the clans into criminal groups."

The new opportunities for trade and business in Moscow and other large cities were already attracting traders and would-be entrepreneurs from all over the Soviet Union. These were opportunities that the Chechen gangs could not resist.

The comparison between the Chechens and foreign mafiosi extended even to their style of behavior. In Moscow, they began to dress like American mobsters from the thirties. "They got their style—zoot suits, slicked hair—from Western mafia films, even though they had plenty of money to buy modern clothes," Nikishin said with amusement on his face.

There was nothing humorous, however, about their style of crime. The victims of Chechen "business methods" were turning up all over Moscow in 1990 and 1991, with bullets holes in the head or back.

Nikishin was instrumental in putting one of the top Chechen bosses into prison, a veteran warlord nicknamed Khosey, which in Chechen means "little bird." Khosey's real name was Nikolai Suleimanov, and he had been arrested once before; but thanks to his "connections" with senior police authorities and government officials, he had served only a few years in jail. In the late 1980s, Khosey achieved enough power to organize most of the Chechen criminal bands under his leadership. The organized crime unit set Khosey up with a classic sting operation, arresting him as he accepted extortion money from a prominent businessman they had wired with a microphone. With Khosey's arrest in 1990, Nikishin's squad believed they were finally making headway against Chechen power in Moscow.

After August 19, 1991, however, everything changed. Among the Kremlin generals and senior bureaucrats who kidnapped Mikhail Gorbachev and established an "Emergency Committee" to rescue the country from democrats was Nikishin's supreme boss, the cold-eyed Boris Pugo, a former KGB chief from Latvia, whom Gorbachev had appointed in 1990 to succeed Bakatin as minister of internal affairs. In the first, tense week of the coup, he was eagerly preparing to carry out the first resolution published by the country's would-be leaders: a war on crime.

Listing crime among the reasons they had decided to put the country back in order, the members of the Emergency Committee pledged "a decisive struggle against the shadow economy [and] corruption," and vowed to "cleanse the streets" of criminals. At 38 Petrovka Street, police were given an early indication of how the committee intended to back up its rhetoric. Nikishin was handed a copy of a secret order establishing a special anti-crime task force of twenty thousand officers. The directive, scheduled to be published August 24, also included a plan to divide Moscow into 33 special military districts, in which police would have extraordinary powers to arrest and detain all those found with weapons or drugs.[3]

At first glance, the Emergency Committee seemed headed in the right direction. Nikishin knew much more than his fellow citizens about the nature of the threat from the criminal underworld, and he was painfully aware of the strain it placed on meager police resources. Like his fellow officers, he doubted the commitment of the Gorbachev government to wiping out organized crime.

But he had mixed feelings about the task force. "If the Committee had won, we might really have cleaned up the gangs," Nikishin conceded. "We knew exactly who the main crime leaders were, and it would have been easy to get them in one swoop. But this would not be democracy; it would be totalitarianism." A number of Moscow detectives, to their credit, expressed the same private doubts. Even those who cared little about politics recognized that the plan was overkill. "You didn't really need twenty thousand troops," Nikishin suggested. "A few hundred trained detectives, with the proper support, could get rid of the crime bosses."

It seemed a large boast, even for Nikishin, but no one got a chance to prove it either way. The coup leaders' plan turned out to be an academic exercise. When their putsch collapsed, Pugo, in disgrace, shot himself, and his fellow conspirators went to jail. A few months later, the Soviet Union was gone, and with it, apparently, any hope of controlling the chaos on the streets of Russian cities.

A week after his disappointing adventure on Sevastopol Street, Yuri Nikishin took me to Moscow's principal stolen-car market. It was no longer at Yuzhny Port, but was now in the center of town, where it occupied a lot the size of a city block. The process of getting a car had loosened up since the days of perestroika, but there were still hundreds of buyers eager to avoid red tape and delivery snarls. The Chechens, who still controlled and operated the business, had expanded to meet the rising demand.

Hoping to be inconspicuous, we entered from a back street called

Mozhaisky Embankment. Nikishin was wearing his usual uniform of black leather jacket and scuffed shoes.

"Don't talk," he whispered urgently. "They'll know you're a foreigner."

We were to pose as car buyers, but after a few moments I wondered why we had bothered taking any precautions at all. Knots of bored men in padded, wide-shouldered suits hovered around the lot. As soon as they saw us, they casually moved away. Nikishin sighed. "I think they probably remember me," he said. "The last time I came here was over six months ago. This place has really taken off since then."

Rows of gleaming new cars filled every available space in what appeared to be an outdoor showroom. Most were Soviet models, but I could see the hood of the odd Mercedes or Volvo poking out. Some of the bored loungers turned out to be salesmen. They watched benevolently as interested buyers kicked tires and slammed doors. But business seemed to operate in slow motion. No money appeared to change hands. In one corner of the lot, I saw a policeman.

Nikishin noticed my astonishment. "He's supposed to be there to register the sale of every car," he smiled. "The municipality has officially licensed this place as a used-car lot; that's why things have gotten so sophisticated. The militiaman gets a lot of money from the mafiya to look the other way."

A stamp on a document miraculously transformed new automobiles into used ones, thereby allowing car owners to get around government red tape limiting the private sale of new cars. The lot charged five thousand rubles for the transformation, but that was only the beginning of a profitable deal for all the parties. If the salesman found a buyer, the owner stood to get back twice or three times what he paid. A Volga sold off the assembly line for 340,000 rubles would be worth one million rubles by the time it passed through Mozhaisky Embankment. Once a sale was negotiated, the lot owners took another hefty commission, and paid a cut to the friendly policeman.

"There's nothing we can do about it," Nikishin growled. "We don't have the resources to pick up every cop on the take."

Besides, as he pointed out, the used-car trade was only a front for the real business of Mozhaisky Embankment. A car stolen anywhere in Russia or the former Soviet Union received a new identity here before it was moved again, either by a profitable direct sale or by shipment to other regions. The salesmen were decoys for what was one of the country's busiest transportation depots. The foreign cars were smuggled in from the Baltic republics, where local criminal syndicates acted as middlemen for cars stolen in Europe, or they were grabbed off the street by rings of increasingly sophisticated car thieves in Moscow and other major cities. According to police figures, between thirty and forty cars disappear each day in the Russian capital. Some are even "hijacked" while the owners are still inside.

As Nikishin indicated, authorities had been forced to ignore the boom in the illicit automobile trade. Only seventeen Moscow policemen were assigned to the unit dealing with stolen cars in 1992. Even if a hijacker fell into official hands, he had little reason to worry. Only 10 percent of the car thieves apprehended were actually sent to prison.[4]

The festering inefficiency and corruption of law enforcement authorities made life much easier for the Chechens and Russia's other post-Communist criminals. "They understood they could make money without necessarily holding a gun," Nikishin said.

Mozhaisky Embankment displayed the irritating paradox of Russia's gangster economy. Although the Chechens had started in the criminal underworld, their success had enabled them to cross the line into legal activity. By 1993, the syndicate operating the stolen-car market had already amassed enough profits to invest in a large automobile assembly plant in southern Russia.

"Once they work out the terms of protection with the local mafiya on the scene, they will have a perfectly legal way of obtaining cars," Nikishin said. "Maybe they will eventually own the factory."

To some Russians and foreigners, the movement of organized crime into legitimate business activity suggested that the "gangster-capitalist" was a natural phase of economic development. Many of the great industrial barons of Western capitalism, after all, had equally unsavory origins. But was the Russian mafiya really capable of leading, or even contributing to, Russia's transition from Communism?

"Some of our economists claim we should legalize our mafiosi because they are nothing more than ordinary businessmen trying to make a living," said Aleksandr Gurov. "That reminds me of how we used to be told that our bright future lay in socialist competition and the Communist Party. I think the mafiya are even more of a threat than the

Communists. Why should they accept a 10 percent profit, when they are used to getting 100 percent?"

Aleksandr Gurov's opinions are hard to ignore—even in "exile." He was working in a paper-strewn cubbyhole of an office in the Lubyanka when I located him in 1992. It was an appropriately symbolic place to find the man who was both the pioneer and the pariah of modern Soviet criminology. The Lubyanka, headquarters of the former KGB, occupies an entire city block in the center of Moscow. Still one of the grimmest spots in Soviet geography, its barred windows cast a gray pall over the busy city square which it adjoins. History has evicted some of the building's most notorious recent occupants (though far from all of them), and under its new names—first the Russian Ministry of Security, now the Federal Counter-Intelligence Service—it retains its forbidding aura as keeper of the state's secrets. Assignment to the old KGB prison and torture chamber was a kind of punishment for Gurov, who, for reasons he would not explain, was trapped in a dead-end job there, handling the security ministry's relations with the press.[5]

A short, squarely built man in a rumpled suit, he was embarrassingly eager to put aside the bundle of dry public communiques he was working on to talk with me. Our conversation lasted almost three hours, and in the heavy silences of the Lubyanka—not even a footstep echoed in the corridors outside his cell—I caught a glimpse of the tragedy that gave birth to the gangster-riddled world of the New Russia. What Gurov told me that afternoon inspired this book, and continues to form the intellectual underpinning of its argument. The scrappy general believed that the criminal order which enveloped Russia in the aftermath of Communism was not accidental. He was convinced that powerful interests had a stake in its success.

"When I released my study, many people understood perfectly well what I was talking about," he said. "But legal experts were so preoccupied with proving how wonderful our Soviet system was, they ignored what was in front of their eyes."

They ignored it, Gurov said, because his message underscored the criminality at the heart of the Soviet system. Instead of following the accepted ideological approach of tracing organized criminal activity to alien (anti-socialist) influences, Gurov placed organized crime at the center of Russian politics. The huge profits that crime lords began to earn in the black market could only have been possible with the tacit approval, if not the open cooperation, of government authorities and police.

"Not a single [organized criminal group] would exist today if it weren't for those links," he said. "After 1985, when the gangs began making ties across republics and even international borders, they began to resemble formal business organizations. As they grew, they increased their corrupt ties with officials. You now see them all over the country. Even in Khabarovsk, for instance [a city in the Russian Far East], the gang structure has links with foreign partners in Japan and South Korea. The Caucasian mafiyas have branches all over the country."

In his research, Gurov concentrated in particular on the generation of criminals that came of age following the Scabs War. Unlike their traditional rivals, the black marketeers of the 1960s and 1970s crossed the line dividing the underworld and the state. They operated in easy and mutually profitable cooperation with Soviet bureaucrats.

"It was bound to happen as soon as our system opened up, and that was in the so-called thaw of the 1960s when [Nikita] Khrushchev was in power," he said. "It was impossible to imagine powerful organized-crime groups under Stalin, because a totalitarian regime destroys any rival organization. What we got after that in our society was the moral code of the plunderer. The code of the black market. And of course it was run totally in the interests of the [Party] bureaucracy. For example, we had a so-called 'trade mafiya' in Moscow with representatives in top Party bodies as early as 1974.

"If I or anyone else had tried to warn people about the danger of the shadow economy then, liberals would have laughed, and the government would have called us crazy. But that was how it all started. And the government allowed it to happen, for reasons that ought to make us think. It began under Khrushchev and developed under Brezhnev. But the Gorbachev era was the period when organized crime really became powerful in our country.

"Once upon a time, even as late as 1982, you could say that the *vory v zakonye* determined all the underground life in our country. But that was before we had cooperatives or bankers. In 1985 and 1986, when the cooperative movement was starting up, 60 percent of those cooperatives were run by former or active criminals, by the new *avtoritety*. When people say these were just entrepreneurs who were trying to make a start in business, they have it wrong. Sure, there were people trying in their own way to make a living, to perform a service, but they didn't have much of a chance against the criminals. These so-called entrepreneurs were people who stole from the rest of us. They cheated in their factories and their production lines and reserved the best stuff for their own private trade. I've estimated that 80 percent of the chiefs of small criminal groups today are former deputy directors, former administrators of factories and enterprises."

These gangster-bureaucrats, or comrade criminals, were to find themselves at the center of the relationship between capitalism, crime, and government in post-Communist Russia. But, as Gurov noted, their extraordinary influence and wealth was already becoming apparent in the late 1980s.

Typical of the type was Anatoli Vladimirov, a thirty-seven-year-old former science teacher in the St. Petersburg Polytechnical Institute. He took over the local subsidiary of a Kiev scientific-commercial firm called Planeta in 1989 and soon displayed a special talent for crime.[6]

Taking advantage of the hazy legal climate of perestroika business, Vladimirov signed contracts to supply goods and cars to various firms around the city without bothering to fulfill them. The buyers never paid any money, but Vladimirov used the signed contracts to obtain bank credit. The banks had no way of knowing—and little interest in determining—whether the contracts were legitimate. On the basis of his credit, Vladimirov took out enormous loans, which he invested in other businesses. Or he presented his bank's credit slip to another bank and immediately redeemed it for cash. Within a few years, Vladimirov had built an enormous and powerful organization out of his false-contract business, which he soon turned into a sophisticated protection racket. Planeta opened sixteen branches around the city, ostensibly as a goods-supply firm. Former police officers were hired to act as enforcers when "clients" refused to sign Vladimirov's contracts. One reluctant businessmen was locked in a food store refrigerator for several hours.

By 1991, Vladimirov's wealth had earned him such a prominent place in the city's social and political scene that he gained a reputation as a philanthropist. Planeta contributed millions of rubles to a fund for restoring old St. Petersburg. Vladimirov even offered to rebuild a district police station, and investigators later discovered that several city councillors were on his private payroll, receiving monthly salaries of two thousand rubles (then a sizable sum). Vladimirov indulged his enthusiasm for science by donating huge amounts of money and high-tech equipment to the city's poverty-stricken Institute of Theoretical Astronomy. In December, 1991, grateful scientists at the institute named star number 4267, which had been discovered twenty years earlier, after their benefactor. They called it Anvlad.

Soon, however, they had to withdraw the name. Vladimirov was arrested on fraud and extortion charges. His star had finally fallen to earth.

Vladimirov's criminal career was short-lived, but many others were to follow the same pattern and to receive the same winking support of officialdom. The successful pursuit of wealth in the late Communist era was tainted with much more than larceny: government was a necessary and silent partner in crime. Vladimirov's story helps explain why "moving to capitalism" can have an entirely different meaning in Russia and other former Communist states from what it has elsewhere. Without clear rules or models, free enterprise is often a license for criminal behavior.

"What we have to remember is that criminal organizations never appear spontaneously. There are always objective reasons," said Aleksandr Gurov. "In the West, the mafiya rose out of purely criminal activities like extortion or bootlegging. But with us, even normal activities—making profits, creating associations without having to ask permission from the state—were illegal. That's why [crime] organizations have been part of our Soviet society from the beginning. If we don't understand that, we can't understand why these things are happening to us today."

4 Comrade Criminal

Seran Akopyan opened his tiny grocery store on Moscow's Krasnoprudnaya Street in the spring of 1992, soon after municipal authorities gave private citizens the right to lease state retail shops. A few months later, he bought a gun.

"It's just a gas pistol," Akopyan smiled, pulling it from the bottom drawer of his desk. "It can't kill anybody. But it's useful in this neighborhood."

In more than five years as a correspondent in the Soviet Union, I could not remember ever meeting an ordinary, law-abiding civilian with a weapon. But I could see Akopyan's point. His business was within bullet range of one of the roughest districts in the capital. The nearby Central Market was a haven for drug dealers. A few blocks away, the Kazan, Yaroslavl, and Leningrad railway terminals attracted runaway children, beggars, drunks, con men, thieves, and prostitutes.

When the stations were built in the early years of the twentieth century, they had been magical additions to the Moscow skyline. Today, their clock towers and soaring fairy-tale roofs look forlorn against the hustle and grime of New Russia.

Akopyan's grocery was a more fitting monument to the new age of Russian capitalism than the railway stations. Most Soviet food stores were grim, cluttered places, where a pushing mob of customers faced sour-looking clerks over counters filled with largely unrecognizable merchandise. Beyond the heavy glass doors of Akopyan's food emporium, however, was a new world. The shelves and floors were briskly swept clean of litter. Clerks in spotless aprons stood in front of rows of tinned food, imported vegetables, and jars of pickled spices—all neatly sorted by category and size. Cellophane-wrapped packages of meat and poultry were piled invitingly in a large, modern freezer, a sight unimaginable in a normal Moscow *produkty* store. Akopyan's store radiated enterprise and profit.

But the shopkeeper's gun was proof that the businesslike atmosphere inside his establishment offered no protection from the predatory world outside. "The other night, there was a shoot-out outside my door," he said. "A bunch of guys just opened fire on each other, like cowboys, and when we came to work the next morning, there was blood all over the sidewalk."

He bought the weapon following an unpleasant encounter with the neighborhood mafiya. A pair of hoodlums walked through his door one evening when the shop was nearly empty and the storekeeper was counting the day's receipts. Smiling at Akopyan, they complimented him on the success of his new business. They wondered whether he would be interested in a long-term "protection" arrangement.

Akopyan is small and wiry, with a black mustache and a combustible temper. When the hoodlums emphasized their point by methodically kicking over chairs and sweeping his papers to the floor, he cursed and lunged at them. Years of lifting heavy crates had put strength in his arms and shoulders. To his surprise, his visitors fled into the night.

As he recounted the story, Akopyan was disconcertingly casual. "Most of the mafiosi in this area don't make trouble for me," he said. "They even bring me some of their stolen goods—imported tape recorders, that sort of thing—and ask me to sell them. I tell them no, and they go away. But some of the groups are not easy to handle, even for me."

According to the mutual friend who introduced us, Akopyan was among the few private businessmen in the city who did not have to worry about satisfying mafiya greed—and it wasn't because he carried a gun. My friend hinted that Akopyan had powerful mob connections.

"He's the biggest food distributor in north Moscow, and he knows everyone," he said. Lowering his voice meaningfully, he added, "To have a food business in Moscow is to have power in a hungry country like ours—and he knows how to use his power."

Akopyan did not mind being perceived as having a secret, darker dimension. "I have always known influential people," he said grandly. "Everyone knows me in this region."

Was the shopkeeper a minor crime lord, as my friend tried to suggest? Or was he an honest man trying to make his way in a world which could be cruel and unforgiving to the timid?

As I continued talking with him, it was apparent that the quest for profit in post-Soviet Russia required a businessman to play both roles.

For instance, he soon found a way to discourage further visits from the gang that had tried to pull him into an extortion racket. The same hoodlums returned to his store a few weeks later, but this time Akopyan was ready. Several large, powerful men were waiting inside his office, and as soon as the gangsters stepped inside, they overwhelmed them in a melee of fists and sticks. The shopkeeper merely had to watch.

Who were these men? Akopyan described them, with an uneasy smile, as his "friends." He said that after the attack he had formed an "association" of 120 strong young fighters, including former policemen, black-belt karate experts, and wrestling champions. "From now on, if I'm in trouble, I know I can always call my friends," he said, "and in ten minutes they will be here to help me." The shopkeeper had evidently learned valuable lessons from Uganov, the Armenian *vor* who had impressed him as a child in Karabakh, in the art of overcoming the obstacles Russia threw up to its citizens—and of profiting from them.

Akopyan soon felt confident enough to expand his business interests. He became part-owner of a cooperative called Melik ("prince" in Armenian), which was soon earning enough money for him to contemplate putting another five million rubles into his shop for improvements. The cooperative had several sponsors, but "we don't always like the way they do business," he acknowledged. Melik, he said, was not a food store, but he refused to tell me what services it provided. "That is a secret," he said.

A few weeks after he developed his private security force, Akopyan was in Grozny, the capital of Chechnya (and the national home of the Chechen mob). When he prepared to board the airplane for his homeward flight to Moscow, an airport official informed him that there were no seats—a transparent attempt to extract a bribe. Strengthened by the newly found "friends" he could call on, Akopyan played the gangster.

"I told the guy he had two choices," Akopyan boasted. "He could let me on the plane and then go home, and I'd be sure to guarantee he had some wine and nice things. Or he could keep me from boarding—in which case he would spend the rest of his life trying to earn enough money to pay his medical bills." Akopyan boarded the plane.

With his "association" behind him, Akopyan no longer feared anyone. "The mafiya provide certain services," he said. "If you need goods, they can find them quickly," he said. "If you're having a problem, they solve it so that you can be sure no one else will get in your way. People need protection. What does it matter who provides it, or who they pay?"

But this picture of the "evolution" of an honest shopkeeper into an aggressive participant in gangster economics was incomplete. There was another reason why the mafiya held no terrors for Akopyan; its tactics were simply an extension of the system he had been working in most of his life.

When Seran Akopyan decided to become a capitalist, at the age of forty-five, he was already manager of one of the city's largest state food warehouses. He tried playing by the rules established under the government's 1992 privatization plan. He wrote a formal letter of application to participate in the bidding for a lease; he paid the registration fee; he obtained references from a bank. But he was getting nowhere.[1]

Then a municipal official he had known for years arrived one night at his door. The two men spent an hour chatting over glasses of *tutovka,* Akopyan's favorite throat-searing cognac from his native Karabakh, in the Caucasus Mountains. Finally, Akopyan's visitor cleared his throat.

"That shop you want on Krasnoprudnaya Street," he began. "It can be arranged that you get the lease. But, you know . . . it has to be bought first."

Akopyan understood immediately. "How much?" he asked.

"Two hundred thousand rubles."

As he conducted me on a tour of his establishment, Akopyan gave me a further education in the ethics of post-Communism. He proudly pointed to a corner of the room where ten-pound bags of rice were stacked.

"In your country, all you need to do is ring up some distributor and say I want so much rice; please bring it around next week," he said, and then he smiled. "That's not how it works here."

Akopyan mimicked someone handing over a bottle.

"So only the person who pays a bribe gets the goods?" I asked.

Akopyan laughed. "No, not necessarily. You have to be known and trusted. Even though I may have the money to pay, that doesn't ensure I will get what I need. Personal sympathy, that's what counts."

He went on to explain. "If you are starting a shop, you still need to get approval for everything you do, even after you come up with the money to buy it. The local district committee wants to see your re-modeling blueprints. The regional food ministry official has to approve the purchase of machinery, and there's the health inspector. But when you go to see the bureaucrat, he's reluctant. He tells you that he's busy, and that things could take a lot of time.

"So you tell him you happen to know there is really good beer for sale at such and such a shop. He's interested. Everyone knows there's a shortage of beer. You ring the shopowner who happens to be a friend of yours, and you tell him to set aside some beer, and of course you tell your friend not to take any money from this bureaucrat but to put it on your account. He goes along with it because he knows someday you could help him. It works perfectly—and you get your approval."

Akopyan smiled again. "People exaggerate when they say you need thousands of rubles to get things done," he continued. "It's often just a question of fitting in with someone's interests. As I said, it's all based on personal sympathy."

Twenty years earlier, Akopyan was considerably less cynical. When he first arrived in the capital from the Caucasus, he was a fervent be-liever in the system.

"I actually wrote a statement to my bosses on my first Moscow job, saying I thought our life in the Soviet Union was the most correct way of life," Akopyan laughed. "I wanted to live like a real Communist, and I even told them I didn't want a big salary, just enough so my family could live. I got those ideals from my father, who was a military engineer—one of those crystal-pure souls who believed that to be a Communist was the best thing in the world. I believed everything he taught me. But it didn't take me long once I came to Moscow to see what was behind all that propaganda."

Akopyan's first job in Moscow was on an assembly line, producing jet engines for Russian MIGs. He worked hard—too hard, he said. His bosses were irritated to discover that their zealous apprentice was earn-ing more in bonuses than they were. They made his life uncomfortable, and he finally left the factory to work as a forwarding agent in a food warehouse. There, he received his initiation in the system's brand of corruption.

"We would get an order to ship 120 kilograms of sausage to some shop, but the shipments we sent out contained only 100 kilograms," Akopyan remembered. "Where were the other twenty? They were shifted into the manager's private stock so he could sell them for his own profit. It was up to us to cover the loss."

The "private stock" made its way into the black market. But the so-called shadow economy was more than a vast private supermarket. It was also the only place real work ever got done. Some Russians now say that the phrases "black market" or "shadow business" are misleading, because they convey a system that thrived on the edges of the real economy. According to Lev Timofeyev, a former Soviet dissident who became active in the reformers' movement in the 1990s, the market was not "black," but "universal." "In the last decades in the USSR, not a single product has been manufactured and not a single paid service has been performed outside the confines of the black market," he wrote in a book published after the fall of Communism, called *The Secret Rulers of Russia*. "[It was] the living blood circulating in a dead organism." The black market is a key to understanding the history of the Soviet Union as well as the trauma of post-Communist Russia. "The entire Soviet system—everything without exception—was nothing more than an enormous black market," Timofeyev observed.[2]

Learning how to manipulate the black market was part of the education of every Soviet manager.[3] A few years after Akopyan arrived in Moscow, the director of his warehouse was fired for "infringement of party discipline." No one explained what his crime was, but he had apparently raised uncomfortable questions with Party authorities about missing shipments of goods. A day after the firing, the astonished Akopyan was asked to take his place. It was an invitation he could not have refused without being subject to the same Party "discipline" as his predecessor. But as he sat around conference tables with colleagues from other warehouses, he began to understand why he was chosen. He was a youthful, upwardly mobile official; he was expected to have no conscience.

"I realized," Akopyan said, "that you needed to lie in order to survive."

He had excellent teachers. During the 1970s and 1980s, the state wholesale food distribution network was one of the country's most corruption-riddled enterprises, and Moscow was its golden hub. The Party and city officials in charge of food supply ran the aptly called "trade mafiya." It was centered in what was then the city's largest *ga-*

stronom (a department store selling fresh food and dried goods) that had in turn served as a popular prerevolutionary store, Eliseyev's.

The *gastronom* was controlled by a bureaucrat named Yuri Sokolov, who used bribes and political contacts to ensure that he received a steady supply of hard-to-get gourmet and luxury foods from state outlets. He sold most of those supplies "from the back door" to favored customers and other retail shops for high prices. He was an extremely rich man, and a generous one. He used his earnings—along with the occasional German salami and bottle of French champagne—to bribe his way into the inner Kremlin circle, where he became a silent associate of luminaries such as Viktor Grishin, then Moscow Party chief and one of the rumored front-runners to become the next Soviet leader following Brezhnev's death.

Sokolov's enterprise came to an unfortunate end. Authorities opened a criminal investigation into his business dealings—but their attention was motivated by politics rather than judicial zeal. Sokolov's patrons were caught up in the internal Kremlin power struggles at the close of the Brezhnev era, and their enemies decided to strike at them through their friendly grocer. Sokolov was arrested, tried, and eventually executed. But it proved to be only a minor setback for the trade mafiya, which was soon thriving again under a new cabal of bosses.[4]

Minor bureaucrats like Akopyan found themselves caught inside the web of corruption merely by trying to follow orders. During the 1980 Summer Olympics, held in Moscow, the government ordered the rush delivery of food shipments from all over the country to the capital to impress visiting foreigners with the advantages of socialism. There were soon so many trucks waiting at loading docks that the food began to rot. "There was nowhere to store it; the fridges were full," remembered Akopyan.

But no warehouse director could refuse delivery of the food without risking the wrath of Party officials. Akopyan, through his contacts in the trade mafiya, arranged for the foodstuffs he received to be sold privately in the Moscow region while they remained officially on his books. He was rewarded with a percentage of the profits.

Similar "special arrangements" were common in every industry connected with food. In a complex scheme operated by the Ministry of Fisheries, top-quality caviar and seafood were sent to special shops around the nation, whose managers immediately sold the foodstuffs privately for amounts five or six times higher than the state price. In their reports to Moscow, they claimed to have received the official price, and they pocketed the difference after paying the required kickbacks to their ministry watchdogs.[5]

Greedy bureaucrats are as familiar as borshch in Russian culture. They cram the pages of Gogol and Dostoyevsky. But the Soviet regime broke new ground in corruption, and few politicians dared tackle it publicly. Mikhail Gorbachev once took his friend and future Soviet foreign minister Eduard Shevardnadze aside during a meeting of Communist leaders at the Black Sea resort of Pitsunda in the early 1980s for a walk and a private conversation that was too delicate for the ears of untrustworthy listeners. Corruption was dragging the country through the mud, he said. Both men agreed that the system had turned "rotten" at the core. Gorbachev later called that conversation the starting point for the entire perestroika crusade. But long afterward, Shevardnadze, who had led his own campaign against bribe takers and influence peddlers in Georgia when he was that republic's minister of internal affairs, admitted that neither of them had understood the roots of the problem.

"As long as there was a shortage of goods, food, and services, no matter how harsh the laws and how brutal the law-enforcement officers, [the] evil would not be eradicated," said Shevardnadze in 1991. "The sources for these ills [were] in the system itself . . . the conservativism in the economy, the centralized system, the monopoly on property."[6]

In office, Gorbachev became the first Soviet Communist leader to provide a public estimate of the shadow economy. During a 1987 speech, he claimed that the annual black-market turnover was 1.5 billion rubles (equivalent at the time to nearly two billion dollars). Most domestic observers considered this a low estimate, but Gorbachev also made the link—unprecedented for a Kremlin politician—between high-level corruption and the booming black market. It was "not accidental," he pointed out, that bribery was a common form of behavior in the Soviet system.[7]

But the limits of what he and senior leaders were prepared to do to stop it became apparent in the case of Boris Yeltsin, who had similarly begun his rise to national prominence as a corruption fighter. Shortly after the Siberian populist was appointed Moscow Party chief in 1985, he went on a much-publicized tour of food shops around the capital. To the satisfaction of Muscovites, he attacked the trade mafiya and accused them of causing shortages. But the trade mafiya soon had its revenge. Yeltsin's defiance of nomenklatura interests, which included firing several top municipal officials for corruption, got him thrown off his job and then yanked off the Politburo itself.

Yeltsin's firing became one of the crucial episodes in the decline and fall of Soviet power. The reason commonly given for his dismissal was the harsh criticism he had leveled at Gorbachev and other Politburo members for their ambiguous policies toward economic reform. But Yeltsin's anti-corruption campaign in Moscow played a significant and unheralded role. His attacks on the Party mafiya isolated him from the support he might have found in the Kremlin's inner circle and made his downfall inevitable. Despite their own attitudes toward the rot eating away the system from inside, Gorbachev and his few reform allies in the government never felt confident about their power to challenge it. Ironically, the course of Russian history might have been different if Yeltsin's campaign had not been abruptly cut short. As Yeltsin wrote later in his autobiography, he was threatened with death if he continued to persecute Moscow's mafiya bosses.[8]

The Yeltsin episode demonstrated the thin line between politics and corruption in the Soviet system. The crooked secret networks were often used after 1985 to sabotage perestroika. Much earlier, some scholars already predicted that the black market would become a stronghold of conservative nomenklatura opposition to reform. "Since the second economy was an important source of income to many in high places, it is likely they will resist and sabotage any important steps towards the formal liberalization of the economy," Gregory Grossman, a historian of the Soviet economy, wrote in 1977.[9]

The sabotage became apparent during the so-called food shortages of the late 1980s. Attempts to liberalize commodity prices were accompanied by the mysterious disappearance of food in the shops. There was widespread talk of an approaching famine, which naturally provided ammunition for conservative opponents of perestroika. These shortages, however, were almost entirely inspired by political manipulation of the food industry. At the height of the famine scare, I visited several food warehouses in Moscow, which were stacked high with produce.

Similar reports came in from St. Petersburg. Akopyan admitted that he and his colleagues were under constant pressure during that period.

"There was a time, for instance, when there was no sugar in the shops," Akopyan recalled. "Some people blamed the anti-alcohol campaign, because a lot of sugar was going into making private [illicit] liquor. Others said it was because of the government's wrongheaded policies. But the truth was, we always had plenty of sugar stocked in our warehouses. We were just told to keep it off the shelves.

"There was panic everywhere, and when we finally started to deliver the sugar, people bought it in such huge quantities that there was a danger of a real shortage. So warehouse directors were told to keep it off the shelves again. Some sold what they had privately to store directors and made money that way. Everyone was happy."

Ironically, perestroika's economic reforms, instead of tackling corruption, made it worse. Since the 1970s, the illegal profits of the bureaucracy had been plowed into jewelry, gold, cars, and luxury goods, or smuggled abroad. A bureaucrat, gangster, or black-market producer could not use his money for anything else. Anyone who tried to deposit huge sums of "unearned" cash in a savings bank risked having his affairs investigated by the KGB or being charged as a speculator. There was nowhere to invest the cash legally—until the government permitted the establishment of semi-private commercial businesses, member-operated cooperatives, and joint ventures for the first time since the 1920s.

Most of these operations were only modest steps on the road to capitalism. The government hemmed them in carefully with restrictions such as limiting shares in a cooperative restaurant to family members. But thousands of tiny firms sprang up around the country, and they soon brought its secret wealth out of the shadows. Party officials and black marketeers joined the rush to "privatize," creating legitimate companies as investments for their earnings.[10]

The rise of cooperatives and small businesses not only offered a way to launder black-market profits; it also directly contributed to a rise in crime, thanks to the conditions under which the country's new businessmen were forced to work. Food suppliers, for example, were prohibited from selling produce to a private restaurant at the cheap subsidized prices available to state-owned restaurants. This was supposedly intended to prevent competition from "destabilizing" the market, but it was actually designed to cushion the monopoly held by bureaucrats who were already selling subsidized food for windfall profits. The profiteers of the black market flourished, as desperate restaurant owners and small businessmen came to them for supplies. A clothing cooperative, for instance, found that no state manufacturer could sell him denim. But the same denim became available at astronomical prices in the shadow economy, where the factory manager had secretly helped underwrite a "private" production line.

The small businessman was also vulnerable to extortion rackets, which appeared at the same time. Mobsters provided a unique form of protection to these seedlings of free enterprise. They were happy to help a businessman collect his bills or stave off unfriendly creditors, but they were also quick to punish any who resisted their help. In the late 1980s, a wave of firebombings and assaults hit dozens of cooperative restaurants and businesses in Moscow and other cities.

"Cooperative owners, even the legitimate ones, had to get involved with illegal activity in some form—they had no choice," said Aleksandr Gurov. "If they wanted office space, they would have to bribe officials; if they needed a loan, there were no banks to go to; and if they tried to get money from customers who didn't pay their bills, there were no courts to come to their side. The only businessmen who didn't go bankrupt were the ones who were associated with the mafiya." [11]

The peculiar nature of perestroika *bizness* was missed, or ignored, outside the Soviet Union, where any form of enterprise that bore a resemblance to capitalism was treated as a brave departure from the command-administrative economy. Western investors who rushed into Moscow to cultivate what they believed were the first shoots of Soviet free enterprise quickly discovered that unless the "new businessmen" they found as partners for their joint ventures were able to pay for bureaucratic or mob protection, or were disguised bureaucrats themselves, the partnership would soon evaporate.

The relaxation of the command-administrative system had done little more than allow enterprising apparatchiks and black marketeers to convert the wealth they earned through the manipulation of the system into "real" money. The bureaucracy showed no interest in making things easier for ordinary entrepreneurs: a competitive marketplace would not only reduce their opportunities for private gain, but also challenge their power. Instead of laying the groundwork for a free market, perestroika merely reinforced the operating methods of the black economy.

Some argued that it had an even worse long-term effect. Long after perestroika had faded into history, one of the former Soviet Union's most prominent political figures said that the government's failure to regulate the black market had doomed the chances for genuine reform. Vadim Bakatin, minister of internal affairs in the Gorbachev government until 1990—and Aleksandr Gurov's boss—admitted that bureaucrats and mobsters not only shared a common interest in blocking the creation of a competitive open market, but had joined forces in terrorizing independent businessmen as well. "The foundation of today's organized crime was the shadow economy, but the roof was our own bureaucratic system," Bakatin ruefully explained to me in 1993. "Our burcaucrats, police, procurators, judges, even the KGB, were merging with the underground world. It was a critical change in the development of crime in our country." [12]

The inevitable consequence was the rise of the unique post-Soviet gangster-bureaucrat: the comrade criminal.

In 1993, I was shown one of Russian law enforcement's most secret, and most embarrassing, documents: a list of eighty leading criminals in Moscow and the surrounding region. Their faces stared triumphantly out of the grainy police mug shots, as if they were celebrating the fact that they were all still at large. But what was especially interesting was that less than a quarter of them were acknowledged *vory v zakonye*. The majority were men in their late thirties and early forties, whose occupations were listed as industrial manager or business director.

If bureaucrats could transform themselves into gangsters, it was no surprise to see gangsters turning up as bureaucrats. A Georgian crime lord, one of the younger generation of *vory v zakonye*, reputedly joined the staff of Eduard Shevardnadze, who by then had left his career in national politics to become president of independent Georgia. (The policeman who informed me of this doubted that Shevardnadze was aware of his aide's background.) [13] Similar sightings of comrade criminals have been reported in other governments of the Commonwealth of Independent States, including Russia.

But the most telling evidence that the gangster-bureaucrat continued to squeeze legitimate business enterprise after the Soviet collapse was in the uninterrupted flourishing of the black market, years after there was any apparent reason for it to exist—at least if one took seriously Russia's proclaimed intention of moving toward a free economy. In 1992, the estimated size of the shadow economy—that is, goods and services for which no taxes were paid—was 2.5 trillion rubles (then worth about 1.3 billion dollars). According to a confidential paper prepared by Russian law enforcement agencies, this post-Communist black market already accounted for 15 percent of the Russian volume of goods and services by the end of 1991.[14]

Comrade criminals, and the shadow economy they manipulate, continue to affect the way Seran Akopyan does business. The Party bosses he once dealt with as a bureaucrat have turned up in Moscow's privatized retail trade as either administrators or practitioners.

"Compared to people like myself, they are the sharks," Akopyan told me. "Everyone operates in the same way as in the old days. The networks haven't changed. I estimate that 40 percent of the old bureaucrats are still there—they're not interested in ideology, but business. For instance, if I ring the Ostankino sausage factory for an order, they might bring me three or four varieties of sausage; but to another [shopowner] they might send ten types." The determining factor was "personal sympathy," Akopyan repeated. "It doesn't matter to the factory that I could do a better job of selling the sausages," he said. "In our country, the producer is not interested in selling his goods fast."

After several conversations with Akopyan, I came away with a grudging respect for the oasis he had created on Krasnoprudnaya Street—and for what it cost to maintain it. Akopyan survived from day to day on the strength of his ability to get along with the city's comrade criminals.

In the middle of one of our chats, an old woman walked into his office, carrying a container of powdered cleanser. She handed the detergent to Akopyan without a word, and he kissed her on each cheek and stored the container away in the same desk drawer where he kept his gun. The woman stalked out, mumbling angrily beneath her breath.

Akopyan noticed my mystified stare and started to laugh.

"We have a special arrangement," he said. "That woman works in a house next door, and she steals the stuff for me because I can't get any myself from the people I know. Tomorrow, I will give her a nice imported chicken."

The shabby edifice of the Soviet Union may have collapsed—but the moral ambiguities it fostered have survived on the New Russia's frontier.

5 Life and Death on the Russian Frontier

Flying east from Moscow to Yekaterinburg, the Aeroflot plane crosses a thousand miles of grassland and steppe before it reaches the Ural Mountains. A few miles further east lies one of the great demarcation lines of the planet, the continental divide separating Europe and Asia. This is a country of blurred endings and indistinct beginnings. There are no obvious landmarks, in the green carpet of pine and birch spreading eastward toward the Pacific, to pinpoint where European Russia ends and Asia begins, just as there are few signs to indicate that this was also once one of the most secret territories on earth—the homeland of the Soviet military-industrial complex.

The plane descends over a strangely empty landscape. Not a car can be seen on the highways that cut through the forests. There are no chimneys belching smoke, and there is little evidence of industry or commerce. On the horizon, if you look carefully, clusters of austere white buildings are visible—military cities, which were designated by numbers instead of names. These cities are deserted. Their strategic usefulness is gone, and they are now hollow memorials to the pride of Kremlin autocrats, who ordered them carved out of a wilderness larger than Western Europe.

But the picture of tranquility from the air is deceptive. A few miles from the airport, the booming city of Yekaterinburg rises out of the surrounding farmland. Home to more than two million people, it is a brash frontier capital. Since the fall of the Soviet Union, it has become the nerve center of one of the fastest-growing regions of Russia. The countryside is rich in natural resources, providing a steady supply of gems, strategic ores, and timber for export overseas. Sprawling factories that once churned out tanks and weapons for the military send trucks, machinery, and drilling equipment into the civilian economy.

In the autumn of 1991, when I first visited the city, Yekaterinburg was in the process of recapturing its former glories. Founded nearly 270 years earlier by Russian adventurers and named in honor of the Empress Catherine, it had been a prosperous merchant city until the 1917 revolution. The weathered, elaborately carved mansions of fur traders on downtown streets had been the only reminders of the city's commercial past until the failed coup of August, 1991. Yekaterinburg had even lost its original name: for more than seventy years it had been called Sverdlovsk, in honor of Yakov Sverdlov, the first secretary of the Communist Party's Central Committee and father of the Party apparatus. Sverdlovsk had been literally sealed off from the outside world. Foreigners were barred from the town, and even Soviet citizens living elsewhere had to get special permission to visit. But after the coup, municipal leaders restored the old name and a sense of mercantile purpose. By 1992, when I returned for a second visit, Yekaterinburg was firmly in business again. Billboards once marked with Party slogans now advertised new banks, stock exchanges, and private shops. Fortunes were won and lost in the space of weeks. Stockbrokers discussed the international price of emeralds and aluminum over cups of strong coffee in the new restaurants near the city market.

One afternoon, on my second trip to Yekaterinburg, I walked into the city's Musical Comedy Theater, a severe building that had been erected for state cultural extravaganzas under Communism. That afternoon, it was host to a fashion show sponsored by a large American soap and pharmaceutical company. Lithe, good-looking men and women dressed in clothing imported from Europe gyrated across the platform to rock music. Some of the models were children. Stepping self-consciously onto the stage in outfits that had never before been seen in this part of the old Soviet Union, they beamed under the applause. Even more striking was the audience, who were as well dressed and as beautifully poised as the models.

The women were dressed as if they were attending a London theater opening, in expensive gowns and dripping jewelry. The men's well-cut suits wouldn't have looked out of place among fashionable circles in Moscow or New York. Perhaps the audience was more self-consciously "nouveau" than "riche," but there was scarcely a trace of Soviet Man or Woman. Gone was the gray, baggy conformism of the Marxist regime, less than a year since its collapse. I was amazed to discover that lifestyles had changed so dramatically in such a short time.

During the intermission, I walked through the lobby, admiring the crowd and listening to snatches of conversation about market prices and fashion. On the fringes, I noticed a few men standing alone, with tell-tale bulges in their jackets, looking like bodyguards. But no one paid attention to them. I struck up a conversation with several members of the audience. A large man in a pinstripe suit introduced himself as deputy manager of Uralmash, a state-owned machinery-building plant and the town's largest enterprise. He was standing with a younger man, who worked for a sportswear import firm that now operated out of an Uralmash division and had co-sponsored the fashion show. A third managed Yekaterinburg's first cable-television station. We began an oddly abstract conversation about Russia's economy and the need for Western investment.

The amiable sportswear salesman admitted he had once been an official of Komsomol, the Communist Youth League.

"It taught me a lot about commerce," he said earnestly. "Most of us in Komsomol have been involved in some kind of business since the late 1980s. All my friends thought Communism had no future."

When I casually dropped the name of Viktor Ternyak, however, the atmosphere froze. The man in the pinstripe suit walked abruptly away. The man from the sportswear shop, after a pause, admitted that he knew Ternyak well and had even been involved with him in business ventures—but he refused to say more.

Viktor Nakhimovich Ternyak was a millionaire investment broker and one of the leading figures of Yekaterinburg's post-Soviet economy. A few weeks before I arrived, he had been murdered. The killing had been performed with a professionalism surprising in a city located so far from Moscow and St. Petersburg. On the morning of September 8, 1992, as Ternyak's white Volvo emerged from the driveway of his apartment building, a man stepped from behind a clump of bushes and fired seven shots through the car windows. Ternyak was killed instantly. His driver and a bodyguard were wounded. The shooting took place in front of dozens of witnesses, but none came forward to assist police. At the fashion show, I had expected to hear expressions of horror and anger at such a blow to the civic image. Instead, I found a morbid fear.[1]

"He was the best businessman in this city, and the one I respected most," the cable-TV manager finally said to me after our companions had moved off.

I asked him whether he would assign his journalists to investigate Ternyak's murder.

"If I did that," he answered evenly. "The same thing would happen to me."

The truth was, Yekaterinburg's good fortune covered a disagreeable reality. The murder of Viktor Ternyak hinted that there was something false behind the glittering clothes and smug confidence of the fashion show audience.

On the surface, the fifty-seven-year-old Ternyak was an impressive advertisement for the new Russian capitalism. A former waiter, he became chairman of the European-Asiatic Company, a prosperous metals-trading firm, after founding a number of joint ventures and a private insurance agency in the 1990s. He was a weighty figure in civic life— a philanthropist who contributed to charities and a man who ardently believed in Yekaterinburg's capitalist future. Only a few weeks before his death, Ternyak had called a press conference to announce plans for a local credit card system.

But there was more to Ternyak's rags-to-riches story than met the eye. He was already a wealthy man in the Soviet era, having served as manager of a state restaurant conglomerate—a position that placed him firmly inside the web of the corrupt food industry. Among his dubious business associates was a man named Konstantin Tsyganov.

A few days after the fashion show, I was told an interesting story about Tsyganov. A businessman from a nearby town had been working on a project to build a block of apartments near the Uralmash machinery complex, in the northern part of Yekaterinburg. The project ran into financial difficulties. When the businessman told municipal authorities about his problem, they intimated that other means of funding were available. He would be informed about them shortly, they said. The mysterious hint puzzled the director, and he braced himself for what he anticipated was sure financial ruin.

A week later, there was a knock on his office door, and a man in his late thirties, with the trim looks of an athlete, asked politely if he wanted to chat. The man introduced himself as Konstantin Tsyganov. He said he understood that the businessman was having financial difficulties. Perhaps he could help?

The businessman invited Tsyganov inside. Two muscled young "assistants" in track suits standing in the doorway behind him disappeared into the corridor at a nod from their boss. Uneasily, the businessman offered tea. Tsyganov shook his head and smiled, revealing a row of gold teeth. He said that he didn't want to waste anyone's time, and invited his host to describe his situation.

The businessman launched into an elaborate account of his affairs. Tsyganov asked sympathetic questions about the project's financing and architectural plans. As the atmosphere relaxed, it might have been a discussion between a neighborhood banker and a prospective loan recipient.

That was exactly what it turned out to be. Tsyganov offered a loan on easy terms to finish the project. There was only one extra condition, he said, almost as an afterthought. It would be "helpful" if several of the apartments in the new building were reserved for his organization to use or rent as he wished, Tsyganov said. The terms were promptly, and gratefully, accepted.

When the businessman later recounted the incident to his local partners, they whistled in admiration. "It was really quite an honor for Tsyganov to come to the businessman instead of the other way around," said the person who told me this story. "Usually, a summons from Tsyganov has the kind of authority that an order from a Party chief had in the old days."

Who was Konstantin Tsyganov?

It didn't take long in Yekaterinburg to find out. Conversations with local police and residents identified him as the leader of the town's most powerful crime syndicate. It was called the Uralmash group because it operated in the same neighborhood as the Uralmash machinery plant.

But there was more than just a geographical connection between the two. For many years, Tsyganov and his friends served as *tolkachi* for the state Uralmash enterprise. *Tolkach,* which comes from the Russian verb *tolkat,* meaning "to push through" or "to hustle," was a familiar word in Soviet industrial life. The *tolkachi* were the unofficial supply officers of state firms. They obtained the spare parts, materials, or anything else factory bosses needed to fulfill production quotas. If a manager needed wrenches to fix machinery, or an extra load of sheet metal, it might take months to obtain them through the bureaucracy—if they ever came through at all. But a *tolkach* would "happen to know" of another factory nearby that could provide what was needed in return for, perhaps, a scarce shipment of industrial oil or several bottles of vodka. Sometimes, the *tolkach* was listed on the payroll as an ordinary worker; often he was someone with good connections inside the black market, or a black marketeer himself, as Tsyganov was.

Through bribery and barter, the *tolkachi* kept factories running, made managers happy—and turned themselves into very rich men. Tsyganov's connection with Uralmash, however, was soon to make him even richer.

In the early 1990s, the Uralmash plant was hit by the catastrophic depression in the Soviet military complex. Although its fifty thousand workers produced bulldozers and machinery for steel mills and iron foundries, Uralmash was also an important manufacturer of military equipment. In the former Soviet Union, the machine-building industry provided a cover for the country's huge defense projects, and Uralmash was one of the largest assembly plants in the country. Like most such enterprises, it faced bankruptcy when orders from the defense ministry dried up in the aftermath of the USSR's collapse. But the solution— selling the plant off to private owners—was politically unpalatable to the managers at the time. Like their colleagues in other regions who ran the nation's industrial behemoths, they feared not only the prospect of throwing thousands of employees out of work, but also the eclipse of their power over the manufacturing sector.[2]

Tsyganov and his older brother Grigori came to the rescue. The brothers used the same technique that later snared the beleaguered construction chief: they offered a no-strings-attached loan in return for the use of Uralmash facilities. The plant could keep nominal ownership, but they would have a cut of the profits. By the summer of 1992, the Tsyganov brothers were running a sportswear business and a small commercial importing firm out of the Uralmash grounds. The gangsters hired their own employees and managers, and were soon numbered among the town's most successful businessmen. Although they acted as if they had repudiated their past, police knew better.

The Tsyganovs' acquisition of parts of Uralmash, in effect, had elevated them to the status of criminal *avtoritety;* and their legitimate business operations only served to enhance the power of their expanding crime syndicate.

What had happened in Yekaterinburg was repeated in hundreds of towns and cities across the former Soviet Union. As Party power and central control crumbled, a new class of warlord rose to claim the spoils of the old system. Life on the new frontier began to resemble an earlier time in Russian history—the period of the Time of Troubles, when the noble boyars feuded among themselves for a place in the new order before the beginning of the Romanov dynasty. Almost four centuries later, another struggle over the future of Russia was being fought, and the battlegrounds were in cities and regions far from Moscow and St. Petersburg.[3]

Sochi, near the Black Sea resort of Pitsunda, where Gorbachev and Shevardnadze had their conversation about the future of Russia, provided a typical illustration. In early 1991, a gang from Arkhangelsk, in northern Russia, was invited there by a resident named Manukian, who knew them from his days working as a barman in the north. Backed by the gang, Manukian became a prominent figure in city commerce. He invested widely in catering businesses and small shops, and his ever-present "associates," who had exchanged their ill-fitting clothes for leather jackets and Adidas running shoes, cowed officials and other would-be businessmen.[4]

But several local gangs united—at the apparent request of Manukian's competitors—to challenge his power. The leader of the new rival syndicate, named Guseinov, started by going after Manukian himself in 1992. Gunmen killed the gang boss as he opened the door of his apartment; a bullet grazed his mother, who was standing behind him. The assassination led to open war. The "northerners" chose Manukian's deputy, named Tremzin, to lead the campaign. For the next several months, the two gang armies conducted swoop-and-destroy tactics on each other's territories. Few city businesses were immune from the fighting, as gunfire erupted anywhere at a moment's notice. In one set-piece battle, the two sides drove to a local football field in separate convoys of Volvos, Fords and BMWs. Dismounting, they fought each other with clubs and fists. In one corner of the field, the two rival gang chieftains squared off like ancient Russian warriors. They swore at each other, and Guseinov at last pulled his gun and fired, fatally wounding Tremzin. The northerners retreated in shock. Guseinov, not content to let his rival bleed to death, put Tremzin into the trunk of his car and spirited him off to a desolate spot in the nearby mountains. There, he chopped off the tips of his fingers—standard gangland practice to prevent a corpse from being identified—put the still-breathing Tremzin back in the car, and set it alight.

A few days later, Tremzin's followers tried to take revenge. As Guseinov left one of his favorite spots in town, a local casino, a gunmen grabbed him and forced him into another car. Guseinov struggled wildly. Although wounded by a gunshot and several stab wounds, he escaped. He went to police and offered to testify about everything he knew about the northern gangs in return for protection. Tremzin's followers were convicted and imprisoned, and the "hometown" warriors were left firmly in control of their territory—and several times richer than when it all began.

Yekaterinburg's experience was especially poignant. It was the political base of Russian president Boris Yeltsin, the city where he first rose to prominence in the early 1980s as a reform-minded Communist Party boss. But the link with Yeltsin provided no immunity from the world of crime.[5]

There were at least four large criminal organizations operating in Yekaterinburg by 1992, including Uralmash. Between them, they directly "employed" more than twelve thousand people—roughly the work force of a medium-sized Soviet factory—as enforcers, soldiers, accountants, and "business managers." Many thousands more were on their unofficial payroll in the municipal offices and police headquarters. They controlled a number of the banks and stock exchanges.

But their most interesting investment was the town's recently completed gambling casino, which was built near the site where Czar Nicholas II, the last Russian monarch, was assassinated with his family, on Moscow's orders, in 1918. This was somehow appropriate. The Yekaterinburg *avtoritety* held the power of life and death over their city, and their supremacy was as unquestioned as that of the czars or Party barons.[6]

"Our political connections have not prevented us from leading the country in either crime or inflation," Maj. Vladimir Koltsov said tartly.

Koltsov, one of the few Yekaterinburg police officers who specialized in organized crime, said that the town was both dazzled and frightened by its powerful gangster barons.

"They are very clever about manipulating public opinion," he told me as we drove through downtown Yekaterinburg. "Some of our crime groups make a big show of donations to charity. One is restoring a church, and another even paid for everyone to ride around free on trains and buses for a whole day."

Koltsov, a tall, slow-speaking man with a scar on his throat—a knife wound from a gangster, he explained offhandedly—said that the average Yekaterinburger chose to ignore the link between their prosperity and the gangs' growing control of the economy. "Some people in town believe this is a step toward a free-market economy, and they don't want to understand that these groups exist only to make themselves rich, not to produce anything," he said.

Yekaterinburg businessmen had no such illusions, however. Shortly after the fashion show, I visited a city *banya,* or bathhouse, to meet someone who claimed to have "special information" about Ternyak's murder. He had little to offer, but as we soaked in the steam room, his friend, who recently had started his own computer software firm, described what it meant to make a profit in Yekaterinburg. "No honest businessman can have any success for long in this town without eventually getting a visit from someone in an 'organization,' " he said miserably.

Koltsov confirmed that this was true. "Everything here is more expensive because every entrepreneur has to pay unofficial taxes to people from criminal structures who come around at the end of every month," he said. "Billions of rubles are collected this way."

Ternyak's murder had the salutory effect of removing some of the illusions about gang benevolence. It also demonstrated that life on the Russian frontier, even for the new boyars, was precarious.

Major Koltsov drove me to an apartment on the outskirts of Yekaterinburg. It was the home of one of his friends, a retired police officer, Col. Leonid Zonov. As we entered the lift, I noticed that Koltsov was carrying a tiny videocassette. In Zonov's apartment, Koltsov immediately walked to his friend's parlor, inserted the cassette into a VCR, and then took his seat, grinning.[7]

"This," he said, "will help you understand what is happening in our town."

Zonov, a courtly man of sixty, laughed along with him. The cassette was a film of a Yekaterinburg birthday party in 1992 attended by some of the city's mobsters. Neither of the officers explained where they had gotten it. As the images appeared on Zonov's television screen, Koltsov provided a running commentary.

The featured players were the Tarlanovs, father and son. Both were Yekaterinburg racketeers, who ran an underground clothing factory and sold black-market gasoline during the perestroika years. According to Koltsov, the father was already a millionaire in the late 1980s, and he was hoping to retire.

His son Pavel, however, had other ideas. He was in the process of putting together a new syndicate at the time of the party, which, as it happened, was a celebration of his own birthday.

The affair, held at the redecorated hotel above the casino, afforded a rare glimpse of most of the town's mobsters in the same room. As later events were to show, it was the last time they were together in such friendly circumstances.

The camera jumped around the banquet hall like an overexcited guest. It focused on well-known Yekaterinburg crime lords, looking solemn in their Soviet-style suits and wide ties. A much sleeker and younger crowd was sitting at tables near the dance floor, sending showers of rubles over the heads of sequined women undulating to the music.

Presiding over it all, at the head table, was Pavel Tarlanov, a stocky, balding young man who seemed to hold himself aloof from the celebration. The camera showed a parade of well-wishers filing up, each one planting formal kisses on both his cheeks and whispering briefly in his ear. Like a prince receiving tribute, young Pavel sat with a scowl on his face. He pointedly ignored his proud mother and father, who were placed on either side of the guest of honor.

Zonov explained that Tarlanov, Senior, was not happy about his son's ambition to become an *avtoritet*. "He was such an old-fashioned conservative that he didn't allow guns at home," said the colonel. "He told me once he begged his son to get out of crime completely, so they could live off their money, but he wouldn't listen."

Pavel should have listened. A few months after his party, on April 2, 1992, he was kidnapped by persons unknown. In despair, the father went to Zonov, who was then a senior crime investigator with the Yekaterinburg militia, for help. He offered a deal: in return for police assistance in locating his son, he would name the leading municipal officials involved in black-market crime in the city.

"It could have been a good deal," said Zonov. "I felt sure I knew who was responsible for the kidnapping. But I was told to stay away by my superiors, for my own safety."

Three weeks after Pavel disappeared, the father was dead. A sniper, perched on a building near the local KGB headquarters, shot through the window of Tarlanov's house and killed him. Pavel was never seen again.

"I have no doubt he's under the ground," Zonov said gruffly. "After he disappeared, Tarlanov's mother and his girlfriend were attacked. No one would dare attack them unless they knew he was off the scene."

The murder of the Tarlanovs coincided with a menacing turn to violence in Yekaterinburg's crime world. As the stakes of the new economy grew, so did the competitive instincts of the gangs. A few weeks after the Tarlanov killings, Polecat, a leading *vor,* was shot dead. Soon afterward, Grigori Tsyganov, Konstantin Tsyganov's brother, was assassinated. Over the next several months, dozens of gangsters and businessmen like Ternyak with disreputable pasts met similar fates. The crack of gunfire broke the quiet of Yekaterinburg evenings for the first time since the Russian civil war of 1918–20. Almost overnight, Yekaterinburgers' initial pleasure at their city's post-Communist revival turned to horror. Gang violence erupted, sometimes literally before their eyes.

Sergei Molodtsov, a local journalist, was returning home from work late one night on one of the city's main boulevards when two speeding cars slammed to a halt just ahead of him. Several men jumped out of each car and began shooting at each other. Molodtsov froze, too astonished to take cover. When the gunfire ended, two bodies lay on the street in widening pools of blood. The gunfighters roared off, but minutes later another car drove up. A man got out, and dragged the bodies into the back seat. Molodtsov hurried on his way. "It was just like an American gangster movie," he told me afterward.[8]

The epidemic of murder continued through the winter of 1992 and through 1993. Oleg Vagin, a leader of the Tsentralnaya gang, and the man who was believed to have organized the killing of Ternyak and the Tarlanovs, himself was shot in October, 1993. But long before then,

Yekaterinburgers could not help associating the violence with the spread of private enterprise and the end of Party control in their city. They wondered whether capitalism was worth it.

"You used to be able to walk downtown at eleven p.m. with no worries," Tamara Lomakina, editor of *Na Smenu,* formerly the town's Communist youth newspaper and now an independent journal, told me in her office. "Now, at night, the town goes dead. People have built metal fences around their houses. This isn't a town any longer; it's a prison." [9]

Lomakina, a quiet-spoken woman of forty-three, was herself a victim. On Tuesday, June 16, 1992, a few days after her newspaper published a series of articles about Yekaterinburg's gang wars, she was severely beaten by gangsters as she walked out of her apartment.

"I left the house a little earlier than usual that day, because we have editorial meetings on Tuesdays," she began. "I should have realized something was wrong, because when I picked up my telephone at 9 a.m. to call my office, the line was dead. My driver, Sergei, usually turns up at my apartment at 9:20. I heard his car as I was saying goodbye to my son and getting my papers together. Then I heard two loud bangs. I looked out the window and saw a person running away down the street. I called over to Sergei to ask what was going on, but he was already out the door of my apartment. I followed him, and ran down the three flights of stairs. In the entranceway, we have a double door. I opened the first one, and then . . . I was already being hit. Someone came flying at me, and hit me hard. I fell over. The doctors tell me they must have hit me with brass knuckles. I didn't even have time to see who was there and how many of them there were. They started kicking me. Mostly they kicked me in the head. Then they ran off. They said nothing. My nose was bleeding. I crawled out into the street. I remember Sergei running up with a baton. It turned out that when he had gone downstairs, three men were standing by our car, aged about twenty-two to twenty-five. One of them had a knife. They started to fight with him, and then, when the others came running out after beating me up, they ran away too."

Lomakina spent six weeks in hospital. She was treated for a severe concussion and bruises. One of the nerves around her left eye was damaged. For a few weeks, doctors thought she would lose her sight in that eye. When I met her, nearly four months after the attack, the police investigation had turned up no clues to her assailants. Lomakina didn't expect it to. "Who would give evidence?" she said with a sigh.

The carnage in the cities across the Urals and the rest of Russia underscored as well the dramatic impact of post-Soviet politics on the old Russian underworld. Before Yekaterinburg became one of the killing fields of the gangster economy, it had been a quiet outpost in the Thieves World. The Urals marked one of the boundaries of the so-called Criminal Zone, the vast Gulag prison empire constructed by Stalin across Siberia and the Far East. For decades, the military-industrial complex had been a feeding ground for the Zone.

The Urals region contained some of the country's most notorious prison camps. Convicts released from the Zone usually settled in nearby towns to maintain their links with the crime lords who ran the Thieves World from their prison cells. The Yekaterinburg district was a lucrative base for small-scale smuggling and thievery. There was often regular traffic between the prisons and the outside.

By the 1970s, Yekaterinburg's proximity to the prison complex ensured that it had a thriving criminal subculture. Two local gangs, Ovchina and Trifon, were the principal rivals for the vodka and timber-smuggling "franchises" in the area. They even fought a brief, violent war. Nevertheless, their quarrels were for the most part waged peacefully and unobtrusively, since the local police and KGB were then carefully guarding the security of all the country's military cities. But in the late 1970s and early 1980s, a new criminal operator appeared on the civic landscape. Taking advantage of the perilous state of the Soviet economy, black-market speculators opened underground "factories" to produce everything from textiles to shoes. *Tolkachi* in state enterprises expanded their operations.

Many of these wheelers and dealers were survivors of the Scabs War in the prisons, and long since had been excommunicated from the established fraternities of thieves for having lent themselves to the war effort against Nazi Germany. Like the Tarlanovs, they ignored underworld prohibitions against trade to exploit the burgeoning shadow economy. Their younger associates, like the Tsyganovs, defied the old *vory* to form gangs of their own. Even Viktor Ternyak, it was said, had done time in the Zone on charges of profiteering. Moved by envy as well as contempt, their former comrades in the underworld dubbed the budding crime tycoons *belye* (whites), to distinguish them from the more traditional *siniye* (blue) gangsters, so called because of the color of the prison tattoos most of them wore.[10]

When the Yekaterinburg economy boomed after 1991, traditional hoodlums found that their old sources of income had been squeezed by the whites. Some even found themselves in the undignified role of mercenaries in the frontier wars of Russian capitalism.

"We have no choice except to sell our fists," complained a gangster nicknamed Bolt. "How else can we feed our families?"

Bolt was a short young man with thinning hair. He had huge arms, which he kept close to his body, as if he were preparing to fend off an attack at any moment. We met in circumstances that were not ideal for a conversation. Five other gang members had gathered with Bolt to meet me under a dim street lamp outside the city's former Communist Party headquarters. They were dressed shabbily, with heavy work shoes, blue jeans, and dirty sweatshirts, and their hostility was unmistakable. One kept his hand over his coat pocket, with the obvious purpose of fixing my attention on the possibility that he had a gun. Another had a disturbing rasp to his voice, and I saw a long ugly scar under his jaw. When he caught me staring at it, he laughed.

"I'm back from the dead," he said. "They thought they killed me." He didn't elaborate.

None of them, clearly, relished the prospect of talking to a foreigner. But they were there under orders. The leader of their gang, one of Yekaterinburg's leading *vory,* was in jail; he had instructed his men to see me at the urging of a local human rights lawyer. The lawyer explained before the meeting that the *vor* was anxious to restore the public standing and morale of his group, which was being squeezed out of its territory by the city's larger gangs. "But to tell you the truth, I think he expects me to get him out of prison," he added nervously. "I have the feeling that I've got myself into a situation I'm going to regret later."

The lawyer's anxiety was catching. I avoided the stares of pedestrians strolling past our little group. A few blocks away, well out of sight of the gang members, Maj. Vladimir Koltsov waited in his parked car. If anything happened, he assured me, he would be there within seconds. But I wondered what would happen if Bolt and his friends discovered there was a policeman nearby. Meeting the Armenian had felt very different. Compared with these provincial Russian hoodlums, the gangsters of Moscow seemed cosmopolitan.

The conversation started on the wrong foot. I asked them the name of their gang.

"No names," one of them spit out.

I asked how long they had been involved in their "work."

"All our lives," said Bolt, suddenly smiling. "We have never done anything else. That's what our tradition calls for. We used to make a lot of money without anyone's else's help."

Although Bolt was the appointed spokesman, the others gradually overcame their wariness. They complained about the change in Yekaterinburg's underworld. It was becoming crowded with newcomers, who arrived from Moscow and the Caucasus with suitcases full of cash and bristling weaponry. Just as disturbing was the fact that the honorable profession of thieves had become cluttered with former Party officials, hustling gangster-bureaucrats, and those they called, with a touch of condescension, "traders."

"We know who we are, and we don't get involved in trade," said one stoutly. "We take our money from the street vendors, and they are usually glad to pay for the protection. Once a shopkeeper refused to follow the rules. He said he used to be like us; he had been in prison. I just shouted at him. You're not like us anymore, I said. I hold you in bigger contempt than a fat store clerk, because you're a traitor. You should know better."

Although no one mentioned it, I detected traces of bitterness inherited from the Scabs War toward those who betrayed the code of thieves. All of them had been born after that bloody conflict in the prisons, but they talked about themselves as if they were figures from a vanishing era.

"Every week we visit the cemetery where our elder comrades are buried," Bolt said. "It is one of our rituals, to show our respect for those who taught us."

Against my instincts, I found myself warming to these wistful mobsters. The life of honorable thieves, for which they had been trained, was no longer applicable to the brutal new world of Yekaterinburg.

"We were the ones who used to keep order here," said Bolt sadly. "The Party people left us alone and we left them alone. Once, when the *musor*—"garbage," the underworld slang for police—arrested me, I told them we were doing a better job of keeping the streets safe then they were. And it was true.

"No one shows us respect anymore."

The group huddled around me under the lamppost added their vehement agreement. I felt they wanted to go on talking. But the man with the scar on his throat raised his hand, and Bolt announced that it was time to conclude.

"We're going to collect our taxes," he said casually. "Do you want to come?"

I said yes, half in jest. But I noticed the lawyer beside me turn pale.

"Maybe next time," I said quickly.

Bolt seemed to take my refusal as another critical acknowledgment of how low he and his friends had gone down in the hierarchy of crime.

"What's going on now is terrible," he said, as we all shook hands. "The old values are gone."

They were, indeed. Bolt and the men of the traditional gangworld had lost more than tactical ground to the new mobsters. The "whites," whose laundered black-market profits had won them a controlling share in the city's boom economy, destroyed the racketeering monopolies of the old "blue" gangs. And they locked in their triumph by moving into politics. Most knowledgeable Yekaterinburgers assumed that the syndicates were protected by officials in the municipal government and the security organs. It soon become obvious that those officials were providing more than protection.

In what became an essential—and generally unrecognized—part of the story of post-Communist Russia, crime structures took over the political role once played by the Party in many areas of the country. By the early 1990s, they were able to penetrate or suborn municipal and district governments. Konstantin Tsyganov evidently learned of the financial troubles of the Yekaterinburg contractor from friendly local officials to whom the contractor had first applied for help. The unofficial alliance between officialdom and criminal syndicates was not a secret. Local businessmen confessed to me—as well as to police—that they were afraid to register their companies with the municipality because they knew the financial information they provided would be passed along to the criminal world and used for extortion activities against them. The leader of one of the city's crime cartels was reputedly a retired Soviet Army officer who served in Afghanistan.

Yekaterinburg's political leaders periodically vowed to destroy the mafiya, "but that," said Sergei Plotnikov, a reporter for *Na Smenu* whose crime articles had provoked the attack on Tamara Lomakina, "is like someone saying he will stick a knife in his own throat."

The fusion of the gangs with the city's political establishment made a crackdown on organized crime even more unlikely, for economic reasons. "The white criminals are putting literally millions of rubles into circulation," Plotnikov said. "Senior municipal authorities have told me that since all this former criminal money is now subject to taxes, it would be silly to do anything to stop it, especially since there is no money coming in from the central government." The participation of officials in the frontier plunder explained the tight-lipped atmosphere surrounding Ternyak's death. No one could avoid the conclusion that Yekaterinburg was run by, and operated for the benefit of, comrade criminals.

Tamara Lomakina believed that the link between authorities and criminal structures was the most disillusioning result of the second Russian revolution. "Everything that happens in this town is being dictated by the mafiya," she said, sitting stiffly in a chair in her twelfth-floor office overlooking Yekaterinburg. "The failure of the coup was supposed to be the dawn of freedom, the start of a new world. Now, when the sun goes down, we are prisoners in our own homes, and the authorities profit from our chaos. When things get back to order, they will quietly leave their offices and be rich men. Yeltsin knows well enough what is going on here and in all the other cities of the region. I think he's honest enough, but things have already reached too large a scale. Even he can't stop it.

"If people begin to equate freedom and democracy with crime and anarchy, they will support political forces who say they can eliminate the *bespredel* by strong-arm measures. And there is really only one political force in this country strong enough to do that right now, together with the army—the fascists."

I wanted to meet Konstantin Tsyganov. But the process involved the kind of delicate negotiations required to see a Party boss in the old days. I had almost given up when, on one of my last afternoons in Yekaterinburg, a young man wearing an expensive, full-length leather jacket and tasseled French loafers, consented to talk to me as a "representative" of the boss. His card introduced him as Aleksei Belyshev, commercial director of Uralsport.

Despite his youth, Belyshev carried an air of authority. His movie-star good looks were slightly marred by hard blue eyes. When he came closer, I smelled cheap cologne.

"The boss is out of town right now," he said smoothly. "But he wanted me to meet you."

The lie was obvious. But Belyshev was an intriguing stand-in for the crime boss. He had been a *fartsovshchik,* a street-dealer selling jeans and smuggled videocameras, in the 1980s. Tsyganov apparently saw potential in him.

"He offered me the chance to manage his sportswear business," Belyshev said, with unconccaled pride. "I think he wanted to help out young people. I did so well that he made me one of his chief assistants."

We sat on a bench in a square in the middle of the city. Several of his associates stood nearby, keeping their hands over their pockets. This was beginning to seem a permanent position for half the town. Except for their more expensive clothing, I might once again have been speaking with Bolt and his comrades. We discussed what Belyshev called the "problems of doing business" in Yekaterinburg.

"They say," I suggested tentatively, "that some businessmen in this town are earning some of their money illegally, even associating with criminals. . . ."

Belyshev chuckled. "Oh yes, there's a lot of that. In a sick society, you have to make money however you can, so the next generation, our kids, will have a decent, honest life. The authorities here do nothing to protect an honest businessman. But that is changing."

The former street dealer admitted that the recent violence had made life difficult for the "business community."

"I think it's calmed down," he assured me.

He gave me a serious look. "You know one of the people in America I admire most?"

"Who?" I said.

"Al Capone. He said it was better to be guided by principles than have to suffer dishonest politicians."

I told him I had not studied Capone's writings, but I would take his word for it.

"Do principles matter more than money?" I asked.

Belyshev smiled. "What matters most is respect," he said, perhaps unwittingly echoing a sentiment shared by Sicilian "men of honor" and by mafia groups the world over. "You have to have respect."

The subject was obviously close to Belyshev's heart. He invited me to a former Komsomol youth center on the Uralmash factory grounds for an expansive lunch. As we walked into the Soviet-style cafeteria, a waiter guided us to a table with the panache of a maître d'hôtel. An enormous spread of cold cuts and vodka was waiting for us. The bodyguards ate with relish, pausing only for the inevitable toasts. Looking benevolently at them, Belyshev said Uralmash had done wonderful things for the town. He made it clear that he was talking about the syndicate, not the plant. He mentioned the fashion show—"we're raising money for children"—and added that his sportswear firm was also sponsoring a girls' football team. By the end of the lunch, Belyshev and I were fast friends. He smiled brightly at me as we shook hands.

"The next time you come back to our city," he said. "I'm sure the boss will be glad to see you."

But that proved impossible. Six months after I left Yekaterinburg, Konstantin Tsyganov was arrested by city police and charged with extortion.

Although this seemed to have no noticeable effect on the violence—several more gangsters and businessmen were shot to death the following spring and summer—Tsyganov's arrest inadvertently exposed the seamless connections between power, wealth, and crime on the Russian frontier.

A group of prominent local business leaders rushed to the crime lord's defense when he was picked up by police. The leader of the group was an entrepreneur named Andrei Pampurin, who had replaced the murdered Viktor Ternyak as president of the European-Asiatic Company. Pampurin admitted that his firm had a close financial relationship with Tsyganov. But he insisted that this was further proof of the crime boss's value to the Yekaterinburg business community.[11]

"[Tsyganov] only wanted to bring positive things to our society," Pampurin told a local press conference. "He's no criminal. The fact is, he provided a kind of balance between business circles of the region, and a guarantee of security and opportunity for foreign investors.

"For instance, there were businessmen from Poland and the Baltic republics who were considering investing in Ural businesses because of Tsyganov's recommendations, and he was due to fly to Washington for talks with American manufacturing firms interested in helping construction projects here and in importing precious metals."

Within a year of his arrest, Tsyganov was free under a court ruling that there was insufficient evidence to proceed with a trial. One local newspaper suggested that this curious ruling was not unconnected with a "recent attack on the Internal Affairs Ministry building of the Sverdlovsk region, which involved a grenade and the beating up of a judge." Nothing could have illustrated more vividly how the greed, corruption and violence thriving on the post-Communist frontier undermined the fledgling market economy. In less than two years, Yekaterinburg was transformed from a closed Soviet industrial city into a community walled off by crime, and the surrounding Sverdlovsk region became one of the most important theaters of operation for the new Russian mafiya. The convergence of interests and opportunities that brought men like Tsyganov into power with little fear of interference from the central government has been duplicated in varying degrees across Russia and the former Soviet Union.

Yekaterinburg's tragedy is only compounded by the fact that its "liberal" economic environment has made it a magnet for Western investment. Without realizing it—or, at least, so one would hope—Western businessmen flocking in to exploit the rich resources of Central Russia end up providing a cover of legitimacy to Russia's comrade criminals.

Pampurin did not bother to explain the techniques Tsyganov used to achieve the "balance" among business circles, and apparently no one needed to ask the question. Who could doubt the credentials of a man who was ready to fly to America for the good of the town?

"The worst thing about his arrest," Pampurin went on, "is that it will damage all the charity projects we were involved in together."

One of the projects had been launched by Viktor Ternyak himself, Pampurin said reverently. It was a formal memorial to the murdered Czar Nicholas II. Russia's comrade criminals could not be accused of lacking an appreciation for their predecessors.

6 The Criminal State

In the heady weeks following the defeat of the August, 1991, coup, Moscow was in an uproar. Crowds roamed the streets day and night, pulling down the statues and slogans of the old regime. The city was swept by rumors of an imminent ban on the Soviet Communist Party. An angry mob gathered behind police lines in front of the offices of the Central Committee on Staraya Ploshchad (Old Square), calling out threats to frightened secretaries and office workers. Inside the building, a high-ranking Party official sat down to write an urgent memo to one of his assistants.

"I've taken one hundred million rubles," the memo said. "Hide it." [1]

In the midst of its worst disaster, the world's largest Communist Party was reverting to its clandestine habits. In Moscow, and around the country, Party leaders were shredding records and files and making preparations to go into underground opposition. Even in forced retirement, though, the Party had better prospects than it did nearly a century earlier, when the threadbare bands of Marxists in Geneva, Minsk, and St. Petersburg first began plotting the overthrow of the czarist empire. In fact, many Soviet Communist Party leaders looked less like reluctant pensioners than like bandits fleeing the scene of a crime: they were moving off the stage of Russian history with a fortune worthy of a czar.

After seventy-four years in power, the Party was one of the world's richest organizations—controlling property and investments abroad worth, by some estimates, billions of dollars. Although the extent of its actual cash reserves was unknown—some insiders maintain that it was much less than critics believe—it possessed the unchallenged ability to treat the Soviet state's financial resources as its own. Greed and corruption marked its final years in power to an extent scarcely suspected abroad. The truth did not become apparent until records of the Politburo and Central Committee—the Party organs that effectively governed the Soviet Union—became accessible to researchers after the aborted 1991 coup.

A complete account of the secret wealth of the Communist state may never be possible, but the impact of that wealth on post-Communist society is just beginning to be clear. There is evidence to suggest that the money now underwrites both left-wing and right-wing opposition to reforms that would open the Russian economy to greater competition and restrict the comrade criminal's ability to plunder the state. Even more ominously, Party funds have contributed to the criminalization of life after Communism.[2] But that is merely a testimony to the enduring influence of Russia's largest and most sinister mafiya organization.

In the 1970s and early 1980s, a series of revelations about murder and corruption in high places shook the Soviet Union. The newspaper accounts and summaries of court cases of the time read like true-crime tales. The cases had one common denominator: they all involved officials who were influential members of the Communist Party.

The mayor of Sochi, for example, amassed such a huge private fortune from bribery and kickbacks that he was able to build a fantasy mansion with a singing fountain that emitted different notes, depending on the height of the water. In the nearby resort spa of Gelendzhik, several high-ranking officials were murdered just before they were to give evidence to investigators about massive influence peddling in the region. Sections of the exclusive vacation compounds in southern Russia and the Baltic states reserved for the Party elite and their families were turned into brothels. Senior bureaucrats even dabbled in drug trafficking and the distribution of pornographic videos.[3]

One of the most riveting scandals came to light in April, 1983, when a search of the home of an official in the fabled Central Asian city of Bukhara revealed a treasure trove of one million rubles, nearly a mile's length of gold brocade, and piles of diamonds, rubies, Swiss watches, and jeans. The official admitted that his wealth came from a complicated kickback scheme that involved falsifying reports about the production of cotton.

Moscow had decided several years before to turn Central Asia into a vast cotton plantation. After a few bumper harvests, the weakened soil could no longer produce enough to fulfill the quotas set by the planning ministries. The region's leaders, however, were not bothered by those details. With the collusion of the Moscow bureaucracy, which feared admitting any failure in agriculture, they continued to report huge crops and were paid anyway. Moscow bureaucrats, who took a cut of the profits, were happy with the arrangement. Everyone could became rich while advancing socialism. The conspiracy spread to include hundreds of officials across Central Asia and reached into the higher levels of the Soviet establishment. Among those eventually implicated in the scandal were Yuri Churbanov, deputy minister of the Soviet Ministry of Internal Affairs (and son-in-law of the late Soviet leader Leonid Brezhnev), and Sharaf Rashidov, the Party boss of Uzbekistan, a candidate (non-voting) member of the Politburo and a close Brezhnev ally.

Some of the Central Asian and Moscow bosses arrested as a result of the investigation were shot, and others received jail terms. But police inquiries never penetrated deeper into the system. The affair was officially regarded as a "deviation" from the moral code of Bolsheviks, and the establishment closed ranks behind the culprits. Yet no one could have any doubt that this scandal, like many others, was traceable directly to the Central Committee of the Communist Party.

"The Central Committee was like a czar's court," said Yevgeni Myslovsky, a former senior investigator in the office of the Moscow procurator (public prosecutor), who worked on the cotton scandal and other cases. "There were about five thousand people employed there, but twenty-five of them were the real unofficial organizers of the corruption that was going on around the country. They weren't really top officials, just deputy heads of departments, special [Party] instructors, those kinds of people. But they acted like a mafiya clan." [4]

It was a mafiya that could dictate which of its members would be prosecuted. As in the cotton scandal, the leadership decided how far any investigation could go. "Every time we wanted to prosecute a corruption case against a bureaucrat, we had to bargain with these people at Party headquarters," Myslovsky recalled. "As soon as we got close to someone they wanted to protect, they removed all the evidence. They had terrible power. They seemed to me like a special caste."

Aslambek Aslakhanov, chairman of the Russian parliamentary commission on law and order until 1993 (and a former investigator with the Soviet Ministry of Internal Affairs), told me a similar story about his efforts to prosecute top officials in the 1970s. After arresting a senior Party figure on bribery charges, a man who boasted of having "three friends" in the Politburo, Aslakhanov was assured by the justice minister that there would be no interference. But the justice minister was fired, and the corrupt bureaucrat was released from prison the next day. "They even showed him on television as a hero," Aslakhanov recalled bitterly.[5]

The special caste that senior officials belonged to—the nomenklatura—was officially unmentionable in Soviet public discourse. Yet no one was untouched by their power.

The nomenklatura were the governing class of the old empire. Occupying the privileged center of Soviet politics, they were to ordinary civil servants what sharks are to goldfish. They numbered, by some estimates, nearly 1.5 million people, and their special authority came from their place on a secret list prepared by the Central Committee containing the names of the most worthy Party members. From this list all the top officials of the state were chosen, from regional and municipal Party secretaries to ambassadors and senior government ministers. The nomenklatura constituted a private club of individuals whose loyalty to the Party transcended any other obligation. And it was their chief, the general secretary of the Communist Party, the first name on the list, who led the Soviet state.[6]

Over the years of Soviet power, the nomenklatura adopted an internal system of rewards and punishments that was as carefully graded as any Sicilian mafia clan's. Relatively innocent gifts, like fruit or flowers, were required to establish key relationships. Raisa Gorbacheva was said to have presented a necklace to Galina Brezhneva, wife of the late Soviet leader, when the couple came to Moscow after her husband had been appointed agriculture chief at the Central Committee. Party memberships went for higher prices. In Krasnodar, they cost between 3,000 and 3,500 rubles; in other regions, the cost of securing a leading position could be as high as 6,000 rubles—then the equivalent of about two years' wages for an average Soviet worker.[7]

Georgi Arbatov, a confidante of Soviet leaders from Andropov to Gorbachev, also used the phrase "special caste" to describe the nomenklatura, in a book called *The System*. As a measure of the fear imposed on its members, Arbatov only felt safe writing about the system in 1991, when it was on its last legs. But he provides one of the most candid records we have had of what it meant to be inside the Soviet establishment.

Arbatov, the son of an ardent Communist imprisoned during the Stalin years, personified the blend of mendacious and meritocratic principles that reigned in the Soviet bureaucracy during the final quarter-century of the USSR's existence. A decorated war veteran, who occasionally had to disguise his father's Jewish background to achieve success, Arbatov rose to the innermost circles of power. Although he was a talented scholar, he could never have risen so high without shutting his eyes to the hypocrisies of the system. As an official in the Central Committee and later as a policy adviser to the senior leadership, he was effectively separated from the real world. The truth was effectively brought home to him in his first weeks on the job, when he brought home foodstuffs picked up from the privileged Kremlin cafeteria, known euphemistically as the Dining Room of Therapeutic Eating. His mother burst into tears at the sight of the food, telling her son she had not seen such variety and quality since the 1920s.

When Arbatov was offered the opportunity to form a foreign-policy think tank, the Institute for the Study of the USA and Canada, some of his friends thought he was mad to leave the sheltered world of the Central Committee. In his new position, Arbatov claimed, he acted as a private gadfly to Soviet policymakers and often fell afoul of his old friends in the Kremlin. But he never considered removing himself from the system: it would have been like leaving his own family.[8]

The system knew how to repay the loyalty of its members. In the 1970s, a senior Party worker named Kulakov received on his retirement the right to free hospitalization for his family, a country dacha, and private cars for as long as he lived. His grandchildren were awarded a monthly seventy-ruble stipend. In a revealing note of cynicism, an anonymous Central Committee official headed the document approving Kulakov's retirement plans, "Easing the Panic of Comrade Kulakov."[9]

The nomenklatura not only took care of its own; it also kept its ranks firmly off-limits to politically incorrect outsiders. Children of high officials went to the same schools and holiday camps, and intermarried with each other. "The *apparat* tried to set up a system of inherited power . . . through an exclusive system of education and then through a system of appointments and promotions," Arbatov wrote, adding that, like corruption, the nepotism originated at the top. Brezhnev's son, for example, became deputy minister for foreign trade.

Despite the titillating revelations of scandal in high places, the Party bosses set clear limits on what the Soviet public could be told about the extent of their criminal activity. When the popular national magazine

Krokodil published an exposé in the early 1980s which linked Communist officials in the Ukrainian city of Dnepropetrovsk with local gangs, the issue never appeared on local newsstands. Dnepropetrovsk happened to be Brezhnev's political base, and allegations of corruption touched sensitive nerves.[10]

Corruption was imprinted in the system's genetic code. "The old administrative-command society [was] organically connected with corruption," wrote Arbatov afterward. "[We had] an enormous and parasitic *apparat* [that] gives or takes away, permits or prohibits, takes care of everything, can fire anybody, demote anybody, often even throw him in prison or, on the contrary, raise him up. And who with such power at his disposal can resist temptation?"[11]

But no one really guessed how lucrative the temptation was. "The budget of the Communist Party of the Soviet Union [CPSU] was always marked 'top-secret,'" said Aleksandr Kotenkov, a state legal official who defended the Russian government's ban on the Party in a 1992 trial. "But we have evidence showing that the CPSU spent hundreds of millions of dollars of the state's money for its own needs alone every year."[12]

To back up his charge, Kotenkov made public at a Moscow press conference documents showing that the Party regularly plundered the state treasury to underwrite foreign Communist groups and terrorist organizations. "There would be a decision of the Politburo on financing a particular group," Kotenkov said. "Then an instruction would come from the Central Committee to the [Soviet] State Bank for a delivery of hard currency. A man would come around from the bank to Old Square with the cash, and it would then be handed over through KGB channels."

There are other versions of how the money went abroad. Former Party insiders have told me that the money was sent directly from the Central Bank to KGB station chiefs overseas. I have also seen memos from the Central Committee archives authorizing the direct transfer of millions of dollars to Communist Party leaders in Europe and North America. (No detail was too small: one 1970s memo authorized the purchase of an expensive fur coat for a loyal Canadian party worker.) The disclosure of such transfers embarrassed the recipients, but no one was surprised by them. The secret flow of cash was central to the Soviet goal of winning friends and financing clandestine movements abroad.

The troubling issue raised by Russian investigators later, however, was how many millions went into private foreign bank accounts held by Party officials rather than the pockets of designated "friends" of the international proletariat. The nature of the clandestine process made it impossible to verify how the money was actually spent. It was not nearly as hard to figure out where it came from. "The Party always insisted that everything it had came from membership dues," Kotenkov said. "But our documents show that the source of all the Soviet Communist Party's wealth came from state property."

In other words, Party and KGB officials were raiding the government treasury for their overseas operations. Formally, this was a violation of Soviet constitutional provisions that separated Party and state. But it was the least of the illegalities associated with the establishment's behavior. "We had," said Aslambek Aslakhanov, "a mafiya of the supreme organs of power."

The nomenklatura's principal attributes—a paramilitary hierarchy, hostility toward outsiders, and a propensity for illegal behavior—established its similarity with the criminal societies of the old Russian underworld. The similarity was no coincidence. The organizational model that the Bolsheviks found so attractive in the Russian criminal bands seventy years earlier was internalized in the modern Communist Party structure.

But the Party possessed an advantage undreamed of in the *vorovskoi mir:* it was the ruling class of the society it ravaged. In the absence of any serious check on its power, it was free to do whatever it wanted, to whomever it wanted.

"In Soviet conditions the decisive mafia [*sic*] role is played by politicians," wrote Arkady Vaksberg, a prominent Moscow journalist who, in a book called *The Soviet Mafia,* described the inner workings of the Party and government bureaucracy in the 1970s and 1980s. "[They used] criminal methods to preserve their jobs and their strongholds." [13]

Vaksberg compared the conspiracy of silence surrounding the nomenklatura to the Italian mafia's code of *omerta,* the blood oath committing each member to take the secrets of the clan to his death. A number of top officials committed suicide during the late 1970s and early 1980s, when the KGB, under the ambitious Yuri Andropov, launched a crackdown on corruption.[14] for example, Gen. Nikolai Shcholokov, a Brezhnev ally and minister of internal affairs, was found shot to death on December 13, 1984. Shcholokov had been at the center of a scandal threatening to involve even more senior figures in the hierarchy. According to one widely circulated version of his death, he was visited in his apartment the night before by agents of the Moscow procurator's office and handed his own service revolver. The officials then silently departed to let him draw the obvious conclusion.[15]

The system was clearly not as monolithic as it appeared from the outside. Behind the walls that kept them separate from the rest of Soviet society, the nomenklatura engaged in fierce internal struggles that were as vicious as those of mafiya clans. From the 1920s on, at the same time as the *vorovskoi mir* was forming, they plotted against one another, murdered one another, imprisoned one another—and even wiretapped one another. Tensions inside the establishment had reached such a point that the KGB bugged the conversations of Boris Yeltsin, Mikhail Gorbachev, and other high officials between January, 1989, and August, 1991.[16]

In the Party's final days in power, another rash of suicides claimed the lives of leading *apparatchiki*. Boris Pugo, then minister of internal affairs and one of the leading plotters of the coup, shot himself and his wife to avoid arrest. Nikolai Kruchina, financial and property administrator of the Communist Party, jumped to his death from the balcony of his fifth-floor Moscow apartment on Aug 26, 1991, only days after the botched coup—and a few weeks before an investigation of Party finances was scheduled to open. In his suicide note, he explained that he was killing himself out of "fear of the future." [17]

It was an intriguing phrase. Kruchina evidently believed that he could not participate in a future without the Communist Party. But the treasurer may also have sacrificed himself in the hope of taking to the grave the secrets of how the Soviet mafiya had guaranteed its own future. Unfortunately for Kruchina, the story—or most of it—is now in the public domain.

The Party's private insurance program effectively began after February 5, 1990. On that date, at a historic plenary session, the Communist Party's governing Central Committee voted to revoke the privilege granted to the Party under Article Six of the Soviet constitution as the state's only legal political organization. The Party did not easily consent to the removal of its seven-decade-long monopoly on political power. It took a tough speech by Mikhail Gorbachev to persuade reluctant Central Committee members that it was "time for us to understand the age we live in." Few in the leadership saw anything but trouble ahead as a result of the decision.[18]

"The whole system was held together by the nomenklatura," said Vadim Bakatin, who, as Soviet minister of internal affairs from 1988 to 1990, was present at that meeting. "They knew if you pulled one nail out, the whole thing was in danger of falling apart." The decision to abolish Article Six was the nail. It was the moment when the Communist Party lost its time-honored right to steal.

"The Party no longer had easy access to state funds," Bakatin told me in 1993. "Now money had to be found somewhere to pay the bureaucrats who had no other jobs apart from Party work. We were faced with a huge financial crisis. The central bureaucracy and the Politburo were already in terrible financial shape. Even the income from Party dues was reduced because so many members were leaving. So instructions came [from the leadership] to invest Party money in commercial structures."[19]

Within months of the February 5th meeting, huge sums of money were quietly being transferred out of Party coffers. Documents from the Central Committee archives made public after the coup have provided a graphic illustration of the Party's miraculous conversion to capitalist enterprise.

In June, 1990, the first of many private banks was established with Party funds. Some thirty-one million rubles (about 1.2 million dollars at commercial 1990 rates) were placed as start-up capital for an operation envisioned as leading to large-scale credit and investment transfers at home and abroad. Officials reported that they planned to transfer an additional five hundred million rubles (about twenty million dollars) from the Party's reserves to the account by that autumn, because of what they called "the deterioration of the economic and political situation in the country." Eight months later, Party treasurer Nikolai Kruchina was so pleased with the bank's work that he deposited, in the name of the Central Committee, another fifty million rubles, at an interest rate of 6 percent.[20]

The banking operation blithely ignored a law of the Russian Federation that restricted the ownership of commercial banks to state bodies. As a political group, the Party did not formally qualify. But this was a minor quibble compared to the arrogance with which Party officials ignored their own ideological proscriptions against "profiteering" from bank interest.

Another document, dated August 23, 1990, disclosed the Communist Party leadership's plan to engage in private business. It was a Politburo resolution entitled "On Emergency Measures to Organize Commercial and Foreign Economic Activity of the Party," and it authorized the creation of several new "commercial organizations." Those organizations included a consulting firm to provide foreign brokerage services and a bank for administering the Party's hard-currency holdings, as well as its investments in international firms controlled by Communist parties abroad. (The document described them as "Friends of the Party," but they were also known as "Companies of Friends," in the Kremlin's special jargon.)[21]

The Soviet Union's military empire overseas was an early source of dividends. According to the Moscow crime newspaper *Kriminalnaya Khronika,* the sale of military property in East Germany during the early 1990s produced huge amounts of Soviet rubles, which in turn were exchanged for East German marks at the artificial rates set by COMECON, the moribund socialist trade market comprising the Soviet Union and its East European satellites. After German unification, the East German currency was exchanged for West German deutschmarks at an enormous profit.[22]

The newspaper claimed that it had proof of an even more notorious scheme in which several Communist-established "private" banks in Russia accepted huge dollar deposits from Panamanian and Colombian drug dealers, converted them to rubles, and then reconverted them to dollars, transferring the money overseas again in return for a hefty commission. "The Soviet Union," the paper said, "was operating as a colossal launderette."

There could be no doubt the Party was aware that its commercial activities were a betrayal of the state it purported to lead. The August 23rd Politburo resolution expressly ordered that the financial structures created under its scheme were to have "minimal visible ties" to the Communist leadership. "Anonymous organizations [will] mask direct links to the Party when launching commercial and foreign economic Party activity," the resolution instructed, with the aplomb of a mafiya syndicate creating front groups.

The fast track to capitalism was authorized at the highest levels. A classified Politburo resolution dated June 11, 1991, which approved the transfer of six hundred million rubles to commercial organizations and banks established by Party bodies such as the Komsomol, was signed by Communist Party general secretary Mikhail Gorbachev. According to the resolution, the funds were to serve as seed money for investment in "modern forms of economic activity, such as shareholding companies and small enterprises." These funds were also to be made available to "reliable" foreigners willing to establish joint ventures with Party enterprises.[23]

Lenin's heirs were not only concerned with preserving their communal wealth. According to evidence presented at the 1992 trial involving the Yeltsin government's ban on the Communist Party, Gorbachev also signed another document just a few weeks before the coup recommending that Party property around the country be transferred into the name of trustworthy "private" owners—all presumably members of the nomenklatura. Officials testified that there had not been time to carry this recommendation out, but the attempt to protect the Communist patrimony was already well under way.[24]

Long before the coup, the nomenklatura's eleventh-hour switch to capitalism produced maneuvers that made the black-market buccaneers of Yekaterinburg look like lowly bank robbers. The paper trail left in the archives shows that top state officials positioned themselves very early for a struggle over the control of post-Communist Russia's financial and industrial base. In one case, senior bureaucrats at Gossnab, the Ministry of State Supply, arranged to buy 142 government-owned dachas outside Moscow for the equivalent of about seventy-five thousand dollars, at prevailing rates, in 1990. A year later, the buildings as well as the land had an estimated value of more than four million dollars.[25]

For those nomenklatura separated by distance and rank from the financial schemes under way in Moscow, there were other means of assuring a secure future. In the final years of the regime, the entire system echoed to the thud of bureaucrats parachuting into comfortable private-sector jobs.

In August, 1990, Igor Gorbunov, then the regional party chief of Bashkiria—a region southwest of Yekaterinburg—received two million rubles from the Central Committee to establish a small cooperative bank. A few months later, the bank moved to Moscow, where it was relocated in a building owned by the Lenin District Party Committee. After the coup, Gorbunov and other Bashkirian Communist Party officials landed jobs at the bank, with monthly salaries of up to eighty thousand rubles, several times the average worker's wage.[26]

What helped these officials enormously, of course, was the fact that they were writing the new rules as they went along. "For a brief time, the . . . nomenklatura both acquired the freedom of private initiative and preserved their entire distributive power over state property," observed Lev Timofeyev.[27]

The measures taken under perestroika to liberalize the economy and reduce state control promoted first and foremost the interests of the Party elite. A Soviet pun in the early 1990s recognized this when it transformed *privatizatsiya,* "privatization," into *prikhvatizatsiya,* "grabbing." One of the major beneficiaries of the government's privatization program turned out to be the KGB. A maverick KGB general named Oleg Kalugin disclosed later that the agency "virtually controlled" the privatization program in the final years of the Soviet regime.[28] This was confirmed by Yevgeniya Albats, a Moscow journalist, whose investigation of the spy agency's activities showed that it invested three billion rubles (about 120 million dollars) in six hundred newly established commercial firms and banks around the country.[29]

Taking advantage of new rules permitting the establishment of "foreign economic associations" with the right to trade abroad, the agency created a Moscow-based export firm named Santa, whose board members were all active reserve officers of the KGB. The general director was a reserve KGB colonel identified only as V. Belousov. Santa lived up to its name. Within a few months, it was distributing generous gifts of cash to other newly created commercial firms inside the Soviet military-industrial complex.[30]

A "scientific industrial center" called Dalvent was set up in Vladivostok, under a general director named Kostyukov, who was an officer in the KGB unit attached to the Pacific fleet. In Leningrad, Santa financed a company called Petrobalt and appointed as its director First Captain Yuri Tkach, deputy chief of the KGB special detachment at the Leningrad Naval Base.

The KGB was an important secret player—perhaps the most important—in bridging the criminality of the old regime with the criminality of post-Communist era. On January 5, 1991, the KGB Third Main Department, the division responsible for military counterintelligence, sent a classified telegram to Soviet army and navy bases around the country. The message, discovered by Russian researchers in the agency's archives and listed as document 174033, relayed coded instructions from then KGB chairman Vladimir Kryuchkov for the establishment of private commercial firms to sell military technology overseas. Document 174033 triggered one of the most important domestic operations in KGB history. Kryuchkov, citing the "deteriorating domestic political situation," outlined the plan's three strategic aims in dry, bureaucratic language.[31] The new companies were to serve as "reliable covers for [KGB] leaders and the most valuable [KGB] operatives, in case the domestic . . . situation develops along East German lines; to provide financial means for the organization of underground work if 'destructive elements' come to power; and to create conditions for the effective use of foreign and domestic agent networks during [a period of] increased political instability."[32]

At the time, the KGB was already doing its best to heighten that instability. A week earlier, on December 20, 1990, Foreign Minister Eduard Shevardnadze had walked up to the podium of the Soviet parliament and announced his resignation. In an effort to call attention to the gathering power of reactionaries in Moscow, he had warned that a "dictatorship" was on the horizon—leaving no doubt that he considered the KGB the main center of conspiracy against the government.[33] Less than a month later, and just eight days after the Kryuchkov telegram was sent, army tanks and elite KGB troops launched a crackdown that left thirteen people dead in the streets of Vilnius, the Lithuanian capital, and raised a firestorm of anger and fear across the country.

As document 174033 suggested, the KGB was far from confident about its ability to prevail over the reformers. Thus, the second stated aim of the KGB operation—requiring agents to obtain the "means" of financing political opposition against a future reform government—was the crucial one.

It was a new twist on an old tactic. Since the early days of perestroika, the agency had used cover firms to spy on entrepreneurs, but this time, instead of funneling its secret earnings into the state treasury, it would use the profits from clandestine military sales to create a private source of wealth to fund its own anti-government activities.

Hundreds of other telegrams and memos similar to document 174033 record the paranoia of the powerful during the empire's final years. They are grist for future historians of the Soviet Union, but their greater importance lies in what they indicate about the sources of wealth and power in post-Communist Russia.

Before Russia's new democratic leaders could get their economic priorities in order, they were faced with a group of powerful opponents who looked disturbingly familiar. The nomenklatura bureaucrats who had invested in the private sector were now among Russia's most influential bank managers, company directors, and heads of commercial enterprises. The Communist Party's well-timed investments had assured the nomenklatura of political influence as well as personal wealth in the era that succeeded them.

"Some of my old friends in the Party are today chairmen of banks and stock exchanges, and they keep calling me up to cut me into deals," said Vadim Bakatin. "They always have something going in Siberia, or Odessa, or some other place. When I say no, they take pity on me. They say, 'Vadim, can I give you a car, for God's sake, you are in a bad way.' I just keep saying, 'No thanks, don't give me anything.' "

Bakatin used to command magisterial offices as a senior member of the nomenklatura. He had been a minister in Gorbachev's cabinet and Boris Yeltsin's chairman of the KGB. When I met him in 1993, his working quarters were so small that if he shifted his big frame slightly, he could reach the pot of withered flowers on the windowsill overlooking the Moscow River without getting up from his desk. He made a modest living, working for one of the handful of "foundations" that have provided safe perches for perestroika veterans. A map of the former Soviet Union, hanging on one wall, provided the only color in the room.

Bakatin, a genial man whose liberal attitudes and square-jawed good looks made him a poster boy for perestroika in the West, typified the best and the brightest of the nomenklatura. Like Arbatov, he had risen on the strength of his intelligence. But once inside the inner circle of power, he became a victim of its ruling ethic. From October, 1988, to December, 1990, Bakatin was the Soviet Union's chief policeman. As minister of internal affairs, he was given the impossible task of keeping law and order in a system that was gradually unraveling. Bakatin read Aleksandr Gurov's research paper and was so impressed that he set up the ministry's special division on organized crime—and made Gurov its head. But he was never allowed to challenge the guiding principles that made the job futile. When he tried to push through some of his ideas about legalizing the black economy to counter organized crime in the late 1980s, he was told by the Party secretariat not to make waves. "They said we didn't need any more problems," he recalled.

He had one accomplishment to be proud of. Throughout his career, which included an unsuccessful run for the presidency of Russia against Yeltsin in 1991 and a brief five-month appointment as chairman of the KGB following the coup, he was never tarnished with any corruption scandals. But that made him all the more defensive about the other members of his class.[34]

"I don't like all this talk about the corruption of the old system," he told me. "It is true we ran the economy ineffectively, and there was an elite which enjoyed limitless wealth. But you can't really call that corruption. The senior Party leaders were gods and czars. They already lived under Communism. They could get whatever they wanted from abroad. They didn't need to take bribes, but it was the order of things that people gave gifts. It was the way power was organized then. But it was a less corrupt system than what we have now."

Bakatin was right in a sense. The scandals of the Soviet regime pale beside the massive corruption and crime of the present era. But like most members of his generation in the former leadership, he is reluctant to acknowledge the formative role played by the nomenklatura in the development of post-Soviet crime.

Other Russians, however, have had no hesitation about doing so. "The criminal party has left the stage, but the criminal state has remained," declared Pavel Voshchanov, a commentator for *Komsomolskaya Pravda* who became Yeltsin's press secretary, in the summer of 1992. "Mafiya habits, embezzlement of public funds, and corruption remain the norms of social relations and penetrate the atmosphere in which the country and each of our citizens lives. Our efforts to present [the defeat of the coup] as a victory for democracy are nothing more than self-deception. On the whole, Communists were defeated by other Communists."[35]

Within a month of the coup, there were as many schisms inside the nomenklatura as there were inside the Russian underworld, as Communists continued to fight Communists for a share of the Party legacy.

Aleksandr Muzikantsky, an official appointed by the Russian government to deal with the expropriation of Party buildings, complained that rival bureaucrats were scrambling over each other in a race to "grab state property." [36]

At a press conference on August 30, 1991, the exasperated Muzikantsky held up a letter he had received from Mikhail Gorbachev demanding title to a building owned by the Institute of Social Sciences, on Moscow's Leningradsky Prospekt. Gorbachev claimed that he needed the quarters for his presidential staff now that he no longer had access to his former offices at Central Committee Headquarters. Gorbachev was not the only top official eager to stake out his claim. Muzikantsky received a curt demand from the new Russian government for transferring ownership of the luxury apartment blocks that had belonged to the Central Committee to the new Council of Ministers. "We need to make sure that property is not handed over from one set of bureaucrats to another set of bureaucrats," Muzikantsky pleaded. "This kind of thing has to stop."

It didn't. The secret financial deals of the last years of the Soviet regime blossomed into open chicanery in the hospitable environment of post-Communism. As one long-term foreign resident put it succinctly following the coup, "There are only two kinds of people with money in Russia: ex-Communist officials, and the men who bribed them." [37]

The two classes remain the principal combatants in the struggle over the spoils of the Soviet system—a struggle whose outcome will determine the future power balance of Russia. "The struggle for power in our country is the struggle for property," Len Karpinsky, editor of the liberal newspaper *Moskovskiye Novosti* wrote in March, 1993. "Capital and wealth are the key to position in the power structure. . . . If the [former] bureaucrat continues to be pivotal to the system, we may well find ourselves living under 'nomenklatura capitalism,' whose despotism will not be inferior to the planned socialist system." [38]

The "nomenklatura capitalists" have financed their struggle with the funds transferred or embezzled from the former Communist state. Long after the coup, laundered Party money was turning up in every sector of the new Russian economy. Russian government investigators found evidence showing that Communist Party money financed more than one hundred commercial enterprises in Moscow and some six hundred across Russia. The investigators traced to the Central Committee more than one billion rubles deposited in Russian banks alone. An estimated fifty billion rubles was believed hidden around Russia and abroad. Considering the senior nomenklatura's freedom to do what it wanted without fear of scrutiny, this may be the tip of the iceberg. According to the Russian Ministry of the Economy, the Soviet Communist Party held 453.5 billion "hard-currency" rubles (freely convertible to dollars) in its accounts between 1981 and 1991, and some one billion dollars in cash. There were many powerful interests anxious to keep that money secret.[39]

Inspector Vladimir Kalinichenko, on special assignment from the government to track Communist funds abroad, ran into the wall of silence erected by the nomenklatura capitalists almost as soon as he began his investigations. When I first called and asked for an interview with him in the summer of 1992, he insisted on meeting me away from his offices in the old Gosplan building, which had once housed the powerful Soviet planning agency, near Red Square. "Too many people listening up there," he said cryptically.

He brought along his aide, Nikolai Emelyanov, one of the few colleagues on the commission he trusted. Hunched like conspirators over a table in the nearly empty coffee shop of the Intourist Hotel on Tverskaya Street, the two men talked in rapid-fire sentences, frequently interrupting each other. The astronomical sums they tossed over the coffee and heavy pastry sounded fantastic against the claims of bankruptcy made by the new Russian government.

"While our leaders go to the West and beg for a few million dollars in aid, I would say many more millions, even billions, are being transferred back and forth through our country," Kalinichenko said.[40]

"We know businessmen who in the course of a month can get together three hundred billion rubles for a deal," said Emelyanov. "I don't think you can collect that much money in the States over a month, but here they can . . ."

"In no time at all," cut in Kalinichenko. "Then they go to the West and change the rubles for dollars. Even at a cheap conversion rate, it still comes back as pure profit. And they know how to use it. The president of one bank came to me and said that if we left him alone we could just name our bank account and he would transfer fifty million dollars to it. That's the kind of money moving around this country now.

"And that's why it's foolish to keep looking for Party money abroad.

We'll never get that back, but the money that counts now is all around us."

The investigations begun by Kalinichenko and Emelyanov were filed away in oblivion when the government anti-corruption commission they worked for was closed down. Subsequent commissions met the same fate. It had become politically impossible to acknowledge the sheer volume of corruption that overtook Russia in 1992 and 1993. According to the two former investigators, the "dirty" money that financed the purchase of a New York skyscraper and numerous other properties in the United States and Europe came from the same secret treasure chest that finances the nomenklatura's growing interests at home.

The Communist Party remains the source of one of the richest accumulations of private wealth in the world, and the ethics of the Party mafiya dominate the post-Soviet world. Konstantin Maydanyuk, a former senior investigator with the USSR Special Prosecutor's Office, noted that it was irrelevant to distinguish the senior leadership and politicians after 1991 as democrats or conservatives. "The people this system [produced] bring their habits with them," he told Lev Timofeyev. "They haven't become different." [41]

Even though Russian president Boris Yeltsin appears to have belatedly recognized the danger, he has proven unable to do anything about it. In the first year of his administration, the principal target of his invective was the organized-crime underworld. But he eventually identified the former Soviet bureaucracy as the main obstacle to Russia's becoming a competitive market economy and a normal society. "Bribery, privatization for the sake of, and by, the nomenklatura, the plunder of natural resources, and nomenklatura separatism threaten the disintegration of Russia," Yeltsin declared in a December, 1992, speech. A few months later, in March, 1993, he added that the "former Bolshevik system . . . has not yet disintegrated [and] is today again striving to renew its lost power over Russia." [42]

The former Communists have enlisted new allies. In the wreckage of Soviet Communism, the *vory* and the nomenklatura have grown closer together. "We can no longer talk about links between the old mafiya underworld and the bureaucrats," Kalinichenko grumbled. "We have to talk about mergers."

The two criminal societies made a natural fit. Already strikingly

similar in organization, they presided over the two major streams of
capital available to post-Communist Russia: black-market profits and
the wealth of the Communist Party. The old formal barriers between the
vorovskoi mir and the Party hierarchy were erased by new alliances of
convenience. The process was most visible in Russia's regions, where
the crime lords and the bureaucrats shared the common aim of resisting the attempts of the central authorities to break the power of the
large state enterprises. This was what Yeltsin meant by "nomenklatura
separatism."

As in Yekaterinburg, regional and local officials turned their fledgling coalitions with former black marketeers and the criminal world into
a new power base. In nearly all the seventy-eight regions of the Russian
Federation, former bureaucrats became the most outspoken proponents
of de-centralization—a fashionable notion in the West, but in Russia a
code word for local resistance to Moscow-imposed economic reforms.

Mikhail Poltaranin, former Russian minister for press and the mass
media, warned in 1992 that the coalition of crime lords, former Communist managers, and local authorities represented a "fifth estate." [43]
By that year, they were already strong enough to defy Moscow's authority. Local governments withheld tax revenue, appointed their own
justice and customs officials, and committed thousands of other violations of federal rules during 1992, and the country's chief law officer
filed more than two hundred thousand formal protests against violators
of local authority. No one expected the trend to be reversed. By 1993,
some provincial bosses were mounting even more pointed challenges to
Moscow. Yekaterinburg, for instance, became the focus of efforts to set
up an "independent" Urals Republic. [44]

When the new Russian government, in an early burst of reformist
zeal, abolished the central industrial ministries and gave enterprises
the right to deal directly with suppliers and customers instead of going
through Moscow, it played directly into the local bosses' hands. Freed
from Moscow's scrutiny, they took control of the huge state enterprises
in their jurisdiction and blocked further efforts to turn them into private
companies. [45]

But the regional axis of power was only one of the combinations
threatening political and economic stability in Russia. Connections between the nomenklatura capitalists and criminal groups have turned up

at the central-government level. On October 18, 1992, a former Party colleague of Vadim Bakatin's named Anatoli Melnik was sentenced to five years in prison for smuggling. Melnik was associated with an Armenian crime lord who imported nearly seventeen thousand bottles of liquor from Germany designated as "humanitarian aid." With new labels identifying the bottles as containing mineral water, the liquor was reexported to Poland and Germany and sold at a profit of nearly 400 percent. According to evidence presented in court, Melnik bribed one of his contacts in the Russian Customs Department to let the shipment leave the country on forged waybills. At the time, Melnik was head of the Russian Interpol office; previously, he had held the rank of colonel in the Ministry of Internal Affairs, to which he had been promoted by Bakatin.[46]

Until he was arrested, Melnik belonged to the circle of Russian government insiders who comfortably administered the transition from Communism to capitalism. He even lived in the same exclusive Moscow building as top officials of the Ministry of Russian Security. Clearly, not every member of the bureaucracy was corrupt. Was it fair, then, to condemn all former nomenklatura because of the excesses of a few? Even the comrade criminals, after all, might well be tomorrow's Russian Rothschilds, Rockefellers, and Morgans. Considering the risks of the Russian marketplace, who could better assure the country's stable passage toward the future than the guardians of the old order? The situation bears an ironic resemblance to the earliest period of the Soviet state, when the leadership recruited czarist functionaries to keep the country running and the empire's military officers to assure its defense.

"If you look at the social make-up of today's *nouveaux riches,* there are an awful lot of former Party and KGB workers, maybe proportionally more than anyone else," said Bakatin. "But I see nothing wrong with it. If we had a normal economy, things might have been different. KGB and Party *apparatchiki* are the leaders in business simply because they are the people who had more information than others, better contacts, more possibilities of getting hold of supplies. They are not stupid."

It is a depressing argument, all the more so because many Westerners appear to have conceded the point on the grounds, perhaps, that no one can keep an old car on the road better than those who know what it looks like under the hood. But it is circular reasoning. The fact that there was no "normal economy," in Bakatin's phrase, to produce an efficient, non-partisan managerial class and civil service capable of presiding over the transition from Communism is hardly an accident of history. Although the czarist functionaries were eventually purged by the Soviet leadership, they never posed a serious threat of subversion to the new order. In contrast, yesterday's nomenklatura—enriched by the Communist fortune and reinforced by its mob contacts—does have the power to subvert the new Russian democracy. And it has had the extra advantage of advance planning.

"The nomenklatura knew years ago that the system would come tumbling down," said Aslambek Aslakhanov. "They prepared themselves for that, and they have obviously been successful. But no matter how high a position they occupy in our country, I still consider them ordinary criminals, because they put their own interests above the interests of the state, just as they did when the Party existed."

Lev Timofeyev, the former dissident, went a step further in his book with a warning that the code the nomenklatura lived by, and which it now shared with its underworld partners, was poisonous to Russia's hopes for a normal economy. "The danger isn't that a former member of the *apparat* becomes a bank president," he wrote. "The trouble is, rather, that this person is . . . bound hand and foot to his social class— [to] the apparat, the military-industrial complex, and the KGB. He is dependent on that trinity in everything he does, because he obtains his property rights from them for a price: a silent oath of loyalty. If he breaks that oath, he will not remain a property owner for long." [47]

Timofeyev went on to predict that those forces that preserved their economic monopoly while holding on to government power would move into positions of greater political authority in Russia and other Commonwealth states. After the December, 1993, Russian parliamentary elections, his prediction was borne out. By February, 1994, the majority of senior cabinet posts in the Yeltsin government was occupied by former Communist officials with deep ties to powerful state industrial and agricultural interests. Russia was well on its way to a form of state capitalism in which former Communists played the commanding roles.

In post-Communist Russia, as in the former Soviet Union, the boundaries between crime and politics have been blurred. That is one reason why Russia's comrade criminals do not represent a law-and-order problem in the accepted Western sense of the term. The comrade criminal carries with him the baggage of the criminal state.

Aslakhanov could find only one reason for reassurance as he surveyed his country's surging corruption and crime. "Russia is still too big and disorganized for there to be one Al Capone," he said. "The spirit of independence is strong among all our different criminal groups. While the chaos continues, they would rather act on their own without having to submit to one criminal chieftain who is in charge of everything.

"The real problem may start when the state actually manages to come to grips with organized crime—when our law enforcement agencies work the way they're supposed to, and when we begin to control corruption. Then the criminal clans and the political clans may try to elect someone who can lead them."

If Aslakhanov is right, the entire "transition period" may be little more than an interregnum between Russia's previous oppressors and its as-yet-unidentified future ones. It is all the more important, therefore, to look at the multifarious and often imaginative ways Russia's comrade criminals are advancing their political and economic fortunes.

II Field of Wonders

I believe you and I are the only people in Russia who don't steal.

—Czar Nicholas I, in a comment reputedly made to his ten-year-old son during the Crimean War

7 Post-Soviet Man

Matrosskaya Tishina Prison, in Moscow, is a long way in spirit, as well as distance, from the penal camps of Siberia. Its name means "sailor's peace," and, compared to the frozen wasteland where the hoodlums of the Thieves World do their hard time, it is almost a hotel. The cells are small, but comfortable. Through the barred windows, an inmate can see the quiet, tree-lined streets near the Yauza River, which winds its way north from the Kremlin walls past grimy factories, derelict churches, and the majestic onion-shaped domes of Andronikov Monastery. Matrosskaya Tishina briefly became world-famous in 1991, when the conspirators of the August coup were jailed there, but it was used throughout the Soviet era as a lockup for so-called "economic criminals"—black-marketeers found guilty of the crime of making a profit.

In 1988, Mark Rudinshtein received his graduate education in business behind its walls. Rudinshtein had been one of the richest businessmen in Moscow in the mid-1980s. A plump, cheerful man who favors double-breasted suits and wide, flowered ties, he was a successful promoter of rock music and films when he was arrested and charged with profiteering. His real crime was to have irritated his business rivals. In most countries, needless to say, healthy competition does not lead to a criminal charge. But Rudinshtein's business rivals were Soviet government bureaucrats.

"Of course, I broke the same silly laws everyone was breaking at the time," Rudinshtein told me when I met him in 1993. "But no one bothered me until some deputy ministers decided I was too successful. They wanted me put away so they could control the business." [1]

Rudinshtein became a successful promoter with the help of bureaucrats in the Ministry of Culture, who were desperately trying to find ways to fill the concert halls built in Moscow for the 1980 Olympics. After spending millions of rubles to construct showcases of Soviet socialism, the state had been left with white elephants and a large debt. Rudinshtein brought in special concerts, generating a profit for himself and his bureaucratic partners. But when he developed a video rental business and then a movie production studio with his share of the earnings, he ran into trouble. Jealous bureaucrats tried to elbow him out by setting up a rival company. When that failed, Rudinshtein found himself behind bars.

Most of his fellow prisoners were so-called "speculators," whose principal offense had been to challenge the state's monopoly of commerce by trading in hard-to-obtain goods like computers and Western sports shoes. Considering how much of the Soviet economy was already in the hands of similar black-market entrepreneurs, it was reasonable to assume that the inhabitants of Matrosskaya Tishina were incarcerated because they either failed to make the proper payoffs or—like Rudinshtein—had grown too rich and powerful for the business interests of the nomenklatura.

Rudinshtein's own cellmates, however, did not fit either category. Like him, they were accused of "economic crimes." But the crucial difference was that they were part of the system that had sent Rudinshtein to prison. In one bed lay the former minister of transport of Kazakhstan. In the other was the former cotton minister of Turkmenistan. The cell next door was occupied by Yuri Churbanov, son-in-law of the late Soviet president Leonid Brezhnev and once the deputy federal police minister. All three were victims of the first major corruption crackdown launched under perestroika. Linked to the infamous cotton scandal of Central Asia, they were accused of accepting huge bribes to falsify production reports.

At first, Rudinshtein was uneasy at being associated with men who had robbed the state. But he arrived at a grudging respect for the former ministers. "If they didn't take bribes, they would have been in even more trouble with their bosses," he said. "The state ended up corrupting everyone who was part of it."

Perhaps only behind bars in the Soviet Union could the pre-capitalist and post-Communist societies achieve a mutual understanding. Rudinshtein said that in prison he learned more about the intricacies of making money under the Soviet regime than he had ever learned on the outside. "Those ministers taught me a lot I didn't know about the system," he said later. "Especially Churbanov. He was a really clever guy. It's strange to say it, but I thought he would probably made a good businessman in a real economy."

Rudinshtein left Matrosskaya Tishina in 1990 an invigorated man. He believed he had learned the secret of success. "Before I went to prison, I had the fear all Soviet people had for the state," he said. "But the fear left me while I was inside. After I came out, my knees no longer shook in fright every time a Party committee sneezed. What more could they do to me?"

He didn't realize how much more. Rudinshtein's sympathy for his bureaucrat cellmates faded when he discovered that their colleagues outside had grown even more powerful—and more larcenous. The bureaucrats who had made his life miserable before he went to jail turned up as owners of "private" film companies and promotion agencies. Their connections with their old colleagues in the Ministry of Culture had by then ensured them control of Russia's expanding private entertainment industry. Moreover, they were able to get access to Party funds through the network of contacts established under the old regime.

Rudinshtein found obstacles wherever he turned. Several theaters refused to distribute his films. It was difficult for him to obtain equipment, while his rivals arranged to get cameras from Mosfilm, the official state film company, that were supposed to have been placed on public auction.

Yet the producer's disenchantment was at first difficult to understand. He seemed to have productive contacts of his own. We met at the former Soviet Ministry of Culture, where he had secured an impressive suite of fifth-floor offices overlooking the Arbat—Moscow's popular pedestrian mall. His company, Kinotavr, produced about six films a year, and several of his films were showing abroad, in Israel and America. But as far as Rudinshtein was concerned, real success—the kind that was measured in soaring profits and an expanding business empire—was permanently beyond his grasp. He believed that his career had been sabotaged by the rise of the comrade criminal.

"One of my biggest competitors, for instance, is an old Communist who calls himself a big businessman," he said. "He can distribute his films in places I can't, and he and his friends stop me from getting the loans I could use to expand and make more movies. People tell me the money is in importing American films—that's what people want to see—but our best studios are collapsing because the profits these people make go into their foreign bank accounts instead of into modernizing our industry. The nomenklatura operate by their own laws. They were dishonest, godless people then, and they are the same now. Thanks to them, I will never have the chance to become a real magnate, and we'll never have a decent film industry.

"I suppose I should be thankful for being able to do as well as I did. But the truth is, in order to be a successful capitalist in this country and get access to real money, you need to have been in the Party for a long time."

Rudinshtein was exaggerating—but the point was worth noting. The millions of average ex–Party members, of course, had little hope of making fortunes. Only those who held senior Party posts, or could obtain favors from those who did, had access to large stocks of capital. Outside the Party, one needed to be extremely tough or armed—or frequently both. Yet these facts were not immediately apparent to anyone who observed the entrepreneurial energy of post-Soviet society. Within three years of the fall of Communism, between forty million and fifty million Russians were participating in the free-market economy, either directly or through a family connection. They were workers in private farms, stock exchanges, privatized factories, cooperatives, and banks. They were also managers, shopkeepers, investors, and entrepreneurs. It was a measure of how far Russia had already traveled from its Communist past. But the figures told only part of the story.[2]

By 1994, Russia displayed the signs of a consumer boom, but the "free market" that underpinned it had little in common with a Western competitive economy. Middle-class Russians crowded shops selling high-priced imported videos and televisions. They had a wide choice of foreign groceries, liquor, and expensive cuts of meats. They lived in expensively restored apartments and took their holidays in Paris or Cyprus. Thriving street markets sold everything from clothes to car parts. But except for the goods brought in by energetic private traders, much of this Western cornucopia was channeled through wholesale trade outlets and importers that resembled the monopolies of Soviet times.[3]

Genuine competition in price and quality was hard to find. Most basic goods were produced by the same large factories and conglomerates of the Soviet era. Even private shops, like Seran Akopyan's grocery store, were at the mercy of supplier cartels controlled by the state or the underworld, or both. More importantly, most of Russia's new wealth was not based on rising productivity, but on the profits generated by currency and commodity speculation in the country's new stock exchanges and brokerages, and on the provision of services and foreign products to a newly affluent and gadget-hungry population. A Russian could become immensely rich on the profits from international trade and the export of raw materials and resources, and so could those who worked for him, but investors were unlikely to put their money in new factories or production lines. Not only were such investments too long-term for a country still nervous about its political future, but high taxation and tight credit policies made them dubious. In a stark illustration of the lack of confidence, industrial production fell nearly 25 percent in the first three months of 1994.[4]

The drive to get rich quickly with as little risk as possible spread from the middle class to most sectors of the population. Nearly 450,000 St. Petersburgers were duped in 1993 by a consortium of commercial firms that promised a 250 percent profit in three months to anyone who handed over a privatization voucher—and then disappeared. (The vouchers were shares in state enterprises given free to every Russian citizen, and could be traded or sold.) Similar scams swindled millions across the country. Perhaps the crowning example of warped capitalism occurred in 1994, when a company called MMM, which sold more than four billion rubles' worth of stock certificates (about two million dollars) to housewives and factory workers, collapsed in Moscow. Thousands of panicked investors besieged the company's offices as the value of their tiny individual holdings plummeted, and the government was forced to step in. An investigation revealed that the company was investing in nothing but itself. The profits from its sales were paid out as dividends in an intricate pyramid scheme. The incident added fuel to national suspicion of "capitalism," but it wasn't likely to dissuade would-be Russian millionaires. "Russians who don't believe in anything anymore—not in the government, not in politicians—are ready to believe an advertisement that promises to make them rich overnight," said Mikhail Berger of *Izvestiya*.[5]

The popularity of such schemes was a symptom of the desperation and uncertainty at the center of Russia's "boom." Although inflation had begun to ease by 1994, and some of the early chaos of the transition period had cleared, many of the ingredients for a real competitive economy were still missing. Ownership of land for commercial purposes was heavily restricted. Governments at every level intruded on all aspects of business operations, from licensing permits to prices. The structures of power, in fact, were reminiscent of the old regime. Russia continued to be governed as the lucrative fiefdom of a paternal state bureaucracy.

In the crucial early years of Russia's democratic experiment, few of the men and women who ran the governments of the post-Soviet nations showed any inclination to create a climate for private investment and free enterprise. There were rational reasons for doing nothing. The breakdown of the Soviet system opened new vistas of opportunity for the public servants of the new regime, who found themselves guardians of a vast patrimony of buildings, factories, tanks, missiles, hotels, ships, and countless other products of the Soviet industrial state. Under Communist management, these products had no intrinsic price; they were blocks of goods that the state shifted around in its accounting books. But with the end of Party control, the goods possessed a tremendous potential market value. Like the assets of a bankrupt firm, they could be auctioned off to the highest bidder or—just as profitably—retained for their value as negotiating chips in the battle for political influence.

Who owned these assets? In Soviet-speak, it was the "people." In post-Soviet-speak, it was the "state," which was just as impossible to define.

Who, for instance, really owned the sprawling Zil assembly plant in south Moscow? The government of Russia, as the legal successor to the Soviet state and, presumably, all of its property, could lay a claim. But Moscow officials could argue that the plant belonged to the municipality that built and serviced it. With perhaps equal justification, the Zil workers' collective could insist that the enterprise was the rightful property of those who had a vested interest in keeping it running.

The tortuous debate over ownership, repeated in thousands of similar cases across the country, produced the chaos of post-Communism. As the competing claims to the Soviet inheritance were pursued in courts, parliaments, city councils, and gangster-dominated streets, the value of the disputed goods continued to climb. The bureaucrat moved to center stage. After all, who knew the property better?

As stewards of the "people's property" under the old regime, officials decided who would live in which apartments, who was entitled to use state recreational facilities, who would repair and run the planes, trains, and research facilities. No one else could provide continuity between the old system and the new. Without their stewardship, they could argue, the property would be at the mercy of rapacious foreign investors or—just as dangerously—the angry masses intent on laying claim to their own piece of Russia. It had happened, everyone knew, once before—during the anarchy of "expropriation" and looting that followed the 1917 revolution.

Until the arguments could be resolved, the nomenklatura made themselves essential to the developing Russian market. It would have been unreasonable to expect a bureaucrat not to translate his steward's role into genuine wealth. And even more unreasonable to think that he would not emerge as the most powerful player in Russia's game of capitalism.

Leonid Zapalsky, a deputy economics minister in Russia, nearly got away with one of the more brilliant maneuvers in the new economy in the weeks following the aborted coup. Appointed head of the Liquidation Commission, which disposed of former Soviet property, he assumed title to the Soviet Economics Ministry headquarters in central Moscow. In the process of "liquidating" the property, he transferred the buildings, along with 50 computers, 220 fax machines, and other office equipment, to the Russian-Japanese University, an institution that he and several fellow bureaucrats had privately set up as a joint venture. When anti-corruption investigators caught up with him, he was preparing to pocket a profit of fifty million rubles. The commissioners recovered the money, but the case never went further. Inspector Vladimir Kalinichenko, of the anti-corruption commission, who investigated the case, told me that Zapalsky evaded prosecution thanks to the protection of a "senior" aide in Yeltsin's office.[6]

The process that turned wealth which no one officially owned into a marketable commodity gave the former Soviet bureaucracy the power to dominate commerce and trade. It was a kind of "privatization," but it bore only a superficial resemblance to programs of the same name undertaken in Western industrial democracies. Valery Chernogorodsky, a senior Russian official, admitted that his country's privatization policies often resulted in "private monopolies emerging from state monopolies," so that "the ordinary businessman [could not] compete."[7]

Bureaucrats proved adept at undervaluing property in order to obtain astronomical profits. The commercial port at Nakhodka, on the Pacific coast, was sold to a private firm for 18.4 million rubles. The Russian State Property Management Committee had priced it at 70 million rubles. According to the conclusions of an anti-corruption investigation, the difference was more than made up in kickbacks. But why sell off what you can own yourself?

Russian justice authorities disclosed that seven hundred state officials were fired in 1992 for using their posts to gain control of commercial enterprises. Most knowledgeable people considered this only a small portion of what was actually going on. The list of top bureaucrats linked to business covered a Who's Who of the Russian political establishment. The regulations governing their commercial activities were so vague that few could formally be accused of doing anything illegal.

Vasili Gromyko, a former deputy health minister, sat on the board of directors of Siemensmedtekhnika, a health care joint venture, when he was still in office. Yuri Skokov, the chairman of the National Security Council and the second-most powerful man in the Russian government until 1993, supervised—among other activities—the Garantiya fund, which enjoyed a monopoly over the sale of raw materials and military property. Former vice-president Aleksandr Rutskoi was chairman of the Vozrozhdeniye (Revival) Fund, a charity for pensioned soldiers, which was later linked to an attempt to smuggle abroad millions of tons of crude oil and refinery products.

In the regions, the army of "civil-service businessmen" reached embarrassing proportions. According to reports in Moscow newspapers, virtually the entire administration of Kalmykia engaged in private commerce in 1992. B. Ilyanov, deputy chairman of the Council of Ministers, was president of the Kalmyk Builders' Association. I. Bugdayev, the minister of agriculture, was president of the board of Kalmytskaya Sherst (Kalmyk Wool), a joint-stock company. The minister of finance, the chairman of the properties fund, the minister of social security, and other high-ranking officials also were part-time capitalists.

The capitalist urge was not limited to Russian bureaucrats. More than two hundred high-ranking officials in Belarus were involved in private companies. According to Eduard Shirovsky, the national security chief, they did not hide the use of their positions for private enrichment. "It's a national disaster," he said. In one typical case, a senior official of the Belarussian Trade Committee arranged for the "privatization" of a state-owned instrument-making plant by selling it to a Swedish-Belarussian joint venture for a token price of eight million rubles. The

Soviet government had purchased the same plant several years before for 10.5 million dollars. The official—along with the plant manager—happened to be on the board of the joint venture.[8]

In Kazakhstan, civil servants quietly transferred dozens of state-owned enterprises into their own names. "All the lucrative state properties have already been seized," charged Serik Abdrakhmanov, a deputy of the Kazakh parliament, at the end of 1992. He added that bureaucrats compounded the plunder of national resources by financing their clandestine acquisitions on cheap credit. "These officials have no trouble [getting money], but an ordinary person cannot receive a loan from the National State Bank," he complained.[9]

In the first years of the post-Soviet era, the Commonwealth of Independent States experienced the equivalent of a gold rush as bureaucrats raced to put down stakes in the new economy. Municipal authorities in Kishinev, the capital of Moldova, secretly invested thirteen million rubles from the city budget in private ventures, according to charges filed by that republic's law enforcement officials in late 1992. In Armenia, President Levon Ter-Petrosyan ordered his officials to begin an inventory of all state property to head off an epidemic of graft. He issued a decree requiring all civil servants to disclose their incomes and bank holdings, but few expected results. "We are seeing a rise in the professionalism of organized crime, and a tendency towards merger with state structures and responsible officials," the Armenian Ministry of Internal Affairs warned.[10]

Meanwhile, in Azerbaijan, Rufat Agayev, the former mayor of Baku and the country's ambassador to Italy, was named by local police as the godfather of a crime syndicate. The internal affairs minister said that other top officials, including a former president of the Azerbaijan Soviet Socialist Republic, a senior official in Azerbaijan's delegation to the United Nations, and a former municipal Communist Party kingpin, were part of the organization.[11]

Felix Kulov, vice-president of the mountainous Central Asian country of Kyrgyzstan, was accused in 1993 of arranging illegal export licenses of copper wire, aluminum, and rare bronze artifacts to China and Russia. The deals were worth billions of rubles, officials said. "The 're-export virus' is making its way from the shores of the Baltic Sea to the Tien-Shan Mountains of Kyrgyzstan," noted the local correspondent of *Izvestiya*. "It has infected commercial enterprises and mafiya structures alike. In Bishkek [the capital], they are stealing copper wire from trolleybuses and aluminum fencing from parks; meanwhile, the lack of metal and lumber has brought construction of housing and schools in the city to a standstill. The customs documents allowing these items to be sold abroad are all stamped, conveniently, 'surplus to needs.' " [12]

In Ukraine, then Prime Minister (now President) Leonid Kuchma disclosed that a rough, unofficial privatization was under way in the region's petroleum industry. Eight million tons of Ukrainian petroleum products had been sold on the black market to refineries in Europe. At the same time, he complained, Ukraine was experiencing such serious oil shortages that fuel from the strategic reserves had to be used to carry the beet harvest to sugar refineries. [13]

Bureaucrats revealed an inventiveness they were rarely permitted to display under Soviet power. Enormous quantities of Russian raw materials and strategic resources began turning up on foreign markets at bargain-basement prices, undercutting government revenues. "Private" Russian crude oil in 1992 was selling at three to four dollars a ton below the government price, and other resources were selling for as much as five to ten times less. A government working group on economic security claimed that eight billion dollars' worth of cobalt had been illegally exported in 1992, much of it stolen from state warehouses. According to the economist Pavel Bunich, Russia was forced to import nearly 50 percent of its bauxite and aluminum requirements in 1992, while nearly the identical amount was "smuggled abroad." [14]

The Tyumen region of Siberia, which contains some of the largest oil and gas reserves of the former Soviet Union, became the hub of a flourishing clandestine oil trade. Russian government officials said that former and present bureaucrats had smuggled a substantial part of the region's oil production abroad in 1992. Local officials denied the charge, insisting that it was impossible to transport the oil in any way except through government pipelines. But government export figures showed an unexplained gap between the amount of oil passing through the pipelines and the amount that actually showed up on world markets. [15]

"We are losing all our strategic resources in big quantities, but the situation with oil is especially catastrophic," Mikhail Gurtovoi, chairman of the Russian Anti-Corruption Commission (which employed Vladimir Kalinichenko and Nikolai Emelyanov), said in an interview with the newspaper *Trud*. "Less than one-quarter of the true value of our oil exports comes back to this country, while profits from the sale of millions of tons of Russian oil are on deposit in the accounts of foreign firms." [16]

In 1993, the Russian government enacted a decree limiting the export of "strategically important" raw materials, which officials hoped would plug the oil leak. But few others expected it to make a difference. Soon after the edict was published, more than three million tons of Russian oil sold to Ukraine, Belarus, and the Baltic states mysteriously ended up in Hungary. [17]

The so-called "oil mafiya" took advantage of new rules designed to encourage joint ventures with foreign firms in the once-restricted energy sector. The government hoped that the joint ventures would attract Western capital to modernize ancient rigs and leaking pipelines, and to improve living conditions for workers. Unfortunately, said Gurtovoi, firms "which were too small and too ill-equipped to extract or develop anything, and had no intentions of doing so," were the main beneficiaries of the change in regulations. One joint venture, approved by the government after presenting a detailed drilling schedule, never drilled a single well, even though it managed to conclude contracts for the sale of 700,000 tons of oil. Its crude actually came from supplies already produced by government wells and siphoned off with the collusion of officials. "This is one reason why we have gasoline shortages in Russia," Gurtovoi complained.

Vladimir Kalinichenko's description of the boggling amount of illicit capital moving around, into, and out of the former Soviet Union was lent added weight by official estimates of the annual capital flow out of the country, ranging between six billion to twenty-five billion dollars. Some Russian economists said that the money was flowing overseas because ordinary Russian investors trusted neither their country's banks nor its new political masters to keep their savings safe. This ignored, however, the more important point at the heart of the post-Soviet economy's problems: there were, in fact, few "ordinary Russian investors." [18]

Most of the wealth was generated by the shrewd manipulation of an economy that remained effectively under state control. Like the crude oil siphoned from existing wells by the oil mafiya, it represented neither new production nor investment. Those making billions were, for the most part, those who made millions in the Soviet era—either by arranging black-market sales of state goods or from the byzantine system of bribery. The old state, in effect, had criminalized the new.

President Boris Yeltsin reported to a February, 1993, conference on organized crime in Moscow that he had discovered a two-billion-dollar "shortfall" between exports abroad and payments returned to Russia in the account books prepared by the Ministry of Foreign Economic Relations. "I would like to know," he scolded, "who in our government is getting rich on this."

If he had been told, it's hard to imagine what he could have done. In early 1992, Aslambek Aslakhanov, chairman of the parliamentary law and order committee, was entrusted with the job of preparing Russia's first law on corruption in the civil service. Eight months later, he was still trying to persuade his own committee members to approve the draft of the bill. "I have been getting phone calls from various people, who say, 'Why get involved? Wait for a year — it's not needed now,' " he told me.[19]

"There are people in the entourages of all the important people in the state who are not interested in seeing this law passed. The aim is to grab and grab, steal, steal, and steal. And when they have stolen so much that they don't know what to do with any more money, when they have all bought huge houses abroad in Germany, when they settle abroad, with the millions of dollars stolen from us, to build their own bright future, then they will 'let' us pass the law."

The government's corruption fighters were not the only ones who lost out to the nomenklatura. Young reformers who had been swept into positions of power and authority by the pro-democracy movements of the late 1980s and early 1990s found themselves quietly eased out of influence. Yuri Lebedev, a parliamentary deputy from Russia's Altai region, near the border with Mongolia, joined the Yeltsin government in 1990. Along with a handful of young economists and political scientists, he was part of the first generation of Russian politicians in decades who were independent of the Communist hierarchy.

Lebedev was an ideal example of what the New Russia might have been. An inventor and entrepreneur, he was a ruble millionaire before he turned thirty-five. He opened a company that manufactured geological equipment across the street from the log cabin where his grandfather had settled after the turn of the century. Fighting local Party bureaucrats, Lebedev built a hotel and a campsite beside one of the area's pristine mountain lakes, the first step in a plan to develop what he called "ecological" tourism. He never joined the Party, and the nomenklatura tried unsuccessfully to derail his campaign for a seat in the Russian Supreme Soviet. After his 1990 election, Lebedev was appointed Russian "minister of innovation," a title he invented to suggest the government's interest in finding alternative ways of spurring industrial development.

Lebedev worked twelve to fifteen hours a day and rarely saw his family, who were deposited in a government dacha in the woods outside Moscow. But he soon found himself at odds with power brokers in the Yeltsin entourage who displayed hostility to anything resembling either innovation or free enterprise. One powerful *apparatchik,* a self-described reform leader in Volgograd (formerly Stalingrad) before coming to Yeltsin's Moscow, became the young minister's nemesis. The bureaucrat was the driving force behind an "environmental" firm established by several well-connected Russian businessmen who hoped to attract Western money for cleaning up the country's poisoned factory towns. With the bureaucrat's sponsorship, they expected to win government grants as well. The corporation founders declared a starting capital of 200 million rubles, which enabled them under new state rules to issue shares in the company for more than twice that amount. The plan came to Lebedev's office for review, and he quickly discovered that the company was a fiction. "At least 150 million of their founding capital didn't exist," Lebedev recalled. "When they received the funds for sale of the shares, they planned to immediately convert them to dollars, transfer them abroad, and then declare bankruptcy." Bitter experience of similar dummy corporations had already given rise to a new jargon word among Yeltsin's young turks. "We called them *panamas,*" said Lebedev.[20]

But when the minister of innovation tried to stop the deal, he began feeling pressure. One of Lebedev's deputies, with close connections to the former Volgograd bureaucrat, called him at home to deliver a thinly veiled warning.

"You are running great risks," he said. "Remember, you have children."

Lebedev obtained bodyguards for his wife and children, and continued fighting. But the company won approval for its plans. After eighteen months of similarly frustrating guerrilla warfare, Lebedev had had enough. He resigned, in order to go back to private life.

"I cannot beat them," he told me despondently. "The old networks, the skeleton of the hierarchy, are stronger than ever. On the one hand, you have people from the old military-industrial sector, the hard-liners, and on the other, you have the more progressive Party people, but they all have access to Party monies. I could imagine getting caught in the middle of the war breaking out between the different clans over control. It was time for me to leave."

Lebedev was a victim of the post-Communist dream—as we all were. Western observers had believed as fervently as Russian reformers that with the end of the Soviet era, Soviet values would peel off to reveal a nascent capitalist democracy. The rejection of Communism was supposed to be solid proof that "they" were just like us. The New Russian was supposed to have replaced "Homo Sovieticus"—Soviet Man—for decades the ideal citizen of Communist society. Although Soviet Man was impossible to find in the streets of any Soviet city, he stood as a symbol of Marxist puritanism, a person who happily sacrificed individual interests to the communal good. However unrealizable his virtues, he had been the moral authority for generations of Soviet citizens.[21]

Perestroika seemed to speed his departure—and make way for what would become Post-Soviet Man. During the 1980s, each moment in the country's passage to what looked like capitalism was celebrated in the West, and in some Russian circles, with intoxicated awe. The first private cooperative restaurant, the first stock exchange, the first millionaire (followed by the creation of a group that even called itself the Millionaires Club), were media sensations. They were regarded as signs of the final disintegration of the Marxist system. But Post-Soviet Man was disappointing. He usually turned out to be a bureaucrat or a criminal—or both. According to the Russian security ministry, in 1993, more than half of Russia's criminal groups had close ties with government ministries and agencies.[22]

"We have something that most of the other countries of the world do not have," Aslambek Aslakhanov told the February, 1993, Moscow crime conference. "A marriage contract between bureaucrats and the most dyed-in-the-wool criminals."[23]

8 How to Steal a Billion Rubles

Toward the end of May, 1992, a police patrol car was cruising slowly down Petrovka Street in central Moscow. A few blocks from the city's police headquarters, a detective noticed men loading heavy sacks into a parked car. As he watched, one stumbled and dropped his sack. Wads of ruble notes spilled into the street.

The patrol car stopped immediately. Policemen raced out and detained the men before they could run away. The car was searched. Dozens of sacks were pulled out of the trunk, and each was stuffed with cash. Later, more than six million rubles, still in bank wrappings, were counted out at police headquarters.[1]

The men loading the sacks were all members of a Chechen gang. They seemed unfazed by police interest. The money was obtained legally, they insisted, and they showed police bank "promissory notes" for additional amounts, which they planned to cash in the next few days. The notes were all written on banks in Grozny, the capital of Chechnya, in the Caucasus, and other financial institutions around the Commonwealth of Independent States.[2]

But the police decided to check further. Several bank directors in Moscow were surprised to get visits from detectives in the week following the arrest of the bag carriers. Yes, they said, with some annoyance—they had indeed handed over sacks of cash to the Chechens. But they had the promissory notes, didn't they? It was all legal. At police insistence, the bankers reluctantly called their counterparts in Grozny. To their horror, they discovered that no notes had ever been issued.

When a few of the bankers anxiously opened their safes to retrieve the questionable vouchers, they received another shock. Nothing was there. Their frightened employees explained that the day after they had handed over the cash, another group of well-dressed men, identifying themselves as police from Chechnya, entered the bank and asked to see the notes. Explaining that they were conducting an "official investigation," they took the vouchers away—removing all evidence of the crime. Inquiries made to police in Chechnya revealed, of course, that no "investigators" had ever been sent to Moscow.

Security ministry officials ordered a Russia-wide investigation. A raid on the Hotel Salyut, in south Moscow, where some of the Chechens were staying, turned up dozens of empty brown sacks. They also found blank forms of vouchers with the seals and stamps of the Grozny State Bank.

A few days later, a Russian citizen was stopped with more than one million dollars in his overnight bag as he was preparing to board a flight to Zurich at Moscow's Sheremetievo Airport. The man was taken back, under armed guard, to city police headquarters, where he admitted that he had used some of the false vouchers to obtain rubles and then convert them quickly to dollars for deposit abroad.

By the early summer of 1992, it was clear that a clumsy gangster had exposed one of the most staggering swindles ever attempted up to that point in Russia. Forged promissory notes worth more than sixty billion rubles (then, about seven hundred million dollars) turned up in hundreds of banks around Russia. Only forty million rubles were actually cashed before authorities intervened, but the "Chechen affair" produced acute embarrassment in government corridors. And violence.

At 2:05 a.m. on June 4, 1992, a bomb shattered every window in a four-story apartment house on Mesheryakova Street. An hour later, an explosion in a building on Matross Zheleznik Boulevard blew open the doors of several flats and smashed the tiny lift. At 4:35 the same morning, residents of a house on Tamozhenny Lane were wrenched from sleep by another blast, this one so large it left gaping holes where the doors of seven flats used to be.

Miraculously, no one was killed or even injured. Moscow newspapers the next day speculated that a new gang war had started. But police found a connection between the explosions and the Chechen scandal. The owners of the three targeted apartments were some of Moscow's wealthiest men. One was chairman of a private bank; the other two were officials of a Moscow commercial firm. All had been deeply involved in secret currency transactions with banks in Chechnya.

Although the Chechen syndicate received most of the attention over the bank scandal in those months, the volume of promissory notes required for the swindle implied collusion with bankers and businessmen elsewhere in the country. Shortly after the explosions, two mysterious murders occurred in Moscow. A police traffic inspector named Viktor Shapov was stabbed to death, and the president of a Moscow trade union bank, Aleksandr Petrov, was shot in the doorway of his home.

Police managed to tie these deaths as well to the bank conspiracy. The traffic inspector was killed, it was alleged, because he had witnessed a payoff between a leading bank official and a mobster. The banker Petrov had been the victim of a squeeze. The Chechen syndicate was reported to have deposited several million stolen rubles in his bank, and then demanded in a telephone conversation that he convert the money to dollars and transfer it to a foreign bank. Russian security agents, who had tapped the banker's phone as part of a separate investigation into the transfer of hard currency abroad, visited Petrov the next day. Unaware that the money was part of the Chechen swindle, they warned that if he went ahead with the transaction, he would be arrested.[3]

The banker heeded the warning, but when his criminal partners discovered that he had "double-crossed" them, they killed him as an object lesson. The tactic worked. The next week, the money was sent abroad by Petrov's deputy.

More than a year later, in 1993, four officials of the Central Bank were arrested in connection with the conspiracy. They were accused of accepting bribes of millions of rubles and "tens of thousands of dollars" to assist in distributing the forged promissory notes.[4]

There were also suggestions that the affair reached inside the Ministry of Finance. Rumor and fact collided in the fog of scandal, but at least one thing was certain. As the shell-shocked Russian government later acknowledged, the fraud would have triggered the collapse of the national monetary system if it had not been discovered in time.

Newspapers and magazines featured the story prominently for months. Politicians and bankers promised that they would lose no time in plugging the loopholes in the promissory-voucher system, as a first step toward a thoroughgoing reform of the banking industry. But memories in Russia can be conveniently short.

In early 1993, less than six months after the bag of money spilled out onto a Moscow sidewalk, a businessman walked into Pragmabank, a modestly successful commercial lending institution owned by a group of Moscow food stores and gas stations, and asked for one billion rubles. He was extremely polite. He showed the clerk a credit note bearing the stamp of the Central State Bank of Russia, which indicated that he was legally entitled to the money (worth, at the time, about 1.8 million dollars). The cash, he explained pleasantly, was for the purchase of "agricultural goods and privatization vouchers."

The clerk saw no reason to question him. The promissory note was backed by the state; it seemed perfectly legal. Besides, she recognized the businessman. He was a regular customer at Pragmabank.

She handed a slip of paper to another bank clerk, who strode over to the bank vault. A few minutes later, one billion rubles in large bills were presented to the waiting businessman. He smiled, thanked everyone profusely, and walked outside. No one ever heard from him again.

Frantic bank officials later contacted the Central Bank. They received an angry rebuff. Of course they had issued the credit note. But why shouldn't they have? The man carried personal references from Pragmabank suggesting that he was one of their most trustworthy clients.

Of course we trusted him, Pragmabank replied testily. He was backed by the Central Bank of Russia, wasn't he?

Forged vouchers reappeared around the country. In July 1993, the Russian Ministry of Internal Affairs claimed that more than three hundred billion rubles (then, worth about five hundred million dollars) had been embezzled from banks over the previous year, using the fake voucher system. They said that over 160 banks and commercial institutions had participated in the fraud. Tellers and bank officials around the country had dutifully cashed the vouchers without question. After all, wasn't that what banks were for?[5]

At the height of the Chechen scandal, I paid a visit to Sergei Yegorov, head of the Association of Russian Banks, in his office near the Bolshoi Theater in Moscow. The gruff Yegorov spent fifteen years as chairman of the State Bank of Russia, the culmination of a career that began in the Altai region on the Mongolian border. He made himself noteworthy among his Soviet colleagues by actually welcoming the rise of Russian private lending and financial institutions. The association, formed by five hundred private banks before the August, 1991, coup, naturally picked him to be the voice of post-Soviet finance. To Yegorov, the Chechen fraud was part of a larger conspiracy by the nomenklatura to undermine Russia's fledgling private banks.

"There's no doubt that criminals are taking advantage of the chaos in our system," Yegorov said. "A banker has to keep his eyes open when he deals with money. But it's not correct to blame the banks alone."[6]

The campaign to destabilize private banking began long before the Soviet collapse, Yegorov said. The first set of edicts handed down by the leaders of the August coup included an order to shut down all non-state banks. "We were the real enemies to them, more than Yeltsin," Yegorov recalled. "We held a meeting here shortly after they'd kidnapped Gorbachev, and we could see the sharpshooters on the roof of the Bolshoi training their guns at us. They still don't want us around."

The anti-bank campaign was conducted on several levels, Yegorov said. Trade union and former Komsomol banks, backed by powerful state industrial enterprises and Party money, quietly lobbied the government bureaucracy to restrict the access to capital of rival banks set up by private businessmen. At the same time, the Russian Central Bank's policy of extending unlimited subsidies and credits to the industrial behemoths of the old regime reduced incentives for private investment elsewhere in the economy. The third level of attack was concentrated inside Russia's parliament, dominated by the state industrial lobbies who opposed in principle any loosening of government ownership.

"It is very easy to strangle the market economy by the throat, especially at the stage when we have a primitive accumulation of capital," Yegorov said. "Simply by blocking every attempt at liberal banking legislation, they make us vulnerable to the black market."

The most dangerous criminal behavior in post-Soviet Russia was increasingly taking place inside the average Russian bank. By 1993, between three thousand and four thousand private banks or banking affiliates were operating in Russia. Most rested on precarious foundations. They were undercapitalized, they offered hardly any protection to the ordinary depositor, and many were fronts for criminal syndicates. Russian police identified more than 360 separate types of bank fraud, ranging from the use of non-existent credits to the manipulation of overdrafts. The lack of adequate legislation and insurance left nearly every bank vulnerable. "In most cases," the Moscow newspaper *Kuranty* commented tartly, "the best that police can do is provide a handkerchief for a banker to weep in."[7]

The conflict between the Central Bank and commercial banks mirrored the struggle in other sectors of Russian life for control of the new economy. "The Central Bank wants to run things the way it always used to," Konstantin Borovoi, director of Moscow's Raw Materials and Commodity Exchange and commonly regarded as one of Russia's richest private businessmen, suggested during a conversation in his office in Kitaigorod, a neighborhood near the Kremlin which was slowly recapturing its pre-revolutionary status as the financial district of Moscow. "They want to keep their monopoly power over the movement of capital. They pass regulations to prevent commercial banks from keeping sufficient cash on hand, which of course forces them to depend on the system of promissory notes." [8]

The Chechen affair revealed the nature of the power struggle. Investigators discovered that many of the faked promissory notes were written on branches of the Russian State Bank or commercial banks subsidized by Party money. One bank, started by the Communist Youth League before the collapse of the Soviet Union, was located in a building once owned by the USSR Supreme Soviet.

"These banks are built on the idea of protectionism," said Borovoi. "They have huge amounts of funds, but they know they cannot survive in a normal atmosphere of free competition. They don't have the specialists. They have no desire to work. They are dangerous, because they will get involved in any form of illegality to keep themselves afloat."

Borovoi suspected that the state bankers, most of whom were the same bureaucrats who had run things in the Soviet era, used these banks to flood Russia with billions of rubles, in order to weaken the country's new financial institutions. They did it using another technique inherited from the Soviet Union's magic bag of accounting practices.

Most Soviet enterprises operated on what was called a "non-cash ruble" system, in which payment for goods and services was achieved by moving sets of figures from one account to another. The fictional currency remained on the books of state banks across Soviet territory after the regime collapsed. Desperate factory managers in former Soviet republics used it to pay bills to Russian suppliers, even though it was not backed up by real cash reserves in their countries' newly created central banks. According to the Association of Russian Banks, more than two trillion rubles of such accounting-ledger money was circulating around Russia in 1992.

"I would never have thought this sort of thing possible in principle," said Garegin Tosunyan, owner of Moscow's Tekhnobank. "But we now have huge amounts of non-existent money injected into the banking system."[9] Moscow wits said that the practice had earned Russia a unique place in the world annals of white-collar crime: it was the first country to make counterfeiting "old-fashioned."

"It is much simpler just to draw a billion or two on an ordinary piece of paper, obtain a few bank codes, and fabricate a stamp," wrote a reporter for *Komsomolskaya Pravda*. The reporter went on to document the case of a Rostov businessman named Sergei Vtorov, who arranged with a Chechen firm to transfer 3.5 billion rubles to his account in return for marking them as a payment of credits to companies to whom the Chechens owed money.[10] The billions never existed. They were "non-cash" rubles drawn out of the accounts of several state enterprises. Vtorov, however, was free to use the fictitious rubles in whatever way he wanted to. It was another miracle produced in the post-Communist looking-glass world. The newspaper said, "The illusory billions set out on their voyage through the wonderland called Russia. Having once entered the Russian banking system, the fake capital spread to dozens of big and small companies and became transformed into hundreds of contracts—finally materializing in luxury cars and other deluxe products. The nonexistent capital is still generating quite tangible profits."

The underground fight waged by the former elite took other insidious forms. A "whispering campaign" was used against several of the most prominent Moscow banks to undermine their reputations. "Our new bankers have had to grow up very quickly," Yegorov added, with a smile. "Only a year ago they were like boys in short pants, and now most of them are professionals. I'm proud of them."

The "international" headquarters of Stolichny Bank are located in an undistinguished three-story building on Pyatnitskaya Street, in a dingy neighborhood near the Moscow River. On the day I arrived, it looked like a construction site. I joined a gang of workers in hard hats moving through the large double doors, only to be stopped by stern guards with a vaguely familiar air of authority. Shouldering their heavy weapons, they examined my identification papers.

"They still look like KGB, no matter how much they try not to," whispered Vladimir Mironov. "They can't help it."

Vladimir, or Volodya, as he preferred to be called, was a young Russian businessman who had arranged an appointment for me with the president of Stolichny Bank, Aleksandr Smolensky. As we drove to the bank, he described the man we were about to see.

"Smolensky is afraid of nothing—his bank spits on the Central Bank of Russia," Volodya said. "He will do operations that smaller banks are afraid to do."

At the bank entrance, the guards spoke into European-made walkie-talkies, and then grudgingly waved us through. A modern, glass-enclosed elevator was in the lobby.

"Not working yet," a guard called out behind us. We walked up two badly scuffed flights of wooden stairs and emerged into—the West.

Track lights on the ceiling cast a soothing glow over an office that could have been in Zurich or London. A large piece of incomprehensible metal sculpture stood in a corner, beside deep red sofas that were so new they were still flecked with bits of plastic packing material. Everything, in fact, looked as if it had only yesterday come out of a crate marked "modern office decor." Even the secretaries appeared to have been picked from the pages of an office catalogue. A pretty young receptionist sat awkwardly behind a desk. She was wearing a pearl necklace, silk stockings, and the kind of high-heeled shoes that were only available in certain Western hard-currency stores in Moscow. As we stood in the reception area, Smolensky came bounding toward us. He was dressed in an elegant houndstooth-check sports jacket that smoothed the contours of his large body. He shook hands quickly and began talking as if he were continuing a conversation started some time before.

"It's easier to build something on the moon than in this country," he grumbled. "Accept my apologies for this construction site." [11]

I still couldn't take my eyes away from the vision of efficiency spread before me. There were banks of telephones and rows of blinking computer screens. I had never seen an office anywhere in the old Soviet Union that looked remotely like it.

"How did you manage all this?"

Smolensky laughed. "State officials ask me the same question. They make it sound like an accusation."

"What bothers them so much?" I asked innocently. "Your premises are the most beautiful I've seen in Moscow."

Smolensky looked ready to embrace me. "Yes!" he said. "That's exactly what I mean! To a Westerner, this looks completely normal, nothing surprising, right? But to them, our success is infuriating."

Smolensky led us to a still-unfinished boardroom. A maid in white came in silently and poured tea into delicate china cups. There were chocolate cookies on a glass dish. The bank president took one, and winked.

"We try not to frighten the geese, but what can you do? They just don't like to see anyone who does well."

He leaned forward and touched my shoulder. "The truth is, everything you see around you, all our success, is not thanks to our wonderful economic laws. It's thanks to the fact that we do not obey them."

Volodya released an appreciative chuckle, and winked at me.

Stolichny Bank, the third-largest private banking institution in Russia, became the target of a whispering campaign almost as soon as it was created. "I heard we were supposed to be bankrupt, or arrested," recalled Smolensky. "We were supposed to be dealing in drug money and weapons smuggling. Then, suddenly, they excluded us from advisory councils to the finance ministry and the Supreme Soviet. They were trying to make us invisible." [12]

Forced invisibility was a familiar experience to the thirty-eight-year-old Smolensky. Like many of Russia's new bankers and financiers, he was an outsider. His background—his parents were Austrian Communists who had taken refuge in the Soviet Union from the Nazis—gave him the taint of "foreign association" even after he had completed his Soviet Army service. Smolensky believed that his non-Russian parentage blocked his attempt to join the Communist Party and therefore left him unable to pursue a serious career. He eventually found work as a minor official in the state construction ministry, but at the beginning of perestroika, he quit to form his own construction cooperative.

The more successful he was, the more problems he had. "The state persecuted me for thirty-three years, first as a boy, and then as a young man who wanted to do something different," he said. "It was as if I were Jesus Christ. When I started up in business, the KGB proposed that I leave the country. Some of my friends who got the same 'offer' decided they might as well accept it."

Echoing Yegorov, he added, "The nomenklatura simply didn't want people like us around. We were like fish bones in their throats. But I was stubborn."

Smolensky, who saw a portion of his bank's funds frozen during the Chechen affair, fought back in an inimitably Russian way. Many commercial bankers have hired policemen as security guards. But Smolensky outdistanced his competitors: he hired former members of the elite Alpha squad of the KGB—thereby becoming the first major Russian businessman with his own private intelligence agency.

"They are fine, patriotic guys," he grinned. "I also pay them what they are worth. They're professionals."

They also had little trouble adjusting to commercial life, since Smolensky kept them busy at familiar tasks. The "Stolichny KGB" eavesdropped on clients, as well as employees, with top-of-the-line equipment imported from Europe. "If you don't control the situation," Smolensky explained breezily, "you can't survive."

A multimillionaire, Smolensky was testimony to the prosperous potential of the New Russia and the youth of its capitalist pioneers. The oldest employee of his bank was forty and the average age was twenty-three. Stolichny Bank had been founded in 1991 with a starting capital of two billion rubles. It already operated offices in fifteen cities around the Commonwealth, as well as in New York, Vienna, and Amsterdam. But it seemed that scoring points against his old nomenklatura persecutors was nearly as important as making a success of Stolichny Bank.

"I used to rent small offices here, from a state organization," he said. "But when I took over the building, I threw all of them out."

His smile widened. "The funny thing was that when we started the renovation, we had to rip up the tiny offices that had been occupied by all those little czars, and we found so many wires and listening devices that it took three dump trucks to haul them away."

Smolensky brushed the chocolate crumbs from his moustache and sat back looking pleased with himself.

"We are in the primitive stage of capital accumulation, so we have to deal with things that could never be tolerated in international banking."

I heard this hackneyed phrase of Marxist economics everywhere I went in post-Communist Moscow. Yegorov used it. So did nearly every businessman I met. It came naturally, of course, to everyone's lips, having been pounded into Soviet schoolchildren almost as soon as they were old enough to read. Now it was repeated like a mantra among the capital's financial and political circles. Somehow, describing the chaos of the new economy as the "primitive stage of capital accumulation" provided comfort to Russia's harassed capitalists. A grisly anecdote recounted by Smolensky was convincing proof that "primitive" accurately described the reality of Moscow's banking world.

A few months before our conversation, Smolensky had signed an agreement with a local district council to purchase a building owned by Mosfilm, the former state film production company. Before he could pick up the keys, the son of the local district council chairman was kidnapped. The kidnappers demanded that the sale of the building be stopped, or the young man's head would be cut off.

"When they told me about it, I decided, okay, we don't need any more office space," Smolensky said dryly. "We canceled the deal, and the son returned home. It turned out the kidnappers were people who were living in the building. I warned the district leader that he hadn't seen the end of it. The kidnappers had his number now, and if he didn't resign, they would end up controlling him."

Smolensky moved his wife and child to Vienna in order to avoid placing his own family at similar risk. He visited them each weekend. "If my family lived here, I would have to give them round-the-clock protection," he explained. "My son would have to go to school with a guard. What sort of life is that? It's hard enough to ensure my own security."

I asked him why he bothered to stay.

"Russia is like Alaska during the gold rush—anyone can become rich with hard work and luck." Smolensky sat straighter in his chair. "You know," he continued, "my experiences here make me sympathetic to the Rockefellers. They faced the same obstacles as we did when they started."

Smolensky's charm, the confidence of his office, even the glancing reference to the Rockefellers, made one temporarily forget the harshness of the world in which the banker operated—a world in which it was necessary to wiretap clients and move family members thousands of miles away to keep them safe. Over the next year, twenty-seven Russian bankers were murdered in gangster assaults. "The new financial institutions are in the gun sights of well-organized bandits armed with up-to-date technical means," Yegorov wrote in a 1993 letter to President Yeltsin that was signed by Smolensky and a number of other private financiers.[13]

Bankers could hope for no protection from a hostile government. Since many of them already operated on shaky foundations, they were as likely to be the instigators of criminal behavior as the victims of it. In 1992, police arrested the president and nine employees of Promstroibank, a construction bank in Stavropol, for corruption. The only unusual aspect of the case was that the bribe-takers were caught. Russian officials estimated that three billion rubles were paid in bribes to bank officials around the country that year, usually in return for not asking unfriendly questions about a loan or for looking the other way when a withdrawal was made from a non-existent account.[14]

The chaos in Russian banking was predictable. Financial instruments of the modern West had been introduced into a state with neither the legal framework nor the cultural experience to cope with them. In the Soviet Union, banking had always been an otherworldly experience. Arranging a loan, even with some of the new enterprise or agricultural banks allowed to exist by the late 1980s, could take months. There were state-owned "savings banks" paying a minimal interest, but checks were unheard of, and credit cards were a fantasy.[15]

It was no surprise to discover that few ordinary Russians perceived banks as having anything to do with their personal financial planning. "A lot of people think a commercial bank is a kind of luxury commercial store, where the employees rake in money with a spade," admitted Yuri Agapov, the thirty-three-year-old president of Moscow's Credobank.[16] Skepticism and fear of future state action also kept most honest investors away. "Everybody concentrates on buying and selling, because it's the quickest and safest way to turn money around," said Garegin Tosunyan. "They think the state will expropriate property and wealth, as it did before."

A large number of the commercial banking sector's clients came from the shadow economy. "Every banker gets calls from people offering to deposit huge sums of money," Tosunyan said. "It is difficult to check who they are. Sometimes they want a seat on the board. Usually we know they just want a place to squirrel away money that is not necessarily legal."

"We often get inquiries from abroad," he continued, "but we know these aren't legitimate foreign investors. Most foreigners have the same fear of investing money in our system that domestic business does." The requests, Tosunyan believed, came from criminal cartels abroad. "We get offers to buy our rubles for dollars at attractive rates, hundreds of millions. They come from America and Europe, through go-betweens. And we know they can turn around and sell those rubles again. You can launder money from *narco-bizness*, for instance, beautifully in our system."

This was, perhaps, the ultimate irony. The creation of a viable banking system ought to have been the centerpiece of Russia's transformation to capitalism. Instead, banks had become the stage for a struggle over the spoils of the former Communist system. Their vulnerability made them a gateway into the new Russian economy for rogues and con men of every stripe.

9 Masters of Moscow

The old women were found dead in their apartments. Most looked as if they had died in their sleep, but by the time the number of deaths reached fourteen, Moscow police had found evidence to suggest a disquieting pattern. Each woman had signed a paper bequeathing her apartment to real estate "brokers" in return for a cash "supplement" to her state pension.

The search for an explanation led investigators to a decree passed six months earlier by the Russian government, in late 1992, awarding all tenants of state housing (which meant virtually everybody) the right to dispose of their apartments as they saw fit. By March, 1993, more than half a million apartments in Moscow—some 20 percent of the city's housing—had been transformed into private dwellings. A truly historic step toward a "homeowners' democracy," it ended the demeaning system that forced divorced couples to stay together and families to crowd into tiny two-room apartments. Under the Soviet regime, living space was strictly regulated. A thriving black market had allowed citizens to swap apartments privately, but the new decree freed Russians from the housing bureaucrats who had dominated their lives. It also brought into the open a strange and unfamiliar phenomenon for Russian society: real estate speculation.[1]

Under the new rules, tenants in public housing could obtain the rights to their apartments without paying anything. They could also sell. Many who lived in cramped, shabby mansion blocks in downtown areas took advantage of the chance to obtain hard cash and move to newer buildings in the suburbs. As space in the center of large cities became available, the country's rich new businessmen jostled foreigners in a bidding war for the choicest sites. A two-room apartment in the center of Moscow that sold for a few thousand dollars in 1992 soared to as much as $120,000 in 1993.[2]

The speculation fever, which soon priced most ordinary Russians out of downtown areas, was encouraged by officials who realized they were sitting on a potential tax revenue bonanza. Investigators discovered that municipal bureaucrats in Moscow and St. Petersburg provided lists of potential sellers to commercial brokers. The possession of such a list in Moscow was assumed to have led housing brokers to the old women. Moscow police drew what seemed the obvious, sad conclusion: the murdered pensioners had been punished for taking too long to pass away and free up their valuable space.[3]

Less violent forms of real estate speculation had already proved equally harmful to the living standards of Muscovites. The curiosity of Yuri Shchekochikhin, an investigative reporter for *Literaturnaya Gazeta,* was aroused when tenants of buildings in the neighborhood of his downtown office complained that their repeated appeals to municipal authorities for repairs went unheeded. Shchekochikhin explained why in a full-page exposé published by his newspaper late in 1992. "When a building is allowed to depreciate in quality, it is listed at lower real estate values on municipal books," he wrote. "Those buildings are then sold off to developers who lease out space at normal inflationary market prices, and earn enormous profits on the difference."[4]

The reporter based his conclusions on an investigation of one prominent real estate firm in the city, a joint venture called Most (Bridge), which he said was connected with senior city officials. The firm purchased more than one hundred commercial and residential buildings around Moscow during 1992 "for a pittance," he claimed. Shchekochikhin went on to charge that Mayor Yuri Luzhkov directly benefited from some of the arrangements. After Most purchased an unfinished building on Krestyanskaya Square at a city auction, the municipality used the proceeds of the sale to renovate an office block on Volgogradsky Prospekt. The prime contractor appointed by the mayor for that job, according to Shchekochikhin, was Most.

Shchekochikhin laced his report with descriptions of meetings in empty offices with informants too frightened to provide their names or speak on the telephone, who burned up evidence as soon as they showed it to a journalist. "It is reminiscent of the days when the KGB was all powerful in our society," Shchekochikhin wrote. "On the basis of these personal observations I can say that . . . mafiya structures have come to power on the back of our young democracy, structures which have already divided Moscow into spheres of influence, and have already sold one another the best parts of the capital . . . behind the smokescreen of democracy and our August [1991] victory."

The accusations in *Literaturnaya Gazeta* were denounced by Russian officialdom. Even Yeltsin issued a public statement defending the Moscow mayor. Shchekochikhin, however, was unrepentant when I visited his newspaper office after publication of the article. He noted that none of his critics had addressed the real issue: the corruption in Moscow's booming real estate market had betrayed the democratic hopes of 1991.

"When the Bolsheviks came to power, they started treating the country like their own private estate," said Shchekochikhin, a small man with flashing eyes. "Frankly, I can't see much of a difference now. It used to be enough to say you were a democrat; everyone knew what that meant. But not anymore. To tell you the truth, if someone staged a new coup tomorrow, I wouldn't know what or whom to defend."[5]

In *Literaturnaya Gazeta,* the journalist wrote that post-Communist bureaucrats displayed a special talent for cloaking their actions in the fashionable jargon of free-market capitalism. "We have three types of capitalists in our [city]," he wrote. "There are entrepreneurs who have been given the chance to make real money, thanks to the changes in our system, and there are criminals who launder their dirty capital in legitimate business. But the first and the second types are mere kids in comparison with our *'biznesmeny'* in the official structures of power. They, in disguise, are the true masters of Moscow."

Shchekochikhin was not the only one to arrive at this conclusion. "Moscow city government is four times more corrupt today than it ever was under the old system," declared Aleksandr Tsopov. "Our city is being bought up by the rich, by criminals, by underground business, by Party money. It is a terrible tragedy."[6]

I met Tsopov, chairman of the Municipal Legal Commission of the Moscow City Council, at city hall. The eighteenth-century baroque palace, which once used to house czarist military governors, was a civic landmark. Lenin had delivered a speech from one of its balconies when the new Bolshevik government revived Moscow as the nation's capital in 1919. A statue of Yuri Dolgoruky (Yuri the Long-Armed), the twelfth-century founder of Moscow, commanded the square opposite the building. Wearing a battle helmet and seated on a giant horse, the figure pointed at city hall as if it were delivering a reprimand. During the 1980s, thousands of pro-democracy demonstrators regularly gathered at the foot of the monument, while municipal Party chieftains peeked from behind their curtained windows in the building across the street.

Now, many of those demonstrators worked in offices behind the same windows. But Yuri the Long-Armed still pointed accusingly in the same direction. Tsopov believed that this was only fitting.

Tsopov bristled with the kind of anger that only comes from disillusionment. A haggard man in his early forties, he had spent many nights in the shadow of Yuri Dolgoruky's statue during the final years of the Soviet era. He was among the crowds who gathered there in frequent pro-democracy demonstrations. As a veteran investigator in the Soviet prosecutor's office, with the rank of major, Tsopov knew better than most Russians how corrupt the system was. He arrived in office as a city council deputy in 1991 on the same tide of reform that carried the liberal economist Gavriil Popov into the mayoralty in Moscow and brought Boris Yeltsin to power in Russia. Popov left office before the end of his term, under a cloud of rumor and mystery. He said that he wanted to help organize a national party of democratic reformers, but a whispering campaign in the capital claimed that he was more intent on promoting his private business interests. Municipal power passed to his deputy, Yuri Luzhkov, who was head of the Moscow executive committee, the capital's municipal authority during the last Communist administration. By 1993, the ranks around Yeltsin had been sadly depleted of reformist faces. Like countless numbers of his colleagues who were left to pick up the pieces, Tsopov felt betrayed.

"I compare our people to a deceived woman sitting by herself in the kitchen, abandoned by all her lovers," he said. "We were screwed by President Yeltsin, by Luzhkov, by Popov . . . all of them, and they don't care what happens to us now."

There are few people more dangerous in Russia than idealists who have lost their heroes. Tsopov's office, on one of the upper floors of the city hall building, was the operations room for a bitter campaign against the reform leaders of August, 1991. Boxes of files were piled on desks and scattered on the floor in disarray. As we talked, other deputies—Tsopov's fellow conspirators—rushed in and out with yet more papers or with reports of a new outrage committed by a municipal baron. A few stayed to listen, muttering assent like a wrathful chorus each time Tsopov grabbed a document from the pile to emphasize a point.

"Here," he said, smoothing the edges of one wrinkled sheet bearing an official stamp and handing it to me. "Look at this."

It was a report from the chief municipal comptroller on an investigation of the Moscow State Property Fund, the agency that reviewed development plans for all residential and commercial housing in Moscow. According to the comptroller, three of the six members of the fund were directors of private real estate firms, in violation of conflict-of-interest regulations. The comptroller passed over the fact that all members of the fund had been appointed by city authorities more than a year earlier. "There should be a review [of this situation]," she concluded.

It seemed a mild rebuke. But to Tsopov, it was a moral victory. "What this document proves," he said, shaking his head, "is that the sellers of Moscow property are also the buyers."

He brought out more documents from his bag, spreading them on the desk as if they were campaign medals. In fact, Tsopov's record of battle victories was pitifully slender. The saddest documents covered the deals that had gone too far to stop. They recorded contracts for the reconstruction or renovation of Moscow's dilapidated housing stock. Dozens of such agreements were being signed every week, testaments to the extraordinary real estate boom under way in Russia's largest and richest city.

Tsopov talked about the list of Moscow properties kept in the desks of some senior municipal officials. He claimed that foreign or domestic developers were charged a "fee" of ten thousand dollars for the privilege of seeing the list. After the would-be developer circled his choices, he was taken to the site. If he approved, a contract would be negotiated. The process, said Tsopov, was a blatant violation of city regulations requiring all properties to be available for public auction. Municipal housing authorities also ignored laws that required them to submit major property deals to the city government or neighborhood district councils, Tsopov said. He showed me one set of documents recording an arrangement between the city's housing agency and a company based in Seattle to develop a seventeen-story building. The Americans promised to pay ten million rubles (about fifty thousand dollars) toward the cost of renovating the structure in return for ownership of half the apartments, which they could then rent out as offices. The remainder of the renovated apartments would be the municipality's, to sell or rent as it wished. The unlucky tenants, of course, had nothing to say about the disposal of their homes. They could either accept the municipality's offer of temporary housing somewhere else in the city or receive small cash payments.

"This," said Tsopov angrily, "is how Moscow is being sold off."

But this discovery was a long time in coming. During the opening years of the new economy, the transformation of socialist bureaucrats into capitalist businessmen was usually hailed as progress.

In the early 1990s, the Western and Russian media unloaded their suitcase of clichés about perestroika to introduce the world to a forty-five-year-old Moscow real estate developer named Andrei Stroyev. Newspapers described him as one of the "new breed" of Soviet millionaires to emerge from the bowels of the Communist system. One American report gushed that he was "the equivalent of Gorbachev or Yeltsin in business." Stroyev even made the cover of *Newsweek*'s European edition. The *Wall Street Journal* called him "the Donald Trump of Moscow—until Mr. Trump himself ran into financial difficulties." *Kommersant,* a respected, new Moscow business journal, which took its name from a famous commercial newspaper closed by the authorities after the 1917 revolution, made Stroyev the subject of a business profile. It declared, "[Stroyev's] ascent to the summit of success brings to mind stories about the American dream." [7]

As the glowing reviews indicated, Stroyev was turning Moscow inside out. A blunt former construction boss, he was the first to exploit the commercial possibilities of the city's architectural heritage. Hundreds of nineteenth-century buildings that once housed wealthy merchants and professionals still stood in central Moscow. Their carved facades and elegant entrances made a pleasing contrast to the cinder-block apartment complexes and offices erected by Soviet builders. But the spacious, high-ceilinged apartments inside had long since been divided up for communal housing. Years of neglect had left hallways dank and plaster peeling from the walls.

Stroyev realized that they could be turned into investment opportunities. He convinced the city to transfer the residents of the old mansion blocks to apartments in newer buildings in the Moscow suburbs, and then he gutted the interiors to create high-rent office space. In 1988, he formed a joint venture with an American real estate firm based in Atlanta and called the enterprise Perestroika. It was an appropriate name. The firm engaged in a form of "reconstruction," not only of Moscow's lost glamour, but of the long-dead spirit of Russian commerce.

By 1991, his firm had already earned an estimated thirty million dollars from its projects. In 1992, the company added residential development to its growing portfolio of projects. On a landfill in the western suburbs of Moscow, Stroyev's workers were erecting 118 units of pre-fabricated American townhouses for the first of what it hoped would be dozens of special "residential communities." Stroyev's talent for cutting through Soviet red tape earned him the sobriquet "shark of socialism." Few paid attention to the fact that one reason for his ability to move easily through every level of bureaucracy was that he was a bureaucrat himself.

When he created Perestroika, Stroyev was already a powerful municipal *apparatchik*. He had risen from the post of site foreman to become head of Mosinzhstroi, the Moscow State Construction Enterprise, in 1987. Mosinzhstroi was a vast, typical Soviet monopoly of the day, in charge of everything that concerned municipal real estate infrastructure. Its thirty-five thousand employees were responsible for office and housing construction, as well as for maintaining the capital's roads, heating lines, and water pipes.

As a private builder, Stroyev might have been expected to leave Mosinzhstroi, so to avoid even the impression of a conflict of interest. But in the hustling optimism of the time, such lapses were overlooked. Much later, Stroyev was sensitive about the point, refusing to acknowledge that his continued association with the municipal bureaucracy was the key to Perestroika's phenomenal success.

"I am not a bureaucrat," he snapped, when I interviewed him in his comfortable Moscow office in the summer of 1992.[8] "Mosinzhstroi has been privatized. I even have my own money in it, so you can't call it a state agency."

This was stretching a point, since he knew as well as I did that "privatization" had not changed the controlling structure of an operation that received all its contracts and permits from the municipality. But it was easy to see why so many foreigners trusted him. A well-built man, his aura of authority was enhanced by a conservative gray suit. He had the salesman's talent for making me feel the focus of his attention, and the bureaucrat's skill at conveying the idea that I was unaccountably blessed to be allowed to take up his time.

"If Mosinzhstroi has no connection with the municipality, why do you need it then?" I asked.

He flashed me an annoyed look.

"Mosinzhstroi is the Russian partner of our joint venture," he said flatly. "Our only involvement with the state is when we apply to Moscow authorities for land allocation or building permission, just like a private developer anywhere in the world."

Stroyev had agreed to see me on the evident assumption that I would provide him with yet another glowing review in the West. He enjoyed reporters, particularly Western ones, who found him a charming change from Soviet bureaucrats. His air of openness and Western vigor seemed to make him a model Post-Soviet Man. But in what was perhaps an unguarded moment, he confided one fact about himself that added a different perspective to his personality. His parents had been notable figures in the Moscow theater world, he said proudly. As a youth, he had even considered going into the theater. I sensed that he was a man who could play whatever role was required.

"No one should try to tell you there are no difficulties in this business climate," he said, putting his hands together and fixing me with a look of utter sincerity.

"The real estate market is risky, and very tiring—sometimes very boring. I will admit to you that sometimes I wonder whether it is possible to keep going. But the fact is, Moscow is a good place to invest."

Stroyev instantly passed from prayerfulness to prophecy. "In the next few years, there will be a real land boom in this city," he said. "I know forty to one hundred large projects just ready to get off the ground now. This is the best time to come to Moscow. You can earn tremendous profits if you know how to take advantage of the fact that we live in a changing society, a changing world."

I refused to let the point pass. "Most ordinary businessmen I've talked to think they're lucky to get anything done."

"Of course, it helps whom you know," Stroyev said with a smile. "I have worked in Moscow for twenty years, I know a lot of people, and they know me. Isn't it the same anywhere in the world?"

In May, 1993, a year after our conversation, *Kommersant* informed its readers that both Perestroika and Stroyev were under investigation by the economic-crimes division of the MVD.[9] Making up for its earlier starry treatment, the newspaper concluded, after a review of official records and interviews with Stroyev's associates, that Moscow's charming real estate tycoon owed his success and good fortune to a conspiracy inside the municipal government bureaucracy. According to *Kommersant,* Perestroika acted as a vehicle for channeling state funds into city real estate. Stroyev's "silent partner" was the first deputy prime minister for urban development in Moscow, a man named Andrei Resin, who sat on the board of directors of Mosinzhstroi. The agency was turned into a semi-private organization principally in order to enter into his joint venture with the Atlanta firm and thereby gain access to Western investment dollars.

There was nothing illegal about the maneuver. In the late 1980s, the Soviet government made joint ventures an important feature of economic reform, but it was careful to limit foreign control. Mosinzhstroi became a majority partner in Perestroika. But it was at this point that the scheme became murky. Although Mosinzhstroi was formally removed from the state bureaucracy, its principal shareholders were Resin, who controlled the city agency that approved all requests for building renovations, the twenty-two directors of the city's largest construction organizations, and managers of several of the giant housing complexes in Moscow.

At the first meeting of the company, Stroyev made clear its underlying purpose. "He said to us, 'Look, guys, the only way we can survive is by getting hard currency to buy new equipment and to keep our buildings going,' " a housing boss who attended the session told *Kommersant.* "He explained that with Perestroika we would be able to keep 40 percent of the hard currency our projects made."

It was an offer none of those present could resist. Mosinzhstroi's shareholders were middle-level bureaucrats who, like Stroyev, were frustrated with the city's Communist leadership. The formation of the enterprise was another step in the complex endgame pitting progressive elements of the bureaucracy against Party hard-liners during the dying days of the old regime. This endgame, in which men like Stroyev made common cause with other municipal reformers, added special irony to the story of Perestroika.

The reform victors of the 1991 municipal elections made a jarring discovery soon after coming into office. Their vanquished opponents in the Moscow Communist Party had been transferring large chunks of municipal property out of state control since February 5, 1990, the date on which the Central Committee agreed to abandon its monopoly on political power. The Moscow barons, like their counterparts across the country at every level, had no intention of allowing the Party's patrimony to slip onto the open market. The city's Party leadership was involved in these machinations literally up to the last minute. A document found in the Central Committee archives after the August, 1991, coup contains a report from the Moscow Party leader, Yuri Prokofiev, certifying the transfer of state property valued at more than one hundred million rubles (then about fifty-five million dollars) to a so-called private "shareholders' association" a few weeks before Gorbachev was taken hostage in his Crimean dacha. Some 70 percent of the shares in the association were held by officials in Moscow's former Communist government. Determined to stop such secret deals, the incoming Moscow administration established its own property agency—answerable only to the mayor—which was empowered to negotiate leases and renovation contracts around the city. The action violated a Yeltsin decree asserting Russian federal control over former Soviet property. But at the time, reformers believed that it was the only way they could regulate their own market.[10]

The new administration, of course, found welcome allies in Stroyev, Resin, and the progressive bureaucrats at Mosinzhstroi. Working together, they could hope to break the Communist grip on the city's real estate. Inevitably, the concentration of political power and wealth proved as corrupting as it had been to the old guard.

Within a year of its founding, Perestroika could command top fees from space-hungry Western businessmen. Stroyev was able to provide prime pieces of real estate, because of his working partnership with the city government, and at the same time arrange for land development and building contracts, through his association with Mosinzhstroi. Government regulations requiring public bids for property were regularly bypassed, as municipal crusaders like Aleksandr Tsopov and Yuri Shchekochikhin discovered. "Everything was arranged in the quiet of [city] offices," said *Kommersant*.

In one typical deal, two foreign companies transferred twenty-one million dollars to Perestroika's foreign bank account to secure a lease on one of Stroyev's buildings. The money represented six years of lease payments in advance, but Stroyev had told his unsuspecting clients that he needed cash in order to buy equipment to finish the job to Western standards. The actual cost of the renovation work, *Kommersant* discovered, was seven million dollars. The developer used the same argument with all his foreign clients. Within a few years, the Cyprus bank account operated in the name of the joint venture filled with hundreds of millions of dollars. "Stroyev's first principle was that he would always charge at least twice what a job cost," said *Kommersant*. "That way, he could keep financing other projects and keep his shareholders in Mosinzhstroi happy."

But the dollars Stroyev had promised to the construction bosses in return for their cooperation never arrived. "We started to receive computers and bulldozers, and even trips to America, and we all shouted 'hoorah,' " said the construction boss who attended the first meeting. "But after a while, we began to wonder, where was all the cash?"

When some of the Mosinzhstroi shareholders tried to find out, they were not amused. They discovered that the developer had purchased a three-thousand-acre tract of land in Tennessee, as well as paid for a number of questionable trips to Europe. Pressure begin to build for an investigation to resolve whether Stroyev was guilty of any fraudulent dealings. Unfortunately, this master of Moscow made no effort to defend himself against his critics. A year after he had told me Moscow was the world's most exciting investment opportunity, he disappeared from the capital. According to rumor, Stroyev was living in America.[11]

He left behind a ruined empire. *Kommersant* reported that the Perestroika firm was near collapse in 1993, and that several of its building projects were on the point of being canceled. Foreign investors who had bought leases from Stroyev faced foreclosure. Meanwhile, the questions raised by the developer's activities remained unanswered. Was he a businessman who had cheated his investors? A bureaucrat who had mismanaged state funds? Or merely a maligned visionary? In any case, the newspaper noted, the reputation of Moscow government had suffered long-term damage from his activities. "This does not contribute to a healthy climate for foreign investors," said *Kommersant*.

Yet the most corrosive effect of the Stroyev affair, and of similar cases unearthed by crusading journalists and politicians, was ignored. Foreign investors, after all, could afford to swallow their losses or move elsewhere. But the involvement of bureaucrats and politicians in real estate manipulation undermined the most important promise of economic reform: a democratic system of property ownership. And it forced every Moscow businessman, regardless of his degree of honesty, to struggle in the half-light between capitalism and socialism.

"There is no legislative basis for any kind of real property market," said Viktor Kalinin, owner of a Moscow apartment brokerage company. "The bureaucrat knows that he couldn't have the same power if there was private property. You can buy an apartment, but as long as the land remains the property of the state, the official has ultimate control. In his secret thoughts, he knows that he can expropriate that apartment, if he has to.[12]

"That's why, when you Westerners speak of Communists, we think of bureaucrats. They have already transformed themselves for the new world, while they keep their old places in the power structure. What they fear is that people like me will take away their authority and influence. Even though I am a rich man, I am more vulnerable than anyone else in our so-called new society."

Viktor Kalinin, as he would be the first to admit, is no saint. No one meeting him for the first time in his elegant home, on the top floor of a yellow, crumbling, four-story walkup on Prechistinka Street (formerly Kropotkinskaya Street) in the center of Moscow, would guess that he had started out in business as a black-market smuggler. A slender forty-seven-year-old with a clipped beard, slippers, and a languid voice, Kalinin was a portrait of a pre-revolutionary Russian aristocrat come to life. A German piano made in 1905 sat in one corner of the room, facing an array of video and stereo equipment. In front of a brick fireplace were two ponderous, velvet-covered divans. A cellular phone was within reach. He smiled as he poured me a cup of strong English tea.

"You are looking at a former anti-Soviet activist," he said.

Kalinin's life story encompassed all the terrors and absurdities of the last decades of the Soviet Union. As a student in Moscow in the 1960s, he became involved with a group of dissident artists and poets and was arrested during a demonstration. Even though he had never dabbled in politics before and his parents were ardent Communists, his life was ruined. He had hoped to become a concert musician or a teacher, but he was branded an enemy of the state and forced to leave the university.

He found a job as a singer in a church choir—a job which, in a state openly hostile to religion, seemed to banish him forever to the margins of Soviet life.

But Kalinin found unexpected sanctuary inside the church. He became fascinated by liturgical music and helped develop the choir into a serious group of musicians. It toured the Soviet Union and even won some critical recognition from Western musicologists. Eventually Kalinin became choirmaster. He married another member of the choir, and by the time he was thirty, he had a young family and a responsible career. "I did all the organizing for our concerts and worked out the fees," he recalled. "I really operated on the principle that we were a sort of business. It's an experience I would never have had if I were teaching in a university or playing in an orchestra. I guess that's when I learned to be a real manager."

But then he made another mistake. He became a religious believer and joined some of the unofficial groups agitating for freedom of religious worship. His church superiors, anxious to avoid alienating their government protectors, fired him. Kalinin once more found himself marginalized. Like other dissident intellectuals, he found menial jobs as a janitor or a street cleaner. But the security organs never relaxed their vigilance. Once, he was dismissed from a sanitation squad that was cleaning the underground pedestrian passage between Red Square and the department store Detsky Mir (Children's World) because an officious KGB colonel decided that he was a security risk: the passageway ran directly underneath the Lubyanka, KGB headquarters.

"The system made it impossible for me to live like a normal Soviet citizen," Kalinin said without bitterness. "But that's probably the reason I became what I am today. The desire to earn money really grew in me."

With nothing more to lose, Kalinin decided to make his way in the black-market economy. He found his first commercial job in a company producing handbags and hats for sale in Moscow's thriving street markets. The company was unabashedly fraudulent. The goods were sold as "Western-made," with labels cut from foreign clothing. The hats were made from men's flannel underwear, cut up and retailored to resemble the models seen in Western magazines. But the devout musician was making more money than he ever had in his life.

In the mid-1980s, Kalinin took his riskiest gamble. With the money he had saved from black-market trade, he bought some secondhand Western computers and resold them at huge profits to his friends. At the time, the government strictly regulated access to information technology, but perestroika fanned the hunger for Western goods. Kalinin contacted middle-level officials in various Moscow ministries who were willing to pay high prices to replace their ponderous Soviet-made computers with Western models.

Kalinin had a unique source of supply. His brother had emigrated to England several years before to establish an export-import business with the Soviet Union, thereby allowing him to travel regularly to Moscow. From then on, his brother added to his Moscow baggage worn-out, used computers he had found at discount shops in London, and Viktor sold them for astronomical profits. "You could sell even a poor-quality IBM clone for ten times as much as a Soviet Robotron," he said.

The two brothers' smuggling activities made them wealthy men. But they shrewdly covered their risks: the black-market computers were sold only to government officials, to ensure that they were not bothered by curious customs inspectors. Everybody gained, until the KGB stepped in once again—this time, not as policemen but as business rivals.

"We started to hear about huge shipments of computers, coming by the planeloads and trainloads," Kalinin said. "This represented huge sums of money, and it was clear that ordinary businessmen like myself couldn't have worked on that scale. There were special joint ventures which entered the business, and it wasn't hard to figure out who was behind them. No one could provide the logistics and protection for transporting so many computers, and arrange the credits, unless he had help from certain official organs."

In the early 1990s, the Kalinins decided to get out of the computer business. Not only was it useless to compete with KGB smugglers; it was clearly imprudent. One of the new partners Viktor had taken on to help run his expanding operation was murdered shortly after he left to start his own smuggling business. Both he and his wife were found in their home with their throats slashed.

"He was always bragging about his important partners," Kalinin said of his friend. "I think he got in trouble because he was too greedy. A businessman has to be cautious if he wants to stay out of trouble in this city."

Kalinin followed his own advice. The next business he chose seemed innocuous enough. "We started trading in property at a time when the market in housing was very small," he said. "Most bureaucrats saw very little profit in it, except for what they could earn in bribes from people who were trying to move into better homes, and the criminal gangs were interested in much larger kinds of business. No one really understood the value of real estate. You could buy a one-room flat for one thousand dollars, which was amazing money at the time but had no relation to what it was actually worth. Then you could fix it and clean it up, and wait until the prices began to climb."

As Andrei Stroyev was discovering at roughly the same time, Moscow's inventory of old buildings and spacious flats would handsomely repay renovation efforts. Kalinin, of course, did not have Stroyev's network of municipal connections, but he was content to occupy himself with selling and redecorating apartments for homeowners instead of re-creating office buildings for foreigners. Nevertheless, he discovered that, just as in the computer business, bigger and more threatening rivals were moving into the game.

"There are certain large real estate firms which can buy entire apartment houses cheaply because they have the cooperation of officials who set the prices as low as possible, and then sell off each apartment for enormous profits," he said.

"You have to imagine the kind of big money circulating when someone buys a building with five hundred apartments and then two weeks later sells the same space at auction. Even in the new housing developments in the [Moscow] suburbs, a square meter of space will sell for two hundred or two hundred and fifty dollars. At fifty square meters for an average apartment, the value comes to six million dollars. And each of those housing complexes has two or three or four buildings. There are many Moscow districts being developed in this way. Sometimes it seems to me that all of Moscow is for sale."

Even if Kalinin wanted to, he couldn't break into the lucrative new housing market. Bureaucrats had completely tied it up. "There is no way any company could obtain as many housing sites for reconstruction as Perestroika did without bribes or powerful backers, or both," said Kalinin. "If I got involved on that scale, I could be an even richer man—or dead."

When I spoke with Kalinin in the middle of 1993, he was no longer confident that his small operation would remain immune from the masters of Moscow. "We have been very careful not to engage in any large-scale vigorous activity," he said. "We don't advertise or go out and look for clients. We have a select group of customers. But the danger is great, very great. It would be easy to destroy us just by forcing us to spend a lot of money on an apartment and then refusing to pay for it. This has happened to others."

Kalinin described one case he knew of, in which a commercial firm purchased several large buildings in downtown Moscow for a rich client. The firm bribed an army of officials to obtain the necessary licenses and permits. But when it presented documents for final approval of the deal, no one in the local district office would sign it. The firm went bankrupt.

"The only conclusion one can draw is that someone very powerful wanted to get that firm out of the way so he could obtain those buildings for himself," said Kalinin. "We could be talking about a bureaucrat or someone very close to him who was able to pay more in bribes to the right people. We could also be talking about a criminal group. Or maybe both working together. Certainly, no one was going to complain. If anyone raised questions, he would have been warned that something would happen to his family. That's the way those things are done now."

Kalinin shook his head. "Everyone knows that the control of organized crime over real estate is increasing. Of course, it's difficult to know by how much, but I have reason to think that [crime groups] now account for more than 50 percent of the market."

Once again, Kalinin was marginalized. Unless he was willing to risk bureaucratic intervention or gangland extortion, he was forced to act like an underground black marketeer. He carefully avoided telling the state how much he earned in his real estate deals.

"The taxes are 40 percent, but that's not the main reason," he said. "I would be willing to pay even higher taxes if I could be sure the state won't give information about my income to people who would have no qualms about robbing me, or that some official will not come to me one day and demand that I just hand over everything I have. It wouldn't be the first time that happened in our country."

My conversation with Kalinin took place six months before Russia plunged into the political turbulence that alerted the world to the failure of the second Russian revolution. But even then, the one-time dissident recognized the signs of trouble ahead.

A few weeks before we met, he was visited in his office by polite men suggesting a "partnership." Friends in the police helped scare them off, and Kalinin paid them for their help, but he didn't know whether he could count upon their future assistance. As the price of remaining in his homeland, he was beginning to consider the kind of "special security arrangements" he had long resisted. Some of his clients were connected, as he put it, to "shady structures," and they would be only too happy to take him under their wing.

"Right now, the lack of security means I have to think twice about expanding my business," he told me. "In fact, security is one of the important questions for me. I don't know whether it is possible for me to develop normally, according to my capabilities, in this country. I have small children, relatives, parents to think of. If I want to stay in this country and expand, it means I will have to do some unpleasant things. It's not just a matter of making payoffs to these criminal structures. It means losing real control over my company. I have to decide what to do."

Countless Russian businessmen had already made their choice. A report prepared by Moscow's Analytical Center for Social and Economic Policies in 1994 said that nearly 80 percent of private enterprises and commercial banks in the country paid up to 20 percent of their earnings in "taxes" to racketeers. The most successful entrepreneurs in post-Soviet society were those who could navigate between organized crime and the corrupt bureaucracy. They were also the ones who stayed alive.[13]

10 "They Can Shoot, They Can Kill"

It was close to midnight on a summer evening in Moscow. Driving cautiously through a quiet residential neighborhood in the north of the city, I tried to make out the address scrawled on a piece of paper.

"Here!" Volodya Mironov suddenly called out. "Turn here. I recognize the street."

We entered a narrow laneway and emerged into a dark square enclosed by tall buildings.

"I knew it," said Volodya. "Look at the cars. We're here."

Three Mercedes and a BMW were parked in the rubble-strewn yard. By now, I knew exactly what that meant. Luxurious Western cars were no longer the prerogative of foreigners. It was possible, of course, that they were owned by legitimately wealthy Russian businessmen. But we were going to a private birthday party held by one of the city's gangs, and the imported automobiles were unmistakable evidence that we had come to the right address.

Volodya, the enterprising young Moscow businessman who introduced me to the banker Aleksandr Smolensky, had secured the invitation. A few weeks earlier, he volunteered to be one of my guides to the Moscow underworld, claiming to know everything there was to know about the Russian mafiya. I was skeptical at first, because of his background.

A dapper man in his mid-thirties, Volodya had worked as a writer for *Kommunist*, the Party's principal journal of ideology, during the Soviet era. Like hundreds of young Russians of his generation, he made a swift passage from Communism to capitalism. After 1991, he became involved in what he vaguely described as "financial services." *Kommersant*, the Moscow business journal which had first praised and then exposed the real estate developer Andrei Stroyev, chose Mironov as the subject of one of its weekly profiles of prominent Russian entrepreneurs in 1992. He was co-founder of an investment company whose subscribers included ninety banks and private financial institutions across Russia. *Kommersant* observed that Mironov moved comfortably inside the country's business and political circles. I wondered what they meant. Each time I arrived at his Moscow office, I found an odd cast of visitors in Volodya's reception room: men in expensive double-breasted suits sat with portfolios on their laps, while more casually dressed people seemed to hover for no apparent purpose.[1]

Volodya would sometimes disappear for days or weeks at a time. He rarely answered phone messages. The English version of the *Kommersant* article, perhaps in an effort to find a familiar reference for a Western audience, described Volodya's style as "schmoozing." If one stretched the word to convey the clubby, faintly disreputable air of an insider trader, this was certainly adequate. But I could not picture any of Volodya's Western counterparts going to a gangland party—or at least making such little effort to conceal their intimacy with dubious characters. I was already learning the different rules for commercial life in Russia. One man's gangster could be another man's business associate.

"All Russian people are undergoing a social conversion, even me," Volodya once confided. "We dropped our so-called good jobs in the system, but in order to survive, we had to get involved in bad business. That's not what we want to do with our lives, of course. It's just a means to an end. In order to survive, none of us can escape being corrupted."

We parked on the square beside the Mercedes. Volodya walked a few steps ahead of me and stopped in front of a shabby apartment block. He rapped twice on the door, which opened immediately, as if someone had been waiting just inside. A man stood in the entranceway. He was short and compact, like a boxer, and he wore a sports jacket over an open-necked shirt. His hair was cut short, in the military style. The sound of someone crooning to a guitar, and muffled laughter, streamed past him into the night.

He looked at me instead of Volodya, and I shifted uneasily, clinking a plastic bag with bottles of expensive vodka I had bought at Volodya's suggestion. After a few moments of awkward silence, Volodya came to my rescue.

"It's not a bomb; it's a gift for the guest of honor."

The man didn't smile, but he turned and motioned us to follow him down a darkened corridor.

"They don't like to take any chances with security," Volodya whispered in my ear. "A man was killed in the yard a few weeks before."

A light bulb was swaying from the ceiling of the room we entered. It left most of the room's occupants in shadow, but I could make out boxes of computers and electrical equipment against the walls. As my eyes grew accustomed to the dim light, I saw young men in various stages of alcoholic stupor sitting around a table filled with bread, cheese, and dozens of nearly empty bottles.

A blond, muscular youth rose unsteadily to his feet. "Everyone is welcome," he shouted, and then collapsed into his chair. Someone laughed.

That was Sergei, I was told. The guest of honor. He was celebrating his twentieth birthday that night. Most of the others were in their teens and early twenties, but a few older men sat, or slumped, on chairs propped against the wall. I counted about fifteen shapes in the room.

The man who ushered us inside snapped out a command, and three tall, plastic glasses were produced. He was about as old as Volodya, in his mid-thirties, but something in his military bearing suggested a familiarity with giving orders. His name, Volodya told me softly, was Igor. Our vodka bottles were opened. Igor poured out two brimming glasses of clear liquid, handed them to us, and then poured an equally large portion for himself.

"What about us?" someone called out from the shadows. Laughing uproariously, the others struggled to their feet as the bottle was handed round.

I stared uneasily at the filled glass in front of me. According to Russian custom, it would have to be emptied in one gulp.

"To our guests!" barked Igor. "We are civilized people here!"

Everyone drank and sat down. Our glasses were filled a second time. A few of the party guests grabbed food from the table, and one of the older men I had seen sitting against the wall picked up a guitar and continued the song we had heard outside. It was a mournful soldier's ballad.

"We used to sing that in Afghanistan," a young man near him said in a slurred voice. The younger people listened quietly, almost reverently.

Igor noticed me staring at them.

"The war killed a lot of their friends," he said.

"Did they serve in Afghanistan?" I asked.

"Not the younger ones," said Igor. "When I found the young guys, they were in trouble with the police. They were washing car windows or hustling stolen bluejeans in the market. But look at them now. I'm proud of them—we're all comrades together. There are a lot of groups in this city, but none are as good as ours."

Igor's tone erased any lingering doubt that he was the leader. I asked what made them special, and he smiled for the first time.

"They can do everything," he said. "They can fight, they can shoot. They can kill."

We drank a third round of vodka. Igor offered to show us around the building, and Volodya and I rose weakly to our feet and followed him back along the corridor.

Despite the building's air of abandonment, it was filled with people. As we passed a room with a half-opened door, two young men inside jumped to their feet. Unlike their companions down the hall, they were completely sober. Igor motioned them to sit.

"This is the company director's office," he said. "We had some trouble here recently."

Behind me, I heard Volodya's intake of breath.

"It's a torture chamber," he whispered to me excitedly. "They kidnapped a businessman who refused to pay his bills and they held him for a couple of days right here. They nearly killed the guy."

As we walked on, Igor apologized for the building's state of disrepair. A large commercial firm had just purchased the structure, he said, and his group of ex-soldiers and street toughs was protecting the site while "renovation" work went ahead.

At the far end of the corridor, Igor motioned us into another large room.

"This is our real business," he said proudly.

The room was filled with copying machines and computer consoles. Books were everywhere, some in piles reaching nearly to the ceiling. A slight, bearded man stood up to greet us.

"This is our computer expert," said Igor.

Igor was clearly intent on impressing me with the fact that his comrades were no ordinary group of thugs. They were full-fledged partners in the firm. As payment for their services, they could run whatever business they chose on the premises, and they had chosen to launch a desktop publishing business.

"What do you publish?" I asked, trying to hide my surprise.

"Mysteries, that sort of thing," shrugged the computer expert.

"Do you commission authors?" I went on.

Igor and his assistant began to laugh.

"Not precisely," said the young man. "All the books are written already. In the West."

He went over to one of the piles of books and picked out a work by a well-known British mystery writer. It had a Russian title. He ran his hands lovingly over the cover.

"We translate them, produce a version on our computers, and then copy them," he said. "It's all legal. The copyright has passed already."

The operation he described was elegantly simple. Since Soviet state publishing houses lost their monopoly on the written word in the early 1990s, Western titles were sold at every street corner. Cheap and often badly translated pulp novels opened up a new world to the avid reading public of Russia. The "publishers" had no need to be concerned with the quality of the writing or the plot: anything from the West would do. If someone brought in a likely paperback, it was translated and pro-grammed on Russian software obtained from their partners. They could publish forty thousand copies at a cost of less than twenty rubles apiece and sell each copy for one hundred rubles. On a good month—and with a popular novel—the assembly line could earn over three million rubles.

"We paid for our equipment," said Igor, although I had not asked him.

"But where did you get it?" I asked, pointing to a huge American-made copying machine in one corner of the room. "I haven't seen a copier like that for sale anywhere in Moscow."

Igor was evasive. I suspected that everything in the building, from the cheap Western novels to the boxes of computers, had been smuggled in for resale.

"To tell you the truth," Igor growled. "I don't know where this stuff came from, and I don't care. We paid for it just like you do in the West. We provide the conditions under which everything you see here can work. Nothing gets done in this city without protection."

In that case, I ventured hesitantly, did he consider his group a busi-ness or a security service?

Igor thought about this.

"You need fists," he said at last, "to allow the brains to work nor-mally."

The guitarist was still playing when we walked back to the party. A few more vodka bottles had been emptied. Sergei was sound asleep. The other youths stumbled to their feet.

The respect for their leader was palpable. As Igor nodded to the youths to sit, there was rough affection in his voice.

"Just look at their eyes," he said. "You can see these are not stupid people. They can get things done."

Igor poured out more glasses of vodka. I said I was impressed by the way he seemed to control his band.

"I learned it in the armed forces," he said proudly. "I was an officer, submarine captain, third grade, in the Soviet Navy."

He smiled at my startled look.

"I wasn't kicked out—I retired honorably," he said. "An officer's pay is not enough these days to support a family, and I have a four-year-old son and a daughter of eleven."

Igor admitted that his "boys" were often in conflict with the police. But he said I shouldn't be surprised that an officer had formed a group of outlaws. There were many who had done the same.

"We have to make use of the opportunities that are given to us," he said. "Maybe later, when we are all rich and there are proper laws in place, we will be honest businessmen. But meanwhile, we have to provide a decent future for our families and children. Right now, there is no way of doing this and staying within the law."

Igor would not tell me his last name. Nevertheless, he agreed to meet me again in a more sober setting, where he would expand upon his singular philosophy of life. Over the next few weeks, Volodya tried several times to persuade him to live up to his promise. But Igor was elusive.

"He really doesn't want to talk to foreigners about what he does," Volodya explained. "It's dangerous to tell secrets in this environment."

He gave me the disappointing news as we were sitting in a private restaurant near the Kremlin, where he had suggested I might run into some of Igor's soldiers.

"Everyone comes here. It's a meeting ground for all the boys."

The restaurant was attached to what had once been a state club for artists and writers overlooking the Moscow River. In the Soviet years, it had been a fashionable playground for the *zolotaya molodyozh*, the so-called "golden youth" who were the children of leading Party officials. There was an ice-skating rink, a tennis court, and even a private gymnasium and sauna. Entrance had been permitted only to those with special passes stamped by the Communist Party Central Committee. But after the fall of Communism, the club became a gathering place for the wheelers and dealers of new Russian finance and for upwardly mobile hoodlums.

None of Igor's men were there on the day we arrived. But as we ordered coffee and sandwiches from a waitress, Volodya directed my attention to a group sitting nearby. A large bottle of French brandy was on their table. Three powerfully built young men, in Western track suits, were happily pouring each other drinks.

When the bottle was empty, they staggered to their feet. One dropped a plastic shopping bag and, cursing, bent to pick it up. But he only succeeded in distributing its contents across the floor. I looked closer. The floor was littered with crisp ten- and fifty-ruble notes.

As we watched in silence, the youths succeeded in stuffing their money back into the bag and wobbled out of the restaurant. They did not appear to have paid their bill.

"Some of these guys have so much money they don't know how to handle it," said the grinning Volodya after they left.

"I feel sorry for them," he continued. "You have to have a goal in life—otherwise money is useless. Take myself, for instance. My real dream is to be a writer."

"Really?"

"Of course. I'm not just a businessman. When I worked for *Kommunist,* I wrote about everything that I was told to—the Marxist theory of history, the ideological shortcomings of our literature. It was all nonsense. Now I can write what I want, but who will pay me to do it?"

"Maybe Igor will publish your books.".

He laughed. "I'll ask him. But a person has to earn a living. That's why I got involved in business."

It wasn't long before I was introduced to Volodya's business. He invited me to a currency auction sponsored by his company and held in the auditorium of a large city hotel. It was an invitation-only affair. About two dozen men were in the audience, bidding on blocks of dollars offered as lines of credit by the Central State Bank. The buyers represented private banks and commercial enterprises, which expected to make a healthy profit by loaning their newly acquired dollars to businessmen at high rates of interest. It was, in essence, a primitive venture-capital market. As I looked over the crowd, I was startled to see Igor's "boys" at strategic places around the room.

A few stood at either side of the platform where the auctioneer led the bidding. This time, they looked fiercely sober. Their ties and jackets made them indistinguishable from other members of the audience. Only Sergei, the birthday guest of honor, showed any sign of recognition. When I stared at him, he winked.

During a lull in the proceedings, Volodya came up to me. I told him what I had seen and asked if he were surprised.

"Of course not," he laughed. "I hired them as security guards. With the kind of money we deal in at our auctions, you can't take chances. Each will earn one thousand rubles for a few hours' work—that's more than a month's salary for most people—and Igor will get two thousand. But these guys are worth every kopek we pay them."

Volodya moved away to mingle with the buyers before I could ask any more questions. This time, I paid closer attention to his movements. I noticed that he was often engaged in conversation with an elegantly dressed businessman. At one point, I heard Volodya introduce him to someone else as his "partner." The man seemed familiar, and I took a closer look. It was Igor, the ex-submarine captain.

When the auction ended, I joined the traders milling around the entranceway. I waited for Igor to come out, hoping to resume our birthday-party conversation. But the boozy comradery had vanished in the cold light of commerce. He walked by me with barely a glance.

Volodya's way of introducing me to the secrets of the underworld was like peeling layers from an onion. The birthday party, the "golden youth" restaurant, and finally the auction led me slowly into one of the secrets of Russian crime. Igor and his outlaw band were not simply outriders for businessmen in the shark-infested seas of post-Soviet commerce. They were the boat itself.

By 1993, hundreds of groups like Igor's were associated with businesses around the country. They often called themselves security agencies or bodyguards, but this captured only one facet of their services. They conducted negotiations, collected debts, intimidated creditors, and resolved disputes about market share with competitors. They had little to do with the formal structure of the underworld, often seeing themselves as the chosen instruments of law and order against the mafiya and the small-time racketeers and hoodlums—*shpana,* in the Russian vernacular—who terrorized neighborhoods. Many, in fact, were former policemen, combat veterans, ex-agents of the security organs or young athletes—*sportsmeny*—recruited from gyms and body-building clubs.

When they first began appearing in Russia's brokerages and stock exchanges, they were considered by many entrepreneurs an unavoidable feature of the transition to a market economy. Since authorities provided little protection to business and there was no legal way of arbitrating commercial differences, these shock troops of Russian capitalism filled an early need for security. But, straddling the line between legal and illegal behavior, they soon grew powerful and influential enough to turn the tables on their employers. They sat in boardrooms and at the back of commercial shops; in the executive offices of hotels, nightclubs, and casinos; and in the counting rooms of banks and financial houses. According to the report on crime presented to President Yeltsin in early 1994, gangs owned or controlled about forty thousand Russian businesses, including two thousand in the state sector. But this activity did not lend itself to easy rhetoric about "organized crime," at least of the kind that originated in the Soviet prisons and the Thieves' World. The leaders of these underground syndicates could be bureaucrats, former black marketeers, army officers, policemen, or even teachers. It was a form of criminal activity run by men who were, to all appearances, not criminals at all.[2]

After Igor broke off communications, I despaired of finding out more about these shadowy groups. They were even more hostile to outsiders than the *vory*. But Volodya telephoned one day and asked me to meet him outside his office.

"I have someone I want you to know," he said.

I picked him up in my car the next afternoon. As we threaded our way through traffic toward the northern section of the city, past Sokolniki Park, Volodya looked pleased with himself.

"It will be up to you to convince this guy to talk, but I've paved the way for you," he said. "He's a real mafiya boss."

"How did you meet him?" I asked suspiciously.

Volodya smiled. "It's very simple. He's my karate teacher."

We parked beside a four-story building with a large sign that identified it as an educational institute. Most of the windows were boarded up.

There were the inevitable foreign cars outside. As I followed Volodya to a side entrance, I passed a Ford jeep and a BMW. We were met by a young man in a loose-fitting white outfit, who led us without a word down a long passageway to a room spread with exercise mats, upon which about two dozen similarly clad young men were energetically throwing each other.

In the midst of the melee, a giant in his fifties, dressed completely in black, called out instructions. He had a powerful body which showed signs of dissolving into fat. But despite his size, he moved with the grace of a dancer, occasionally stopping at one of the sparring pairs of youths to demonstrate a hold. When he saw us, he glided across the room, wiping sweat from his black moustache.

To my astonishment, Vladimir bowed.

"Hello, teacher," he said quietly.

The teacher answered with a solemn bow of his own. He examined me with glittering, shrewd black eyes.

"I am Kasyanov," he said in a deep voice.

A woman almost as tall as he came running up and gave his shoulder an affectionate pat.

"This is Ted," she said to me, in perfect English. "Don't let him frighten you. I'm Elena, his wife."

At her touch, Kasyanov softened. He turned back to me.

"First I must finish this exercise," he said. "Then we will talk."

As I watched the youths perform more acts of violence on each other under Kasyanov's alert gaze, Elena moved close to me.

"Don't be frightened of him," she said, taking my arm. "He acts like a big bully. But it's just an act."

She cast an adoring glance at her husband. I asked where she learned English.

"I used to be a government interpreter," she smiled. "I don't translate any more, but we needed the money when we were young. Now that Ted is finally being recognized for all the good works he has done, I can stay home and be a housewife."

Before I could ask about her husband's good works, Volodya pointed out a muscular woman whom Ted was just then lecturing on the gym floor.

"That's Kasyanov's daughter," he said. "She's almost as good now as the teacher."

She was the only female in the class. We watched her execute a maneuver that sent her partner flying onto the mat. Elena informed me that the partner was her daughter's husband.

"She has so much talent," said Elena. "Our whole family comes to the gym every day. Except me, of course. I'm just not built for that sort of thing."

She left us momentarily, and I nudged Volodya, who was absorbed in the martial-arts display.

"I thought you were bringing me to see a mafiya boss," I whispered, "not a karate teacher with a strange family."

"Be patient," Volodya replied. "He's no ordinary karate teacher. He's chairman of the Russian Karate Federation, and he has 245 branches of his school around Russia. He also has his own security service, Cassius, which he fills with his students. Can you think of a better basis for a syndicate?"

I was skeptical. "What about his good works?"

Vladimir only winked at me and put his finger to his lips. Kasyanov was approaching.

The man in black grabbed my arm and felt it for muscle tone. "You could use some exercise," he said.

I immediately changed the subject.

"Your students seem very eager to learn," I told him. "Do they come from local schools?"

Kasyanov and Vladimir smiled knowingly.

"The school they come from," boomed the teacher, "is the school of life."

He waved his hand at the rows of panting combatants, who now were looking at us.

"Hundreds of young people come to me and say, 'Teacher, I want to learn how to fight like you do.' They brag to me that they are tough, that they have already been on the streets and have learned to defend themselves very early in life. But I look at their faces very carefully. I look in their eyes."

"What do you look for?"

Kasyanov patted his moustache again. "Something more than toughness. I also give them a simple test before they join me: I ask them what they would do if they had twenty million rubles and had to divide it among ten people. If they say they would divide it equally among everyone, I tell them to go home, maybe find work in a bank. But if the person says he would take a little extra for himself, because he had performed the work of getting the money, that's who I want."

I asked if all his students measured up to his standards.

"Even after I accept them, some kids don't last the course," he admitted sadly. "They go off to work for evil people."

Kasyanov looked at his watch. "My students are waiting," he said. "We have to begin another exercise."

I asked him, tentatively, if we could have a longer chat. To my surprise, he nodded. "Call me any time," he said.

Volodya was triumphant as we left. "He liked you," he said, and added, with needless emphasis, "Kasyanov is not an easy man to know."

Then, as we headed back to his office, Volodya peeled off another layer of the onion. He told me who Kasyanov really was. During the Soviet era, the teacher had been a martial-arts instructor for the army and the KGB. He had continued his contacts with friends in the intelligence services after 1991, and it is reputed that they had helped him to expand his karate school. In return, Kasyanov's gym had served as a "training academy" for the new security agencies. But the teacher was ambitious and broke with his partners. He was eager to go into business for himself, and he formed the Cassius Security Agency.

"He started to offer the services of his students directly to restaurants and shops around the capital," Volodya said. "Of course, it was a kind of protection racket. But the teacher was so respected, no one dared to cross him. He began earning a lot of money, and he opened up more of his clubs around the country. The trouble was, he didn't know how to go further. I know he wanted to buy a restaurant, and I tried to help him, but he doesn't have a head for business. He calls himself a businessman, but if he had a clever business mind, he could have become even more of a powerful man in this city. Unfortunately, his experiences have made him a very disappointed and bitter person. Perhaps he agreed to talk with you because he can't get anyone else to listen to his troubles any more. I have the greatest respect for the teacher, but I worry about him."

With this sobering introduction, I telephoned Kasyanov a few days later, and he invited me to his home. Volodya didn't join me or, rather,

I didn't get the chance to ask him to: he was off on another of his mysterious business errands.

The Kasyanovs lived close to the karate school, in a colorless block of flats with a courtyard whose asphalt was badly cracked from the previous winter's snows. Elena met me at the door when I emerged from the rickety lift. She was wearing an apron, and her fingers were whitened with flour. Several pairs of flannel slippers were in the hall. I bent to take off my shoes and put on a pair, and then walked into the carpeted parlor, past walls lined with pictures of family members, paintings of Russian scenes, and reproductions of icons. For a mafiya boss—if that was what he was—Kasyanov lived in modest comfort. Instead of his formidable black costume, he wore a frayed track suit and slippers and sat on a sagging old sofa reading a newspaper.

He motioned me to join him. Elena brought out a tray of meat pies.

"Eat," she urged me. "I won't make them for Ted anymore because he doesn't know when to stop. He'll just put on weight."

Even in "civilian" clothes, Kasyanov radiated a disturbing energy. He put down his newspaper and watched with impatience as I savored the meat pies. Finally, he pulled my arm. "Come," he announced. "I will show you something."

He led me to a hall closet and opened the door. I stifled a gasp. Inside the closet was a small arsenal of the most exotic weapons I had ever seen. Kasyanov proudly picked up each one and described it to me. There was a curved Uzbek dagger, a blade from a Red Army–issue M-16 rifle, Chinese metal throwing sticks, and Chinese bracelets that could break a man's wrist.

"I love weapons," he said. "I can spend hours looking at my collection. Other people like guns, but for me cold-steel weapons are like the difference between water and fire."

Elena came up behind us. For the first time, I noticed, she seemed disturbed.

"Ted, you talk too much," she said. "No one can understand you."

He went on as if he hadn't heard. "These weapons are not just for show," he said. "I use them myself. And I teach my students, when they are ready for them."

"Why are they necessary for karate?" I asked.

"You don't understand," said Kasyanov smoothly. "What I teach is a way of life. I teach people hand-to-hand fighting of a Slavonic character. Cold steel. We don't need weapons like your ordinary hoodlums. With these things, my boys can beat people with machine guns. They can scare them to death. This is how we fight the mafiya."

"You fight the mafiya?"

"Absolutely," he said.

Elena looked exasperated. "Why are you boring our guest?" she said. "He still hasn't finished his lunch."

Obediently, we trudged back to the parlor. But Kasyanov was eager to talk. He cast what seemed like an imploring glance to his wife, and she shrugged.

"Tell him about the time they invited you to lunch," she said, resignedly.

"Who invited you to lunch?"

"The mafiya," he said. "I know a lot of these guys. We were all kids at the same time."

I asked him what he meant by the mafiya.

"There is a big difference between your mafiya in the West and ours," he replied. "The Cosa Nostra are noble people. Who could be against well-organized societies? But our mafiya are not organized, at least not as they should be. That's why everything is in disorder here. Nobody knows whom to obey. When there is no order, there is *bespredel*, and people cannot lead normal lives.

"Our mafiya have no culture. They are simply uncultured, stupid people; you cannot reason with them. One should be more afraid of our mafiya than of yours. They kill without batting an eyelash. And you know what makes them more brazen? Why they have become involved in dishonorable things like drugs and prostitution? It's because they have decided to merge with our government *apparat*. They think no one can fight them that way. But they lost the most important thing—the respect of the people.

"In the old days, before the revolution, the mafiya really worked for the people. There was a group that once kidnapped Lenin. But they didn't believe it was really him, and they let him go. They should have shot the bastard then—we would never have had the Communist nightmare. Communism was a criminal idea to begin with. It was unnatural to think that I should be interested in your well-being before I care about my own. It should be the other way round."

I asked him to tell me about his lunch with the mafiya.

"Four of these mafiosi invited me to one of their restaurants near the Taganka," he began, naming a popular theater in central Moscow. "Of course, I went without weapons. I'm not afraid of them. I have always told them to their faces they were bandits, and I told them this again, at the lunch. I said I always have been and always will be against you. You are *bespredel*. You have robbed everyone, no one has anything left. Who are you going to rob now, one another?"

Kasyanov's tirade apparently did not prevent the gangsters from asking for his cooperation. "They kept sniffing around me," he said. "They offered me a lot of money, a lot of money."

"What did they want you to do?"

He pretended not to hear the question. "Of course, I turned them down," he went on. "Two of them immediately got up from their chairs and left. I heard one of them say to his friend, 'why did you bring this guy?' They thought they could intimidate me. But I was very calm. I knew I could just call my men if there was trouble, and we would finish them off.

"I have a lot of friends. Do you know I used to work with the KGB? I went out on drug raids with them on the Afghan border. I taught those guys everything they know . . ."

Kasyanov looked sad. "Everything they know," he repeated, "and no one is grateful."

I was beginning to feel dizzy from the man's jarring mixture of boastfulness, moralizing, and melancholy. Elena, perhaps sensing my discomfort, shoved the tray of meat pies in my face.

"Eat," she said.

I nibbled on one of the pies, while Kasyanov observed a long, stony silence.

"They are all *mraz i svoloch* [scum and swine]," he said at last. "*Mraz i svoloch*. That's why I have decided to fight the mafiya myself."

He glared at me. "I don't know why I'm saying all this to you. Actually, I find the topic of the mafiya very uninteresting. It's like asking a person who cleans toilets to talk about his work."

"But how do you go about it?" I asked. "How do you fight the mafiya yourself?"

Elena tried to be helpful. "The Federation does a lot of charity," she said. "It helps orphans, for instance."

Kasyanov smiled at her. "For the last twenty-five years, people have been calling me for help," he said. "People always remember me when they are in a mess. Mostly they want money. But sometimes they need protection. Just the other day I got a telephone call. 'Teacher,' they said to me. 'There has been an attack on a restaurant. You must come.' So I took weapons and went to get some of my boys. By the time I got there, more of our people had arrived from various corners of Moscow. Boom-boom-boom, and that was that," he said, in an imitation of gunfire. I did not remind him of his distaste for guns.

"Can you imagine the head of the New York mafiya going himself to a *razborka*?" he said, using the gangland term for the settling of accounts. "But for my friends, I will do these things."

A deep sigh came from the chair where Elena was sitting. "He does it so he won't be out of practice," she said, apparently having given up on promoting her husband's benevolent side. "If you ask me," she said crisply, "he's getting too old for this."

But Kasyanov was in full flight. "All I have to do is whistle," he bragged. "And people will come from everywhere. People think they can get away with anything in this time of *bespredel*. So you have to protect yourself. A man has to act. Let me give you another example. I have my money in a certain bank, and I went to the president of the bank and asked him to transfer that money somewhere else so I could settle a bill. Fine, he said. But I found out he was more interested in loaning my money to someone else so he could earn more interest. He was screwing me, and I had a big deal depending on that money."

Kasyanov smiled at me. "How did I get it back? Simple. I went to his office with my weapons." He stretched out his arms as if he were carrying a gun. "I told him, 'Asshole, give me my money, and my interest as well.' And I got the money. He won't complain. These things are done in such a way as to make it difficult to investigate."

It seemed futile to ask how such actions contributed to fighting *bespredel,* much less the "mafiya." But there was no doubt that, for all his disappointment, Ted Kasyanov occupied a profitable niche in the world of Russian "protection services." He confided that he was planning to buy his own airplane, in order to pick up "intelligence" from the 245 clubs of his Karate Federation scattered across the country.

"In Moscow, we have analysts who go over the information and meet with me to decide what to do, but I always need information," he said.

"I am a businessman, and you know, of course, that proper intelligence is essential for business."

Elena was beginning to look restless. We had already been talking for several hours, and I decided that it was time to leave. But as he escorted me to the door, Kasyanov was still discussing his plans. He invited me to visit again. "I'll be away from Moscow for awhile," he said. "But you can call in a month."

I asked him where he was going. "Kamchatka," he said, naming the peninsula in the Russian Far East. "Our intelligence tells us that Korean gangs are getting the upper hand there. I was asked to help out."

"Who asked you?"

Kasyanov winked. "They have a lot of guns out there," he said. "But I am stronger. They will learn to respect me."

I never saw Ted Kasyanov again. A few weeks after we spoke, he was arrested and charged with attempted murder and kidnapping. The case caused a minor stir in the Russian press.

Details were hard to confirm. Instead of going to Kamchatka, Kasyanov had gone to the city of Kazan, the capital of Tatarstan, where one of his strongest "clubs" was located. Something happened in Kazan. An argument. A shootout. It wasn't clear. But Kasyanov fled back to Moscow, one step ahead of the local police. Kazan authorities applied to Moscow police for assistance, and a surprised Kasyanov was taken prisoner in the courtyard of his apartment block. The authorities, evidently, feared trouble. They had placed sharpshooters on the roof of Kasyanov's building, and a small army of riot-squad officers with machine guns and bullet-proof vests made the arrest. They stormed into his flat and even confiscated his cherished arsenal of cold steel, while a weeping Elena looked on.[3]

Kasyanov was taken to Kazan under guard and placed in solitary confinement. Meanwhile, his friends tried to put the best face on his predicament.

"I have known Ted Kasyanov for years, ever since he began his karate school," wrote a sympathetic journalist, Olga Belan, in *Sobesednik*, a weekly Moscow newspaper. "He pleased us with his simplicity and his straightforward formula for life, which was nothing more than every man must be able to defend himself, his home, his country, and he must be strong and healthy."[4]

But the journalist had to concede that her friend was caught crossing the line between his business activities and gangsterism. "Willingly or unwillingly, he became a puppet in the hands of mafiya groups that are in the midst of serious financial disagreements," she reported.

What was Kasyanov really up to when he was arrested? Elena, who gave me a tearful account of the arrest and her own subsequent trip to Kazan, insisted that she didn't know. "It's a frameup by one of his old students," she said. "Ted is no criminal, and now they are making him suffer in prison. When I saw him, he had already lost thirty kilograms."

"Can't the Karate Foundation come to his aid?" I asked.

"I can't tell you anything more," she said miserably. "I was warned several times that if I speak too much, I will be killed."

Volodya was even less forthcoming when I finally made contact with him. "You need muscles and brains to survive in Russia—muscles and brains," he repeated, echoing Igor and implying once again that his karate teacher had too much of one and not enough of the other.

Meanwhile, Igor was apparently doing better than ever. He had become director of his own company. "He sends you his regards," said Volodya.

Kasyanov was lucky in at least one respect. It was better to be caught by police than by an unfriendly rival. In 1993, the year Kasyanov was imprisoned, there were 29,200 murders in Russia. Many, according to police, were related to gang disputes concerning business. But what I found surprising was the equanimity with which everyone who knew Ted—except for Elena, of course—accepted his fate. "An entire generation is growing up for whom this situation is normal and who . . . will not turn to official authorities but to unofficial ones [for help]," noted the authors of the 1994 report to Yeltsin. "People are more likely to hire a murderer to punish a guilty, or even an unpleasant, partner than to go to court or arbitration."

Kasyanov himself recognized that in the New Russia, there was no room for pity. "You see," he had told me patiently the day we first met in his gym, "we live in cruel times. You have to be more than just tough to survive—you have to know what you want, and then be prepared to get it, even if other people suffer. Maybe you would call this selfishness, but a person aware of his selfish nature is a person who knows himself. He is a person capable of finding harmony between his acts and his thoughts."

In the ersatz Zen philosophy of Ted Kasyanov, one could hear Post-

Soviet Man struggling to free himself from the baggage of Communist culture. In order to survive in Soviet society, a citizen performed in public as if he had no private thoughts. As a child, he recited devotional poetry to Lenin and joined the Octobrists and Young Pioneers to prove his eligibility for Soviet adulthood. As an adult, he allowed himself to be herded along with his workmates to May Day parades to demonstrate his reliability. Only by conforming to the standards of public life could he enjoy the luxury—and safety—of a private one. This enforced "disconnect" between action and thought fed the deep cynicism of the final years of Soviet society. Acting in a way that corresponded to one's convictions was a luxury available to dissidents and criminals, perhaps, but to few others.

The end of the Soviet system put Kasyanov's ideal of harmony within the grasp of millions. For the first time in the lives of most Russians born after 1917, they were free to express their private hungers and ambitions—and to act on them—without fear of the state's intervention. The problem was that Russia itself had not changed. The nation's new leaders seemed to have the same moral or legal standards, or the same absence of them, as their predecessors. "Democracy" merely turned the underground culture of the black market into standard above-ground behavior for the new society.

The mobsters and racketeers of post-Soviet Russia were far from being isolated and temporary by-products of the nation's passage to capitalism. They flourished in fertile soil. To thousands of Kasyanov's compatriots, criminal behavior was a legitimate, if not a necessary, form of survival. The breakdown of the Soviet Union's oppressive system of social control had freed the ordinary citizen to become as larcenous as a Party first secretary.

11 The Smugglers

In 1992, Moscow's Sheremetievo International Airport received an odd unofficial name. Newspapers dubbed it the "field of wonders." This was a play on a phrase made famous in a popular 1930s translation of the Pinocchio tale by the Russian writer Aleksei Tolstoy. At that time, *polye chudes* served as a code to mock the megaprojects that were supposed to transform feudal Russia miraculously into utopia, but which never seemed to get beyond the blueprints of Stalinist planners.

The real miracles, it turned out, were left to a much later age. You could witness them every day at Sheremetievo, whenever a flight arrived from some foreign country. In the crowd of tired passengers lining up before the customs inspectors, it was always easy to single out the Russian faces. They wore curious expressions of anticipation and unease. Unlike their foreign companions, they were overwhelmed with luggage and boxes of every size and description. No one had to ask what the boxes contained. They were vivid advertisements of how these Russians had spent their time outside the Motherland—exotic cheeses and cognacs from Paris, children's bicycles from Dubai, Japanese stereos and VCRs picked up in the bargain shops of Frankfurt, discount American computers from Prague. The owners of these goods faced one last hurdle before they brought their prizes home. They had to talk their way past an insufferably rude customs inspector, who needed to be persuaded that the four brand-new laptop computers were actually for the personal use of relatives waiting at home. If the explanation were accepted, unease would fade before the smiling anticipation of the miracle to come: an ordinary worker who had left Russia a few days earlier with all the savings he could muster was about to be transformed into a wealthy merchant.[1]

In the post-Soviet era, millions of Russians turned to smuggling as a passport to quick riches. Sheremetievo was not the only field on which the miraculous transformation from Soviet proletarian to capitalist entrepreneur occurred. Thanks to the legal chaos created by the breakup of the Soviet Union, it wasn't necessary to go abroad in order to make a reasonable investment in risk and initiative pay off in huge rewards.

In the confusion of the Soviet collapse, there had been no time to work out customs rules or even erect proper markers along the borders of the fifteen former Soviet republics, which had declared themselves sovereign countries. The new Commonwealth of Independent States (CIS), initially comprising ten of the republics, treated the borders between them as transparent. Goods and people freely crossed the old boundaries as if they were still the dividing lines between republics of one country. Even when customs inspection points were established, the enterprising smuggler had little to fear from police once he got his contraband safely across "national" lines. The laws of one former republic were usually ignored by its neighbor, which meant in practice that goods obtained illicitly in Russia were magically transformed in Ukraine or Estonia into items for sale in the legal marketplace.[2]

Mass smuggling turned the entire territory of the former Soviet Union into a field of wonders. The roads between Russia and its neighboring states became superhighways for con men and would-be capitalists. It was hard to tell the two varieties of entrepreneur apart. A Russian factory machinist and his family would stuff bottles of vodka bought under the counter or stolen from local warehouses into the back seat of their Lada and journey across the border for a weekend visit to "relatives" in Ukraine—who would pay valuable dollars for the carload. Armenians living in Moscow packed gold into their suitcases to barter for luxury goods or food when they traveled home to Yerevan. The train from St. Petersburg to Tallinn filled every night with enterprising "tourists" carrying copper wire in their suitcases or even under their coats. If the police didn't foil their plans, the wire would soon be in the eager hands of scrap-metal dealers in the Baltics.[3]

"We stop between twenty and thirty smugglers a week, but there's no way of knowing how many get through," Edgar Aaro, head of the Estonian Border Guards, told me, with a gesture of weary resignation. "Each enterprise, each factory, each farmer, is trying to grab as much as possible. That's how the collapse of the Soviet imperial system changed all our lives."[4]

The smuggling phenomenon of post-Soviet Russia represented a kind of coming-of-age for the Soviet black market. During the 1970s and 1980s, the Soviet Union was already enmeshed in furtive commerce.

As many as twenty million people actively participated in the so-called shadow economy—one out of every fifteen Soviet citizens. Although this "second economy" was often considered by outsiders to be an embryonic laboratory of capitalism, proof that Soviets were avid free-marketeers under their Party clothing, it corrupted everyone who participated in it.[5]

A few perceptive Western scholars have openly questioned for years whether the second economy was a boon or bane for the development of Russian society. Soviet officialdom, not surprisingly, set the tone for the entire underground enterprise. They secretly encouraged and profited from the services available in the illicit private sector, while harassing any of its participants who refused to share the dividends of the black market. The "crimes" of people like the promoter Mark Rudinshtein or Viktor Kalinin, the importer of computers, chiefly resided in the fact that they had become dangerous competitors for the bureaucratic mafiya.[6]

It was therefore no surprise to discover that the clandestine economy nurtured the morality of the thief and embezzler. It was a place where every civic value was determinedly and conscientiously flouted. Cheating the government was considered normal—even expected—behavior. "The average citizen felt no compunction about stealing . . . from his factory, for instance, [even though] he would never rob his neighbors," the exiled Soviet academic Valery Chalidze wrote in 1977.[7]

Less than twenty years later, this split psychology was to underpin post-Soviet life. The state remained a wily and tyrannical competitor of the would-be entrepreneur. Smugglers, in particular, considered their activities a legitimate form of competition with officialdom and the police. Most of the smuggler-entrepreneurs, in fact, were young. According to a study of arrests conducted by the Russian security ministry in 1992, the average smuggler was a male, aged between nineteen and thirty, who considered himself a "businessman." He usually had a higher education and no previous criminal record. Needless to say, he did not consider himself a criminal. He was only, after all, stealing revenue and goods from a government that otherwise would steal from him.[8]

Five or six times a year, a young man named Mikhail left his apartment in Moscow, stepped into his white Nissan van, and drove one thousand miles across southern Russia and Ukraine to deliver a load of stolen ikons and art treasures to buyers in the West. Mikhail had dreamed of becoming a dentist. He was lucky enough to be alive at a time in Russia when he could also dream of opening his own dental clinic upon finishing university. He needed more than luck, however. The costs of buying and equipping a clinic in the post-Soviet inflationary economy were beyond the possibilities of a poor Moscow student. In order to achieve his dreams, Mikhail followed hundreds of his fellow Russians into the trade of art smuggling. To him, it was the most natural progression in the world.

"Everybody in Russia today is trying to make money," he told me. "I can earn in one trip as much as I can earn in a year at anything else. This way, I can provide for my family, I can save for my dental clinic, and also have a comfortable life. I've got nothing to be ashamed of." [9]

But he was not free from anxiety. He would tell his story only if I agreed not to use his real name. I found him one evening sitting in the front seat of his van, which was parked on a tree-lined street in one of the capital's southern districts. The friend who had arranged our meeting motioned me into the back seat. Throughout our conversation, I saw only the back of Mikhail's head, but in the dim light of the dashboard I glimpsed the features of a large, mournful-looking man. He said he was thirty-two years old. As he spoke, his hands nervously twirled the wheel.

The life of a smuggler was hard. Mikhail had to face inclement weather, poor roads, the lack of gasoline along the way—and bandits. Parts of southern Russia and western Ukraine were patrolled by armed men who preyed on travelers like the highwaymen of czarist times. The practice had become so common that few commercial drivers ventured on the highways of the old Soviet Union without extra money, a spare carton of cigarettes, or a bottle of vodka to pay a "toll" to the local lords of the road. On one of his trips, Mikhail was forced to stop on a deserted stretch of highway between the cities of Belgorod and Kharkiv. Two cars were parked in the center of the road. As he waited in his van, men carrying machine guns emerged from the cars and rapped on his window. No words were exchanged. He handed over two bottles of vodka, and at a signal the cars separated to let him pass.

There were other human obstacles besides highwaymen. On a normal journey, he could be stopped as many as fifty times at militia posts outside large towns by policemen whose curiosity was aroused by his

Moscow license plates. They would ask to examine his van. Mikhail knew what they were after.

"Look," he would say. "You're doing your job, I'm doing my job. We both have to live."

The militiaman would smile knowingly—and wait until Mikhail had pulled a ten-dollar bill from the glove compartment, stepped out of the van, and shook his hand. When Mikhail returned, the ten-dollar bill was gone.

He carried several hundred dollars for each trip. Sometimes a highwayman would refuse the vodka bottle or cigarettes, and Mikhail would have to part with more of his stash of bills. The bribery never fazed him. The money wasn't really his, and as long as his highway encounters remained peaceful, he felt secure. He knew that none of the predators would touch the cargo he carried in his van. Although it was worth far more than any of the tolls he paid on the road, the ikons were useless to the bandit or policeman hungry for quick profits.

It took two or three days for an average journey. Mikhail slept in the homes of people he had met in different cities during his career, people who would be discreet and helpful in return for some of the dollars in his glove compartment. An art smuggler was only as good as his contacts along the road, and Mikhail had one of the best networks in the business.

The best part came when the trip was nearly over, and Mikhail's van was negotiating the winding turns of the Transcarpathian countryside in western Ukraine. In the spring, the drive through those weathered mountains was one of the loveliest on the Eurasian continent. The road climbed through forests of oak and beech toward the subalpine meadows. If he decided to hurry, he could reach the Ukrainian border town of Chop before noon, in time for a good spot in the line of cars and coaches waiting to pass international customs inspection for entry into Hungary.

Here, Mikhail would earn the high fees he was paid by the men who ran the country's art-smuggling trade. As he approached the customs post, he would keep his eye out for tourist buses. On any day of the week, there were usually several lumbering to a stop ahead of him.

It had been a long time since any of those buses carried tourists. Black-market traders hoping to sell cigarettes, vodka, or fruit in the small towns on the Polish, Hungarian, and Slovak borders had long since replaced the Soviet factory workers heading for a holiday in one of the "sister" lands of socialism.

Mikhail would stop his van and walk up to the closest coach. Sometimes the driver would know him, making his job easier. But it took only one hundred-dollar-bill to persuade a new face to accept the box of ikons from Mikhail's van. While the passengers stretched their legs outside, the driver would help Mikhail load the box into the cargo compartment, along with the bundles of produce and cheap goods headed across the border. The compartment was usually safe, but if word filtered through the queue that the customs guards were "curious" that day, a good driver could always find special nooks for valuable cargo.

Mikhail would follow the coach through the international border. To some of the customs and immigration inspectors, he is a familiar face. He has told them that he is a businessman looking for deals in Hungary. Usually, they wave him by without a word, but sometimes he stops to share in the griping about rising prices and corrupt politicians. At dusk, he would drive slowly until he caught sight of the coach parked near a restaurant on the side of the road, where the passengers had stopped for dinner. The smiling driver would be waiting for him outside, and together they would carry the box back to Mikhail's van. Sometimes, he would enter the restaurant and reward himself with a good meal.

But more often, he would be back on the highway at once, driving fast through the flat, pleasant countryside of Hungary. For the first time in his journey, the knot in Mikhail's stomach would be gone. He would be in Budapest that evening, and after delivering his cargo to the "businessmen" who were impatiently waiting for it, he would head off for dinner and a refreshing sleep in a luxurious hotel. While he slept, the shipment of art and ikons would be repacked in crates for another, and much easier, journey to an art collector in Europe, Asia, or the United States.

The next day, Mikhail would head home to his wife and young child with as much as one thousand dollars in cash. And Russia would have lost another small portion of its artistic heritage.

Even in the dim light of the car, I sensed both pride and defensiveness in Mikhail. He conceded to occasional twinges of conscience about his participation in the cultural robbery of his country.

"Once, God punished me, because, after all, I guess we are doing something which is sinful," he said in a soft voice. "I had an accident one winter on the roads before Lviv, which are normally pretty bad anyway. I was traveling with no lights, and my van hit a stretch of ice and overturned. It fell on the side that contained the ikons, under the paneling of the bus. I wasn't really hurt, but the stuff was damaged." He gave a sad shake of his head. "Yes," he said. "It was God who punished me."

But momentary guilt did not prevent the young dentist from enjoying his ability to survive in the chaos of post-Communist Russia. He was the perfect *muzhik*, the earthy Russian peasant, who used courage and cunning to get along. Mikhail first began working as a "courier" with a small network of friends in 1991. It was the ideal moment to join the trade. With the collapse of Communism, art smugglers like Mikhail were able, in effect, to privatize one of the oldest state criminal monopolies.

During the Soviet era, the illegal export of cultural valuables was controlled by government officials, who invested the wealth they earned in bribes in the purchase of stolen ikons and antiques. The business was as old as the Bolshevik revolution. The commissars operated a thriving market in relics of the religion they had contemptuously banned. The painted ikonic figures of saints, revered for centuries as talismans, found a ready market among art lovers abroad. By the 1960s, according to the estimates of police experts, at least a fifth of the art sold in the Latin Quarter of Paris came from the Soviet Union. According to police figures, more than 90 percent of Russia's ikons have disappeared abroad since 1916. Officially, the Soviet government maintained strict controls on its art heritage. But an inventory at the world-renowned Hermitage Museum in St. Petersburg in 1993 revealed that almost twenty thousand priceless articles, including unique cut-glass chandeliers, Gobelin tapestries, rare china pieces, silver vases, and paintings by old masters, were missing. Most of the items, the museum believed, had been taken years before the Soviet collapse.[10]

Arkady Vaksberg, in his classic account of the Soviet bureaucratic mafiya, described the art trade as a conveyor belt run by Soviet diplomats and the KGB that linked collectors in Europe with the remotest Russian villages. Members of government delegations reportedly smuggled Russian art abroad in order to pay for official receptions. And most villages in Russia received visits from official plunderers.[11]

"In those days, a car would drive up to our village with fake or blacked-out number plates, and with two or three people inside," re-called Father Mikhail Ardov, who served for many years in a tiny Russian Orthodox parish near Moscow.

"The first place they headed was the streets where the town's drunks could always be found. The car would stop, someone would get out with a dozen bottles of vodka and say, 'If you want this, go find us some ikons.' The drunkards, of course, knew where everything was. And they knew which old woman had just left her house to go to the market, and because they were local people, they knew where she hid her key. In the 1980s, ikons were constantly disappearing from our homes." [12]

Father Ardov had no doubt that the only "art lovers" who had the authority to obtain fake license plates at the time were the "authorities" themselves. "My guess is that they were connected to the security organs," he said.

The breakdown of law enforcement and the promise of easy money after the fall of the regime turned art smuggling into one of the most democratically inclusive forms of post-Soviet crime. Shopworkers, students, farmers, and even villagers themselves thrived on the trade. Artists raided churches and museums in Siberia for antique religious carvings they could sell to finance their own work, and businessmen slipped ikons into their luggage to help smooth negotiations with their partners abroad.

But it was only a matter of time before "professionals" enlarged their interests beyond art. Between July and December, 1992, Russian border police intercepted trucks and cars carrying a total of 1.5 million tons of oil and petroleum products, 77,000 tons of metal, 43,800 cubic meters of forest and timber materials, and 2.4 billion rubles' worth of industrial chemical products. The enormous traffic left no doubt that sophisticated, organized criminal groups had entered the business. According to a police report in late 1992, more than two hundred gangs with ties across the Commonwealth and to Europe and America were involved in the smuggling of gems, precious metals, and petroleum. "There is a well-regulated system of acquiring and transporting strategic raw materials and other licensed goods and products from Russia overseas," the police concluded.[13]

Within a few years, the art smugglers' field of wonders had become a severely restricted pathway. When I met Mikhail, neither of us needed to mention the reason he could not let me see his face. If the crime bosses who controlled the art smuggling trade ever learned he had talked to me, his wife would soon be a widow.

Mikhail had become a small cog in an immense criminal machine. According to the Supreme Soviet Commission on Culture, more than five thousand priceless art objects were stolen from museums, exhibition halls, churches and art galleries in 1992 and are presumed to have been smuggled out of the country. In 1993, art thefts went up by a startling 848 percent. The Russian Ministry of Internal Affairs considered the "illegal export" of cultural valuables one of the largest sources of income for the post-Soviet criminal world. The trade brought in an estimated thirty million dollars a year.[14]

According to the Russian Ministry of Internal Affairs, forty groups in Western Europe were involved in art smuggling from Russia, most of them run by emigre Russian citizens. They serviced a sprawling network of five hundred shops in Berlin, Frankfurt, Rome, and Milan. Inside Russia, they had an equally complex network of scouts, buyers, and couriers like Mikhail.[15]

Mikhail had been working long enough to consider himself a professional. "I know more or less what things are worth," he assured me. "And I always make sure that I know what I'm carrying. I can date some of the artwork by century and by the style of painting. I might even know the name of the ikon. It's my business to understand value."

The goods were usually delivered to him by unofficial brokers called *perekupshchiki*. In the smuggling syndicates, the brokers collected the artwork from museums, galleries, and homes after they were stolen by small gangs around the country—sometimes to specific orders from abroad.

"Occasionally you get a customer abroad who knows exactly what he wants and makes an order for it," said Mikhail. "But unless it's something so valuable that it can't be held long in the country, we wait until there's a decent haul, and all the arrangements are made for collection abroad before we plan a trip."

Mikhail charged 10 percent of the total value of every load carried. He was paid half before he left and the rest when he successfully brought the goods across. Like any professional craftsman, he still had pride in his work.

"If you know what you're doing, you can take anything out of Russia," he told me. "The borders are like a sieve."   He couldn't resist boasting, "I could even take *you* through the border without any documents."

I heard a similar boast from another young man I met a few days later on a crowded street in central Moscow. He was similar to Mikhail in several respects. He refused to tell me his full name—"Call me Borisovich," he said, as I slipped into a car beside him—and he had also become rich by funneling goods across the unguarded borders of the former Soviet republics. But whereas Mikhail had only plundered his country's past, Borisovich was destroying its future. His commodity of choice was drugs.

In the late 1980s, Borisovich was a student at the Moscow Institute of Engineering and Construction, struggling to support a wife and new baby, and impatient to leave his mark in the world. He was already making a modest living on the side as a *fartsovshchik*—a black-market peddler of jeans, T-shirts and pirated American records. But he was ambitious. Dropping out of school, he took his little family on an extended holiday to the Black Sea. He hoped to find a better market for his goods in the freer atmosphere of Russia's resort region.

He raised the capital for his new venture by pawning his parents' jewelry. "I was sure I could earn enough to get the stuff back before they noticed," he told me. It didn't happen. When Borisovich returned to Moscow, poorer and considerably disillusioned, one of his old student acquaintances tried to comfort him. As they shared a marijuana joint one evening, the friend told him that drug dealing was the business of the future.[16]

"He said anyone could do it," Borisovich recalled. "I saw how much money he was making at the same thing, and I thought, why not?"

It was 1989. The changes in Russian society were having a profound impact on the young—but not quite in the way their elders hoped. While idealistic reformers in their thirties and forties marched for democracy, the Russian twenty-somethings opted out of politics. The children of perestroika were sharply cynical about the reforms that excited their parents. People in their thirties and forties far outnumbered younger people in the crowds cheering on the reformers and democratic activists of the late 1980s. I often encountered skeptical or hostile looks from young Russians whose opinions I sought about political events. Most were convinced that politics was irrelevant to their lives. Their older brothers and cousins, who had returned angry and scarred from the Afghan War, only further confirmed their desire to be left alone by anyone in authority, whether democrat or Communist.[17]

Drugs, along with Western music and videos, provided an outlet from the crushing hypocrisy of the system. Hashish and marijuana were already beginning to circulate in underground youth clubs. The Afghan veterans also came back with new drugs, including *mak,* a weak opium derivative created from poppy straw and used extensively in Afghanistan and Central Asia. "To tell you the truth," said Borisovich. "Drugs were the only thing that made our lives interesting."

Borisovich had found what was for him an ideal occupation—one that combined the thrill of upsetting the prudishness of Soviet society with the lure of profit. And he discovered that he had a natural aptitude for business management.

He located a source of supply in fields outside Moscow, where the *maslichny mak,* or oily poppy, grew wild, and recruited local women and young men willing to harvest the plant for a few rubles. The goods were dried and prepared by Borisovich at home, with several of his friends. At first, he supplied small quantities to his circle of rock musicians, students, and artists. A glassful sold for only ten rubles (or about eighteen dollars) in 1990. Two years later, the market price had kept pace with Russia's astronomical inflation rate. A glass of poppy straw was selling for four thousand rubles in 1992 (about twenty dollars).

After the Soviet collapse, however, increased sales helped Borisovich find his own field of wonders. He transformed himself from a freewheeling merchant of oblivion to the Soviet counterculture into a narcocapitalist. Expanding his area of operations to Kharkiv, in Ukraine, where friends had located likely fields and willing farmers, the onetime university dropout became the boss of a sophisticated smuggling network. Instead of a few agreeable farmers, he now had a network of villages funneling a regular supply of opium to his headquarters in the capital. Hundreds of people depended upon him for their livelihood, including local villagers who harvested his private plantations, assistants in Moscow who prepared the plants for use, and students who delivered the final product to "retailers" around the city. He traveled in style to oversee his far-flung operations, making regular "business trips" to inspect his fields in the spring and returning for the harvest at the end of the summer.

"I can come and go any time I want," he bragged, "No one bothers me."

The year I met him, he had sold twenty kilograms of poppy straw at fifty thousand rubles a kilogram to his dealers, giving him a gross profit of one million rubles. After paying off his various employees, he was not quite a millionaire. But he expected the price to double in the next harvest, as demand outpaced supply. A million rubles was worth only about two thousand dollars at the prevailing rate, but he already earned enough to give him a lifestyle beyond the imagination of most of his compatriots.

Borisovich was no more than thirty years old, and he would have looked even younger without the few days' growth of blond stubble on his cheeks. We shook hands when we met. His fingers were as soft as a child's, and when he extended his wrist, a gold Rolex watch jangled loosely. He had pulled a toque over his ears—to protect himself, I supposed, from easy identification—and he wore a long gray overcoat with the insignia of the old East German border guards, "Grenz Truppen der DDR."

Borisovich considered himself an instrument for healing his country's spiritual sickness. "Drugs are one of the best inventions of mankind," he assured me, with the missionary fervor that used to be associated with the drug culture in the West during the 1960s. "I don't agree with those who say drugs are terrible. If they started selling drugs at every corner, it wouldn't be such a bad thing."

I asked him how he felt about reports that youngsters as young as thirteen were taking drugs.[18]

Borisovich frowned. "I am a person of moral principles, and there are certain things I will not do, like selling drugs to kids."

"But what would you do," I asked, "if someone tried to sell drugs to your son at school?"

"That would not be pleasant," he said, pronouncing each word slowly. "I would personally deal with anybody who did that. But look, if I find drugs in my son's pocket when he's seventeen or twenty, I'm not going to hit him with a strap. That would be hypocritical. It's his affair. I don't know any drug addicts who are bad people, or criminals. At least, they are not more likely to be criminals than someone who never uses drugs."

Later, I looked up the statistics. In 1991, police recorded twenty-nine thousand drug-related crimes in Russia. By 1992, according to police, 60 percent of property crimes in some regions were committed by addicts, and nearly 40 percent of the violent crimes in Moscow were ascribed to drug users. Crime related to narcotics use was not yet at the plague levels reached in some cities in North America, but this was an indication of a serious transformation in Russian society. Just twenty-four drug-related crimes were reported for all of Russia in 1964; twenty years later, the figure had increased to a modest 320.[19]

Statistics were unlikely to alter Borisovich's point of view. Having recently rediscovered his roots in the Russian Orthodox faith, he even managed to find heavenly reinforcement for his business. "Religion is now at the center of my world view," he said. "I don't go to church every Sunday, but it is a deep conviction with me."

If Borisovich really believed his own homilies, he was tragically deceiving himself about the nature of his enterprise   which was making its own special contribution to the sabotage of Russia's fledgling democracy. But he was not quite as ingenuous as he liked to appear. As we chatted, he kept glancing out the window, and frowning.

"We could drive somewhere else," I suggested.

"No, no," said Borisovich. "I wanted to meet you near my home. I am expecting a few telephone calls, and my cellular phone isn't working."

"Is there no one else at home to take the calls?" I said.

"My wife," he said, with a dismissive gesture. He explained that she was too busy with their seven-year-old son to answer a ringing telephone. "Besides, she wouldn't know what to say."

"Does your wife know about your business?"

Borisovich picked some lint from his coat and smiled. "She knows I go off on a lot of trips," he said, "and she knows that these days all entrepreneurs have to travel. So she thinks I'm a kind of cooperative businessman. I tell her I buy precious stones and gold. And then she says, well, where is her gold?" He chuckled. "So I buy her some."

"Why don't you tell her the truth?"

He looked curiously at me. "What's the point?" And then he added, "I don't want to worry her."

When I asked him whether she had reason to worry, considering what he did for a living, he laughed.

"I am a cautious person by nature," he insisted. "And now that I am with the *organizatsiya,* things are safer."

The "organization" was the key to Borisovich's prosperity, and it was the gun—whether he was prepared to recognize it as such or not—aimed at his heart.

Borisovich admitted that he worked for one of the Chechen gangs.

"They found me through some of my dealers," he said. "I was really impressed with them. They were very polite and businesslike. They told me if I wanted to continue what I was doing, I needed to have them as partners. They didn't make any threats, but obviously if I refused, there would be trouble."

Borisovich sighed. "I didn't even think twice about joining them," he said. "Usually, it's the Azeris who are involved in drugs, but the Chechens are so powerful they even take tribute from the Azeris. And they have been very good to me. It's better that I'm with them."

"A lot of people are afraid of the Chechens," he went on. "But they are very good people when you get to know them. They are loyal. They don't double-cross you, and they are honest people. I even call some of them my friends now. We go out to restaurants together and have great times. If I told them tomorrow that I wanted to stop what I was doing and take up music, they would say, fine, go ahead and do your music."

Like an addict boasting of his ability to kick the habit, Borisovich said he could quit at any time. But things were going too well. "You have no idea how big a market Moscow is becoming," he boasted. "Practically all the young people, all the vocational school students, want drugs. No matter how much I bring in, my dealers keep telling me they need more."

It was easy to predict that Borisovich would become expendable as the profits of the Russian narcotics market continued to increase. For the moment, the Chechens were content to keep their young branch manager, but their record of loyalty to associates was not encouraging. Borisovich confessed that he handed over 10 percent of his crop, either in cash or kind, to his Chechen patrons.

"The *organizatsiya* is getting bigger every day," he said. "You can see them in their cars—the latest models of Mercedes, BMWs—all without license plates. They don't worry about the police. They can do anything. If I needed a driver's license, tomorrow they would bring me a new license. If I needed legal help, or someone to fix a problem with my apartment, they could help out, too. They are really serious people. I'm convinced they are the masters here. Not the politicians, or the deputies."

Borisovich already had sufficient proof of his friends' power. When a Moscow militiaman began asking questions about his source of income, a word to his Chechen colleagues ensured that the policeman would never return. The young dealer actually seemed to relish his connection with the gangland way of life.

"I once was visited by two guys who claimed I owed them money," Borisovich recalled. "I told them, 'Listen guys, I don't have any money now. Come back in three days.' Then I called the Chechens and described these people. I don't know what happened to them, but I never saw them again." Perhaps the drug smuggler realized that the same thing could happen to him one day, but it was hard to penetrate his breezy confidence. He appeared to believe that under the benevolent protection of the syndicate, he could go on earning money indefinitely.

Mikhail, on the other hand, was beginning to have second thoughts. Corporate-sized smuggling syndicates had turned life on the road into something less than an adventure.

"It used to be much safer," he admitted. "When I started, everyone knew everyone else on the road. Now there are lots of people I don't recognize, and I don't like the looks of them. People in the art trade are civilized people, but the people who deal in gems and metals or drugs are very different. They are gangsters."

The change in atmosphere had already convinced Mikhail, as he put it, to "retire." He had saved enough of his smuggling profits to buy equipment for one room of the apartment he planned to use as his dental clinic. "I need to think about my future," he told me seriously.

No such concern ruffled Borisovich's cool exterior.

"I'm the kind of person who lives for today," the drug dealer declared. "I don't care about what happens next year."

The contrast between the two young men was perhaps a matter of degree, but at least Mikhail seemed to understand that it was time to end his flirtation with criminality. Borisovich, on the other hand, was a willing recruit to the darker and more destructive criminal forces that were beginning to envelop his country.

12 *Narco-Bizness*

In February, 1993, customs officials in Vyborg, a Russian city on the border with Finland, broke open a large container labeled "Meat and Potatoes," which was addressed to a commercial importing firm in St. Petersburg. They found twenty canisters stuffed with Colombian cocaine. The entire shipment weighed nearly a ton, making it among the largest single hauls of cocaine anywhere in the world. Yet St. Petersburg seemed a surprising destination: it would take years for the small number of cocaine addicts in Russia to consume such a large amount. Investigators guessed that its final destination was Western Europe, where it would have a street value of two hundred million dollars.[1]

There was a tragic inevitability about the incident in Vyborg. Soon after the breakup of the Soviet Union, police around the world detected signs that international drug cartels were focusing on Eurasia as a new transit corridor. More than fifty tons of narcotics from Central Asia destined for Western Europe were seized by Russian police in 1993. Emissaries from the Medellín cartel had already been observed in the Russian capital. In the fall of 1992, Czech police broke up a drug ring in Prague and arrested a Colombian citizen named José Duran, who was said to be in the process of negotiating a deal with Italian and East European mobsters to market cocaine in Western Europe. It seemed only a matter of time before the Colombian syndicates took advantage of the porous borders and frontier mentality of the former Soviet Union.[2]

But no one could have predicted the extent to which enterprising former Soviet citizens would insinuate themselves into the front ranks of the global narcotics industry. The Eurasian shift in the global trade came to fuel a substantial part of post-Soviet Russia's prosperity. "We estimate that 40 percent of the movement of capital in Russia is now linked with narcotics," said Col. Valentin Roshchin, who led the Moscow Police's Anti-Drug Squad until he was promoted to a senior post in the criminal-investigation division in 1993. "Organized criminals abroad have discovered how easy it is to launder drug profits through businesses and banks here."[3]

Efforts to uncover the connection between international drug syndicates and Russian mobsters have been frustrated by the involvement of officials at senior levels of the Russian government, said Inspector Vladimir Kalinichenko. The inspector pursued a case in 1992 that linked a Pakistani businessman suspected of acting as a front for Italian narcotics traffickers with a Russian gang. The businessman's name also turned up as one of the founders of a trust fund in Switzerland. When the investigators tracked the man's movements, they discovered that he was having regular meetings with a deputy minister in the Russian government. "That's where we had to stop," Kalinichenko grumbled, hinting at high-level intervention. "We weren't allowed to go any further." [4]

Roshchin confirmed that the Russian mafiya was becoming one of the most valuable players in international drug dealing. "The Colombians would never have shipped their cocaine to St. Petersburg unless they were confident that a strong Russian network was there to assist them."

I met Roshchin on a chilly spring day in 1993. He had escaped briefly from a session of the Russian parliament, where rising crime was again at the top of the agenda. Along with other top police officials, he was required to attend the sitting in case legislators wanted information. But no one asked him any questions. He found that typical.

"Our legislators don't have the faintest idea what's going on," fumed Roshchin, whose face showed traces of Tatar ancestry. "While they sleep, drugs and drug money are destroying us."

Yet just a few years earlier, the idea of a narcotics industry in Russia was beyond anyone's imagination. Drug abuse barely figured among the principal social problems of the Soviet Union. Strict control over borders and a repressive police apparatus kept much of the sprawling Soviet land mass out of bounds to foreign drug merchants. But it was a problem waiting to happen. Once the barriers between Russia and the rest of the world fell, the market principles of supply and demand did the rest.

On the supply side, the old Soviet Union was an extraordinarily rich, untapped source of raw materials for the drug trade. An estimated one million hectares of cannabis grew wild in Russia alone. Central Asia and parts of Trans-Caucasia were home to enormous fields of opium poppies. There were reports that hemp was being cultivated as far north as Yakutia, which stretches into the Arctic Circle, and in the lands of the Russian Far East.

The infrastructure—or lack of it—left behind by the former Soviet regime made Russia one of the world's most attractive financial centers for crime. The disintegration of the central banking system made it easy for drug traffickers to find safe havens for their money. The Russian government possessed only a rudimentary ability to regulate the movement of capital in and out of the country, and the new private and commercial banks were able to launder huge amounts of criminal profits without fear of monitoring by officials.

Russia fulfilled seventeen of the twenty-two conditions on a hypothetical "money launderers' shopping list" drawn up in 1994 by the U.S. State Department's Bureau of International Narcotics Matters. The lack of effective bank regulations made Russia a dream location for the post–Cold War global criminal.[5]

Until 1994, any Russian with one hundred thousand dollars could open a banking institution. The required starting capital was later raised to about 1.2 million dollars, but by then drug profits provided enough funds to get around this obstacle. The Soviet highway, air, and rail grid that connected nearly every corner of the Eurasian continent gave Russian traffickers a sophisticated transportation network unavailable to their third-world counterparts in the jungles of Peru and the poppy fields of Asia. And as dealers like Borisovich discovered, the collapse of Communism opened a potentially giant market at home.

The Soviet Union used to claim smugly—but correctly—that it had avoided the drug epidemic sweeping the capitalist nations of the West. Needless to say, the puritanical commissars had little patience for any kind of opiate that would distract from the revolution—it was hardly a coincidence that religion was equated with opium as a subversive agent—and they took draconian measures against addicts during the early years of Soviet power, including forced incarceration and corporal punishment. The principal drug of Soviet society was alcohol, followed closely by cigarettes (modern Russia has one of the highest percentage of cigarette smokers in the world), but the increase in reported addiction cases following the second Russian revolution was nothing short of remarkable.

It was as if the breakdown of the authoritarian system released former Soviet citizens from the final taboo. In a survey taken by the Russian Ministry of Education in late 1992, 1.5 million Russians admitted using some form of narcotics at least once a month. This was low by world standards; yet just three years earlier, only 130,000 chronic drug users were registered. Although Soviet statistics are notoriously unreliable, this figure seems a reflection of reality. Soviet police and the KGB effectively sealed off the country from the international drug trade. The collapse of the Soviet system and the widespread corruption of law enforcement agencies and bureaucrats has dramatically changed the landscape. Russian medical specialists have predicted as many as 7.5 million drug addicts before the middle of the decade.[6]

"Drug use is spreading, especially among young people, even the fifteen- to sixteen-year olds," admitted Igor Chenikh, who runs Addiction Clinic No. 17 in Moscow. According to the education ministry survey, 70 percent of those admitting to regular drug use were under thirty—and nearly 9 percent were under eighteen. "And, unfortunately, it's easy to predict it will increase," Chenikh continued. "I blame the lack of stability in the country." [7] Fifty-four percent of drug users in the survey were unemployed.

General Aleksandr Sergeyev, head of the MVD's Division for the Control of Drugs, said that the survey probably underestimated the actual figure. "There has been a dramatic 'narcotization' of the population over the last two years," he told reporters at a press conference in Moscow in May, 1993. "I believe that a lot of people would not admit to using drugs even in an anonymous questionnaire. The psychology [from the old regime] hasn't changed all that much, and many Russians haven't realized that drug use is no longer a criminal offense." [8]

This was the most ironic factor contributing to the rise of the Russian narcotics business. In an attempt to respond to international human rights concerns, the Soviet parliament, in one of its last acts in December, 1993, removed criminal penalties for drug use. Until then, anyone caught taking a narcotic substance faced up to fifteen years' hard labor in penal colonies. Oddly, the possession of drugs remained technically illegal, but under the law it incurred only "administrative punishment," which usually meant fines if the quantities were small. The sale and transport of narcotics continued to be a criminal violation. But the legislators' attempt to "humanize" the law effectively expanded the potential market for professional drug traffickers.[9]

By 1992, a Muscovite could find drugs at any farmers' market. Opium straw and marijuana were available by the "glass."

"All you need to do is walk around inside one of the markets until somebody approaches you," a sixteen-year-old Moscow opium addict named Sergei Basurin told me. "The sellers always change, so you can't identify them later. They bring you over to where a crowd of guys are, and you give them the money. It's easy."

Dozens of sidewalk cafes offered *anasha,* or hashish, for sale in tiny matchboxes. Amphetamines and other synthetic drugs were available to wealthier customers with a telephone call to certain Moscow hotels.

The Moscow drug squad, the country's largest, expanded from eight to thirty-five detectives in 1992, but it could not cope with the problem. "The growth of drugs on the street is frightening," recalled Roshchin. "In the old days, we would seize a few grams of marijuana or hashish at a time; it would be amazing to pick up a kilogram. But we're starting to confiscate hundreds of kilograms."

Drugs became the second most profitable post-Soviet commodity, after stolen guns. According to one police estimate, every ruble invested in *narco-bizness* earned a profit of one thousand rubles. In early 1993, the income from the production and sale of opium, hashish, and synthetic drugs was estimated at more than sixty billion rubles (about 120 million dollars) a year, and several hundred thousand people were employed at every step of the drug chain, from the cultivation and processing of narcotics to its transport and distribution.[10]

The new drug trade efficiently employed the entire territory once encompassed by the Soviet Union. Nearly half of the twenty-two tons of drugs seized in Russia in 1992 were "imported" from other former Soviet republics. Opium grown in remote, fertile river valleys on the borders of Kazakhstan and Kyrgyzstan, an area that both foreign and domestic narcotics experts have equated with the "golden triangle" in Southeast Asia, was sent to laboratories in Baku for processing and then shipped thousands of miles north to dealers in Russian cities. Trains left Moscow every night with dried hemp bound for Riga and other Baltic ports, where the produce was shipped onward to Scandinavia and Germany. Poppy straw grown in western Ukraine and Lithuania turned up in secret military airfields near Kaliningrad on the Baltic coast, from where it was flown south to Poland. And *khimka,* a south Manchurian hemp product cultivated on more than 3.7 million acres in the Maritime and Khabarovsk regions—the once-closed border zones of the Pacific coast—crossed the continent by air and rail to Siberia and Central Russia, or was shipped out on cargo boats and fishing trawlers to Japan and Australia.[11]

In the process, the drug industry has become a significant factor in local politics. According to police and researchers, the cultivation of hemp in the Russian Far East and Pacific saved the local economy from collapse. Collective farms in regions such as Khabarovsk negotiated formal contracts with drug syndicates for the delivery of hemp seeds. In the Central Asian nation of Uzbekistan, where one acre of opium poppies was fifty times more valuable than one acre of cotton, largely because of the artificially depressed prices imposed by Soviet agricultural overlords, rural farmers took advantage of the irrigation systems built during the Stalin and Khrushchev eras.

They were naturally reluctant to give up their windfall. When police appeared at one cooperative farm in a remote area of the country and began to burn opium fields, they were confronted by a delegation of concerned farmers.

"If you pay us the salaries that the state has owed us for seven months, we'll destroy the fields ourselves," the village spokesman said.

The officer leading the raid was unmoved. "They haven't paid *me* for three months," he snapped.[12]

But there were few such examples of police conscientiousness. Law enforcement authorities in Azerbaijan and Central Asia rarely bothered to reply to requests from Russia for the extradition of known drug lords. Frustrated Russian police blamed their problems on the "liberal" political climate created by the new drug laws, on Western influence, and in particular on the gangs from the Caucasus region, who they said controlled 80 percent of the drug traffic in the Russian Federation.

The syndicates based in Azerbaijan and Chechnya were easy to single out as scapegoats. According to police, there were more than fifteen thousand Azeri gang members in Moscow, of whom a large proportion were involved in managing the city's narcotics trade. Behind such accusations, however, lay old Russian prejudices.

"You do not see Georgians or Armenians getting involved in drugs," insisted Roshchin. "Those people are Christians, and Christians are superior in culture and morality to the Muslims, who are too lazy to get involved in anything else."

In fact, the early hold of the Azeri and Chechen gangs on the drug trade came about by default. The Russian *vory,* like the traditional mafiya dons of Sicily and the United States, at first kept themselves contemptuously aloof from *narco-bizness.* The thieves' code banned traffic in drugs.

Inevitably, the potential profits from drug trafficking made many of the new crime lords restless. A proposal to break the Caucasian gangs' monopoly over the narcotics trade was on the agenda of the December, 1991, meeting of *vory* outside Moscow. It set off an internal struggle that recalled the Scabs War between returning veterans and their old criminal comrades across Soviet prisons in the 1950s.

When a young Moscow gangster named Emil was arrested for drug dealing in 1992, a senior *vor* named Valeri Dlukach, who operated under the name Globus, circulated a letter to prisons around the country demanding his removal from the mob hierarchy. "Anyone who deals in drugs cannot be a leader in the *vorovskoi mir,*" he declared in the letter. For good measure, Globus added the names of three of Emil's allies in the criminal fraternity, including several middle-ranking *vory.* All, he said, had broken tradition and no longer deserved the *vor*'s crown.

But Globus's attempt to steer the crime world back to its traditions proved fatal. Two weeks after he sent the letter, the mobster was shot dead while leaving a popular Moscow discotheque. Witnesses told police that they saw four men fleeing in a late-model Lincoln automobile. By the end of 1993, at least eight of the leading Thieves-in-Law of Russia had been murdered.

"In the past, the drug gangs were small and fragmented," said Lt. Col. Vladimir Khairedinov, who took over Roshchin's post as head of the Moscow Drug Squad. "They were in permanent competition. But it's not true any longer." [13]

Khairedinov, of Azeri origin, did not share his predecessor's prejudice against Muslim Caucasians. He said that the Moscow drug world was run by four syndicates—two of them dominated by Russians. "We believe all the groups are in turn subordinate to one top leader, who is a commercial businessman."

In St. Petersburg, Russia's second city, the drug trade has led to a similar consolidation of mob power. "Drug dealers are a new breed here," a police undercover agent named Kolya told a Western reporter. "They're armed, wealthy, and extremely dangerous. But they're impossible to prosecute." [14]

The post-Soviet drug industry could never have reached its remarkable level of profit so quickly without the close involvement of "civilians." Corrupt bureaucrats, law enforcement authorities, and customs officials ensured that the drug network remained largely free of interference. A senior Russian customs official was interviewed by police during the investigation of the Vyborg cocaine haul, after some of his subordinates suggested that he had applied "pressure" on them to pass the shipment without inspection. But the official was never charged. Police explained that even if the accusation were true, there was no evidence that he knew what was inside the canisters.

It was a lame excuse. Few sectors of Russian society have been left untouched by the narcotics trade. Directors of military-industrial plants provide facilities for the clandestine laboratories that make synthetic drugs and trucks for shipping them. Private bankers accept deposits from known drug profiteers without asking difficult questions; commercial managers eagerly take their investments. Meanwhile, *narco-bizness* is attracting some of the best research minds of the younger generation.

In early 1993, the rector of the Moscow Institute of Chemical Technology was handed a paper documenting the scientific work of four young prisoners. He was impressed. "If you free them immediately," he joked to police, "I'll award them all doctorates in chemistry and put them to work at my institute."

There was little chance of that happening. A year earlier, the four prisoners, all under thirty, had been chemistry students at the leading science college of Kazan, capital of the Russian autonomous province of Tatarstan. They were regarded by their teachers and fellow students as the most brilliant in their class—so brilliant, in fact, that they soon grew bored with their formal studies. Working in the school laboratory after hours, they produced an extraordinary drug. It was a dry white powder several times more potent than heroin and almost impossible to detect when mixed with water. The drug was trimethyl phentanyl, often called "3MF" by Russians.[15]

What began as a student lark became a thriving criminal enterprise. Their work came to the attention of Moscow gangland figures, who offered them a contract for as much of the drug as they could produce. Soon, the university laboratory became part of an intricate drug chain. The students themselves brought their work to Moscow, whence the drug was transported to secret refining labs in Azerbaijan. There, it was mixed with distilled water and processed into five-milliliter capsules. Thousands of the tiny capsules were soon making their way around Russia. Selling for five thousand rubles a capsule, 3MF was the drug of choice for the elite by 1992. It was eagerly consumed by the country's new millionaires, athletes, rock musicians, politicians—and even discriminating gangsters.

In late 1992, several dozen mobsters gathered at a swank restaurant in Moscow to honor a member of the criminal fraternity who had died of natural causes in Germany, where he had controlled a smuggling ring. He was given an elaborate funeral in Moscow and, in the standard gangland tradition, the leaders of Moscow's *vorovskoi mir* went to the restaurant wake for a feast. They sat at tables spread with dishes of black caviar and fresh salads. Hundreds of bottles of vodka, champagne, and Armenian cognac moved them to sentimental toasts.

"Around this room, we have gathered the very best people of our brotherhood," said one *vor,* who shakily raised his glass toward the end of the evening, as one informer later told police. "But it is a great shame that the majority of us are seriously addicted."

When he spoke, the room was already half-empty. Most of the party were in the toilets taking 3MF.

The addiction of the gang world to its most profitable product was destroying its veneer of discipline. The Armenian, the crime boss I met in his hotel in south Moscow, admitted that he feared sending some members of his gang out on jobs because they were likely to be in too much of a stupor to aim a gun. "I would say that in the average [criminal] group in Moscow, seven out of every ten members take some form of drugs," he said, with thinly concealed disgust. "When these guys are high, you can't control them." [16]

When police followed the 3MF trail back to the student chemists, they were stunned. "These youngsters were real professionals, just like intelligence agents," said Col. Arkadi Kuznetsov, deputy head of the MVD's drug-control division. "It took us a long time to get them, because they eluded our surveillance. Once, they passed the powder to their business partners by throwing it through the closing door of a Moscow subway train to a contact waiting inside."

Kuznetsov displayed a grudging respect for his captives. "We put them in different detention cells when we finally got them," he recalled. "Within a couple of days, we got separate requests from each one, in neat handwriting, for scientific literature on chemical synthesis. They obviously wanted to perfect their knowledge."

The breakup of the student drug ring came too late. Moscow was being flooded with thousands of 3MF capsules a day, long after the young chemists went to prison. By then, their secret formula was guiding the work underground laboratories from Baku to Riga. The story of 3MF proved that the credit for Russia's drug boom belonged not just to domestic gangsters, bureaucrats, and scheming international drug lords. The children of the New Russia had earned the right to share in it.

Six months after the ton of Colombian cocaine was discovered at Vyborg, the trail had grown cold. Only one arrest had been reported. A Russian emigre with Israeli citizenship was detained when he arrived to claim the shipment. The Israeli, who worked for the St. Petersburg firm to which the shipment had been addressed, was released for lack of evidence tying him to the drugs. Police had managed to discover that the cargo was destined for the Netherlands. But at the end of 1994, the case had still not come to trial.

Although those responsible for arranging the Colombian "connection" eluded Russian law enforcement, police began finding evidence that foreign drug cartels were solidifying their business interests in Russia. Around the time of the Vyborg cocaine haul, Moscow detectives intervened in an attempt by a figure identified only as a "notorious international drug dealer" to open a Moscow hotel through dummy partners. In October, 1992, the Russian MVD similarly prevented an American "businessman" from participating in a joint venture after he was identified as the target of an American drug investigation. There was also evidence that European criminal syndicates were exchanging their drug profits for vouchers sold as part of Russia's privatization program. And drug money was reportedly used to purchase Russian raw materials, which were resold in Europe for profits that ended up in numbered Swiss bank accounts.[17]

Commercial firms and banks in Russia, hungry for investment, often provided cover for domestic and foreign drug tycoons. Vladimir Kalinichenko described one deal that he discovered in the early 1990s, in which a company owned by Russian emigres in Western Europe offered modern milk-production equipment at a discount to a dairy located in the Urals city of Chelyabinsk. In return, they proposed that the dairy set aside a certain amount of casein, a colorless liquid used for making glue.

"We can turn it into glue and export it to Germany," the representatives explained.[18]

The eager dairy managers saw nothing wrong with the idea, and they signed a contract. A few months later, Russian investigators arrived to close them down. The liquid they had carefully preserved for glue production at their partners' request had been mixed with powdered drugs from Central Asia by collaborators inside the plant. Diluted with water, the drugs indeed resembled a thick white glue. They were duly sent abroad in sealed boxes with customs certificates valuing the goods at one thousand dollars a ton. In Germany, however, each container had a street value of several million dollars.

The scam was discovered only after German police alerted their Russian counterparts. The Moscow Drug Squad's Vladimir Khairedinov, like his colleagues in every major Russian police agency, devoted more and more time to the exchange of information with police agencies in Europe and the United States. But foreign intelligence proved of little help in exposing and prosecuting the real godfathers of the Russian drug industry.

"When I was in England, Scotland Yard officials told me there were huge amounts of money being transferred to London bank accounts from Russia," said Khairedinov. "They know this is black-market money, drug money, and they cannot understand why the Russian government doesn't try to find out where the money comes from."

The Moscow policeman knew the answer, but he was too cautious to make it explicit to foreigners. In other former Soviet republics, the intimate connection between drug profits and government revenues was not hard to ascertain. Why should Russia be any different?

"Many officials in Central Asia have told us quite openly that they are going to go on developing plantations of hashish and opium," said Khairedinov. "They said there was no other way to improve their financial situation."

The focus on drug revenue, however, ignored one of the most insidious consequences of official reluctance to crack down on the narcotics industry. Drug dealers had become a factor in post-Soviet politics. In January, 1993, correspondents for *Rossiiskaya Gazeta* reported that narcotics trafficking had increased during the violent civil war between the government in Tajikistan and its opponents.

"The narco-mafiya is clearly benefiting from the war," the correspondents wrote. Opium from Afghanistan and Iran was flowing into southern Russia because of the inability or reluctance of Tajik government authorities to control their borders. Drugs imported into Tajikistan appeared the next day in the Kyrgyz capital of Bishkek, a few hundred miles to the north—and from there were taken by courier to Moscow. One implicit conclusion of the *Rossiiskaya Gazeta* report was that the drug mafiya worked with politicians across Central Asia to keep the trade flowing smoothly. Russian journalists, not for the first time, wondered whether civil unrest in troubled regions of Central Asia and the Caucasus was fueled in part by territorial quarrels between criminal groups.[19]

This was impossible to prove. But the contribution of the drug trade to the instability on Russia's frontiers was hard to dispute in at least one respect. Narcotics revenues were being used to buy the stolen and imported weapons employed in the ethnic wars. "We have seen plenty of examples where the profits from drug sales in Russia are used to buy Soviet Army weapons," said Khairedinov. "Then the weapons turn up in the conflict zones."

The relationship between drugs and politics was fueled, in other words, by post-Soviet Russia's biggest and most dangerous criminal industry: the illicit arms trade.

13 The Guns of Grozny

One evening in 1993, Moscow police were called to the sauna of a popular new sports complex in the capital. They were greeted with what was by then a familiar scene. The bullet-ridden corpses of two Moscow businessmen were lying on the floor. Blood was splattered on the walls. Frightened clients of the sauna had long since fled, and the manager had disappeared almost as soon as he led the police inside. Two submachine guns—one for each corpse—had been placed beside the bodies.

This wasn't carelessness on the part of the murderers. The guns were the standard calling cards of Russia's elite corps of contract killers. "Real professionals use each gun only once," noted *Moscow News,* in a study of post-Soviet gangland assassins. "If a killer is caught with the same pistol or submachine gun even a year or two after the murder, there will be no end to his trouble." [1]

Russia's murder rate continued to climb—according to police figures, one person was murdered every eighteen minutes somewhere in Russia in 1993—but there was an even more ominous increase in one special type of crime: gangland murder by contract.

Some 100 people were eliminated in professional mob assassinations across Russia in 1992. The following year, the number was 250. The evidence for a contract killing was always the same: the telltale gun left purposely beside the corpse. If that rate of increase continued, an observer might reasonably wonder whether the calling-card tradition would eat into the financial resources of Moscow's underworld. A standard Kalashnikov weapon, after all, was selling for up to three million rubles (about 2,400 dollars) on the Moscow black market in 1993. To add to the rising cost of Russian gangsterism, the number of people killed by expensive explosives—such as hand grenades, mines, and even artillery shells—also went up dramatically, to about eighty-three. Considering the country's grave economic problems, the Russian way of death was costly. [2]

But Russian murderers could afford to be profligate. The thriving weapons trade not only ensured a constant replenishment of the tools of their trade; it also provided a substantial source of income.

No single factor has done more to transform the landscape of the

former Soviet Union than the easy access to guns. There are an estimated thirty million unregistered firearms across the Commonwealth
of Independent States, including one million in Moscow alone. The
figure is remarkable, when one realizes that gun control was once taken
for granted by Soviet citizens. As in all Communist states, the Soviet
leadership protected its own security by prohibiting citizens from possessing any firearm more lethal than a hunting rifle or sporting pistol.
In the chaos of post-Communism, however, the new Moscow government was forced to reconsider the policy. Despite police objections, in
1992, Russians were allowed to obtain licenses for certain "self-defense
weapons," such as gas pistols, and large businesses and banks were
permitted to keep guns on their premises. It was a tacit recognition that
the state could no longer protect its citizens in the most fundamental
matters of life and death.[3]

The breakup of the Soviet state accelerated what had been a small
trade in stolen military hardware during the Soviet era. When the status
of military bases in the newly independent republics came under review,
some divisions were abruptly withdrawn, and others were downsized.
The new states were allocated part of the arsenals left behind, but many
of the leaders, who faced civil strife at home, argued for a greater share
of the Soviet military inheritance. What could not be negotiated was
stolen or bartered. The unstable southern republics of the old Soviet
Union, such as Tajikistan, Georgia, Armenia, Azerbaijan, Moldova,
and the Russian provinces of the northern Caucasus, effectively became
a sellers' market in military hardware.

The gun trade was as much cause as effect in the disorder that overtook former Soviet republics after the fall of Communism. In the disputed Trans-Dniestr region of Moldova, Russian separatists fighting the
nationalist Kishinev government obtained artillery shells and ground-
to-ground missiles (as well as troops) from the local army base. The
bitter civil war in Tajikistan during 1992 was fueled by stolen weapons
brought in from army bases across Central Asia or smuggled in from
Afghanistan.[4]

"Many of our military commanders found it profitable to leave behind a lot more of their weapons than they were supposed to," said Yuri
Yudin, who in 1993 was head of the parliamentary commission on army
corruption. "They sold to anyone who could pay a good price."[5]

According to figures of the Internal Affairs Ministry, more than 70 percent of the unregistered guns circulating in the former Soviet Union were stolen army weapons. A Western analyst estimated in 1993 that the artillery stolen in the Trans-Caucasus Military District amounted to four times the stored artillery of the British army. Many of the thefts were simply staged. "When robbers break into a base, we fire a few wild shots to make it look good," one officer in a Caucasus garrison admitted. "But the commanders have already received what they think is a fair fee for their trouble." [6]

The army was not the sole supplier of illegal weapons. Many factories in the military-industrial complex shipped ammunition and weapons unofficially to the south, and posts operated by Internal Affairs Ministry troops sold guns and equipment out the back door. In some areas, complete underground armaments industries sprang up. The middlemen for this flourishing new trade belonged to criminal organizations. "Usually," said Yudin, "the best prices were paid by organized crime."

The connection between post-Soviet gangsters and the armed forces was one of the least publicized aspects of the nation's new crime problem. But it was the one with perhaps the most dire effect on post-Soviet politics. Yudin, a burly, former lieutenant of the Soviet Internal Affairs Ministry, was not naive about the mercenary instincts of his country's soldiers. During the Afghanistan war, he admitted, military garrisons sold guns in local bazaars or smuggled them back into Russia. The collusion between provincial military officers and criminals, however, threatened the line of command from Moscow that had been taken for granted throughout the Soviet era and was the cornerstone of hopes for civil stability in Russia. "If this gets worse, it will be a national catastrophe," Yudin said.

And, of course, it could only get worse. Georgians and Abkhazians fought each other in 1993 with weapons obtained from army warehouses and garrisons. The trade was so open that it resembled an industry more than a "black market." In Lithuania, where private arms sales were legal, police counted more than forty organizations shipping guns from local garrisons across the former Soviet Union. Authorities admitted that they were virtually powerless. "We have checkpoints along the entire Russian border, but we cannot effectively control the smuggling of weapons," wrote Vladimir Yegorov and Alexander Trifonov, two senior officials of the State Customs Committee of the Russian Federation, in 1992.[7]

It was the ultimate post–Cold War irony: the superpower arms race had been replaced by a domestic one. Although the armaments were clearly on a less lethal scale, the quarrels inside and between former Soviet republics left the old slogan of Marxist-Leninist "internationalism" in tatters. The gun trade turned ex-Communists and reformers alike into deterrence theorists.

"Every leader is talking like a warrior chief," complained Aslambek Aslakhanov of the former parliament's law and order committee. "Everyone wants arms to protect himself against his neighbor, and his neighbor obtains a gun for the same reason. Unfortunately, our wheeler-dealers are well equipped to meet the rising demand. They keep the Caucasus and other areas on the brink of war."[8]

The authorities' lack of control was not always a result of poor intelligence or insufficient manpower. As in drug trafficking, there were increasing signs that government officials were implicated no less than army commanders in the profitable business of smuggling guns.

Late one evening, in the summer of 1992, members of the Moscow organized-crime squad gathered in front of a building on Kutuzovsky Prospekt where a hostage, the manager of one of the capital's prominent joint-venture clothing shops, had just been freed. Several men who had been holding the manager came out with their hands in the air. While some of the detectives frisked their new prisoners, an officer went to a corner telephone and dialed the home number of Capt. Yuri Nikishin.

A sleepy voice answered, "Nikishin."

"Yuri," said the officer, "the hostage situation is over."

Nikishin was about to compliment him when the man interrupted. "We have a different problem," he said. "We picked up two *chornye*— "blacks"—just up the street. They had nothing to do with the kidnapping, but they're loaded with guns, and they're pissed off. You'd better come."

Nikishin was dressed and in his car, racing down Moscow's deserted streets, before he was fully awake. When he reached the underpass on Kutuzovsky, near the building where the late Soviet leader Leonid Brezhnev had lived, Nikishin saw two handcuffed Chechens surrounded by a dozen policemen. The Chechens were dressed in suits, and they were shouting.

Nikishin recalled the scene later in a conversation with me. The policeman who had telephoned him took the captain aside. "We picked them up as they were getting into their car," he said, pointing to a black Mercedes. "They claim that one of their employees was the hostage. These guys are armed as if they are going to a war—we found electric batons and stun pistols in the back of their car."

Nikishin's attention was drawn to one of the Chechens, who was sputtering with rage.

"You know who you are dealing with?" the Chechen shouted into the expressionless faces of the police. "You stupid bastards!"

An officer handed Nikishin a sheaf of papers. "We took this from his wallet," he said. Nikishin remembered looking at it with a sense of dread. The papers identified the two men as brothers. One was director of the store where the hostage-taking incident had just ended. The other worked for "Alfa Security Agency."

Only weeks earlier, Alfa, which was headed by a former KGB intelligence official, triggered a controversy in the press when some of its employees were seen acting as unofficial guards for the Russian parliament. The agency also provided security for Vozrozhdeniye, a charity foundation for Russian soldiers whose honorary chairman was then Russian vice-president Aleksandr Rutskoi. One other assignment was supplying security for the joint-venture store where the hostage incident had taken place.

It was an awkward moment. The two brothers had presumably appeared on the scene to look after the interests of one of their clients. Yet how had Alfa—supposedly a respected security agency close to the government—gotten mixed up in circumstances that bore all the marks of a typical gangland quarrel?

Nikishin understood he would get no answers that night. But his anger began to build when he saw the "special permits" for two 9-mm Makarov pistols found in the brothers' possession. The permits were each signed by the head of the Internal Affairs Ministry's licensing office. At the time—before parliament's expansion of the gun licensing laws—only policemen were allowed to carry lethal weapons.

"You'd better let us go," said the Chechen who had spoken to Nikishin, "or you're in for trouble."

As Nikishin recounted the story later, he struck the man in fury. "I really wanted to beat the shit out of him," he told me grimly.

But at that moment, another Mercedes drew up. The passengers stalked out of the car, with pistols drawn. Nikishin's head began to swim. He recognized most of the faces. They were all former KGB. How were they associated with these Chechens?

As the Moscow detectives went for their own weapons, one of the men who got out of the car quickly motioned his associates to put their guns away. Gingerly, he approached Nikishin.

"It's all over, officer," he said. "We can see you've resolved the situation. Let's just forget about this and go home to bed."

"The hell we will," Nikishin said. "Tell me what you're doing here."

The man grinned. "We are protecting our interests. Do you want to see our gun permits too?"

Nikishin exploded. "You can stuff the permits up your ass." But he motioned the police to take the handcuffs off the Chechens.

The next morning, angrier than he could ever remember being, Nikishin paid a call on his superiors at the Ministry of Internal Affairs.

"How can you authorize these gangsters to have guns?" he shouted.

The general sitting across from Nikishin grimaced. Without a word, he pulled open his desk drawer and handed the policeman a file.

When Nikishin began to read, he received another shock. The file contained a record of permits issued for the Makarovs as well as seven imported Albatros pistols. On each permit, the approving officer had noted that the guns were "gifts" from the criminal investigation department of the Internal Affairs Ministry branch in Chechnya. "It's all legal, unfortunately," the general said.

But it wasn't. Someone in the ministry ordered a further investigation. It was soon discovered that the Albatros pistols were part of a shipment of guns smuggled in from Argentina by diplomatic pouch. The Chechens had picked up the shipment at the airport and distributed some of the guns to top ministry officials in gratitude for their "cooperation." The most valuable gun—a Colt-45 pistol—turned up in the possession of Aleksandr Rutskoi himself. The internal-affairs official who had signed the false permits was fired after the investigation showed that his wife was also working for the joint venture. But the affair was quickly hushed up. Rutskoi refused to give up his gun, telling police that they "must have more serious things to do." [9]

"It turned out these [officials] were so eager for the pistols that they didn't care what they had to do to obtain them," Nikishin told me bitterly. "With protection like that, it's not surprising that gun smuggling is impossible to stop."

That was the real source of Nikishin's rage. During the previous months, he had been devoting his energies to a campaign aimed at halting the capital's gun trade and neutralizing its most active merchants—the Chechen syndicates. Nikishin was hardly naive about the hidden relationship between government officials and organized crime, but the hint of involvement at such a high level with Chechen mobsters, who were supposed to be every Russian authority's favorite enemy, seemed to undermine everything he hoped to achieve. At the time, in 1992, an estimated ten thousand stolen weapons were moving out of Moscow every week, south towards the Chechen capital of Grozny in the Caucasus mountains.

The most ambitious operation had taken place only a few weeks before the hostage taking. Every southern exit on the Outer Ring Road, the highway encircling the capital, had been closed off by police patrols. "We knew that the Chechens were taking out enough weapons every month to stock an army," Nikishin told me. "We've even seen them trying to drive off with armored personnel carriers on the back of their trucks. If we closed the roads, we had a chance of choking them off. That's why we called the operation "Python.""

It was a formidable operation. A police helicopter circled above, while Internal Affairs Ministry troops and a special force of Moscow militiamen established an armed perimeter around the capital. Police stopped every truck with license plates from the Caucasus that was leaving or entering the city, and hundreds of stolen guns were confiscated, along with gold bars, VCRs, and several million dollars in cash. But the haul was disappointing—less than police had expected. Nikishin and his men suspected that the Chechen gunrunners were tipped off ahead of time by police whom they had bribed. But the discovery of the smuggled Argentine weapons was painful proof that even the Chechens had friends in powerful places.

"We will never get anywhere," Nikishin confided to me, "as long as there is a highway to Grozny."

It was an elliptical comment, but I knew what he meant. Since late 1991, the tiny capital of Chechnya had been a staging point for the organized criminal subversion of Russian democracy. It would take more than an "Operation Python" to cut off the flow of guns, goods, and illicit money between the Caucasus and Russia's cities. When Moscow finally decided to act, however, it sank into the worst military quagmire since the invasion of Afghanistan.

On December 11, 1994, a combined force of Russian army, air force, and Internal Affairs Ministry troops launched an assault on Grozny. President Yeltsin gave two reasons for the action. He said that Chechnya was the focus of an armed rebellion against the Russian Federation and it had become, in effect, the former Soviet Union's first mafiya-controled state. In the Russian mind, crime and political subversion had become interlinked in the Caucasus. A few intelligent policemen, like Yuri Nikishin, came early to an understanding of the connection between Chechen gangsters' activities and their historic grievances with Russia. But the Chechen involvement in the Russian bank scandal of 1992 was a wake-up call to Moscow democrats. Since then, the Grozny syndicates had only gotten wealthier and more powerful, allying themselves with opponents of the Yeltsin government and often operating as a fifth column inside Russia.

The military response, however, backfired. Russia's political, law enforcement, and military institutions were already too weakened by corruption to act effectively. At this writing, Russian soldiers are bogged down in the winter mud of Grozny in a fierce guerrilla war, and the Chechen war has become the most tragic example of how crime has imperiled Russia's experiment with democracy. The danger signals should have been obvious from the beginning.

In the autumn of 1991, I was in a bus filled with cold, exhausted, and irritable Western reporters heading toward Grozny. We were on our way to cover what seemed at the time just another of the odd stories connected with the overthrow of Communism and to interview one of the colorful figures of the new era. He was Chechnya's self-declared president, a former Soviet air force general named Dzokhar Dudayev.

Dudayev was one of the few Chechens to reach a senior military rank in the Soviet armed forces. After a series of assignments in Eastern Europe and the Baltics, the forty-seven-year-old general gained a distinguished reputation as a pilot and a garrison commander. He also endeared himself to Baltic independence movements by quietly resisting attempts to use his troops in anti-nationalist exercises during the 1990 quarrel between Moscow and the Baltic republics. Dudayev was deeply affected by the independence fervor in the Baltics. A few weeks after the August, 1991, coup, he spent his home leave in Grozny, which was then the administrative center of the Russian Federation autonomous region known as Chechen-Ingushetia. While visiting his family, he received an invitation to a conference of Chechen "elders" to discuss the implications of the coup for their homeland.

At the conference, he was asked to speak. To everyone's surprise, including perhaps his own, Dudayev delivered a stirring speech that recalled the long troubled history of his people, from their defeat in the guerrilla war against czarist troops in the nineteenth century to the wartime deportations ordered by Josef Stalin. He reminded the delegates that he was born in 1944, the year that marked the beginning of exile for thousands of Chechens. The future Soviet general was packed off to Central Asia with his family. When he returned as a teenager, he said with deep emotion, strangers were living in their old home. The speech earned him a tumultuous ovation, and before the conference ended, the assembled elders had elected Dudayev their leader. The general never returned to his command in the Baltics, though he was not to resign his commission until later. He repaid the elders' confidence by declaring the republic "independent" of Russian rule. Chechens greeted the news with a mixture of jubilation and surprise.

The surprise, at least, was shared in the north. The new democratic leaders in Moscow were happy to support the nationalist aspirations of the Baltic peoples, with whom they had forged alliances against the hard-line Communist leadership during the 1990s. A small minority could even grudgingly accept Ukraine's claim to independence. But there was no sympathy anywhere in the new Russian political establishment for secession movements inside the Russian Federation. The Chechen declaration of independence set an alarming precedent for dozens of other ethnic groups inside Russia who were clamoring to break away from Moscow's control.

After a short-lived attempt at negotiation, the Yeltsin government responded to the Dudayev rebellion with the overbearing imperial methods for which it had often criticized its predecessors. Thousands of Russian troops from nearby bases in the north Caucasus were ordered to reinforce the Grozny garrison. It was the first test of Yeltsin's leadership in the new democratic Russia, and it was nearly a failure. For a week, Dudayev's paramilitary forces kept Russian troops bottled up inside their camps, threatening to shoot anyone who ventured outside. Fearing civil war, Yeltsin submitted to a resolution from the Supreme Soviet ordering that the troops be withdrawn, and the nation relaxed.

But the struggle was not over. Russia's leaders, noting Dudayev's military background, believed that his "independence movement" was linked to hard-liners in Moscow who were planning a new coup. To neutralize him, they slapped an economic blockade on the Chechen territory, and the maverick general was notified that he faced charges of treason. Not for the first time in the history of Russian involvement with the Caucasus, Moscow misread local politics. Dudayev's defiance of Yeltsin won him the status of a folk hero and set in motion a nationalist rebellion across the region.

Each of the mountain peoples—Ossetians, Dagestanis, Ingush, Abkhazians, and dozens of others—revived claims to territories that had long ago been annexed by Russia. The politicized geography of the Soviet Union had left their homelands divided among various republics. Some challenged Moscow to help them recapture pieces of territory that were now in independent countries like Georgia. Others threatened to leave the Russian Federation completely. In the process, many of the mountain peoples found themselves at war with each other, and the north Caucasus became a cauldron of violence. Dozens of paramilitary groups were conducting operations in the mountains by the autumn of 1991. Aided by Russian mercenaries and stocked with Soviet military equipment, they were virtual armies. Chechnya, the most powerful and most militarized territory, assumed the political leadership of the entire region. Grozny was transformed from a political backwater into a crucial stop for journalists in Moscow, and Dudayev suddenly become an important player in the theater of post-Communist politics.[10]

That was why I found myself on a bus navigating a twisting road through the Caucasus Mountains one afternoon, three months after the August, 1991, coup. Intermediaries in neighboring Georgia had arranged a rare interview between the general and a small group of foreign journalists. But our hunt for an exclusive story nearly ended before we arrived.

For a bone-jarring two hours since leaving Tbilisi, the Georgian capital, we had been driving through some of the most rugged landscape of the old Soviet Union. It was a country of wild beauty. The bus wound its way east along hairpin mountain curves and past gorges where guerrillas had ambushed czarist soldiers a century earlier. Everywhere the eye traveled, sunlight glinted off white peaks of the Caucasus range. An occasional truck squeezed past us on the road, but the only sign of human habitation was a few shepherds grazing their flocks. Fifty miles from the Chechen capital, a uniformed man with a gun stepped into the road and ordered us to stop.

"The road is closed," he said.

We straggled outside. Other men with guns watched us from a small wooden hut marked "Customs." It was now almost dusk. We were in a bleak, windblown mountain pass. Ahead of us, the road twisted out of sight behind a cliff.

"What's going on?" we asked.

"The road," the man repeated dully, "is closed."

Outraged by what we considered a lingering example of Soviet bureaucratic mentality, we all began to talk at once.

"We have to get through," someone said, in the authoritative tone that Moscow-based foreign reporters often considered necessary to hide their vulnerability in the provinces. "We are journalists, and we have an appointment with General Dudayev."

The uniformed man sighed.

"He can wait," said the man. "If you keep going tonight, you may not get there at all."

Our skeptical looks goaded the customs guard into volubility. He said that the road continuing on from there bisected a piece of land under dispute between the Ossetian and Ingush peoples. The previous week, the dispute had broken out into violent warfare, and a curfew had been imposed on the entire area.

"After dark, Ossetians come down from the mountains and attacked everything that moved on the highway," he said. "We had to impose a curfew. A few nights ago, they hijacked a truck and took the poor driver's clothing. He had to walk naked the rest of the way, and he almost died from exposure."

Someone laughed, and the man turned toward him with a scowl, his patience with Moscow reporters suddenly at an end. "He was lucky they didn't kill him," he barked at us. "They'll get you, too, if you keep going tonight. You can cross tomorrow."

Those in our group who still had romantic notions about post-Soviet democracy were swiftly disillusioned by this introduction to the murderous politics of the Caucasus. Some said that we should turn back. But we voted to wait out the night in safety before going on. We found accommodations in a crumbling, bug-infested hotel in a village close to the customs post, keeping alert for the sound of gunfire. We heard nothing. But the next day, as we set out on the road, a new customs officer told us we would see evidence of previous battles ahead. A few miles further, our bus passed the wreckage of a jeep with Georgian plates lying at the bottom of a gorge. It had been hit by machine-gun fire from the nearby cliffs.

More signs of the region's quarrels greeted us when we emerged from the mountains. As our bus passed through the farmlands of Ossetia and Ingushetia on the way to the Chechen republic, we saw dozens of men in civilian clothes lounging by the roadside with guns strapped to their hips. At a few places, we saw army patrols from nearby garrisons who had been assigned the impossible job of keeping the peace in these picture-postcard territories.

Grozny, when we reached it at last about midday, was even less reassuring. The dusty city combined the atmosphere of a decaying Soviet provincial town with Muslim fervor. Since the local declaration of independence, Islam was experiencing a revival in Chechnya, and the central square was filled with knots of people gathered around mullahs in turbans and brown robes. Green banners with Arabic script hung from the offices of the former Communist Party municipal committee. In an even odder contrast, black Mercedes limousines cruised slowly up the pot-holed streets. Mercedes seemed to be the favorite means of transport; I saw only one Soviet car, a Zhiguli, in the square. And each automobile was filled with hawk-faced men. It was hard to ignore the preponderance of guns. Every male inhabitant seemed to be carrying a machine gun or a rifle.

The old Communist Party headquarters were now the offices of the president. A crowd of men, some wearing *kinjals*—the dagger of the Caucasus—in their waistbands, loitered in front of the main door. Only the children, who swarmed around our party trying to sell us pins and tiny Chechen flags, were unarmed. Two men carrying submachine guns escorted us up to the second floor, where we found Gen. Dzokhar Dudayev in a dark, wood-paneled office.

He stood up to welcome us. When we described the trials of our journey, he scowled. "It's all the Russians' fault," he said.[11]

He was a trim man, with an erect military bearing and deep black eyes. While preparing for the meeting in Moscow, I saw a photograph in a newspaper that made him look like a 1930s Hollywood villain, in a black fedora, a suit with padded shoulders, and a pencil-thin moustache. For his encounter with journalists, he had decided to look presidential, in a gray suit and somber tie. But it was hard to ignore the distinctly unpresidential "aides" who had crowded after us into his office, all of whom were packing large guns.

We arranged ourselves around a large conference table. Dudayev sat down with us. "I am ready for your questions," he said gravely.

"You've spent all your life in the Soviet military," one of the journalists began. "How is it you suddenly identify yourself as the leader of a separate nation?"

"Would you ask the same question to someone in the Baltics?" he responded, with a touch of anger. "This is my heritage."

In a more soothing voice, he added, "Of course, I have to admit that when I became president, I hardly knew about this country. After all, I was a young man when I left for military service, and I only came home after that on leave. And I stayed away from politics. But these new times have changed all of us."

Dudayev said that he had begun Islamic studies, to return to the faith of his parents. "I even swore my presidential oath on the Koran," he boasted. "And the mullahs are always near me."

The next hour or so was spent in detailed discussion of Dudayev's grievances with the Yeltsin government. Moscow newspapers had already quoted him at length on the subject, and he seemed reluctant to go beyond what he had already said. At one point, he repeated a threat to cut the pipelines carrying Chechnya oil to Russia—the territory was a substantial supplier—and then became conciliatory. "I don't understand why we can't come to an agreement," he said. "I have the greatest respect for President Yeltsin, but he is being influenced by my enemies in Moscow." Dudayev seemed strangely uneasy, as if he could not forget that he had once been a loyal Soviet officer. He kept glancing at the armed men in the room.

Finally, someone asked the question that had been bothering all of us.

"There no longer seems to be a threat of violence with Russian troops. Why are there still so many armed men in the square?"

"Everybody has a gun here," the general replied tersely. "That's our culture, and if I tried to disarm the people, I would be in trouble. Of course, I can't allow hooliganism. The Russians say we're all gangsters, but they really don't understand us. How could a gangster swear on the Koran?"

Someone asked whether he feared assassination. He slapped the desk with his hand.

"The Russians have taught us a good lesson over the past three months," he said crisply. "I have so many enemies I must sleep with a pistol under my pillow every night."

When we walked back to our car after the meeting, there were more limousines parked by the square opposite Dudayev's office. I suddenly realized why all the men were milling around. They were buying and selling guns.

Two years later, dissidents in Dudayev's entourage charged that the general was at the center of one of the largest arms-dealing rings in the former Soviet Union, and added that some of the Chechen syndicate bosses occupied senior positions in Dudayev's cabinet. In 1992, a member of the president's personal staff was caught escorting a shipment of machine guns to Russia. The man was later released, and no other evidence of the charges against Dudayev came to light. But by then, there was little doubt that the gun market in Grozny was the Commonwealth's largest black-market clearinghouse for weapons. A reporter from *Moscow News* who visited Grozny in 1993 described hearing submachine-gun bursts everywhere he went in the city. "Everyone wants to test his purchase—it's different from the usual sound of a Caucasus bazaar," the reporter wrote dryly.[12]

"Weapons were always part of Caucasus life," he continued. "But things are a little different now. Beside the Kalashnikovs, you see long-barreled mortars and anti-tank guns."

The local commander of Russian forces estimated more than 150,000 firearms were at large in the Chechen capital, a city with 400,000 inhabitants. The president's bodyguards and advisers were often seen replenishing or adding to the inventory on the square. Much of the arms dealing took place a "five minutes' walk" from Dudayev's office, the *Moscow News* observed.

To an increasing body of local Chechnya opinion, it was hard to distinguish between the activities of the crime syndicates and government officials. "The leadership here doesn't fight the criminal underworld, [because] it belongs to it," asserted Salambek Khadzhiyev, a leader of the so-called Round Table Opposition in Grozny in 1993.[13]

Whether or not the Dudayev government directly profited from the illicit arms trade, it made little effort to stop the business. In Moscow, police traced the Chechens' swift rise to power in the post-Soviet crime world to their profits from the sale of drugs and weapons. Within two years of Dudayev's appearance as president, the Chechens were the premier arms dealers of post-Communist society. They owned more than five hundred flats in the capital, as well as an estimated 140 businesses and joint ventures and half a dozen hotels. Although no one could come up with a conclusive link between the syndicates and the government in Grozny, there was circumstantial proof of their mutual dependence. The timing of the Chechen gangs' transformation from small bands involved in petty extortion and stolen-car rackets into sophisticated crime conglomerates trading in guns and drugs coincided with the rise of Chechnya as a financial and political force. By mid-1992, according to police, the three principal Chechen clans in Moscow jointly owned a bank with reserves conservatively estimated in the hundreds of millions of rubles.[14]

The Russian Ministry of Security claimed that between ten million and fifteen million rubles in cash were funneled from Moscow every week and deposited in government-controlled banks in Grozny. The gangs effectively undermined Moscow's economic blockade, since they were able to transport food, fuel, and goods on the same underground network that sped narcotics and guns through the Commonwealth.

Whether or not the Chechen gangs were the appointed instruments of Chechen government policy, their activities neatly dovetailed with Grozny's determination to take revenge on Moscow. Behind the 1992 promissory-note scandal, which nearly bankrupted the Russian economy, were Grozny banks as well as the Chechen syndicates. And the discovery that Russian Central Bank officials were also involved illustrated the way in which Chechens were able to manipulate internal

Russian politics to their own advantage. Moreover, the gun-smuggling connection that Yuri Nikishin and his detectives stumbled upon during the Moscow hostage-taking incident had suggested a link between the circle of supporters around the Russian vice-president, who was even then in open opposition to Yeltsin, and the Chechens. At first glance, this was the strangest link of all, since Rutskoi's erstwhile political ally, parliamentary speaker Ruslan Khasbulatov, was a Chechen who had aroused the special enmity of Dudayev when he supported applying military pressure against Grozny in 1991. But while it may have been impossible to decipher the shifting alliances inside the Russian leadership, Chechen gangster politics was slightly more straightforward. If one could profit from the Russian economy while undermining it, it was the best of all possible worlds. One well-informed Moscow business leader told me darkly that he had seen evidence of a Chechen attempt to corner Russia's gold reserves.[15]

The Chechens' ability to act as both a criminal and political force set them apart at first from their Russian counterparts—but it established a pattern that would soon be followed throughout the post-Soviet underworld. "The Chechens were really the first mob group to successfully penetrate the post-Soviet economy," said Igor Baranovsky, a *Moscow News* journalist who specialized in the Chechen gangs.[16]

But the key to their success remained the former Soviet army. The Chechens would never have been able to establish their financial base without the collusion between gun brokers and the armed forces across Russia. In January, 1993, police in Novosibirsk and Russian Security Ministry agents arrested three senior Russian officers from the Siberian Military District as they tried to unload radio-controlled mines to a group of Caucasian traders for twenty-thousand rubles apiece.[17]

As the trade expanded, the dealers began to conduct their business by telex and telephone without setting foot outside Grozny. In another celebrated case, agents from the Moscow military prosecutor's office intercepted ten railway carriages filled with control panels for artillery units, radio transmitters, advanced navigation aids, and night-vision devices, all destined for the northern Caucasus. The goods had been certified as "tractor parts." The investigators discovered that the shipment was organized by one of the units of the elite Missile Artillery Department, in cooperation with a private Moscow commercial firm and bureaucrats in several defense production ministries.[18]

The Chechen connection clearly was not confined to the ranks. Oleg Teziev, the prime minister of South Ossetia, charged in 1992 that six of the top commanders in the Trans-Caucasus Military District were pivotal to the region's gun trade. "They are now the six richest men in the Russian army," he said.[19]

Yet for all their money, even the Chechens were, in the end, only junior partners in the military's expanding commercial operations. By then, it was impossible to disregard evidence that military criminal enterprise was condoned, if not encouraged, by officials in the country's defense establishment. In June, 1993, an army colonel serving in a garrison town about one hundred miles south of Moscow was arrested in the act of trying to sell eighty-two detonators for mines to Russian underworld contacts. The detonators were cleverly concealed inside ballpoint pens. When investigators opened the colonel's suitcase, they discovered how ingenious he really was. Inside the suitcase were thirty silver crosses and four hundred pairs of men's gold cufflinks—all, as police discovered later, made from melted-down military equipment.[20]

Under questioning, the colonel admitted the obvious: he didn't work alone. The investigation uncovered a ring involving senior military officials, including bureaucrats in the Russian Defense Ministry. The leader of the ring was a general who was found with jewels, gold, ammunition, and a mold for making crosses in his private safe. Investigators also discovered papers showing that the general was running his own private company from inside a munitions plant. He had not stopped there. The documents indicated that he had helped set up similar "private" firms in three other military bases to manufacture weapons for the black market.

Hard, slogging detective work had produced a remarkable success. But, like Capt. Yuri Nikishin, the security agents who cracked the case soon found their efforts undermined by forces beyond their control. After presenting their findings to the military prosecutor, they waited months for news about when the case would come to trial.

Finally, they received a memo from the senior military command informing them that no one would press charges. A spokesman for the Russian Security Ministry gave a somewhat pained explanation to the press.

"We were told," he said, "that we were displaying an unhealthy interest in this case."

14 Red Army Bazaar

The managers of a plant in the military city of Arzamas-16 in Central Russia are still laughing about a letter they received in early 1993. Maybe it was a hoax, they said. But it was a good one.

The letter, in stilted Russian, requested delivery of an "atomic bomb." The plant managers were not to worry about any problems with payment, the letter said. Its author had thoughtfully provided specific details about how the weapon was to be delivered. The letter was signed "Islamic Jihad." [1]

The joke is no longer so obvious. An estimated thirty thousand strategic and tactical nuclear weapons are located in Russia. There have been, so far, no documented cases of "private sales." No one, though, appears to know with any degree of certainty how many of these warheads are under secure control.[2] There were unconfirmed reports around the former Soviet Union during 1992 and 1993 of police interceptions of attempts to sell nuclear armaments abroad.[3] There is no report that Arzamas-16's polite correspondent contacted the plant again. But perhaps he realized he could satisfy his needs more easily without buying a complete "bomb."

The security of the vast stockpile of fissile material accumulated by the USSR is even more uncertain than the guardianship of nuclear warheads. There are 189 separate sites in the former Soviet Union exclusively devoted to the manufacture and mining of nuclear raw materials—including 151 in the Russian Federation—and dozens of "research institutes" that store and handle various grades of uranium and plutonium. A growing body of evidence suggests that some of these sites are the launch pads for a clandestine global trade.[4]

On March 9, 1992, two Russian emigres were arrested in Bavaria after trying to sell three pounds of weapons-grade uranium for nearly two million deutschmarks. A few months later, Italian police arrested a businessman from Milan who had offered to sell two Israelis a consignment of uranium, plutonium, and deuterium. He refused to say where he had obtained the material, but he hinted at "contacts" in Russia. Also that year, a firm in Norway received a business proposal by fax from a small enterprise in Volgograd offering to sell eight tons of "heavy water" for 440 dollars a kilogram. By the end of 1992, ninety-five separate attempts to smuggle Russian uranium had been reported in Germany alone.[5]

In 1993, there were about three hundred seizures across Europe of various types of radioactive material offered for sale. Neither the source nor the destination was clear, but most of it seemed to come from the former Eastern bloc. Then, in the summer of 1994, a series of highly publicized sting operations in Germany elevated the issue to international attention.[6]

On Wednesday, August 10, 1994, a thirty-eight-year-old Colombian citizen named Justiniano Torres was arrested in Munich airport moments after he had arrived on a Lufthansa flight from Moscow. He was carrying a suitcase containing between 300 and 350 grams (10.6 to 12.3 ounces) of plutonium-239.[7]

The arrest ended a cloak-and-dagger story that had begun several weeks earlier. Two Spaniards, who proved to be Torres's accomplices, offered to deliver a total of 8.8 pounds of plutonium, approximately half the amount needed to make a nuclear bomb, for $250 million to German agents posing as businessmen. To prove their veracity, they offered small samples of the material and indicated that they could get as much as they wanted from their Moscow "source." Torres, who had lived for many years in Moscow as a student, was bringing the first installment of the shipment. Investigators found the plutonium in a shielded cylinder inside his suitcase.

Not only was it the largest single amount of black-market plutonium intercepted since the collapse of the Soviet Union, but it was the third such seizure in four months in Germany. The Germans, who had documented more than 123 similar cases since 1992 (and another 118 cases of fraudulent offers to sell nuclear material), felt that this was enough to demonstrate their long-standing charge that a "nuclear mafia" operating between Germany and the former Soviet Union was a conduit for underground shipments of bomb-grade material to the Third World. As if to prove their point, a few days later, police in Bonn raided seven apartments where they claimed to have found evidence of the planned or successful shipment of plutonium to Pakistan.

But the problems presented by this case were only beginning. German analysts first claimed that the plutonium came from weapons laboratories or military installations somewhere in Russia. The Russian Atomic Energy Ministry, MINATOM, promptly denied the claim, insisting that careful checks of its inventory showed nothing missing. Then American experts weighed in with a finding that the plutonium-239 was only 87 percent pure—weapons-grade material is at least 93 percent pure—which they said indicated that the material probably came from a civilian research institute. Although it wasn't bomb-grade, it was still dangerous. A small quantity would be enough to poison the water supply of a medium-sized city, and as one expert has written, "all forms of plutonium can be made into weapons." Nevertheless, this disclosure took some of the edge off the nightmarish scenario painted by newspapers around the world, in which nameless terrorists were importing miniature atom-bomb kits with the help of organized criminals from Russia and the West.[8]

The issue, however, was still serious. Soviet production of weapons-grade uranium officially stopped in 1989, and plutonium production was scheduled to end in 1995, but there is plenty of "idle" inventory on hand. The Soviet Union's yearly requirement of uranium ore was 8,800 metric tons, according to government officials, but in 1990 alone some 26,000 tons was mined. In 1992, the United States estimated that Russia possessed a stockpile of 1,100 tons of highly enriched uranium and 150 tons of weapons-grade plutonium. There are also sizable quantities of other strategic and radioactive materials, including those earmarked for Russia's large civilian nuclear program. In Torres's suitcase, police also found two pounds of lithium-6, a non-radioactive substance used to enhance bomb yields. Most of the military stores may in fact be closely monitored by security police, but the combination of Russian frontier capitalism, loosely guarded borders, and an eager market has helped add the nuclear trade to the list of lucrative criminal enterprises in the former Soviet Union.[9]

The effort to get to the bottom of this trade requires an answer to the all-important question in any criminal conspiracy: who benefits? The Russian government suffered an additional embarrassment from the 1994 plutonium seizure when its deputy minister of atomic energy, Viktor Sidorenko, was discovered to have been a passenger on the plane carrying Torres to Munich. German police hastened to say that they thought it was a coincidence. They guessed that the smugglers had hoped that his visit (concerning official talks on civilian nuclear sales) would allow them to slip past airport security. But the awkward juxtaposition of Russia's legal and illegal nuclear commerce vividly illustrated the thin line separating the two. Sidorenko's bosses and the shadowy architects of the plutonium deal back home in Moscow had several things in common. They had access to the same pool of supplies, and they were equally concerned with earning large amounts of hard currency overseas. Considering the close cooperation already taking place at home between Russia's criminal and official worlds, it would be foolish to assume that they always operated independently of each other.

What further blurs the difference is that a significant amount of nuclear material shipped abroad from Russia is not clandestine at all. It is sold through channels created during the Soviet era to provide parts and fuel for Soviet-built power stations in Eastern Europe. Arkadi Chuvin, deputy head of Tekhsnabeksport, the Russian agency in charge of nuclear exports, admitted in 1992 that it was impossible to check the ultimate destination of nuclear materials. "I can give no guarantees that uranium or plutonium we supply to the Czechs, for instance, won't be sold to a third party," he said. It is not unrealistic to consider the possibility that such "third-party" sales may occasionally be part of the original deal.[10]

Chuvin's comments seemed to have been forgotten in 1994, when the Russian government, in its efforts to belittle Western concerns about the clandestine trade, pointed out that one of the samples of plutonium seized by German police in May came from Bulgaria. But American intelligence officials have suggested that the use of this third-country route may have already delivered reprocessed plutonium to countries like North Korea, Iraq, and Iran.[11]

The blurring of legal and illegal nuclear exports goes to the heart of the criminalization of post-Soviet society. After a week of huffy denials, Russians were willing to admit that there was a problem of security in their civilian nuclear installations. Some fifty thefts of lower-grade radioactive materials had been recorded by 1994. Officials at Gosatomnadzor, the State Atomic Energy Inspectorate (known as GAN), a national agency set up in late 1991 to monitor nuclear installations, confessed that they were having a hard time keeping track of inventories. This put the stiff assertions by the bureaucrats at Russia's Atomic Energy Ministry that nothing was amiss in the military arsenals in a slightly different perspective. Military and civilian technology in the nuclear field were at least as closely related in the old Soviet Union as they are in the West—if not more. This was demonstrated by the 87-percent-pure "finding" in the Munich plutonium case. Reprocessed plutonium normally has a lower grade of purity, and even though the batch discovered in Torres's suitcase was not up to bomb standards, it was a sign that it may have originated at a military source and was in the process of being downgraded for commercial export.[12]

The black-market plutonium, then, could have been stolen or expropriated by anyone with access to the material once it left military stores, and that included a broad range of people from government officials, army generals, and security police to lowly, ill-paid technicians. The trade, arguably, could not flourish without the connivance and support of sectors of the Russian military-industrial complex. Nuclear smuggling, like other big-ticket contraband from the Soviet Union, is the province of the comrade criminal. This would not surprise most Russians. They have already learned the extent of corruption and criminality inside what was once the largest and most formidable military machine in the world.

Russian Armed Forces Day, 1993, will be remembered as one of the humiliating moments in the nation's military history.

On that February 23rd, Defense Minister Pavel Grachev appeared on national television to announce that forty-six senior military officers, including a number of generals, were to be court-martialed for corruption. He said that an additional three thousand officers had already received disciplinary charges for "illegal business dealings," which ranged from the smuggling of weapons to the black-market sale of military equipment.[13]

"A large part of the officer corps has become soiled by corruption," said Grachev, who was a respected paratroop commander before he replaced Marshal Dmitri Yazov, one of the conspirators of the August, 1991, coup.

It couldn't have been an easy confession, but it seemed sadly inevitable. The Soviet army had entered a decline before the end of the Soviet era. Defeat in Afghanistan and withdrawal from Eastern Europe had left deep psychological wounds. But unlike the two other pillars of state power—the KGB and the Communist Party—the armed forces earned the renewed respect of millions of Russians when middle-level commanders like Grachev rallied to President Boris Yeltsin's side during the coup.

Grachev's public recognition that times had changed was long overdue. Several months before his television appearance, military prosecutors charged the commander of the Baltic Air Fleet, Colonel A. Simanov, with operating a "systematic commercial operation" that smuggled fuel and scrap metal overseas for several years. Under Simanov's direction, pilots moonlighted for a private aviation company which, coincidentally, was owned by the former head of the fleet's aviation cargo department. The business involved some of the armed forces' most elite units in a network of supply depots that extended along the Baltic coast from Kaliningrad to Tallinn. Another scandal erupted in the Pacific command, where a top-secret air force base in the Maritime Territory was exposed as the center for a high-flying commercial "taxi service." Military planes at the base were hired by private firms to ferry commercial goods between China and the Russian Far East. In return for their services, the pilots and commanders received cash and scarce consumer items like televisions and VCRs.[14]

This was a different level of corruption from the arms-peddling carried on by provincial garrisons. As Grachev's list indicated, the most senior officers of a force that once considered itself the ultimate defender of the world's proletariat were now acting like capitalists in uniform. Like their bureaucrat counterparts in civilian life, they openly mixed business and official duties. At the elite submarine base in Kaliningrad, on the Baltic coast, for example, more than five hundred serving officers worked as employees or directors of commercial firms. One navy captain even managed two shareholding companies directly from his office on the base.[15]

Some army leaders awkwardly tried to rescue the reputation of their institution by blaming the temper of the times. "What is going on in the armed forces is only a reflection of the general instability in society," Valentin Panichev, the chief Russian military prosecutor, suggested in March, 1993.[16]

The offenders, however, felt that no apology was needed. "Why should I, a general, receive thirty thousand rubles a month while [businessmen] grab millions?" said air force general Vladimir Rodionov, who had been arrested in connection with the Pacific scandal.[17] "I have no apartment and no prospect of one," complained the general, a decorated airman who headed the long-range bomber division in the Far East. "Am I alone in this? Practically the entire army has been forced to dirty its hands to survive."

It was true that the lives of thousands of officers and enlisted men had been thrown into disarray by the worsening financial state of the armed forces. Many of the troops withdrawn from Eastern Europe were still without housing for their families. But Rodionov also reflected the deeper anger of a military class that had lost its special entitlements. Soviet professional soldiers used to be ranked alongside the senior nomenklatura in their privileged access to the best food stores, housing, and equipment. When they retired, they could look forward to a comfortably pensioned old age in any one of a dozen special communities. But inflation had made military pensions virtually worthless.

Many of the nation's military men faced real impoverishment, and this seemed further proof of their diminished social status. Thus, in Rodionov's words, officers who dabbled in crime and commerce were simply "restoring justice." It was a revealing phrase. There was no reason why a military uniform should continue to command the perks and automatic deference it enjoyed in the Soviet era, but most Russian civilians still found it hard to question the self-regard of men like Rodionov. Soviet culture was in many respects militarized as a consequence of decades of martial propaganda and massive spending on arms, and the post-Soviet armed forces basked in the admiration of the sort of uncritical constituency that would now be inconceivable in the West. The aggrieved Soviet officer—with neither a clear role nor a secure standard of living—was a political time bomb.[18]

Grachev's decision to make a public acknowledgment of the army's fall from grace was, therefore, a calculated gamble. It might alienate a public that was still uncertain about the military's role, and it might exacerbate the army's resentments. But Russia's transition to a post-Communist democracy depended to a large extent on whether the army would stay out of politics, and if soldiers and officers succumbed to the lure of profits, they would inevitably become caught up in the struggles for economic advantage in Russian society. At the risk of tarnishing the military image, Grachev hoped to reassert control over his commanders in the field. In the same address, he took the opportunity to accuse some military officers of trying to "blow apart" the army by dragging it into dangerous political debates. It wasn't clear what he was referring to, but the officers who ran their divisions and bases like private corporations had become the equivalent of independent warlords. In the most worrying threat of all to the army's tradition of non-partisanship, the capitalists in uniform had struck alliances with provincial politicians and crime syndicates.

Russian observers noted that in some cities, such as St. Petersburg, the military had already set up financial structures that could provide a "Latin American-style power base." The week of Grachev's announcement, Anatoli Zhilin, editor of the *Russian Army,* a right-wing weekly, warned that "disgruntled officers are now prepared to be led by any politician who succeeds in finding them the image of a new enemy." Although this may have exaggerated the strength of political activism in the military, President Yeltsin admitted more than a year later that one-third of the military vote during the December, 1993, parliamentary elections was cast for the neo-fascist Vladimir Zhirinovsky.[19]

"Our top officers are better placed than a lot of other people in our country to take advantage of the nation's instability," Yuri Yudin, head of the former parliament's commission on military corruption, told me during a conversation in his sixteenth-floor office in Moscow's parliamentary building, a month after Grachev's speech. "They have equipment, communications—a whole network." [20]

In his televised statement, Grachev traced the army's problems to a January, 1991, decision by the Soviet Defense Ministry allowing military personnel to take part in limited commercial enterprise. "Some did so on an honest, proper basis," he said. "But a large part of the officer corps . . . to put it bluntly, spent more time on commerce than combat preparation."

Even Grachev seemed to have been caught in this dilemma. Four months after his statement, a parliamentary commission accused the defense minister of questionable behavior in connection with the purchase of fourteen Mercedes-Benz automobiles. According to Special Prosecutor Nikolai Makarov, the automobiles were bought with profits earned from the sale of Soviet military property in the former East Germany and shipped to Moscow for Grachev and his top aides. The ministry claimed that the cars were purchased to replace the "aging" fleet of vehicles assigned to the army command. But under a presidential decree, all funds from German military sales were earmarked for new army housing. Investigators also disclosed that the cars had been brought into the country under false pretenses: they were registered to a non-commissioned officer named Pronin, whom nobody could identify. "This whole affair was immoral and illegal," the commission charged.[21]

The accusations against Grachev were never tested in court, but they were soon overshadowed by another scandal linking military bureaucrats to the allegedly illegal disposition of Russian military property in Germany. Twelve high officials, including the former head of the Ministry of Defense's trade department, were charged with "abusing their official positions" in connection with that case, and two deputy ministers were forced to resign.

Mounting evidence pointed to the military establishment's involvement in questionable activities at home and abroad. In February, 1992, the *Financial Times* of London reported that two containers holding nearly forty thousand Soviet Army Makarov pistols were seized by customs officers in Estonia and Finland. The shipments, listed as "sports pistols," were on their way to a Helsinki company owned by a Russian citizen and his wife. The company was incorporated in the Isle of Man a year earlier, and an investigation by the *Financial Times* established that the Finnish address was a fiction. According to the newspaper, the weapons' destination just off British shores suggested that the ultimate customer was a terrorist group such as the Irish Republican Army.[22]

This case, in particular, offered a clue to a dimension of military corruption that Grachev had avoided mentioning. The impounded pistols came from a factory in Izhevsk, five hundred miles east of Moscow— a factory known as one of the country's main producers of small arms for the military. The weapons smugglers, in other words, were connected to the vast interlocking network of factories that fed the military arsenal and ensured the corrupt generals a steady source of supply for their sales activities. The military-industrial complex, which had dominated Soviet politics for so many decades, was playing a pivotal role in post-Communist military crime.

Like the army, in the new era, the former Soviet defense production industry had lost many of its privileges and much of its influence. At its peak, the military-industrial complex had comprised more than 1,500 enterprises and employed over seven million people. Now it was in a fight for survival.

Military plants across Russia became a key battleground in the struggle between the old nomenklatura and government reformers. Defense managers—allied with conservative factions in parliament, regional politicians, and elements of the old Party and KGB establishment—represented the most powerful opposition to Russia's transition to an open market. Their campaign benefited from the fact that the ambitious program for "conversion" of military plants to civilian production, launched during perestroika, had gone nowhere.

Even in the West, it was proving difficult to transform economies closely wedded to the priorities of the Cold War. But Russian armaments factories faced the additional problem of retooling production lines run by central planners who had never concerned themselves with finding a market. Few companies had the equipment or design sophistication to successfully compete with Western imported consumer goods. In 1990, as the conversion program was getting under way, I visited a MIG-29 assembly plant in Moscow that was lauded as a model for the new era. Part of the plant was still dedicated to building airplanes, but a substantial portion had been reallocated to civilian production—in a manner of speaking. Directors proudly showed me a new line of food mixers three times as large and cumbersome as any sold in the West. Nearby, employees sitting at long benches painstakingly sewed piecework clothing at machines that had been used to make parachutes. If this was the archetype for conversion, I could imagine the state of plants elsewhere in the country.

Civilian defense workers were in the forefront of those resisting conversion. They had been the most privileged workers in a society that had valued the production of tanks higher than that of refrigerators. Employment in a military plant usually carried with it the right to extended vacations in southern resorts, better housing and food allotments, and shorter waits to get cars. But the insular world of the military-industrial complex fell victim to the same economic realities that destroyed the privileged life of the armed forces.

Six months after the USSR disintegrated, defense orders had dropped by more than 40 percent, and 350,000 workers had lost their jobs. A year later, there were so many idle plants that an estimated one million workers received pay for doing nothing. The defense industry suffered its heaviest blow in 1992, when government spending on arms procurement fell nearly 70 percent over the previous year. Factories were caught in an impossible squeeze. They would either have to go out of business, throwing additional thousands of employees out of work, or try to sell their production in any market that would have them.[23]

In the city of Yekaterinburg, where about a quarter of the labor force, or some five hundred thousand people, worked for military industries, local gangs were some of the most important clients for the grenades and rocket-launchers that once went to the state. The mob lords and black marketeers also provided the muscle and international contacts necessary to market strategic raw materials, weapons, and metals abroad.

An enterprising factory manager in Verkhnyaya Solda, a tiny mining community just north of Yekaterinburg that produced 80 percent of Russia's supply of titanium, found a way to compensate for the reduction in government orders. After accumulating more than eleven tons of the metal for private use by falsifying his production reports, the manager found a partner in a private export firm that had a license to export strategic metals abroad. He arranged to ship the metal secretly to Yekaterinburg with the help of an officer in the former Soviet Army Strategic Rocket Division. The Yekaterinburg firm negotiated a separate deal for the illicit titanium with a foreign buyer, who agreed to pay part of the cost in advance with cars and video players. A few of the luxury Western goods eventually turned up back in Verkhnyaya Solda, in what appeared to be a payoff to local mafiya bosses who had helped arrange the transport. Russian military intelligence, acting on a tip, intercepted the shipment as it left the Verkhnyaya Solda factory.

But, remarkably, the deal still went through. The foreign buyer, insisting that he had signed a contract in good faith, threatened to sue the Yekaterinburg firm, and the titanium was released for export. "There are dozens of such deals happening all the time," said Sergei Plotnikov, who investigated the story for the newspaper *Na Smenu,* in Yekaterinburg. "They start off with the stain of the underworld on them, but they quickly become whitewashed because so much money is involved, and end up being legal."[24]

The alliance between criminal syndicates and the former Soviet military-industrial complex may represent a greater danger to the future of Russian democracy than corruption in the armed forces. The military is at least formally subject to civilian control, but military bureaucrats belong to a separate power structure that is transforming itself into an independent force in Russian politics. As late as 1990, nine separate

Soviet ministries were involved in military production, and an additional eight "industrial ministries" supplied military parts and components. The managers and directors of this enormous bureaucracy were already participating as a secret political lobby in the struggle between reformers and hard-liners before the Soviet Union collapsed.[25]

After 1991, their activities became more blatantly political. The trade in military hardware provided cash to finance their opposition to government reforms designed to break the defense establishment's grip on the post-Soviet economy. "This free capital," the *Moscow News* charged in 1993, "is used to 'orient' public opinion and subsidize election campaigns."[26]

The trade prospered with the connivance of officials in Moscow. "The directors of big [military] plants and factories use their contacts in the government to export weapons, military hardware, and even strategic raw materials without having to pay attention to official regulations," Aslambek Aslakhanov, of the former parliament's committee on law and order, told me in 1993. "They obtain licenses for commercial exports and then send out a shipment labelled 'children's toys,' for instance. But when you open the shipment up, it's all military-industrial hardware inside."[27]

Scandals inside the Moscow ministries assigned to develop arms exports received less attention from the Russian press than reports of gun smuggling and military entrepreneurship, but they illustrated one of the ways in which post-Communist Russia's law-and-order crisis was becoming an international threat. In May, 1993, a former Russian vice-premier was accused of trying to smuggle armaments out of the country. The following month, the parliamentary anti-corruption commission reported that an agency created to implement "military reform" and headed by one of Russia's senior generals was selling military technology in partnership with a foreign joint venture. In July, 1993, security agents in Ukraine intercepted an attempt to sell to an unidentified foreign buyer anti-tank guided missiles capable of destroying a multi-story building at a distance of fifteen miles. The six-foot-long missiles were being offered for two billion rubles apiece.[28]

Such cases helped explain why so much Soviet military hardware was turning up in the shadowy international arms market. As early as 1992, the heavy traffic in Russian weapons abroad began to alarm experts.

"This has got the potential to be the biggest and most dangerous arms bazaar in history," Paul Berever, publisher of *Jane's Defence Weekly,* told the *Observer* of London.[29]

It was not surprising to find that the overseas bazaar featured more worrisome products of the old Soviet arsenal than missiles.

Until 1994, Russian nuclear officials consistently denied that there was a security problem in their warehouses. In 1992, Aleksandr Mokhov, head of the security department of the Russian Ministry of Atomic Energy, claimed that his inspectors had noticed no "significant" depletion of uranium stores.[30]

Literaturnaya Gazeta, which investigated nuclear smuggling in 1993, found a simple explanation for this. It pointed out that under international safeguards agreements, "it takes a fairly considerable amount of product loss to consider it a leak, twenty-five kilos of uranium 235, for example, or not less than a ton of heavy water."[31]

"Why should I need to steal this stuff by the ton?" the newspaper was told by a self-described Russian uranium "entrepreneur." "A kilo is enough to make you a millionaire."

The difficulties involved in nuclear contraband merely challenged the resourcefulness of Russia's post-Communist criminals. "I have yet to see a customs point in the former Soviet Union fitted with devices for measuring radiation levels," the entrepreneur told *Literaturnaya Gazeta.* "All you need to do is give twenty dollars to a customs officer, and your vehicle won't be inspected."

Literaturnaya Gazeta found one smuggling ring that employed the ancient caravan routes in Central Asia for this peculiarly twentieth-century crime. The leader, identified only as "Sasha," picked up enriched uranium from a middleman in Tashkent, the capital of Uzbekistan, and delivered it to a buyer in Afghanistan. Leading a small group of men, each carrying a fifty-pound knapsack lined with lead, he made an arduous trek across the Pamir Mountains at least once month. Sasha claimed that he didn't care about the potential danger to his health.

"It's just money to me," he explained. "I earn the most, about eight hundred dollars, because I am caravan-*bashi,* the leader. The other guys get six hundred for the walk."

Sasha had no idea where his uranium came from, or who provided it—but other cases suggested that the nuclear *bizness* enjoyed powerful official sponsorship. In the early 1990s, senior officials in the Yeltsin government were accused of endangering national security by selling a substance called, in English, red mercury. The mysterious substance, which appeared in countries as far apart as Germany and Canada, sold for as much as 240,000 dollars a kilogram. In the controversy that erupted in Russian newspapers over red mercury, the substance was called the last secret of the Cold War.[32]

There was strong evidence to suggest that red mercury existed only in the imaginations of certain journalists and opposition politicians. Even its name was a source of confusion. Red mercury appeared to be the anglicized shorthand for redistilled mercury—*peredistilirovannaya rtut,* in Russian—a mixture of antimony and mercury. The Moscow press compounded the problem by translating the English word back into Russian as *krasny rtut* (literally, red mercury), thereby making it appear an entirely different and more menacing substance.

Russian scientists made clear that neither "redistilled mercury" nor "red mercury" occurred in nature, but they admitted that a substance fitting that description was developed in Soviet research labs, in 1968, as a coolant for an experimental breeder reactor. The substance, it was said, performed below expectations. The Soviet ministries of Defense and Nuclear Energy, however, believed that it had commercial value. Small amounts of the substance—whatever it was—were offered for sale abroad, and the trade became a profitable source of income for what *Komsomolskaya Pravda* termed the "top echelons of the former Communist Party bureaucracy." The post-Communist government, which apparently stumbled upon the red-mercury arrangement by accident, asked a Yekaterinburg military research firm called Promekologia to develop the product commercially. The firm signed a twenty-four-billion-dollar contract on March 17, 1993, to supply eighty-four tons of red mercury to unidentified Western customers.

The contract was approved by Gennadi Burbulis, then the second-most powerful official in the Yeltsin government. Burbulis, a native of Yekaterinburg, was believed to have close ties with directors of Promekologia, and Yeltsin's opponents, such as Vice-President Aleksandr Rutskoi, seized on his involvement as ammunition for their campaign to discredit reformers. The central issue raised by the red-mercury case, however, was buried.

"The principal responsibility for this scandal rests on the shoulders of former Communist Party apparatchiks who are still entrenched in the government hierarchy," commented *Komsomolskaya Pravda*. "We have a situation in which people in high places, who were supposed to be custodians of state secrets, are making those secrets available for egoistic and economic reasons."

Specialists finally concluded that whatever was being sold abroad as red mercury possessed no military application. Nevertheless, the affair underlined a graver question: how secure was Russia's vast nuclear and conventional arsenal when the politicians entrusted to guard it were susceptible to the lure of profit? The red-mercury case demonstrated how difficult it was to separate official connivance and criminal entrepreneurship on the New Russian frontier. There were plenty of other examples.

In 1992, employees of a metallurgical plant that produced enriched uranium in the Russian territory of Udmurtia decided to go into business for themselves. Led by a thirty-two-year-old named Sergei Suvorov, they worked out an ingenious scheme that exploited plant regulations allowing for a four-percent "leakage" of inventory.[33]

Over several months, they were able to accumulate nearly fifty kilograms of uranium without alerting plant managers to the loss. Workers hid the stolen uranium in empty beer barrels and storage sheds, smuggling it out of the plant when they could no longer camouflage the growing supply. Police later found the radioactive material in garages, apartment bathtubs, and even buried in a cemetery.

The workers opened their sales campaign by sending one of their number to Moscow, where he aroused interest from a Lithuanian "businessman." The Lithuanian was so impressed by the quality of the merchandise that he immediately bought the samples he was offered, and the ring arranged to supply him with a larger consignment. But the plan was foiled by a curious policeman at the Leningrad subway station in Moscow. Even then, authorities had no idea what they were dealing with. The militiaman thought he had apprehended a drunk, who told him an elaborate story of having been offered "zirconium" by a friend as repayment of a debt. The "zirconium" was confiscated and kept in a box at the local militia station for several months, until police were finally told what it was.

Undeterred, Suvorov's ring found other customers. A commercial firm in nearby Izhevsk—the city from which weapons had allegedly been shipped to the Irish Republican Army—bought ten kilograms for 270,000 rubles.

The most promising sales market involved a "Polish connection." An accomplice traveled to Brest on the Belarus border to make contact with a group willing to buy an unlimited supply. Several members of the ring immediately set off for the border with a small amount of uranium in the trunk of their car. They expected to sell their cache for almost seven hundred thousand dollars. Already anticipating the deal that would make them all rich, they celebrated the night before in a Brest hotel. The celebration was their undoing. Polish police, called to the scene by hotel guests incensed by the rowdy Russians, broke up the gathering and discovered the uranium among their belongings. Within a few months, all fifteen members of the ring were behind bars.

The most striking aspect of the case was the credulous behavior of plant officials. "It never occurred to them that someone from inside the plant would steal uranium," said *Sovetskaya Rossiya,* one of the Russian newspapers that delighted in recounting the tale. "Their security system was geared toward protecting the plant from outside infiltration, not from an inside job. The four-percent allowance for leakage turned out to be a hidden employee benefit. [But] perhaps that wasn't a bad thing, considering the economic situation of the country."

Reforms in bookkeeping and tighter inventory control were no guarantee of the security of Russian nuclear and chemical plants. The reduced status of the military-industrial complex affected the country's estimated 110,000 nuclear workers just as keenly as those who manufactured conventional armaments. Behind the fences guarding nuclear installations at the twenty-odd former "closed nuclear cities" across the country were hundreds of would-be entrepreneurs.[34]

Cases of "disappearing" materials filled the pages of the Russian press throughout 1992 and 1993—long before they were picked up by international media. At the Fosforit chemical plant near the Russian border with Estonia, three containers filled with cesium-137, a dangerously radioactive substance, disappeared in the fall of 1992. In March, 1993, Russian border guards discovered a kilogram of mercury, whose estimated market value was more than ten million rubles (about ten thousand dollars), hidden in the ceiling of a sleeping compartment on the Moscow-Tallinn train. In the St. Petersburg region alone, some five thousand enterprises worked with radioactive isotopes. "All of the plants are potential weapons because of the sloppiness and negligence of those responsible for their proper storage and protection," observed *Izvestiya*.[35]

But the post-Soviet Russian government consistently failed to address the problem. Perhaps because of its own vulnerability to corruption charges, the new leadership had by 1994 dropped most of its efforts to tackle the power of the defense bureaucracy. Soon after Yeltsin set up GAN (the State Atomic Energy Inspectorate) in 1991, it was attacked by defense managers who refused to allow "unauthorized" civilians on the grounds of nuclear installations. GAN continues to be virtually ignored by the bureaucracy. With a budget of less than seven million dollars, it has been unable to hire the inspectors or buy the equipment it needs to do its job properly. Stanislav Loutsev, GAN's deputy head of safeguards, told a Western reporter in 1994 that it would take at least one billion dollars and at least five years to create a viable inventory of Russia's nuclear materials. But in late 1994, the agency's role had still not been formally approved by the Russian parliament.[36]

Corruption, embezzlement, and theft in the defense industry were bound to increase in lockstep with Russia's economic difficulties. Yeltsin continued to promise higher pay and better living conditions to the military, but this appeared to have little effect on the secret trade in weapons and strategic materials. Instead, the Russian president found himself under a new obligation to his army commanders after they (grudgingly) secured his government by putting down the rebellion at the Moscow White House in October, 1993. One clear sign of the new balance of power was Yeltsin's submission to the army command's demand for a new "military doctrine" in late 1993 that purported to defend "Russian interests" across the former Soviet Union. The military-industrial establishment's increasing weight in Russian politics made it even less likely that the government would undertake serious investigations of its criminal activities. "I don't know whether to call these people old nomenklatura or new nomenklatura," Aslakhanov, of the law and order committee, said in reference to the corrupt arms bureaucracy, "but they still exert the same power."

Soldiers who sold guns and hired themselves out as mercenaries in ethnic and territorial conflicts outside Russia, or generals and defense managers bent on "restoring justice" by operating commercial enterprises, were not just enriching themselves—they were undermining one of the promises of the second Russian revolution.

Among the encouraging consequences of the Soviet Union's collapse was the early acceptance by Moscow of individual republics' claims to sovereignty. Moscow's reformers pledged not to interfere in the internal problems of their neighbors in the "near-abroad"—the term used to describe the newly independent states that had once formed the Soviet federation. But there were now serious questions about whether Russian diplomacy was being circumscribed, if not influenced, by Russian military "entrepreneurs."

The political dispute between Russia and Ukraine over the division of the Black Sea fleet during 1992 and 1993 contained an important, if unspoken, economic dimension. There were huge potential profits at stake in the sell-off of navy stores, ships, and equipment in the Crimea. And Russia's long-running quarrel with the Baltic countries over the withdrawal of troops and the disposition of military bases reflected the military's commercial interests as much as political concerns over the fate of ethnic Russians.[37]

Since early 1992, officers in the Baltic garrisons had been making small fortunes smuggling metals and oil from military warehouses. Hundreds of tons of copper had been stripped from communications cables for sale abroad. In one remarkable case, two torpedo ships were sunk in shallow waters at the Paldisky submarine base near Tallinn, the capital of Estonia, in order for divers to strip them of titanium, copper, and aluminum. Up to the last moment of its occupation in the Baltics, the Russian military was cheerfully taking full advantage of being located in the military-industrial establishment's richest private outlet to the rest of the world.

15 The Baltic Connection

To Westerners who lived in Moscow during the late Soviet era, a stay at the Palace Hotel in Tallinn, capital of the republic of Estonia, was as good as a vacation. The glass-and-concrete Palace would have been considered average in most northern European cities, but it was the Ritz of state socialist hotel-keeping. This was only partly explained by the fact that it was one of the new joint ventures of the perestroika economy, financed with private Scandinavian investment. The atmosphere of the place, like the tiny Baltic country in which it stood, was a gently rebellious statement about the rest of the Soviet Union. The staff smiled at guests, the telephones worked, the beds were comfortable, and every item on the restaurant menu was available. I traveled to the Baltic region regularly in the years since I first arrived in Moscow in 1987, and the Palace soon came to symbolize for me a certain brisk, quiet hope in this forgotten wedge of Sovietized Europe.

After the Kremlin regime fell, the Palace no longer stood alone. Opulent hotels—including some restored to their nineteenth-century grandeur—reappeared in Moscow and St. Petersburg. Yet the little hotel in Tallinn had lost none of its subversive charm when I returned to Estonia in the spring of 1993. The coffee in the gleaming art-deco expresso bar was even better than I remembered it, and a cosmopolitan air had swept away the last vestige of colonial insecurity. German and Swedish businessmen made deals quietly around the tables. I paid for my coffee with neither rubles nor dollars, but with the safe, easily convertible Estonian kroon. As I stepped outside the Palace's electrically operated glass doors, I saw late-model Western cars with Estonian and Scandinavian license plates. Across the central square, shops displayed the latest fashions from Stockholm and Helsinki. A stroll through the cobbled streets of Tallinn's old town, once gloomy and bleak, revealed cafés and antique shops selling Russian ikons to a steady stream of tourists.

Evidence of the country's prosperity also filled the pages of a local magazine I thumbed in the hotel lobby. New businesses, advertisements for restaurants, food shops, discotheques—even a sex shop—vied for space with photos of earnest officials in well-tailored Western suits. Tiny Estonia even boasted thirty private banks. After so many years of stale homilies from Gorbachev and his advisers, who had treated all three Baltic republics like rebellious teenagers—unable to make it on their own without the Kremlin's paternal guidance—this was truly a refreshing change.[1]

Yet if Estonia was more prosperous than anyone might have dreamed possible a few years ago, it was not entirely because of its technical prowess and "Western" work ethic. The Baltic countries sat at one end of the principal smuggling route of the former Soviet empire. The bulk of Russian contraband in raw materials and metals passed through Latvia, Estonia, and Lithuania. The "black commerce" in drugs, weapons, and stolen cars through the three nations on the Baltic Sea rivaled in quality, if not in quantity, the trade in those items along the second major route, leading south from Moscow to the Caucasus and Central Asia.

Estonia was one of the most interesting spots in the post-Soviet field of wonders. In early 1992, six months after it had regained its independence, the northernmost Baltic country rose to sixth place among world exporters of non-ferrous metals. What made this especially miraculous was that not a single ton of metal was produced in an Estonian factory.[2]

Smuggling was the key to Estonian prosperity. According to the Estonian Security Service, successor to the Estonian KGB, more than half a million dollars' worth of illicit metal passed through Estonia every day during 1992. The huge commissions earned from the sale of aluminum, copper, silver, titanium, and other materials whose production had been controlled by the Soviet military-industrial complex were invested in local banks and businesses, which in turn produced the tax revenue that made the Estonian kroon one of the most stable currencies in Europe.[3]

The Baltics were also the main transit corridor for Russian oil and petroleum exporters eager to avoid export duties. In September, 1992, the Department for Economic Crimes in the Russian Internal Affairs Ministry maintained that the flow of unlicensed oil to Europe, primarily through the Baltics, cost the government 190 billion rubles (about 950 million dollars) in lost revenue. The Russians claimed that Baltic officials added insult to injury by charging kickbacks for their help in moving the shipments. "We have heard that the export of one ton of oil costs exporters two dollars in bribes, which goes to officials in various organs of power," said Vyacheslav Soltaganov, chief of the MVD's economic-crimes department. "This comes to more than one hundred million dollars per year." [4]

But the beneficiaries of the smuggling trade were not limited to the Baltic side of the border. In what Russian police said was a typical case, a railway station manager in the Pskov region accepted a bribe of five hundred thousand rubles and a Lada car in exchange for closing his eyes to a trainload of fifteen thousand tons of motor fuel bound for Latvia in 1992.

The most obnoxious profiteers on both sides of the Baltic-Russian border dealt in human cargo. Latvian police sent nearly six hundred refugees back to Russia in 1992 after they were caught on ships heading across the Baltic Sea. But thousands more illegal immigrants successfully turned the Baltics into the Third World's newest gateway to the West. Iraqi Kurds, Somalians, Palestinians, Vietnamese, Lebanese, and Pakistanis traveled a complex route that began in Turkey and then took them across the Black Sea to Moscow, where they spent months in dingy hotels until they were stuffed into cattle trucks for the ride over the Western frontier to Riga or Tallinn. The final and most perilous leg took them in leaky tramp freighters or fishing boats across the rocky Baltic Sea.

The Baltic nations did not completely shut their eyes to the criminal commerce across their borders. "Among the former territories of the Soviet Union, Estonia has the most stable legal order and the fastest economic development, while in Russia we find a deepening social chaos," Estonian president Lennart Mari told a NATO forum in Brussels in November, 1992. "The pressure on the Estonian border will be increased by economic refugees, organized crime and the smuggling of drugs and weapons." [5]

He left out, oddly enough, the metal trade. Although the Estonian government officially condemned metal smuggling, it did little to prevent private citizens from making enormous profits from it. Dozens of private brokerage companies flourished, despite the government's official monopoly over metal exports. Between independence and the middle of 1993, each of the three successive administrations in Estonia passed a resolution banning private trade in metals, and each time the ban was lifted. Tiit Madisson, a former dissident appointed head of a government anti-corruption commission, claimed that his efforts were regularly sabotaged by authorities. "It's clear that officials want to preserve illegal smuggling for both material and political reasons," he said in early 1993. A few weeks later, his commission was disbanded.[6]

Among Tallinn's community of metal traders, a woman named Tiu Silvas stood out in both success and intrigue. In 1993, she was regarded as Estonia's richest businesswoman. Her company then had nineteen affiliates in Estonia and the former Soviet Union and an estimated annual turnover of ten million dollars. Silvas kept aloof from the local press, but her mysterious career excited widespread rumor and speculation. She was said to have started out as a flower seller on the black market during perestroika. Some believed that her rapid rise to wealth was assisted by Party money, and Tallinn residents darkly noted that she had retained former top officials of the Estonian KGB on the company payroll. No one had ever produced evidence of illegal activity, but any government clearly had to think twice before tangling with her. An Estonian cabinet minister who went to her home in Tallinn was brusquely turned away at the door by a security guard after Silvas sent word that he had failed to request a formal appointment. "She says it is discourteous of you to visit in this way," the guard told the stunned minister. No one denied that Silvas seemed to have a curious power over officialdom.[7]

"Every time the government suggests that it wants to investigate her company, she gets mad and threatens to move out of Estonia and take all her wealth with her," said a well-connected Tallinn journalist who told me the story about the snubbed minister. "It always works. The government does not want to kill a goose that lays such golden eggs. Metal trading has made this country rich, so it's in no one's interest to probe too deeply."

A four hours' drive south across the border, in the Latvian capital of Riga, the change looked equally remarkable to anyone who remembered the days of Soviet power. Prosperity had dramatically transformed the landscape. Riga's cobbled streets and squares, where campfires were lit by residents determined to prevent attacks by Soviet forces during the anxious months of 1991, were now lined with shops and elegant restaurants. Currency houses and exchanges stood on nearly every downtown corner. If you switched on the television in the local Swedish-financed hotel, you got commercials for escort services. Latvia's "economic miracle" also earned gestures of support from foreigners. Coca-Cola announced that it was investing fifteen million dollars in a Riga plant to serve all the Baltics.

But as in Estonia, smuggling smoothed the passage to capitalist success. Latvia's metal traders similarly thrived with little government interference. "The government always claims it can't harm free trade," a Latvian journalist confided to me. "But it evades the issue. We have had top government ministers implicated in scandals which in other countries would have forced people to resign. Not here. They just say, prove we did something wrong."

Daily newspapers were filled with advertisements from private companies offering to buy scrap metal. Again, as in Estonia, the companies thrived, despite a government monopoly. Although state-owned shipping organizations claimed that they accepted no metal of "questionable origin," few questions were asked. "Many small metal-buying companies are actually funded by the state firms," said Sandis Metuzans, an official of the Latvian defense ministry. "So everyone is protected, and the profits can be as much as one hundred percent." [8]

The contradictory legal codes of Russia and the Baltic governments provided additional protection to the canny smuggler. Russian law required an export license for shipping raw materials, but not manufactured goods. As a consequence, metal from industrial enterprises appeared at the border crossing as "plumbing fixtures" or "nails." Scrap timber was turned into wooden platforms or cheap furniture. Once inside Baltic borders, the material was shipped out again as "unfinished goods," to avoid import duties in Europe. If the smuggler was pressed for time, a wad of bills slipped to a customs official on either side of the border miraculously changed the nature of goods listed on an export certificate.

Often, such elaborate ruses were unnecessary, for the law assisted even the clumsiest attempts at contraband. In 1993, an Estonian border guard stopped two trucks at the border crossing with Russia. The drivers claimed that they were carrying onions from Ukraine to the market in Tallinn. "Show me the onions," said the guard. Grinning, the driver of the first truck jumped from his cab and walked to the back, motioning an assistant to help him. They pulled off a heavy tarp covering the load. The guard reached inside. He felt onions rolling in misshapen bundles.

"Unload them," he told the startled driver and his assistant. "It's late," they protested. "We have a job to do, just like you."

But the border guard refused to listen. He watched patiently as hundreds of onions tumbled to the ground, and then looked inside the truck again with his flashlight. At the bottom, he found large, heavy containers, still flecked with the dust of the road. He looked at the driver and the assistant. Angrily, they turned away. When the containers were broken open, more than twelve tons of copper were inside, bearing the marks of military-industrial enterprises in central Russia and Ukraine.

It was a good piece of detective work by an alert guard—but it wasn't the end of the story. The onions were loaded back onto the trucks, the drivers were told to return home, and the copper was held in a border warehouse. Two months later, the owners of the load arrived at the customs post and paid duties that came to 18 percent of the load's real value (as assessed by the Estonian customs officers). They immediately sold the copper to a Tallinn firm, which resold it to a large European trading house. Within days, the metal was on its way across the Baltic Sea.

Edgar Aaro, head of the Estonian border guards division, told the story with a mixture of pride and frustration. "The fact that the copper was stolen was legally not our concern," he said. "Once they pay the duties, they can do what they like with it." [9] Under Estonian law, only goods related to the commission of a crime—like drugs, or weapons—can be confiscated. Since Estonia does not regard the possession of scrap metal from Russia as a criminal act, regardless of how it was obtained, the smugglers are perfectly legitimate once they cross the border.

"Our legislators remember that the Soviets punished people by confiscating their property, so they excluded confiscation from our criminal code," explained Aaro, a former lieutenant-colonel in the Soviet armed forces. "Under our rules, property is sacred."

So, apparently, was profit. The Baltic governments' ability to close their eyes to the source of much of their good fortune turned them into something close to an offshore financial haven for their neighbors and former masters. In one of the shrewder decisions that turned the Baltic region into a laboratory of post-Communist economics, all three states stepped outside the "ruble zone" after independence. As well as giving their tiny economies a chance to integrate with the European market, this effectively sliced the umbilical cord to the flailing Russian economy. The new Baltic currencies were pegged to the dollar and the deutschmark, which in turn were allowed to trade freely on local currency markets, in the hope that the region's technological skills and liberal financial climate would provide an attractive base for investment.

Inevitably, the facility of free currency conversion on Russia's northwestern frontier attracted the rubles and dollars generated by gangster capitalism across the former Soviet Union. Currency auctions in Tallinn and Riga were regularly attended by Commonwealth wheelers and dealers. Once deposited in Baltic bank accounts, rubles became "real money," available for investment back home or convertible to dollars at attractive rates for investment in Russia or abroad.[10]

Accordingly, smuggling hard cash into Russia was as profitable as sending metal in the other direction. One enterprising business group stuffed more than four hundred million rubles obtained from a Lithuanian cooperative aboard two Yak-42 airplanes and flew the load to Yekaterinburg. Since there was no international customs post in that city in the Urals, the money smugglers avoided currency declaration requirements. Their "free" rubles were quickly plowed into real estate, commercial businesses, and the purchase of raw materials, which were then resold for hard currency.

Yekaterinburg police caught up with the operation too late to do anything. The money was "illegal" only when it was in transit. No one could be arrested for having rubles in Lithuania or in Russia. Frustrated investigators in Moscow claimed that there were dozens of such cases in 1992 and 1993. Baltic officials argued that they were helpless to prevent the use of their banking institutions and exchanges as money laundering facilities for Russia's white-collar criminals. It was up to Russia, they insisted, to clean up its own house.

The Baltic smugglers, however, plainly shared with their Russian counterparts an affinity for local nomenklatura capitalists. A Russian task force charged in 1992 that white-collar crime was supported at a "fairly high government level" across the Baltics. According to the report, the Baltic nomenklatura cooperated with their old comrades in the former Soviet Union to prevent any restrictions on the flow of contraband.[11]

Russian police suspected that Baltic white-collar criminals and smugglers were also connected with government officials in Moscow. "Our operative information indicates that the smuggling of raw materials (from the Baltics) is being reinforced at the highest level in Moscow," Boris Baturin, deputy head of the Russian MVD organized-crime division, told a Moscow newspaper in July, 1992. "We know there is a well-organized Baltic crime syndicate run by former Party nomenklatura and former KGB and police officials, which uses its connections inside the Russian leadership to monopolize export operations." [12]

Baturin gave no details, but the same month, Russian and Lithuanian investigators broke up a ring of army officers and senior government officials involved in a conspiracy to smuggle aluminum pipe from Russia to the Netherlands. The pipe was "purchased" by the Moscow International Center for Cultural Relations and "sold" to the Lithuanian Central Trading House in Kaunas. Russian military officers in the Baltic garrisons were listed on the customs invoice as receivers of the shipment, which thereby freed the shippers from paying Russian duties on shipping to non-Russian organizations.

The aluminum filled 340 railway cars, but investigators were only able to catch up with 115. They later found a telex from a Russian customs official in Moscow requesting that the International Center in Moscow transfer four hundred thousand rubles to a joint-stock society headed by his son. "Such a heavy flow of metals means there can be no doubt about the involvement of people at very high levels," said Metuzans.

A number of senior officials of the Soviet era have turned up as prominent Baltic bankers and businessmen. Indrek Toome, the former prime minister of Estonia and secretary of ideology for the republic's Communist Party before he became a leader of the independence movement, became chairman of the board of the Union Baltic Bank. The head of the Estonian Credit Bank was the former president of the State Bank of the Socialist Republic of Estonia, Rein Ottason. Former functionaries of the republic's Ministry of Foreign Trade and Gosplan (the department responsible for state economic planning) were now prominent brokers and company directors.

The prosperity of the nomenklatura was of course no proof of wrongdoing—just as the presence of the KGB in the company run by the mysterious former flower lady of Tallinn was not evidence of chicanery. But some of the new Baltic capitalists had a disturbing habit of falling victim to violence. A former Latvian foreign minister who went into business had his car blown up, and another former minister's car suffered six separate explosions. Adding to the suspicion that such men had more than casual associations with the world of Baltic white-collar crime were mounting reports of financial scandal. Several prominent Latvian banks failed during 1993. Bank officials claimed that it was because they did not get proper support from the government, but police suggested that they had become involved in shady financial operations.[13]

"There has been a lot of criminal money laundered through our banks," asserted Juri Pihl, the director of the Estonian security service. "Perhaps the officials weren't aware of this, but everyone knows that private banking is not exactly a tradition in our part of the world, and it's also easy to get around law enforcement organs, who don't know enough about how these tricks work." [14]

Pihl, a former senior police investigator who took over the old KGB offices in Tallinn, suspected that his predecessors were among his principal opponents. He made a point of noting the former KGB's involvement with Tiu Silvas' metal-trading operation. "I am not allowed to say anything about it," he announced crisply. "You draw your own conclusions."

In passing, he noted another case where the ties between business and officialdom raised awkward questions. In 1991, the Estonian division of Aeroflot privatized itself with the help of the Russian military—and the chairman of the new firm was the former commander of Russian air defense forces in Estonia.[15]

The enthusiasm of outsiders for Estonia's economic miracle was largely unaffected by such cases. "No country in the whole of the (former) Soviet bloc has had such success at the early stages of privatization," Herbert Schmidt, a German financial expert, said in 1993. But for some businessmen in Estonia and the other Baltic nations, the privatization boom carried unsavory consequences.[16]

There were thirty-one murders in Tallinn during the first seven months of 1992, which gave the city a murder rate proportionally eight times higher than an equivalent city in England. Contract killings in which mercenaries slit throats and raped their victims were regularly reported in newspapers. By then, Baltic law enforcement agencies could no longer ignore the clues pointing to a connection between smuggling, official corruption, and organized crime.[17]

"Since independence, we discovered a new kind of crime problem, related to unemployment, economic decline, privatization, whatever you want to call it," Col. Laimonis Liepinch, chief of the Organized Crime Investigation Department in Riga, told me. "On Freedom Street there are even young kids collecting 'taxes' for crime groups." [18]

I met Liepinch in his offices in the former KGB offices of the Latvian Socialist Republic. The irony of the location did not escape either of us. Leipinich, a lean, taciturn man, spent twenty-six years in the Soviet Ministry of Internal Affairs, ending with the rank of colonel, until the independence of his native country changed his life. He spoke slowly, pausing before each sentence, as if he were walking through an unfamiliar landscape.

"This is all new for us," he said. "We never had to worry about being afraid on the streets before. Now we have to use our weapons every day. Last year, I even had one of my policemen killed. These criminals all have the best weapons, which they buy for hard currency. And their murder techniques are getting more sophisticated. There have been cases where people were found wrapped in barbed wire in the river.

"Maybe this is normal. The same mess happened in 1919 when Latvia first got its independence. But I happen to think that things are worse now, because the moral level has fallen. People are not just insecure about the future—they don't care what they do.

"There is corruption from top to bottom. I have to live here, so I don't want to say what I think of our government."

The trail connecting organized crime and Baltic officialdom originated, like everything else, in Russia. In September, 1991, an ethnic Russian named Viktor Obakumov was killed by a bullet to the head in the Latvian capital of Riga. One of the city's leading gangsters for most of the 1980s, Obakumov was found slumped over the wheel of his car in the center of the city. The car had been rigged to explode.

Obakumov's death was followed over the next three months by a wave of violence. Cars blew up in the streets, kiosks were set on fire, and there were several assassinations. The violence shattered the long-standing tranquility of the Baltic underworld. Organized gangs were as deeply rooted in Baltic life as they were in Russia. Several *vory* controlled the region, and they were in turn controlled by more senior crime lords in Moscow. But until the final years of Soviet power, violence was rare.

"Criminals had a totally different mentality in the Baltics—more businesslike, you could call it," said Yuris Blaumans, editor of the city's leading crime weekly, *Pilnigi Atklati* (Totally Candid), and an observer of Baltic organized-crime groups for more than twenty years.[19]

The Baltic crime lords had a business specialty that made them particularly valuable to their partners in Russia and other areas of the former Soviet Union. Their control of the Soviet Union's closest outlet to the West set the scene for a unique smuggling operation. Prostitutes were sent from Moscow, Minsk, and Kiev to the Baltic ports to seduce foreign sailors, with the aim of marrying them and obtaining visas to live abroad. The so-called *interdevochki*—"intergirls" (international girls)—would remain on the mafiya payroll once they arrived in Scandinavia, Germany, or America. Their job was to apply for visas for their "uncles," "fathers," and "brothers" back in the Soviet Union. As a result, numbers of Soviet mafiosi escaped to the West, while local crime lords grew prosperous from their new overseas connections.[20]

Prostitution proved to be a crucial element in the expansion of Baltic crime. In his travels to Sweden, Finland, and Germany during the 1970s and 1980s, Blaumans was surprised to run into many mafiya bosses he had known at home. They proudly admitted that their visas had been arranged by intergirl "nieces."

"They were the same faces I used to see in Riga and Moscow, but they were organizing bigger stuff abroad. That's how Germany, especially Berlin, became a center for Russian organized-crime groups. It started right after unification in 1989. And their wealth really was made by smuggling stuff out when they left. They would even smuggle gold by putting it into the screws of an engine."

The expansion of the smuggling industry after the Soviet collapse changed the operating climate for Baltic crime lords. Obakumov's murder was the opening shot of a vicious struggle for control of an industry that promised wildcat fortunes.

Across the Baltic region, the competition turned violent. Lithuania officially recognized the existence of organized crime in 1992 after a 50 percent increase in the crime figures—to some fifty-six thousand separate incidents. The Lithuanian mobsters were heavily armed. During a raid on a gang hideout in Vilnius, the police found submachine guns, plastic explosives, and anti-tank grenades. Mob violence was threatening to become as much a part of reality in the Baltics as it was in Russia.[21]

In Riga, Blaumans was offended by what he perceived as the uncharacteristically murderous greed of his compatriots. "I suppose when you free a prisoner, he wants to take everything he can, as fast as he can, when he leaves," he said grimly. "We were all prisoners of the Soviet Union, used to a certain routine, certain rules. We were completely unprepared for freedom."

As in other parts of the old Soviet state, the most successful Baltic criminals had already forged alliances inside the nomenklatura. Since the onset of perestroika, much of the wealth obtained through official corruption and racketeering was laundered through legitimate businesses such as cooperatives. Meanwhile, prostitution had advanced far beyond the old intergirl days. So many private "firms" were involved in the business—one estimate was seventy—that the Estonian government was reportedly considering legalizing brothels.

Baltic investigators believed that with help from gangs abroad and from Russia, the Baltic racketeers had consolidated into one or two large syndicates operating across the region. According to the Estonian security service, the syndicates had strong links to gangs from St. Petersburg, the Urals, and the Caucasus.

Many expatriate mafiosi returned to the Baltics after independence. One boss, who emigrated to Sweden several years ago, operated a casino in Riga as a Swedish citizen. A prestigious club for foreigners in Riga was said to have been organized by a former intergirl.

"You can't say they are returning to the criminal world, because those businesses are all now legitimate," said Blaumans. "But the old connections haven't changed."

The establishment of a free-market oasis outside the Commonwealth of Independent States created the Baltic connection. While no one would admit it publicly, the wealth earned from Russia's economic disarray was seen as a kind of revenge for fifty years of occupation. As long as Russia's legal and economic systems remained a mess, there was little any of its neighbors could do about it, even if they wanted to. But the accompanying violence and insecurity presented to Baltic peoples the same moral dilemma confronted by Russians: was smuggling and white-collar crime a satisfactory basis for national prosperity? Even

Estonian border guard chief Edgar Aaro, despite his patriotic interest in extracting as many taxes as possible from smugglers, conceded that tolerance for illicit behavior would leave permanent scars.

"Smuggling is a very good way to get very rich," he said. "But it's corrupting all of us."

The evidence suggested that the price of the passage from Communist control was higher than anyone could have anticipated. This was a lesson, however, that still had to be learned in the West.

The networks established by the Baltic criminals in Europe added a special element to the Baltic connection. As comrade criminals continued to thrive, their ambitions led them beyond the borders of the old Soviet Union. Toward the end of our conversation, Col. Liepinch mentioned that some of Latvia's crime lords attended a meeting near Warsaw in the spring of 1993 with their counterparts from the Baltics, Eastern Europe, and Russia.

"We found out that they were meeting to divide Poland into spheres of influence," he said. "But the strange thing was that a conference of anti-crime officials from various European countries was going on at the same time nearby." He smiled thinly. "Maybe," he said, "the criminals were trying to tell us something."

16 The Evil Empire Revisited

Ruslan and Nazarbek Utsiyev impressed everyone they met when they arrived in London in December, 1992. The two brothers possessed a taste for luxurious living and an apparently bottomless bank account. They paid £995,000 in cash to purchase a four-bedroom penthouse apartment on Baker Street and promptly installed a jacuzzi and sauna. Neighbors could barely pronounce the place they came from—a country named Chechnya in the former Soviet Union—but they seemed to have outstanding credentials. The brothers called themselves "economic advisers" and said they were in the process of establishing a London consulate. They solemnly informed the British Foreign Office of plans to print passports, postage stamps, and new currency. One was a personal aide to the president, Dzokhar Dudayev. It was hard not to notice, however, that their lifestyle afforded them little time for diplomacy. There were loud parties nearly every night in their new home. Women were seen entering and leaving at late hours.

In March, 1993, a London courier was called to the brothers' penthouse to pick up a heavy, six-foot-long cardboard box and deliver it to a house in Middlesex. The box smelled strange. After the courier dropped off the box, he called police, who discovered that it contained the corpse of Ruslan Utsiyev sealed in polyethylene, wrapped in a carpet, and bound with tape. The thirty-nine-year-old Chechen had been shot three times in the head. A few hours later, investigators broke into the Baker Street apartment and found Nazarbek Utsiyev in bed, with three bullets in his skull. A German prostitute was discovered cowering in an adjoining locked bedroom.[1]

The murders caused a brief flurry in the press, but the meaning of what happened took time to sink in. A sinister new figure had suddenly appeared on the police blotters of Western countries—the post-Communist gangster.

After 1991, it was hard to find any nation in Europe that had not felt the impact of Russia's crisis of law and order. One-third of the serious crimes reported in Poland in 1992 was attributed to the "Russian mafiya," and 153 of the 250 foreigners jailed in Polish prisons that year were citizens of the Commonwealth of Independent States. More than one thousand CIS citizens were arrested in Hungary, and Budapest earned the label of "Beirut on the Danube" in 1992 because of the violent behavior of Russian criminals there. In Prague, struggles between Russian and Ukrainian groups regularly erupted in violence. In Sofia, Bulgarian police reported that it was virtually impossible to open a business without paying protection money to Russian gangsters. Over an eighteen-month period between 1991 and 1993, Russian gangs were responsible for at least a dozen murders in Berlin.[2] "We have learned to faultlessly identify the hand of the Russian mafiya, by its extreme cruelty," Hartmut Koschny, head of the Berlin police unit combatting Russian organized crime, told the *Moscow News* in May, 1993.[3]

At the start, Eurasian gangsters operated as a kind of bargain mob-for-hire. "Former Soviet citizens are highly prized by foreign crime groups," said Mikhail Yegorov, head of the organized-crime division of the Russian internal-affairs ministry. "They work for much less money, they are efficient, and they know how to depart the scene of the crime quickly."[4] Russian-speaking mobsters committed murders in New York City for less than two hundred dollars and the price of an air ticket from Moscow. Nikolai Shirokov, director-general of a Russian firm called Ural Region, was shot in Hungary by a professional assassin from Moscow in December, 1993.

But post-Soviet hitmen did not spend all their time killing each other abroad. As they grew accustomed to the capitalist working environment, post-Soviet criminals often pushed aside their local competition. The Armenian—the gang boss I met in the spring of 1993—boasted that the Russian mafiya already controlled prostitution in Italy. "That's why you see young Russian girls in nightclubs all over Europe," he told me. "We buy an interest in the clubs or casinos, and it costs very little to keep the girls there, near our rich clients." Russian criminal activities in foreign countries were not limited to drugs, prostitution, and racketeering. "Many people are investing actively in Holland and Belgium," the Armenian said.

Nor did they all originate in Moscow. Members of the gang that controlled the casino in Yekaterinburg told one of my informants that they planned to open a branch in Hamburg, where several wealthy Russian mobsters were already searching for apartments.

According to Russian police, crime syndicates based in the former Soviet Union conducted business in twenty-nine nations in 1993.[5] It was an eerily familiar problem. For decades, the Soviet Union had sent money and weapons to client states across Eastern Europe and the Third World. When the regime passed into history, most Westerners assumed that the channels of Soviet subversion would dry up. But the international activities of post-Communist mobsters gave new meaning to Ronald Reagan's hoary Cold War rhetoric about the "evil empire."

The former Soviet Union now exported professional hitmen, ikons, gold, drugs, and radioactive isotopes instead of spies—but the political impact on its neighbors was no less profound. Smuggled Soviet weapons and hardware fueled trouble in hot spots from the former Yugoslavia to North Korea. Smuggled strategic materials and metals threatened to destabilize the global economy. Russian aluminum and nickel appeared in such enormous quantities abroad that world prices for both commodities dropped in 1993. The glut was also held responsible for the lost of five thousand American smelter jobs in 1994.[6] Comrade criminals seemed poised to replace the KGB as the nemesis of Western governments. They were even pursuing their own mergers and acquisitions policy.

In the middle of 1993, a group of Russian and Italian mobsters held a summit meeting in Prague. The Russians secured a "franchise" to launder Italian drug profits in Russia, in return for a commitment to protect the new narcotics transit corridor between Eurasia and Europe.[7] The Prague summit, like dozens of similar meetings reported around Eastern Europe since 1992, testified to the new importance of post-Soviet gangs in the international hierarchies of crime.

On July 2, 1993, two chartered airplanes carrying passengers from Turkey, the United States, Germany, and Italy landed in Yerevan, the capital of Armenia. The passengers, all representing foreign criminal organizations, had endured the discomforts of a journey to the embattled Caucasus in order to attend the funeral of Rafael Bagdasarian, better known by his gangland pseudonym, Rafik Svo. Local authorities, in deference to the "international guests," closed certain streets for the funeral procession and even paved a road leading to the childhood home of the deceased. Evidently, the visitors were to be left in no doubt about the city's appreciation for one of its most accomplished native sons.

Rafik was a leader of Russia's Thieves World. Thirty-four of his sixty-three years were spent behind bars, but that did not prevent him from rising to become one of the Soviet Union's most powerful crime bosses. As the presence of foreign crime lords at his elaborate funeral showed, Bagdasarian was no ordinary vodka-swilling mob chieftain. He was the gangster equivalent of an international diplomat.[8]

In the councils of the Russian underworld, he argued for expansion into narcotics trafficking, real estate, and other areas that would bring Soviet gangsterism into the new age of capitalist crime. Rafik was among the small group of *vory* who recognized the opportunities the post-Communist Russian economy offered to foreign crime syndicates, and he turned into a shrewd and tough negotiator. He worked with his foreign counterparts to carve out new territories for the sale of drugs and arms in Eastern Europe and the Near East. He had been an active sponsor of the condominium established between the Russian and Italian syndicates seven months before his death; some said he even worked out an arrangement with the Colombians. But Bagdasarian never lived to see the fruits of his labors. The respect he commanded among his peers had saved him initially from the fratricidal war that broke out in 1992 over the issue of whether honorable thieves should deal in drugs, but he was murdered in prison a few days after being arrested in Moscow on a minor weapons offense. The killer, according to gang world sources, was hired by a rival who could not forgive Rafik's break with tradition.

By then it was too late to stop the movement that Bagdasarian and others had begun. Moscow, St. Petersburg, Vladivostok, Kiev, and other cities across Eurasia were providing private banking facilities for some of the world's wealthiest cartels in bids to become international crime capitals in their own right. The cozy relationship between gangsters and bureaucrats in Russia made it easy to guarantee a trouble-free investment. With such high-level support, Moscow even threatened to supplant banking cities like Zurich as the favored financial shelter for the international crime world. One 1992 case, in which seven billion dollars in suspected drug profits were brought from Europe to Russia, exchanged into rubles, and then reconverted to dollars for transfer to Switzerland, elicited a kind of backhanded compliment from Swiss authorities after investigators tried unsuccessfully to prove Russian official involvement. "It is difficult," the examining magistrate, Jean-Louis Crochet, responded dryly, "to make a distinction between private and official parties [in Russia]." [9]

London police faced a similar problem pursuing the story of the unfortunate Utsiyev brothers, in whose homeland the line between officialdom and gangsterdom had long since been crossed. The Chechen gangs began their international networking well before the Soviet Union collapsed; their stolen-car operations made them contacts in Turkey and Eastern Europe. After 1991, their improving financial base in Russia and their ties to the new government in Grozny allowed them plenty of scope for new business adventures elsewhere. One group of Chechens was believed to have set up an international money-laundering operation in an office building in Frankfurt. Authorities in Grozny appeared to back up the Utsiyevs' claim to diplomatic status by declaring that the murders had been committed by Russian intelligence agents as part of the Yeltsin government's campaign to discredit Chechnya. Another Chechen and a Georgian were originally arrested for the Utsiyev killings. But later investigations focused on an alleged plot by the brothers to ship two thousand Stinger anti-aircraft missiles bought in London to Azerbaijan for help in that country's war with Armenia. Two Armenians linked to Armenia's secret police agency were arrested for the murders. One hung himself in prison. The second was given two life sentences. Other evidence that came to light afterward strengthened the impression that the brothers had not been entirely truthful about the nature of their "economic mission." [10]

According to a report in the *Times* of London, the brothers met a U.S. businessman identified as Joseph Ripp shortly before they were murdered. In the midst of their hectic social schedule, they seemed to have found time to negotiate construction credits in return for the promise of deliveries of Chechnya oil. Ripp was reputed to be no ordinary businessman: the *Times* said that he had connections with the American mafia. [11]

If the story was accurate, it demonstrated how Russia's economic and political turbulence was being exported to the West. The Chechens were killed just as they may have been preparing to break into the most profitable overseas market of all for post-Communist criminals—North America.

On May 5, 1993, thirteen Russians and Americans were indicted in Newark, New Jersey, on charges of tax evasion, racketeering, and money laundering. According to the indictment, they were part of a ring that distributed gasoline and fuel oil across the eastern seaboard of the United States through a chain of fake companies, thereby evading an estimated sixty million dollars in sales taxes. It was a landmark of sorts in American criminal history. The accused were members of American mafia families and Russian syndicates. Michael Chertoff, the U.S. district attorney for New Jersey, called it "a snapshot of how traditional and emerging organized crime [groups] operate together." [12]

But it was only a snapshot. American police failed to connect the rise of Russian criminal activity in the United States with the collapse of the Soviet Union. This was a fatal oversight.

A year before the New Jersey indictments, the Russian ministry of internal affairs informed American law enforcement authorities that a crime boss known by his underworld nickname, Yaponets (Japanese)— or its diminutive, Yaponchik—was en route to America. "He applied for a visa from the American embassy, claiming that his profession was film director," Col. Anatoli Zhoglo of the MVD organized-crime unit told me. "We passed word to the FBI that if they wanted such guests, it was their affair. But we thought they would rather not have this kind of tourist visiting them." [13]

American police sources have denied to me that they had received the warning, but they conceded that it was astonishing that a man with Yaponets's reputation passed unnoticed through U.S. State Department red tape in Moscow. Aged fifty-one or fifty-two at the time of his visa application, Yaponets was the leading crime boss of the Russian Far East. He was regarded as one of the senior *vory v zakonye* in the Soviet Union. In late 1991, he was released from prison in the Irkutsk region, where he had been serving a long sentence for hooliganism and racketeering. By then, Yaponets had become identified with the crime faction arguing for more aggressive participation in narcotics trafficking. He was a leading advocate of a war to dislodge the Chechens and other

Caucasian gangs from their drug monopoly. His closest friend and ally was Rafik Svo.

There were more intriguing aspects to Yaponets's past. Like other Russian mobsters who came to prominence in the final decades of Soviet power, he had formidable political connections. He was said to be a friend of Yuri Churbanov, the former Soviet deputy internal affairs minister (and son-in-law of the late Leonid Brezhnev), who was later convicted of corruption. His friendships extended into the post-Soviet era. According to police, Yaponets's early release from prison was granted on the recommendations of a high official of the Russian Supreme Court and a leading reform politician in the Pacific region.

If U.S. investigators had been aware of it, the December, 1991, gathering of mob leaders at Vedentsovo, outside Moscow, would have given them an important clue to Russian gangsters' designs on America. Yaponets was at the meeting, making his first appearance since leaving prison. His sympathetic colleagues gave him an assignment that would keep him safely out of reach of local police while advancing their collective business interests. At Vedentsovo, the assembled *vory v zakonye* agreed to send Yaponets as an emissary to the United States, where he could investigate commercial opportunities. To protect his affairs while he was away, the crime lord named Rafik as his proxy representative.[14]

Considering Yaponets's authority, background, and official connections, his mission to America resembled the infiltration of a senior KGB spymaster at the height of the Cold War. American authorities may have been caught napping, but Yaponets's assignment was soon no secret in Russian-speaking communities in the United States.

"To the traditional articles of Russian export to America must now be added organized crime," *Novoye Russkoye Slovo,* the dominant Russian-language newspaper in New York, announced in the middle of 1992. "American mafiosi have already had the good fortune of becoming closely acquainted with 'colleagues' who emigrated from the former USSR, [but] we have also begun to see many new crime leaders traveling here from Russia, including *vory v zakonye*."[15]

The newspaper referred to Yaponets in particular. Calling him the "Red godfather," it declared that he had already achieved control of the Soviet emigre crime network established in the 1970s and 1980s among the thousands of Russian Jews who fled Soviet persecution. A subculture of crime and violence had long since attached itself to large Russian communities in neighborhoods like New York's Brighton Beach. But few American policeman were prepared for the "second wave" of Russian criminal immigration, one that would ultimately prove much more dangerous. "For a long time what we were seeing was . . . low-level thugs [from Russia]," Brian Taylor, an organized-crime specialist with the Federal Bureau of Investigation, remarked in 1994. "What we're beginning to see now [are] the professionals." Police in Miami, New York, Los Angeles, and other major cities began to detect a new professionalism among Russian gangs. In addition to the budding alliance with American mafia families, they found evidence of sophisticated bank fraud, counterfeiting, and money laundering. A group of Russians in southern California was arrested after setting up a string of fake medical clinics that earned them more than one billion dollars, the largest medical insurance fraud in U.S. history.

There was also a more professional tone to the violence. On January 26, 1992, a young Russian immigrant, Andrei Kuznetsov, was found murdered in his apartment in West Hollywood. His fingers had been chopped off and placed in a glass of beer to erase fingerprints—one of the telltale signs that this was a Russian gangland murder. Kuznetsov was later tied to an organization that smuggled computers and electronic equipment back to Russia. A newspaper investigation in Russia discovered that Kuznetsov had close ties to government officials. American police admitted that they might have to pay a heavy price for their late start in recognizing the threat from the former Soviet lands. "We're at a very rudimentary level," said Bill Doran, who formed a special unit at the FBI office in New York in 1994 to examine the new Russian criminals. He noted that the FBI did not begin targeting Asian criminal gangs until the mid-1980s, and "we only began having real success against them twelve or eighteen months ago." European authorities were a bit quicker off the mark, but it wasn't clear how much of an advantage they really had. "We are at the spider's-web stage," David Veness, then head of Scotland Yard's organized-crime unit, said in a 1993 BBC radio interview. "[Commonwealth] criminals are engaged in reconnaissance and are building their structures within Western capitals." [16]

Veness was more categorical in remarks he made to a conference of international law enforcement experts the same year. "In five years' time I have absolutely no doubt the major threats confronting the inner cities of the United Kingdom will be Central [European], Eastern European, and Russian criminals," he said.[17]

Nevertheless, the message was hard for the general public in Europe and America to digest. Amid the optimism—and relief—following the end of the Cold War, raising the specter of a new Red scare seemed impolite. Even those who focused on the criminal violence in Russia argued that post-Soviet gangsters were more of a threat to their compatriots than to their neighbors. But the list of criminal activities in which former Soviet citizens were caught outside their borders between 1991 and 1993—ranging from drug trafficking and money laundering to the smuggling of nuclear materials—allowed no credible excuse for inattention.

By 1994, Russian gangs were buying real estate and legitimate businesses around the United States and Europe. It was alleged that they were responsible for a mini–real estate boom in London, according to one source, who described Russians arriving with suitcases full of cash. "They are driving up prices everywhere," the source told me. Russian gangsters were also exploiting their countrymen, who were taking advantage of the removal of travel restrictions to seek opportunities in the West. Sweatshop owners in London's East End who employed illegal Russian immigrants were paying them protection money, and even Russian hockey players on teams abroad admitted that they were forced to pay off the mob. A U.S. law enforcement official told me confidentially that seven "major crime groups" from the former Soviet Union had been identified in America. In April, 1994, they met in Miami to discuss dividing up spheres of interest, in a gangland summit that the official compared to the "Appalachian" meeting of American mafia dons in 1957. Presiding over the Miami meeting was none other than Yaponets.[18]

"Organized crime in the former Soviet Union is fast becoming not only a law enforcement nightmare, but a potential national-security nightmare," Senator Sam Nunn, chairman of the powerful U.S. Senate Permanent Subcommittee on Investigations, said at a May, 1994, hearing in Washington that focused on Russian nuclear smuggling.[19]

If post-Soviet criminals seemed to be repeating the geopolitical games of influence and subversion played by the old Soviet empire, it was more than a coincidence. They enjoyed easy access to sophisticated channels long ago developed by the Kremlin.

For example, the KGB was long a secret source of weaponry for terrorists around the world. Communist Party records made public during 1991 and 1992 have documented this, and further proof was supplied in May, 1994, when President Yeltsin told the *Sunday Times* of London that Soviet agents had agreed to supply the Irish Republican Army with machine guns, rifles, and pistols during the 1970s. The same month as Yeltsin's disclosure, a British businessman told the newspaper that he had been asked by Russian gangs to serve as a middleman for the sale of anti-aircraft guided-missile systems, tanks, and explosives to the IRA. One of his business "partners" turned out to be a former KGB colonel.[20]

The vast Soviet military establishment in East Germany, which once provided a launching pad for Kremlin spies in the West, proved even more crucial to the export of post-Soviet crime in the 1990s. Under the terms of the agreement negotiated between Germany and the former USSR on the withdrawal of Soviet forces, the Russian army was allowed duty-free importation of goods and commodities worth up to six billion deutschmarks a year. The agreement provided a perfect cover for smuggling. Goods purchased ostensibly for army needs flowed in from Russia to the new customs-free zone. Before Russian forces left Germany in August, 1994, the garrisons and military installations were a major source of cheap black-market civilian goods and military equipment in Europe. German police were embittered by the easy success of the entrepreneurs from the East. The wide range of illicit goods passing through the old corridor of East Germany may explain why they seized on the 1994 arrests of nuclear smugglers to draw international attention to the larger problem of Russian criminal penetration of their country. "The Russian mafiya not infrequently succeeds in what seems to be utterly impossible," said Koschny. "[They] bribe German officeholders and customs officers, who are allegedly noted for their incorruptibility." In 1992, profits from organized-crime activities in Germany were estimated at 438 million dollars.[21]

The globe-trotting comrade criminal suffered from no shortage of funds. His activities were well financed by the shadowy network that connected government and crime back home. The strength of that network, and the goals it served, were demonstrated by a case reported in the Canadian city of Toronto.

In early 1993, a twenty-nine-year-old Russian, Dmitri Yakubovsky, turned up as the owner of a mansion in one of the most exclusive neigh-borhoods of the city. He claimed to be a successful businessman—a claim that aroused little curiosity despite his relative youth. Toronto's Russian-speaking emigre community of fifty thousand was the second largest in North America (after New York),and had made the city an important hub of trade with Russia. Since the fall of Communism, thou-sands of Russian immigrants had passed through Canadian immigration, and hundreds had already become rich by exporting Western goods back home.

Yakubovsky was a man of substantial means. The young Russian paid for his luxury house with five million dollars in cash. He quickly began to install security arrangements that were noteworthy even for that prosperous section of the city. His gabled house, set on a large, wooded estate, was fitted out with television surveillance cameras. security guards patrolled the grounds twenty-four hours a day.

But Yakubovsky's neighbors were not aware that he had turned his home into an armed camp. One afternoon, a frightened woman walked into a firearms control office in downtown Toronto, carrying an arm-ful of guns. The woman, who was accompanied by a thick-set man, gave her name as Marina Krasner. She wanted to register her thirteen handguns and rifles as a gun collector and a member of a local gun club.

The clerk who took the application said later that it was an impres-sive armory. The weapons included an AK-47 assault rifle, an M-16 semi-automatic rifle, a 10-millimeter semi-automatic pistol, several .38 caliber Smith and Wesson revolvers, and two nickel-plated .45 caliber revolvers. Krasner's friend seemed to be in control of the situation. "He was talking to her in Russian, like he was telling her what to do about the guns," the clerk recalled. "It was odd that a woman who didn't seem to know much about firearms would have all those guns." [22]

The man who accompanied her was her husband, Dmitri Yakubov-sky. He had a good reason for accumulating so much weaponry: two weeks earlier, someone had fired three shots at the gate of the Yaku-bovsky mansion. The incident was investigated by local reporters, and it provoked a brief flurry of attention to activities of the Russian-emigre mafiya in Canada. Yakubovsky hired his own local consultant to shield him from media queries. From then on, when he left his house in one of the Mercedes Benz cars regularly parked outside, he was accompanied by bodyguards. His enemies, he hinted to reporters, were more sophisticated than the local emigre criminals. A handwritten note in Russian left at the gate of his home after the shooting had warned Yakubovsky to stop talking about "A.I." and "B." if he wanted to remain alive.

Yakubovsky's friends told unsuspecting Western reporters the "A.I." stood for the first name and patronymic of then Russian vice-president Rutskoi. In fact, Rutskoi's name was Aleksandr Vladimirovich. The discrepancy was passed over in the attention paid to the other initial on the death threat. "B" was said to represent Boris Birshtein, a Lithuanian native who had settled in Toronto several years before Yakubovsky and had developed profitable connections in his former homeland as founder and chairman of a Swiss-based multinational firm called the Seabeco Group.[23]

The cryptic letter heightened the mystery surrounding Yakubovsky's presence in Toronto. After investigations into his background by Canadian and Russian journalists, it became clear that the young "businessman" led several parallel lives. Shortly before coming to Canada, he had been deputy director of Birshtein's company in Zurich. But his qualifications for international business were open to question. Before 1991, he was a junior aide to the Moscow procurator (one report said that he had been a janitor). Yakubovsky's charm and a certain native shrewdness won him introductions to several officials in the Yeltsin government, who began to use the young man as a go-between in various projects to obtain international financial assistance for Russia.[24]

Some of those projects, including the establishment of a fund for disposing of Soviet military property in Germany, later became the target of accusations of fraud by government critics like Rutskoi. But Yakubovsky seemed to have a special talent for changing adversity into fortune. By the time he turned up in Canada, he held the rank of general in the Russian security service.

Yakubovsky confided to reporters that not only had he quit his job with Birshtein, but he was now actively working with the Russian government to bring his former employer to trial in Moscow for arranging the illegal transfer of state funds. According to Yakubovsky, one of Birshtein's clients was Russia's vice-president. He gave the press a photocopy of what he claimed was an authentic copy of a transfer order of three million dollars in Rutskoi's name to a private account in Switzerland.[25]

When these charges became public, Birshtein immediately launched a libel suit against Yakubovsky. There were obvious political interests at work: Rutskoi at the time was leading a heated campaign charging top Yeltsin ministers with corruption. The Russian government, searching for a way to strike back, apparently decided to put Birshtein on its list of hostile foreign businessmen. One official at a Moscow press conference called Seabeco a "terrible shadow" over the Russian economy. But the shots fired at Yakubovsky's home suddenly gave the whole thing a more sinister air.[26]

As in London, Russia's domestic quarrels and criminal conspiracies were beginning to spill into the West. Canada was a natural target for comrade criminals. The U.S. State Department, in its 1994 narcotics survey, identified it as one of the world's high-risk countries for money-laundering activities.[27] Yakubovsky suddenly became the object of intense interest from Canada's security service as well as local police. Urgent messages passed between Toronto, Ottawa, Washington, and New York, as investigators began comparing notes about the influx of huge sums of money from Russia and the other former Soviet republics. Much of this money was coming from dozens of businesses and firms based in Russia which could not be traced, and the Yakubovsky-Birshtein case helped alert Western law enforcement agencies to Russia's growing prominence in underground global finance. Another twist came from unconfirmed reports out of Moscow that the anti-corruption commission was looking into charges of gun smuggling related to the affair.

Then, as if following a bad Hollywood script, Yakubovsky turned up in Moscow in July, 1993, where he held a secret meeting with the Yeltsin government's latest anti-corruption commission, set up after the previous one, manned by Vladimir Kalinichenko, fell apart. What Yakubovsky told his interlocutors was made public in sensational headlines across Moscow. He accused the Russian procurator-general, Valentin Stepankov, of plotting the murder of the new anti-corruption commission's chairman, Andrei Makarov. Yakubovsky played a tape recording he had secretly made of a conversation between himself and Stepankov in which the alleged plot was discussed. Stepankov, perhaps coincidentally, was already disliked by Yeltsin's circle, because he had been pressing to investigate Rutskoi's corruption charges.[28]

A week later, Yakubovsky was back in his Toronto mansion, having been spirited out of Russia by a circuitous underground route to avoid, according to insiders, the assassins who were still gunning for him. He did not stay long. After refusing persistent requests for interviews that might clear up what was going on, he left his home—and, apparently, his wife—in order to resettle in Moscow, where he is, according to acquaintances, once again working closely with the Yeltsin government. As of this writing, none of the charges and countercharges—ranging from Birshtein's libel suit to Rutskoi's financial dealings—have come to trial.[29]

The Yakubovsky affair was a signal that the fallout from the struggle for power and wealth in post-Communist Russia had reached the West. The Seabeco case and Yakubovsky's charges coincided with the resignation of Security Minister Viktor Barannikov, First Deputy Internal Affairs Minister Andrei Dunayev, and Prosecutor-General Valentin Stepankov. Dunayev's and Barannikov's wives allegedly took a shopping trip to Zurich at Birshtein's expense. Also fired was the minister of foreign trade, Sergei Glazev.

The principal loser in the affair was Rutskoi, whose efforts to weaken Yeltsin's reform allies by the manipulation of corruption charges had backfired. The vice-president was now vulnerable to an examination of his own questionable links abroad. In June, 1993, a month before Yakubovsky told his story to investigators in Moscow, the FBI arrested two Russian emigres on charges of conspiracy, extortion, and tax evasion. The two men, Dmitri Belokopytov and David Shuster, were accused of evading taxes totaling fifteen million dollars by reselling private heating oil in New Jersey and Pennsylvania, a similar scheme to the one that exposed the connection between Russian gangsters and the American mafia.

Freed on bail, the men fled to Russia. David Shuster, nicknamed "Dodik," turned up in the Moscow offices of a joint venture called Eurocom—which happened to be located in the same building as Vozrozhdeniye. The common address was more than a coincidence. Shuster's business partner and close friend was identified as Akop Yuzbashev, the vice-president of Vozrozhdeniye and reputed to be one of the men who helped arrange the smuggling of the Argentine weapons found a year earlier by Moscow police captain Yuri Nikishin.[30]

The Yakubovsky and Shuster cases indicated the growing tendency of comrade criminals in Moscow to manipulate their shadowy political and business connections abroad into sources of profit and influence. Few

Western authorities suspected how lucrative such connections were. According to Gen. Gennadi Chebotarev, of the Russian MVD, at least twenty-five billion dollars were transferred from the Commonwealth of Independent States to Western banks by Russian organized criminal structures by late 1993.[31]

The penetration by comrade criminals of Western economies may already have reached a level beyond which government action can have any effect. "The leaders of organized crime in our country are very intelligent people," Aslambek Aslakhanov, of the former parliament's law-and-order committee told me. "They can react instantly to political, economic, or other changes in Russia and overseas. They are much quicker than our own politicians. In fact, they have their own politicians working for them, as well as economists and lawyers."

To Inspector Vladimir Kalinichenko, assigned by the Yeltsin government to trace the flow of Russian funds abroad in 1991 and 1992, the degree of financial sophistication among Moscow's gangster-bureaucrats was remarkable from the start. "We would follow transactions from Moscow to South America, then to New York, then to a bank in Paris or Monaco," he told me in 1992.[32]

The sudden appearance of global financiers in the former Soviet Union, a country that had never seen a stock exchange before the beginning of the decade, defied simple explanations. There were many genuine entrepreneurial talents liberated by the collapse of Communism, but the knowledge, experience, and capital necessary for dealing in the international banking world was markedly lacking. Kalinichenko believed that he found one explanation while investigating the activities of a Moscow company that formed a partnership with Russian emigres in America. The firm established a one-billion-dollar credit line through its new partners for the purchase of Western consumer goods and used the promise of credit to raise nine billion rubles from "investors" in Russia and Ukraine.

The Moscow businessmen obtained a letter of guarantee from the Russian government in order to qualify for the credits and gained backing from a parliamentary committee. The investors' funds were deposited in an interest-bearing account in a local bank, and dollar loans obtained on the basis of the credit guarantee were deposited in interest-bearing accounts in the United States.

But not a single item was ever purchased for delivery to Russia. Instead, both accounts were closed after a few months; the loans were repaid, and Russian investors were given back their original funds, with the explanation that the deal had collapsed. The American and Russian partners pocketed the interest. Kalinichenko discovered that not all the nine billion rubles raised in Ukraine and Russia had been returned to the original investors: two billion rubles had been distributed to factories associated with the military-industrial complex. "I believe that was part of the Communist Party money which we spent so much time and made so much noise searching for abroad," Kalinichenko said.

According to the investigator, the deal covered a scheme to launder some of the Party money locked up in banks at home and abroad after the collapse of the Communist regime. The "investors" had set up dummy companies in order to serve as a screen for freeing the funds. Once the money had passed through the Moscow bank as an investment, it could be returned to its rightful owners. The two billion rubles sent to military-industrial managers gave the game away. Some of the participants in the scheme, Kalinichenko believed, were too impatient to wait for another bank transfer and wanted their money immediately. Meanwhile, the American account would continue to be a handy reserve for channeling funds back to Russia.

"The whole idea was to get the money back working inside Russian banks and commercial deals as soon as possible," Kalinichenko said. "It was good starting capital for a lot of projects these bureaucrats are interested in—from commercial ones to political ones."

Kalinichenko couldn't prove his theory. Like most of his other cases, the investigation was squelched as soon as it appeared to implicate someone at a high level, and he believed that one of the comrade criminals involved was allied with either a minister or a deputy minister. (The Moscow company, after all, had no trouble getting a letter of guarantee from the government.) Arranging easy credit and quick money transfers was a skill refined to an art by Communist Party mandarins and senior KGB officials who needed large amounts of funds for activities abroad or secret assistance to foreign sympathizers.

"They have changed their names, but they haven't gone away," Kalinichenko told me bitterly, long after he had left the anti-corruption commission. "I remember one incident that happened after we actually managed to stop a couple of international transfers. We were feeling pretty happy about it, and I got a visit from a KGB man I know, but who didn't really know what I was working on. We were chatting, and he suddenly said, 'Some bastard has destroyed four of our transfer operations.' That told me everything."

Kalinichenko had little expectation that such maneuvers would end—and even less that the West would understand how its institutions were being used to sabotage Russia's transition to democracy. "A healthy law-abiding majority keeps the mafiya limited in the West," he said. "We have nothing like that. I divide our country up between people who work in places where they can steal and those who work where they can't steal anything. In this sort of environment, the people who were in official posts can still do whatever they want. They don't even have to get back in power, although some of them already are."

Listening to him, I wondered how much of this bleak perspective was the result of Kalinichenko's anger over his treatment at the hands of uninterested government officials. But in the years since we first spoke, Russia's increasing corruption has borne out his pessimism.

Despite the widening impact of post-Soviet organized crime on the West—from smuggling, gun dealing, and international drug trafficking to the laundering of Communist Party money—the comrade criminal's main interest was his homeland. Russia's field of wonders offered enormous riches and a path to economic and political influence in the new economy. The gangster-bureaucrat's ability to use the breakdown of the Soviet regime and the vacuum of legal authority to amass wealth and power ensured, ironically, that the old system would never return—even as it transformed the character of the second Russian revolution.

The price of success was high. It was set not only in the number of dead and wounded in gang wars and assassinations, but also in the damaged illusions of those who believed that the revolution was supposed to have brought a better life. The anger and disappointment of millions of Russians had become a new political force to be reckoned with. The backlash threatened not only Russia's democratic future, but also the dream of a peaceful, post–Cold-War international order.

III Crime Fighting in Utopia

"Nothing is impossible in Russia but reform."

—Oscar Wilde

"Today is not the time to stroke people's heads;
today, hands descend to split skulls open."

—Vladimir Lenin, letter to Maxim Gorky

17 Cops and Commissars

Perhaps no country deserved an honest, capable police force and a trustworthy system of justice more than Russia did after December, 1991. The Soviet Union had been the world's most heavily policed state. Security and law enforcement functions were concentrated in an awesome troika—the Ministry of Internal Affairs (MVD), the State Security Committee (KGB), and the Soviet Procurator's Department—which by and large placed the interests of the Party ahead of the security of the citizen. Millions of policemen, plainclothes agents, highway sentries, informers, militia troops, state investigators, and public safety "volunteers" kept (or tried to keep) the same unblinking vigil over society as their czarist predecessors had in the centuries before the 1917 revolution.

The streets were safe, yet the state was essentially lawless. As long as citizens didn't openly threaten authorities by competing for power or wealth, they were free to cheat or challenge the state's innumerable petty regulations, on the often-correct assumption that few authorities, least of all the mandarins of the Party, followed those regulations themselves. This paradox of a police state and a corrupted populace was not exclusive to the Soviet regime, but it was virtually institutionalized during the final, troubled years of Communist power. A 1989 booklet on the Soviet justice system defined criminal behavior as being whatever was considered "socially dangerous"—a phrase that in Soviet-speak generally meant anything construed as a challenge to state authority. Since it allowed officials to ignore a multitude of other offenses at their discretion, the concept was considered far superior to more "formalistic" Western types of justice. "Soviet law has never had a formal approach to [defining crime]," boasted the booklet's authors. "That is why an action or lack of action which, formally speaking, has features of an act described in the criminal code, but is not socially dangerous because of its insignificance, cannot be recognized as a crime." [1]

Such Orwellian definitions allowed Soviet authorities to develop the myth that they lived in a crime-free state compared to the sinful, capitalist West. "After 1917, our crime rate grew just like everywhere else in the world," Vadim Bakatin, the country's last chairman of the KGB and its penultimate police minister, confessed to me. "But around the time of major anniversaries and holidays, it would suddenly dip. At anniversaries, you see, everyone had to report something positive." [2]

Soviet legal sophistry turned crime into an ideological construct rather than an unfortunate by-product of human relations. The role of police and legal bodies was at the same time both impossibly broad and narrowly restricted. Every citizen was a potential criminal until all vestiges of capitalist society were eliminated. But economic enlightenment rather than a police force was regarded as the ultimate corrective tool. "We thought that as socialism was perfected, the social base for crime would gradually disappear, and crime would disappear as well," Bakatin observed. "So there was no point in spending money on criminal justice, on modernizing the police, on training prosecutors, or even on improving our courts. That attitude left us vulnerable to everything that has happened since." [3]

Post-Communist Russia's descent into criminal anarchy was, in other words, a crisis waiting to happen. The formidable network of Soviet police and security organs had collapsed like a deck of cards. Centralized files and a hierarchical organization in which all orders and decisions were made in Moscow disappeared, and one-time Soviet legal officials suddenly found themselves enforcing the orders of new authorities from Estonia to Armenia. Moreover, police and judges were shorn of the political protection that had covered over their inefficiencies. They were forced to confront gangsterism and corruption as real crimes rather than as ideological offenses. And they were faced with an unfamiliar new constituency: instead of placating Party bosses, they had to respond to the outrage of millions of people who no longer felt safe in their homes and neighborhoods. At the very moment when an emerging political and economic regime needed protection, police found that their power and authority were as devalued as the ruble.

There were two ways to deal with such an all-encompassing crisis of law and order. One was to use the opportunity to build the foundations of a new civil society. The other was to reconstruct some of the Soviet institutional approaches to crime fighting, minus the ideological bag-

gage. This included some of the repressive police-state techniques that
had been familiar tools of czarist authorities: searches without warrants,
detention for long periods without trial, arbitrary forms of punishment.
As Russia's crime rate grew to overwhelming proportions, frustrated
authorities adopted the second option. By 1994, the governments of
Russia and other former Soviet republics had discarded most of their
early commitments to legal reform. A new civil society required a new
consensus, as well as new laws—a transformation of the official habits
and popular attitudes that had developed in response to systemic abuses
of power by government in Russia. Centuries of cynicism about the
law could not be wiped away in a few years. The police state (albeit
in a milder form) was on its way back, this time blessed by popular
approval.[4]

The inevitability of such an outcome should have been obvious
from the beginning. Stanislava Gorodenskaya, a Moscow psychologist,
warned a month after the country broke apart that the essential conser-
vatism of Russian society left few people prepared to cope with dramatic change. "The Russian has lived for centuries with a strict sense
of social correctness and hierarchy,' she said. "We are not used to the
idea of freedom of choice."[5]

But to their credit, Russia's democratic leaders gave the first option a
courageous try. In the phrase of John Hazard, an American legal scholar
and a longtime observer of Soviet legal institutions, a "fresh breath"
entered Russian jurisprudence for a few exciting years.[6]

In October and November, 1991, the Russian parliament adopted
two documents designed to be the basis for new legislation enshrining
a civil society guided by the rule of law. The Concept of Judicial Reform and the Declaration of the Rights and Freedoms of the Individual
and Citizen marked dramatic departures from Soviet legal custom. Followed by papers outlining similar new "conceptions" of criminal law
and procedure, they sought to bring Russia's legal system into line
with accepted principles of Western jurisprudence. They provided for,
among other things, the presumption of innocence, the right to a fair,
speedy, open trial, an independent judiciary, legally imposed limits on
the use of force by police, and the protection of private property. The
documents also sought to "decriminalize" many of the previously un-
enforceable (and ideologically inspired) crimes of the Soviet era, such
as speculation and hooliganism. Finally, the reformers set themselves

the ambitious task of rewriting the functions of the state's principal law enforcement bodies. Some of these ideas actually found their way into formal legislation. Many dropped by the wayside, and even more—in time-honored Russian tradition—were corrupted, weakened, or simply ignored in practice.[7]

The most sweeping changes occurred in the complex and byzantine Ministry of Justice, whose bureaucracy ran the courts, wrote legislation, and set the pace for the judicial system. On June 26, 1992, judges were formally awarded life tenure upon election by local and municipal bodies. This crucial reform was intended to sever in one stroke the former dependence of the judiciary on the Communist Party and protect it from the whims of politicians. Judges were required to swear oaths of office, pass qualifying exams, avoid the appearance of impropriety, and even wear robes. Later amendments to the legislation mandated that judges hear most cases alone, without the presence of the so-called "lay assessors," who had formed part of the system of "people's courts" under Soviet power. Along with the establishment of an independent professional judiciary, the new government established clear demarcation lines for civil and criminal cases and strengthened special judicial proceedings such as "arbitrage courts," which had been used in Soviet times to settle disputes between state enterprises, so they could rule on all cases involving private commercial issues. The government re-introduced the concept of twelve-person jury trials, first established by Russian legal reformers in 1864 and eliminated by the Bolsheviks, for all crimes carrying sentences of more than a year.[8]

When members of the American Lawyers Committee for Human Rights visited Russia in 1992 they discovered, however, there was still a large gap between judicial reality and the dreams of reformers. Often they found that the new structures had merely been grafted onto old attitudes. Judges in the city of Vladimir, for example, complained to committee members that they still depended on local councils and the ministry for their housing. One said that the tyranny of the Party had merely been replaced by the tyranny of legislators. The Americans found this point underlined when they attended a Moscow trial in which police were accused of killing an innocent women (having broken down the wrong door). The judge in the trial was visited regularly by a policeman who happened to be a member of the Moscow City Council. After handing down a ruling against the police, she was informed that an apartment she had expected to receive from the city was no longer available.[9]

When they returned home, the American lawyers nonetheless concluded that a "revolution" was under way in Russian jurisprudence. They felt comfortable making that conclusion on the basis of their comparison with the previous system, which, as they wrote, "combined an image of legality with an underlying vacuum of legal guarantees." But they were not sanguine about the prospects of change. "It is tempting," they wrote, "to imagine that the contradictions between the rule of law and the interests of the governing elite have vanished now that the Communist party no longer enjoys a formal monopoly of power. But this is hardly the case. Many of the contradictions which plague the reform process today are the same contradictions which beset the Soviet Union under President Gorbachev's leadership. By and large the people in leadership positions are the same people, the dominant governmental institutions are the same institutions, and the 'mind-set' of the majority of those in power is the same 'mind-set' as it was under Soviet power." [10]

I was able to judge for myself the effects of the lingering Soviet system when I paid a call in 1993 on Zoya Korneyeva, chief judge of the Moscow Appeals Court. The court, which sits at the apex of thirty-three regional criminal courts in Moscow and oversees 470 judges, is located in a rundown building on Kalinichovskaya Street, in the central district of the capital. Korneyeva's office, on the third floor, is accessible by passing through grim corridors crowded by relatives of the accused. Every available space on the wooden benches was occupied. Several people were sitting on the stairs. By contrast, Korneyeva's corner office was elegant and comfortable, with a large antique samovar on one of the glass shelves in the corner. She sat behind a green desk, an expensive amber pin prominently fixed to her dress. A self-assured women, who conveyed the special guarded and smug air of a member of the elite bureaucracy, the chief judge thought that the reforms had gone as fast as they should—perhaps a little too fast.

"There are so many new laws, it's hard to keep up," she said. "People always get access to lawyers, and we are careful to protect the accused. I admit that the individual and his problems were always somewhere in last place." [11]

Korneyeva also admitted it was hard to cope with the rising crime rates—she had recently been the victim of a mugging (someone attempted to grab her necklace in a city street)—and it was difficult to fill vacancies in the court system because of low pay and the threat of violence.[12] But she seemed to blame the rapid introduction of Western concepts of legal procedure for the chaos in her courtrooms. "People are getting such an attitude now," she told me stiffly. "Judges are not called 'your honor' any more. People tend to think automatically that whatever we had before was bad."

Whatever the merits of court reform, the system was clearly paralyzed by rising crime rates. Suspects were often released because of the backlog in cases. Of the 2.7 million crimes registered in 1992, 871,000 were "solved," and some 611,000 people were tried and convicted. Although the murder rate climbed that year, the number of murder convictions actually dropped by 2 percent from the previous year.[13]

But Korneyeva's nostalgia for a simpler time was an important part of the "mind-set" of other legal institutions which successfully resisted change. In January, 1992, the Russian parliament passed a law that purported to reform the procuracy system. The procurator was the lynchpin of Soviet justice. With no real parallel anywhere else in the world, he served as judge, policeman, and prosecutor—conducting the official investigation into a case, signing the warrants for arrest, and then presenting the evidence in court as attorney for the prosecution. The three functions were not seen by Soviet jurists as contradictory. The procurator was regarded as the ultimate guarantor of due process and the rights of the accused. But in practice, he was the state's (and, by extension, the Party's) principal legal official. Once he had marshaled the evidence of guilt, there was little for the judge and the defense attorney to do except argue over sentencing. His primary function was, in effect, to be a watchdog over individuals, government bodies, and state organizations (except those of the Party) who threatened the state's interests—a function first established in the time of Peter the Great, when the procurator was called "the eyes of the czar." The Soviet procurator-general, like his czarist forbears, led an enormous hierarchy that assigned procurators at every level of government, from regional and municipal to republic. The procurators had their own police force of investigators, who wore distinctive uniforms and were empowered to make arrests.

Despite the obvious potential for abuses in a system that effectively usurped the judiciary's role, post-Communist officials were loath to discard the tradition. As regional and municipal governments rebelled against Moscow, the procuracy proved essential to the security of the uncertain democrats in the Kremlin. In the first eighteen months after the fall of Communism, procurators overturned almost two hundred thousand decisions made by local authorities that contradicted central-government decrees.[14]

Post-Communist lawmakers, accordingly, left most of the procurator's powers unchanged. If anything, the escalation of corruption and organized crime turned him into an even more pivotal figure in the justice system. Uniformed "prosecutors" in every city pursued investigations of criminal syndicates that often put them in direct competition with police. The two law enforcement bodies were, of course, supposed to cooperate. But with each jealously guarding his prerogatives against the other, the fight against organized crime began to appear like a Keystone Cops version of justice. It grew so bad that by 1993, the deputy chief of the MVD's organized-crime squad directly accused procurators of destroying investigations or refusing to take cases to court that they had not been involved in. "People say we have bad laws, but certain officials aren't even bothering to enforce the laws we have," fumed MVD general Gennadi Chebotarev.[15]

The MVD was perhaps the enforcement body left in the weakest and most disorganized shape by the collapse of Soviet justice. As administrator of the nation's police forces and prisons, the Ministry of Internal Affairs was a cumbersome, shapeless bureaucracy, whose power depended on its numbers and its reach across the country's eleven time zones rather than on the support of vested Party interests inside the Soviet system. Although this ensured the *militsiya* (militia) or ordinary police officer a grudging respect never given the security organs, the MVD was always the poor cousin of Soviet law enforcement. At the same time, its police powers were largely unchecked. Post-Soviet reforms did little to change either aspect of the MVD's situation.

A law adopted in April 1991 set out the role and duties of the militia, but its sole significance was that it publicly endorsed the powers that police had been awarded secretly under Soviet rule. There were provisions prohibiting any link with the Communist Party and enjoining police against committing abuses of office, but the law established no procedure for complaints. In March, 1992, the Supreme Soviet approved a law on criminal investigations that only further codified the old Soviet investigative "techniques." According to the Lawyers Committee, the legislation contradicted the guarantees pledged in the "conceptual" documents on individual rights that had been approved with a flourish the previous year. A police officer, for instance, was allowed to use deadly force at his discretion, if he certified that his life was endangered, but there were no provisions setting out a procedure for checking the veracity of police accounts.[16]

The continuation of their previous powers, however, gave no comfort to police, who argued they were weak and defenseless against Russia's modern criminals. In many respects, they were right. The organized-crime bands were far wealthier and better equipped than their adversaries. They had fast Western cars, cellular phones, and foreign-made machine guns. Internal Affairs Ministry officials admitted that it would take twenty-five years for police to match the arsenals of the mafiya under their current reequipment schedules.

Despite inheriting what was supposedly one of the world's most efficient systems of surveillance, Russian police were also deprived of many investigative instruments available to organized-crime investigators in the West. There was no witness protection system; and though Soviet police had been able to riddle dissident groups with informers, there were few trained undercover agents capable of infiltrating the mobs. Russian detectives were left to battle one of the world's most sophisticated and well-armed organized-crime networks with the modern equivalents of slingshots and prayers.

"Most of the time, our only weapons are our heads," Capt. Yuri Nikishin, of the Moscow organized-crime squad, told me. "We have to deceive criminals into thinking we're better than we are."

The average Russian policeman encountered working conditions that would have been intolerable to his counterparts in the West. Police pay was already at the lower end of the scale during the Soviet era; afterward, it was in the realm of the absurd. A Russian militiaman in May, 1993, put his life on the line every day for thirty thousand rubles—about thirty dollars—a month, a lower wage than many factory workers received. The once-guaranteed access to special housing for militia workers fell by the wayside in the cash-strapped New Russia. Thousands of policemen and their families were forced to live a hand-to-mouth existence in communal flats or filthy hostels while they waited years for apartments that were unlikely to materialize.[17]

Their uncertain economic status made it difficult even for honest cops to concentrate on their jobs. "Every time you go out on an operation, you are thinking, what if someone kills you, and your family is left alone without food?" Nikishin said. "You know that no one can guarantee they will be taken care of when you're gone. You keep thinking and thinking, and after a while, you no longer feel anything. You get blunted and hard, or you go crazy."

The Russian policeman was tragically underequipped. His gun was usually an older model, no match for the Western arms available to organized criminals. There was never enough ammunition. His car radio often didn't work. Sometimes he couldn't even be sure there would be a car at all. In 1993, the MVD admitted, one out of every four police vehicles needed to be replaced. Even in Moscow, police officers were reduced to tailing suspects by bus. Police were short of the necessary flak jackets and handcuffs by as much as 70 percent, and they had less than 40 percent of the computer, audio and video equipment they needed to fight crime. Even when protective equipment was available, it was not always dependable. During a shootout on August 20, 1993, in Moscow, an officer died after two bullets pierced his "bullet-proof" vest.

The number of personnel in the MVD's operative divisions was an official secret, as it had been in Soviet times. Some estimates placed it at more than two million, which made reports of a high turnover even more alarming. According to ministry figures released in early 1994, nearly 250,000 recruits had joined the force—but as many as 100,000 had left. With the danger of their jobs added to the low pay, the turnover of officers was understandable.[18]

Across Russia in 1992, 318 policemen were killed and 567 wounded in skirmishes with gangsters. According to officials, the death rate of Russian police that year was proportionally five times higher than it was for police in Germany, and eight times higher than the United States. In 1993, the number of deaths dropped to 183, but the number of those seriously wounded remained at roughly the same level, at 572.[19]

Privately, police commanders complained that "carelessness" was one of the reasons for the high casualty rate. Training was haphazard, and there were no background checks on recruits. A different kind of intellectual carelessness left police ill-equipped to deal with the new varieties of crime associated with an emerging capitalist economy. With police training, in the words of one leading officer, "often divorced from reality," few understood white-collar fraud or the intricacies of dummy corporations. Even the *vorovskoi mir* was a foreign subject to most Russian policemen. Since the Soviet state had declared organized crime non-existent, police knew little about the codes and structures that stood behind the bandit groups they were expected to fight.

It took a special kind of cop to probe further. Col. Anatoli Zhoglo learned most of what he knew about the underworld from interviewing gang leaders in prison. "In my training I was taught all about robberies and petty violations of the law," Zhoglo told me in 1993. "But nothing about professional crime. The majority of police still don't even know what a *vor* is." [20] One of the sadder consequences of such institutional blindness is that the reader of this book will know more about Russian organized crime than the average Russian policeman did in the early 1990s.

The lack of adequate equipment and training left law enforcement agencies far behind their adversaries. But police complained most loudly and bitterly about the absence of a legislative framework to fight the sophisticated criminal forces of post-Communist Russia.

Russian police had to battle the post-Communist criminal in a legal system still dominated by the Communist machinery of justice. Under the Criminal Code of the Russian Socialist Federated Republic, which continued to apply through 1994, police could arrest a gang of felons who robbed a bank on a charge of "banditism," but it was hard to make any charges stick against the gang leader if he was far removed from the scene. A provision of the code enabled prosecution of those found complicitous in the commission of a crime, but there were no guidelines to help law enforcement authorities prove, much less define, complicity. It was virtually impossible to move against the business-man, bureaucrat, or accountant who profited from criminal activities behind a front of legitimate behavior. The Western legal concept of a criminal conspiracy—as it applied to organized crime—did not exist.[21]

While the gangs swelled in power, legislators spent nearly three years dawdling over proposals for a new Russian criminal code. In the spring of 1993, Procurator-General Valentin Stepankov took the extraordinary step of publishing his own draft code in hopes of ending the deadlock. His suggestions vividly demonstrated the inadequacy of the govern-ment's legal instruments against the sophisticated techniques of Russia's crime cartels. He called for dropping, once and for all, the Soviet-era statutes corresponding to "crimes against socialist property," which had in effect treated robbery or fraud against a bank or private business less seriously than the theft of potatoes from a collective farm. His new code proposed the establishment of new white-collar offenses, such as company fraud and price fixing. He would formally make criminal syndicates subject to prosecution as a "group," thereby scrapping provisions that limited police to going after individual members of gangs. Just as significantly, he proposed widening the legal basis for bringing charges of corruption. Under the existing code, only top officials were liable. "It's a mistake to think corruption only goes on at the top," he wrote. "It's just as easy to bribe the secretary as the boss, and you get the same result." [22]

Unfortunately, this was putting the cart before the horse. Even the modest reforms of the early post-Soviet era were undermined by corruption on a massive scale. And the problem began with the very people and institutions who were pledged to turn Russia into a state based on the rule of law.

In January, 1993, President Boris Yeltsin announced a "full head-on assault on crime, bribery, and corruption" at a conference of Russian law enforcement officials and government authorities in Moscow. Sitting in the audience, earnestly applauding his words, were Vice-President Aleksandr Rutskoi, Moscow mayor Yuri Luzhkov, and Security Minister Viktor Barannikov. By the end of the year, all three men had faced accusations of corruption. Two of them—Rutskoi and Barannikov—were in jail for their part in leading an armed rebellion against the government.

The contradiction between what the government said and what it had become was not lost on Russians. The moral authority won in August, 1991, by the reformers who stood up to the tanks of the old regime was gone within two years. It was impossible to take seriously the leadership's heated rhetoric about battling crime when so many of its representatives were themselves profiting from the legal chaos of New Russia. In 1993, more than forty-six thousand officials from all levels of government in Russia were brought to trial on charges relating to corruption and abuse of office, according to Acting Procurator Aleksei Ilyushenko.[23]

Few believed that those figures covered the extent of criminal behavior inside Russian government institutions. "The Communist Party robbed the whole country," said Mark Masarsky, president of the Association of Russian Enterprises, a group set up to protect the interests of small businesses. "But they took bribes in accordance with their rank in the hierarchy. Now everyone takes bribes as though it is his last day at work." Cynicism toward the new government, not surprisingly, was pervasive. "Only lazy people do not take bribes these days," commented *Komsomolskaya Pravda*.[24]

As a measure of how bad things had become, the new leaders of Russia earned the barbed admiration of their predecessors. The former prime minister Nikolai Ryzhkov remarked gleefully that his colleagues had been "nursery school kids" compared to the current crop of bureaucrats. Even the number of corruption cases uncovered by police was misleading. Only 9 percent of those found guilty of embezzlement or abuse of official positions were sent to prison. "The law," a St. Petersburg police inspector named Tsyganok said, in a comment that perfectly summed up the climate of public opinion, "punishes only those who lack imagination."[25]

Perhaps the most debilitating corruption was lodged in the law enforcement bureaucracy itself. Consider the tale of Aleksei Kochetov, director of a large brewery in north Moscow. In the summer of 1992, an explosion blew apart the door of Kochetov's apartment. Shards of wood and metal flew into the parlor. No one was injured, but the brewery director had reason to suspect that his assailants were intimately connected with the police. Only a few days earlier, he registered a complaint at the militia station in his neighborhood about racketeers who were shaking down his drivers. A friend passed his story to Moscow's organized-crime squad, and Kochetov received a visit the week following the blast from Capt. Yuri Nikishin.

Nikishin arranged to post armed police guards around the brewery, and he visited Kochetov every week to give him moral support. On one of his visits, Nikishin brought me along. Sitting uneasily at his desk, the brewery director was clearly grateful for the captain's help, but charged that he was the victim of police corruption. Nikishin did not dispute him.[26]

"Every criminal has connections in the police and officialdom," he conceded. "I would guess that about 90 percent of the militiamen who operate out of local police stations in this city are on the take."

The corruption penetrating every level of law enforcement suggested that there were other reasons for the failure of police to move effectively against crime besides the deficiencies in legal instruments, training, and funding. To a greater extent than their fellow citizens, police were exposed to the temptations of gangster capitalism in their daily working lives. From traffic patrolmen who openly demanded huge bribes of speeders to district chiefs who received kickbacks from commercial enterprises, the country's poorly paid and underfunded law enforcement authorities succumbed in large numbers to the lure of *bizness*. Foreign journalists discovered that there was a price on most things related to the justice system. Some police stations charged thousands of dollars to television crews for accompanying detectives on their evening patrols. (Police argued that it was the only way they could buy new equipment for themselves.)[27]

More than two thousand Russian policemen were charged with crimes in 1992, a figure that most experts considered a small proportion of those actually operating outside the law. In one notorious case, detectives of the Moscow criminal-investigation division arrested a group of businessmen on trumped-up charges, brought them down to the station house, and demanded a payoff of six million rubles. When the businessmen refused, they beat them up. Other policemen secretly worked for mobsters as enforcers or "consultants." One police captain in Vladivostok even became head of his own gang.[28]

Many policemen left the MVD to work as bodyguards or security consultants, or joined the country's fast-growing private detective industry. Others became involved in commercial joint ventures while staying on the force, provoking charges of collusion between law enforcement professionals and white-collar criminals. According to one Russian investigative commission, more than half of the 239 senior law enforcement officers charged with crimes in 1992 were collaborating with criminal gangs. Corruption reached into the upper levels of the ministry itself. In 1994, the government broke up a ring of senior Internal Affairs Ministry officials who received regular kickbacks from top mobsters.[29]

Nikishin admitted that he avoided, whenever possible, telling his superiors or colleagues in other divisions about impending operations. "There have been too many times when criminals mysteriously disappeared just when we were ready to arrest them," he said.

Police corruption was only one link in the chain of greed that enveloped the entire state. In Russia, some of the most blatant economic abuses were openly committed by senior officials. Even the procurator-general charged for interviews.[30] The leadership found the corruption increasingly difficult to ignore. In a speech to the newly elected Russian parliament, called the Duma, on February 23, 1994, Boris Yeltsin promised again (as he had the previous year) action against bribe-taking bureaucrats as well as organized criminals. "There is too much irresponsibility and arbitrariness [in government]," he said, in a comment that could perhaps have been made any time in Russia during the past four hundred years. "Federal authorities are spending colossal sums to make themselves comfortable, with surprising ease." [31]

Brave words. But neither Yeltsin nor his audience seemed to notice that this was at least the fourth "war on crime" announced by the Russian government in less than two years. In October, 1992, Yeltsin established with much fanfare an "Inter-Departmental Commission on Combating Crime and Corruption" and placed Vice-President Rutskoi at his head. He followed in January with a complete anti-crime package. The Rutskoi commission soon turned into a political weapon for the vice-president and his political allies, who began charging reformers inside the Yeltsin government with corruption. Rutskoi enlisted the newly appointed commissioners on his side to collect evidence, but whatever the merits of the charges, it was hard to separate them from Rutskoi's political ambitions. Yeltsin's ministers used their allies in the procurator-general's office to come up with countercharges of corruption against Rutskoi and his friends.[32] The accelerating spiral of mutual accusations culminated in the smoking ruins of the Russian White House.

Even before the new parliament met, Yeltsin tried again. In November, 1993, he unveiled a new anti-crime package, which empowered police to conduct spot checks on people anywhere in Russia, increased police salaries, and improved protection for judges. With almost unconscious ease, authorities began hauling out the methods of the regime they had once fought so bitterly against. They reflected a growing body of opinion among police and the public at large that considered crime-fighting strategies designed for a totalitarian utopia better than none at all.

The decisive moment in Russia's backward movement occurred the previous month. On October 3, 1993, tanks and soldiers entered Moscow for the first time since August, 1991, to put down a rebellion by conservative legislators, led by Rutskoi and parliamentary chairman Ruslan Khasbulatov, who had occupied the Russian parliament. While the October events may rightly be considered to have preserved Russia's democratic government, they also led directly to the abandonment of the legal ideals and principles that had been introduced with so much promise in 1991 and 1992.

When the city's military commandant announced in triumph that only 126 crimes had been reported under the military curfew imposed during the crisis, the country's leaders realized that they had been given an irresistible opportunity.[33] They expanded the army's mission to include a cleanup of hoodlums from city streets. Thousands of flak-jacketed soldiers were deployed, along with MVD troops, around the capital. This was soon followed by a decree deporting from Moscow all "unregistered" persons—most of them from the Caucasus.

A coalition of police and municipal politicians had been lobbying for this move since well before the October events. They had sharply opposed a Russian government decision to phase out the system of residential registration, which required all citizens to obtain a permit, or *propiska,* for their domicile. The drive to abolish the *propiska,* one of the most hated legacies of Stalinist totalitarianism, had been another encouraging sign of Russia's passage to a civil society. Opponents of abolition, however, argued that it was one of the few effective weapons left to authorities for fighting organized crime. They insisted that it was the only way to keep track of members of the Caucasian gangs who now traveled freely between Moscow and the "crime capitals" in Chechnya, Dagestan, and other southern provinces. After October's successful sweep of the streets, no major official found it politic to argue the point.

In the first twelve days following the assault on the White House, nearly 3,500 unregistered persons were summarily expelled from the capital. An estimated ten thousand others fled. Meanwhile, army-police patrols made more than six thousand arrests. Over the next month, the crime rate dropped precipitously.[34]

Operation Signal, as it was called, was the object of ecstatic praise. Yet it had almost no impact on Russia's organized-crime syndicates. The most powerful Caucasian gangs, including the Chechens, suffered at best only a temporary curtailment of their drug-trafficking and gun-running operations, having long since diversified into legitimate enterprises such as banks and commercial structures. Leading Russian mobsters in Moscow kept their people off the streets, while privately welcoming the setbacks suffered by their competitors from the Caucasus.

Igor Baranovsky, a journalist with sources in both the underworld and the police, reported that none of the top *vory* were affected. "Important mafiosi are worthy, respected people," was Baranovsky's dry comment. "And everyone knows that you don't go around threatening them."

The majority of the non-resident "aliens" turned out to be traders involved in nothing more illegal than importing unlicensed fruits and vegetables for the city's commercial markets. But this seemed immaterial. The operation gave full expression to Russian frustration over rising crime, not to mention simmering xenophobia and racial prejudice. Human rights activists pointed out futilely that anyone who looked non-Russian had become a target.

"The [authorities] are appealing to some of the basest instincts of Muscovites," complained Rachel Denbar, of the Moscow branch of Helsinki Watch, as police began acting like right-wing terror squads. Members of one special-forces unit broke into a Moscow apartment and beat up refugees from Tajikistan. When an apartment dweller showed the *propiska* that established him as a legitimate resident of Moscow, police tore it up in front of his face.[35]

Authorities did not bother to apologize for returning to the blunderbuss approach of the past. The effect of the post-coup "war on crime" was to further encourage those who believed in dangerously simple solutions to Russia's law-and-order crisis.

Law enforcement officials led the way in demanding a "disciplined" approach to criminality. After two frustrating years of watching the government expend, in their opinion, more energy impressing the West with its human rights credentials than fighting crime, police officers yearned for the old ways of administering law and order. They looked back on the politically inspired anti-crime campaigns of the Soviet era with nostalgia. Policemen and prosecutors trained under the Communist system could not help concluding that order was, in the end, to be more highly prized than democracy.

"The totalitarian system had negative elements, but at least it restrained crime," Col. Dmitri Medvedev, an assistant director of the MVD's organized-crime division, grumbled one afternoon in his Moscow office. "I may appear to be conservative, but our leaders are mixing up human rights and the rights of the criminal. There are a lot of sicknesses in our society, but there are some sicknesses you can't treat. You just have to get them out of the system." [36]

Russian policemen argued that democracy had accomplished little more than the removal of the restraints on their compatriots' behavior. Medvedev was furious about legislation giving citizens the right to own "self-defense" weapons (gas pistols) and decriminalizing the possession of drugs. "It seems to me we are learning from the West the wrong lessons," he said. "We are reinventing the wheel, and a very bad wheel at that."

It should have surprised no one that the old wheel was soon reattached. After the October, 1993, events, the MVD prepared a draft decree giving police the right to search enterprises without a warrant if they suspected criminal activity. The authors of the decree blithely ignored the fact that a similar measure, passed during the last days of Soviet power, had achieved little except the political intimidation of private businessmen. [37]

The decree was leaked to the press, and after an outcry from the country's small group of human rights activists, Yeltsin said that he would not sign it. But a month later, the president announced an anti-crime package containing many of the same provisions. Law enforcement officials now reasonably considered themselves free from the "human rights" restraints of the previous years. On January 20, 1994, a new "interdepartmental commission" was established to coordinate activities against organized crime and corruption, this one headed by Russian justice minister Yuri Kalmykov. But it was no more effective than its predecessors.

By the summer of 1994, Russia was once again in criminal turmoil. June of that year was an especially bloody month in Moscow. A car bomb ignited by remote control near the Paveletsky railway station destroyed a passing Mercedes Benz that carried the manager of one of the city's largest car dealerships. The manager survived, but his driver was decapitated. The same day, the director of a small company had his right leg blown off by a car bomb. A few weeks later, gunmen opened fire with automatic rifles on four men traveling in an automobile through central Moscow. One man was killed outright. Two others were shot dead as they tried to flee. The violence was also taking a toll on innocent passersby. Six pedestrians had been injured in the Paveletsky explosion, and an eight-year-old boy was killed by a blast intended for a businessman. Whatever effect authorities presumed their new "hard line" was having, Russia's criminals were notably unimpressed. In the first five months of the year, crimes involving firearms and explosives were up 45 percent in Moscow. The homicide rate across Russia had increased by 50 percent since 1993.[38]

A frustrated Boris Yeltsin vowed to "cleanse the country of criminal filth." He ordered his top law officials to come up with yet another anti-crime program. The Ministry of Internal Affairs, in cooperation with the Justice Ministry, proposed legislation providing three trillion rubles (1.5 billion dollars) for hiring more police and improving police pay. Any lingering hesitation about taking draconian measures was sidelined in the new draft legislation sent to the Duma. It gave police the right to detain suspects for up to a month without charge, search offices and dwellings without a court order, and examine the financial affairs of anyone suspected of involvement in organized crime. In addition, regional officials were empowered to adopt "emergency measures"—in other words, a state of siege—if they felt it necessary. Finally, the army was to be ordered to back up MVD forces.[39]

Yeltsin did not wait for the legislation to be passed. He incorporated the same measures in a government decree made public in June, 1994.

In 1991, dedicated policemen like Yuri Nikishin could still persuade fellow officers that methods like those outlined in the coup plotters' memo to put twenty thousand soldiers in the street to fight crime represented a distasteful throwback to old ways of thinking. Then, democracy seemed more valuable than the efficiency of a police state. But not any longer. On June 22, 1994, a two-day operation called "Hurricane" put twenty thousand MVD troops and police onto the streets of Moscow. Some 2,200 people were arrested after sweeping searches of hotels, businesses, and banks. The conspirators of 1991 could be forgiven for wondering whether their victorious opponents had merely pulled their anti-crime plan out of the filing cabinet.

As a sign, however, that the original ideals of a rule-of-law state had not completely vanished, Yeltsin and his police allies found themselves under furious attack for violating the rights and freedoms guaranteed by the revolution—and enshrined in the new Russian constitution, which had been approved by the Russian people only six months before. Put on the defensive, officials insisted that the measures were only "temporary."

Sergei Stepashin, head of the newly reorganized Security Ministry, made the argument in terms that few Russians who had experienced the previous three years of criminal anarchy were willing to dispute. "Will there be violations of human rights?" he asked rhetorically. "Probably, but only in the interests of 99 percent of the remaining population." [40]

The point was not lost on his audience, however, that similar explanations had accompanied the "temporary" police-state measures imposed by the Stalinist regime in the 1930s. Nor could it be ignored that the person advancing the argument represented the most unreformed branch of the old Soviet security machine, the agency that used to be known as the KGB.

All the afflictions that plagued post-Soviet legal institutions—inefficiency, corruption, and balkanization—were written large in the nation's vast secret army of intelligence forces.

In May, 1991, the Soviet-era parliament adopted a law that allowed the KGB to continue most of its clandestine functions at home and abroad. In the words of the Lawyers Committee, it legitimized "most of its previous infringements on liberty." Soon after the collapse of the regime, the agency was split into domestic and foreign espionage units. But the domestic security agency, known after December, 1993, as the Federal Counterintelligence Service, represented little more than a face lift. Its powers of action and its freedom from real political oversight continued. Most agency personnel were still in place. [41]

Yet despite their continued importance as the elite praetorian guard for the government, security agents were among the most restless and unhappy of all the former Soviet Union's enforcement personnel. They felt ignored and badly used, particularly in the fight against organized crime—for which they assumed a special proprietary interest. The KGB had always performed a domestic crime-fighting role. In fact, a book published in 1994 made the extraordinary claim that the KGB was the first to identify organized crime as a threat to the state in the 1980s, even defeating a plot by crime lords to assassinate Mikhail Gorbachev. They also regarded themselves as the government's principal bastion against corruption.[42]

In the 1970s, Yuri Andropov, then chairman of the KGB, launched an anti-corruption crusade that put many senior Party officials in prison. No one believed for a moment that the KGB had suddenly uncovered a vast new pool of lawbreakers, or even that the unlucky *apparatchiki* caught in the sweep were more culpable than the majority of their grafting comrades. It was a campaign motivated purely by political considerations. The ambitious Andropov was determined to frighten his rivals and persuade his Politburo colleagues of his leadership credentials. The KGB's manipulation of politics and anti-crime activity left a useful legacy to its senior officers.

In the post-Communist era, KGB resentment at being sidelined was channeled into political opposition. The agency's secret network of informers and its well-stocked clandestine treasury, which was invested in numerous front organizations, banks, and commercial enterprises, continued to make it a powerful player in the New Russia. And its special position at the nexus of the black market and officialdom during the 1980s made its activities particularly ambiguous. It was widely believed inside the MVD that former KGB officers acted as mercenaries and instructors for some organized-crime groups in the 1990s. None was ever caught, but several agents were exposed as comrade criminals. A number of senior agency officials were fired in 1992 for illegal commercial activity.[43]

Meanwhile, large groups of former agency employees turned up working as "consultants" for businesses. Leonid Shebarshin, a former top official appointed head of a prominent shareholding company in 1992, argued that his intelligence expertise served the political as well as the security needs of Russian business. "My task is to create conditions which will make it possible to avert the threat to Russian and foreign businesses which may affect our customers reputation and commercial secrets," he said.[44]

The KGB's shadowy presence on both sides of the war against crime served the political ends spelled out long ago by former chairman Kryuchkov in his secret memo (Document 174033) of January 5, 1991:

"to create conditions for the effective use of foreign and domestic agent networks during [a period of] increased political instability." [45]

Some prominent intelligence operatives joined forces with the parliamentary rebels inside the White House during October, 1993. Former security minister Viktor Barannikov led a group of armed, right-wing demonstrators in an attack on Moscow's central television station that month. Even before then, security agents had played a prominent part in demonstrations against the government. "The opposition is influencing support groups in the organs of law enforcement and security," noted Arkadi Cherechniya in *Rossiiskaya Gazeta* in July, 1993. "Some are infected with racist sentiments, while others are acting out of a desire to ingratiate themselves with those they consider to be the future masters of Russia." [46] Needless to say, the KGB were not alone. Several militiamen joined the White House occupation, and Andrei Dunayev, who had been among the first senior MVD officials to issue a public warning about the mafiya, was among the 140 rebels arrested after the building was stormed. He had accepted an appointment as internal-affairs minister of Rutskoi's alternative government. The rebels of October were freed abruptly and surprisingly by an amnesty granted by parliament in February, 1994. Nikolai Golushko, a career KGB officer who had been appointed head of Yeltsin's new counterintelligence service, signed the order letting them go, over Yeltsin's objections. Golushko was promptly fired.[47] But nothing could have made clearer how the nation's secret police establishment had became a driving force behind the conservative backlash against reform.

18 General Sterligov and His Friends

Gen. Aleksandr Sterligov sat in the wooden chair of a cramped Moscow dining room without moving. His black shoes, polished to a gleam, rested squarely on the floor. He spoke so quietly that I had to lean forward to hear him.

"The danger is real, and we are the only ones who fight it," he was saying, in the tone of someone weary of the world's treacheries. "Policemen are more aware than most people of how criminal capital penetrates all spheres of our economy. We know, for instance, that the mafiya have not only bribed a lot of officials, but they have become officials themselves." [1]

I nodded, not wishing to disturb his icy composure with an objection. The general wore a double-breasted gray suit that looked as if it had been pressed with a knife. His silvery hair was combed straight backwards, in a way that emphasized the bony, Asiatic cast of his features. A jeweled pin in his tie and a white handkerchief peeking above his vest pocket offered the only comforting signs that the man was human enough to be vain. He delivered his next words even more softly, but with a distinct edge.

"Unless the democrats completely clear out the criminals on our streets, in our businesses, and in politics, our support inside the police and security forces will grow, and we will have to take action," he said.

The threat was so cleverly worded that I almost missed the way the general drew a line between himself and the "security forces," as if he possessed two separate identities. This was his private fiction, but many people in Russia were eager to accept it. A few months before we met, in the summer of 1992, Aleksandr Sterligov retired from the KGB, where he had been one of the agency's senior experts in counterintelligence, to become a leader of the "Red-Brown coalition," a group of former Communists and ultranationalists who over the next year were to plunge Russia into violence. He admitted to me that he was still a member of the KGB "reserves," where he continued to hold the rank of major-general (although everyone called him "general").

A KGB man was always a KGB man, whatever identity he chose to assume in the confusing New Russia of democrats and business entrepreneurs. Sterligov considered himself liberated by the collapse of the old regime, since he was now free to pursue the causes that really mattered to him without worrying about the rules imposed by rigid political ideologists. "I am merely continuing the political concerns I always had," said the forty-nine-year-old general. "The security organs were always composed of patriotically minded people who fought to prevent the destruction of our nation. Many of my former colleagues are doing the same as I am."

Indeed, Sterligov's move from the world of the Soviet secret police into the theater of Russian politics was not unusual. It was even predictable. The KGB's role as the self-described "sword and shield" of the Communist Party was only superficially ideological. The agency defended the Party as long as it was synonymous with the state; but it defended the state above all. If the state's new enemies were no longer dissidents and spies but mafiya gangsters, that had not changed the mission. Sterligov illustrated the way in which the debate over law and order became a battleground for competing visions of the nation's future.

Such men were not easy to dismiss. The general's scorn of the "democrats" in power had nothing in common with the knee-jerk hostility exhibited by the dispossessed old guard of Communist politics. His commitment to rooting out the criminal plague in Russia and his hatred of corruption began long before the system crumbled. Like most KGB officers, he was intimately aware of the extent to which crime penetrated the Soviet political establishment. In 1983, he was assigned by Yuri Andropov, then KGB chairman, to investigate corruption in the Ministry of Internal Affairs. The investigation was, of course, motivated by politics inside the Kremlin, but Sterligov plunged into his job with missionary zeal. His work led to the downfall of the police minister, Nikolai Shcholokov, and other Brezhnev cronies, and earned him a reputation for integrity and dogged efficiency. When Russian prime minister Ivan Silayev went looking in 1990 for someone to head a special division created by the Council of Ministers to monitor corruption,

Sterligov was a natural choice. He stayed on to work with the post-Soviet government, but he quickly became disillusioned by the venality of the country's new leaders.

"I had to resign, because I realized that if I continued, I would have had to share the responsibility for what was being done to our country," he said, with a pained expression.

Sterligov became founder and chairman of the Russian National Assembly, a fiercely anti-government movement, which claimed to have sixty-nine branches across the Commonwealth of Independent States. Its first congress, held in the spring of 1992, was attended by more than one thousand delegates from 117 cities. The numbers were relatively small, but the fact that many of the Assembly's members were serving officers in the Russian intelligence service and the MVD gave it a special resonance on the right.

Sterligov and his police comrades considered Russian democracy a national disaster, a view which, as time progressed, hardly distinguished them from the mass of the populace. Their professional qualifications for making such a judgment could not be disputed: they had experienced the breakdown of law and order on their watch. This was one of the principal reasons why the so-called national-patriotic movement was able to link the personal insecurity of millions to the vulnerability of the nation.

Crime transcended questions of economic reform because it threatened rich and poor alike. A February, 1992, nationwide public-opinion poll illustrated how profoundly the comforts of a communal society had been shattered. More than half the respondents said that they anticipated being the victims of crime. Another survey disclosed that three out of four Muscovites admitted they were afraid to walk down the streets at night.[2] And people had only to open their newspapers to read the latest accounts of government scandals and chicanery. "Just a year or two ago it seemed that if only we could get rid of the Communists, everything would fall into place," a Moscow resident named B. Aleksyutkin wrote in a December, 1992, letter to *Stolitsa,* a weekly. "The boil was lanced; but the doctors, instead of taking care of the patient, are too busy going through his pockets."

The Red-Brown coalition of neo-Communists and right-wing extremists is a unique contribution to the political lexicography of the post–Cold War world. It is hard at first to make sense of this mixture of Communist red and fascist brown, particularly in a nation that lost so many millions of its people to the war against Nazi Germany. But both evoke a nationalist spirit whose roots go deeper in Russian history than either Communism or fascism. Members of the Red-Brown coalition regularly celebrate individual Communists as "honest patriots," even while condemning the old Soviet Communist Party as an evil product ow Western philosophy. The briefly imprisoned leaders of the August, 1991, coup were transformed into martyrs—they were, after all, only fighting for the unity of the state.

The same mysterious alchemy turned fellow travelers like Gennadi Zyuganov, an undistinguished former bureaucrat who became leader of the reorganized Russian Communist Party, into nationalist paragons. Sterligov believed that Russia could rely on Zyuganov's Communists in its hour of danger, particularly, he pointed out, since they had abandoned their predecessors' misguided commitment to centralized economic planning. "We can find a common language with him [Zyuganov]," the general said. "It is not really important to us whether someone belongs to the Party. After all, those who are leading us now were some of the biggest defenders of the old ideology, and they are the same people who are selling us out. The only thing that really matters to us is whether someone is willing to help preserve Russia."

The Red-Brown coalition was often portrayed in the West, and in Russia itself, as a bizarre fringe group of neo-Nazis and frustrated *apparatchiki* in baggy suits. But it represented the oldest strain of Russia's intellectual heritage, one that has traditionally emerged in response to the call to "preserve Russia" against its foreign and domestic enemies. Russian nationalist xenophobia was born out of the geography of a vast land mass on the crossroads of Europe and Asia that was permanently vulnerable to attack and assimilation. Over one thousand years of Russian history, the threat has varied in intensity and character—from the Mongol hordes, to the Western advisers and merchants imported by Peter the Great, to the "cosmopolitans" who challenged Stalin's closed society. The newest danger was considered no less potent. The corruption and crime ushered in by Western capitalism threatened to destroy the messianic and holy quality of Russianness, which could redeem a sinful world if allowed to flourish unsullied but was always at risk from the predatory and seductive West. Although this has created some poignant conflicts in Russian literature, it has often translated into the politics of fear and repression.[3]

"The world is trying to destroy the Slavic peoples," said General Sterligov. "This process already began in the Soviet period, when we lost our whole intelligentsia. But we have no intention of letting it get any further. Russians make up 82 percent of the population, but our present government ignores our interests. Can you blame us for being angry? We are called Slavic nationalists, but we take pride in this name."

It was no contradiction for a senior KGB officer to speak like a nationalist. The KGB had been in the forefront of Soviet campaigns against the supposed intrigues of outsiders against the motherland. In one of the bizarre (to foreigners, at least) episodes of the final years of Soviet power, KGB chairman Vladimir Kryuchkov accused Western aid agencies of poisoning the meat sent to Russia. Sterligov and his friends knew how to tap the same fears, and they were assured of a receptive audience.

The collapse of the Soviet Union left Russians feeling as vulnerable as they ever had felt in their history. What the West perceived as a historic opportunity for democracy, patriotic Russians regarded as a breach in their ancient defenses. As post-Soviet Russia plunged into a state of criminal chaos, it was a message few could resist. "Nationalism is a kind of beast sleeping in the soul of every Russian," Volodya Mironov, my sophisticated guide to the Russian underworld, once told me. "Even in my soul, this beast sometimes stirs. But I try to control it, because I know that if this beast awakens, it will be terrible for all of us."

But it was people like Mironov who provoked the beast. The criminals and swindlers he casually affiliated with—and enriched—in the process of making his own fortune were the very enemies who sent patriotic ideologues rushing to the barricades. To the Red-Browns, Russia's new capitalists represented the suspect values of the West. A few months after the aborted 1991 coup, thousands of Communists and nationalists staged a march through Moscow to protest the new government. They carried placards pillorying the principal democratic reformers as members of the mafiya and as "Zionists." One marcher held a poster caricaturing Moscow mayor Gavriil Popov—who is of Greek ancestry—as a Jew. I went up to him and asked why he thought Popov was Jewish.

"What else can he be?" the man said, with an ugly smirk. "Look what he's done to us."

Few took those demonstrators seriously at the time. But many of their leaders were the same people who, a year later, led the gun-wielding mobs who helped occupy the Russian White House.

As corruption and crime spread through post-Communist society, it became easier to blame the nation's problems on the traditional scapegoats of Russian nationalism—Jews and other ethnic minorities, like the Azeris and Chechens, who seemed to be managing better than others the transition from Soviet life. A number of successful entrepreneurs and prominent democratic politicians were Jewish by descent.

The producer Mark Rudinshtein believed that anti-Semitism accounted for some of his problems with the nomenklatura capitalists who dominated the film industry. "It can get ugly," he said. "When I ask distributors why they refuse to take my films, they won't look at me. 'Just be patient,' they tell me. 'It's better not to rock the boat.' But I know what's going on. I have received threats as well, and they use the fact that I am Jewish against me. I thought some of this had gone with history—I was beaten in school in Odessa for being a Jew—but obviously not."

Official anti-Semitism was concealed behind "anti-Zionist" committees during the Soviet era, but there was no need for such tact in the New Russia. A number of prominent black-marketeers and businessmen were Jewish, and police had found evidence tying international gem swindles to joint ventures owned by Russians who had emigrated to Israel. A former Russian who became an Israeli citizen had signed for the shipment of Colombian cocaine that was discovered at Vyborg in 1993; and, according to police, the ikon-smuggling trade was dominated by Russian Jewish emigres in Vienna and Frankfurt. For nationalists, this was heady ammunition. Needless to say, the majority of comrade criminals were Slavs. But anti-Semitism was a convenient means of linking the Red-Brown coalition's fixation on crime with its crusade to protect "native" Russian values.

General Sterligov firmly told me that Jews were responsible for the corruption of local governments. "They are always trying to push out the Russians and seeking the dominating positions," he said. "Even an ancient Russian city like Nizhni Novgorod has been completely destroyed because it is run by a Jewish administration."

I asked him how he knew they were Jews. Sterligov said there was no doubt about the matter—many of the local leaders had Jewish patronymics.

"But how is it you don't consider them Russians as well?" I wondered. "Aren't they just Russians who happen to be Jews?"

"It is impossible to consider them in that way," he said flatly. "They simply don't act like Russians. It is an open secret that the Jews are desecrating our basic values."

So, in the view of the patriots, were the *chornye*—"blacks"—the street name for the Azeris, Chechens, and others from the Caucasus who were crowding into the major cities. The Moscow crackdown on traders from the Caucasus following the October, 1993, crisis was another sign of the intolerance fueled by the nationalists' anti-crime agenda.

"Why should Russians have to fight for the most fundamental things, like the protection of our culture?" Sterligov demanded. "Why should the labor of my fathers end up in the hands of Jews or Azeris?"

Any hope that such views were confined to a small minority was dispelled by the racist rhetoric that increasingly became a part of the Russian law-and-order debate. In February, 1993, the leading ultra-nationalist newspaper, *Sovetskaya Rossiya,* published an article written by Bishop Ioann, metropolitan of St. Petersburg and Ladoga, warning of a "dirty war" against Russia. The Russian Orthodox bishop was already a prominent voice in the nationalist movement, but his article set a new low in national political discourse. He used passages from the "Protocols of the Elders of Zion"—a pamphlet concocted by the czarist police in the early 1900s to falsely implicate Jewish "elders" in a purported Jewish master plan to take over the world—in order to justify his argument that crime and democracy were the joint products of an international conspiracy against Russia. It was the first time the "Protocols," promulgated by Nazis and other anti-Semites throughout the twentieth century, appeared in its full length in a Russian publication.[4]

Ioann smoothly acknowledged that some people doubted the authenticity of the "Protocols." But he also observed that they explained a phenomenon recognized by every Russian. For centuries, he wrote,

Slavs had been forced to defend themselves against attacks by "alien peoples and creeds . . . determined to put to death our moral and religious way of life." Russia's trials during the twentieth century were so extreme that they could only have been organized by an outside force. There was the long dictatorship of Marxist-Leninism, which everyone "knew" was the result of a Jewish-Masonic plot. Then, as soon as Russians heaved away the Communist yoke, they fell under the sway of another tyranny, led by criminals, democrats, and immoral government officials. In an intellectual sleight-of-hand worthy of Sterligov, the bishop refused to accept that Russians bore any responsibility for their own problems. Since the result was so clearly anti-Russian, only non-Russians could have inflicted such damage.

"In my opinion, the destructive plan outlined [in the Protocols] has clearly come to pass," wrote Ioann. "This is a well-financed, secretly planned, and relentless war to the death [and] it is run by diabolic plotters who want to destroy our country and its true religious principles."

Ioann let his readers draw their own conclusions about the identity of the "diabolic plotters," but he left them in no doubt about the proper manner of defense. The full-page article opened with a quotation from Czar Alexander II: "Russia has only two genuine allies—the army and the fleet." Then the bishop made clear that he believed there was yet a third ally: the church itself.

Not one leading church authority disavowed the article. Many churchmen privately disparaged Bishop Ioann as a figure unworthy of serious attention; nevertheless, few found it necessary, or politic, to challenge his views.

The Russian Orthodox Church had survived Communism to become the country's leading spiritual institution, but it felt more threatened than ever by the spread of Western material values, for which gangster capitalism was a handy vessel. Ioann only carried to an extreme the fears and prejudices of the entire post-Soviet religious establishment.

"We have simply been inundated with filth from the West," said Father Mikhail Ardov, a Russian Orthodox priest who had moved to Moscow in 1993 after administering a tiny village parish for more than a decade. "In my village, young children freely swear in front of their teachers. What else can this be but the result of things like pornography and rock music? We have not only lost respect for religion, but for any concept of morality. The logical result is crime." [5]

On first impression, Father Mikhail was worlds apart from the xeno-phobic Bishop Ioann. A journalist and essayist, he became a priest at the age of forty-two, in 1979, and instantly lost the privileges he had enjoyed as a member of the Communist intelligentsia. He was the type of believer who would have been eagerly taken up by Westerners in the days when the church existed in Soviet purgatory, for he cherished poetry and the life of the mind. As a young man, he served as personal secretary to Anna Akhmatova, one of the century's best Russian poets, whom he credited with arousing the first shoots of religious feeling in his soul. A small, articulate man with a kindly face, he conveyed the impression of a worldly sophisticate, more at ease in a literary salon than in a parish church. When I met him, he eagerly pressed on me copies of his articles and stories, including a humorous parody of the style of the nineteenth-century writer Nikolai Leskov. The apartment where we met, the home of a well-known Moscow actor, was filled with paintings and books. After he swept inside, absent-mindedly accepting a kiss on his hand from the actor, Father Mikhail went immediately to the bookshelves, stroking the old volumes with sighs of pleasure.

As our conversation proceeded, I discovered that Father Mikhail pos-sessed a worldview very similar to Bishop Ioann's. But where the bishop was direct and open, the priest was subtle.

"Of course, there are good things about the West," he assured me. "I have nothing against Western businessmen coming here. But Russians are taking the worst of foreign cultures and destroying their own. This started with perestroika, when people began to concentrate on making money and nothing else. Our democrats have stolen more than the Com-munists did over seventy years. At least the Communists were afraid of each other; now, everyone steals like there is no tomorrow."

Slavic fundamentalists cheerfully pandered to the church's fears about its place in post-Communist life. "We must restore the role which the church always used to have in our society," Sterligov told me piously. "In our opinion, the only guarantee that the Communist system will not return is a nationally oriented government that has restored its links with the Orthodox faith."

There were many priests, of course, who thought such assurances odd coming from men who had devoted their professional lives to ma-nipulating religion in the Soviet regime. But large numbers accepted the seemingly miraculous conversion of their former persecutors without question. Priests were often welcomed at official functions of Red-Brown organizations.

In 1991, church dignitaries invited representatives of the newly re-established "Black Hundred" organization to the rededication of a shrine in the central Russian city of Nizhni Novgorod. The Black Hundred, responsible for bloody pogroms in the early years of the century, was a paramilitary group sponsored by the czar which used the "Protocols" as a guide to action. They were revived at a meeting in the House of the Soviet Army in Moscow on August 1, 1990, in circumstances that suggested they were once again the recipients of official support.[6]

An even more significant event for Russian patriots and churchmen occurred on May 29, 1992, in St. Petersburg. On that day, Grand Duke Vladimir Kirillovich Romanov, heir to the Romanov throne, was interred in his family crypt near the historic Peter and Paul Fortress. It was one of those moments in Russian history when the past overwhelms the present. The grand duke, who was born in exile shortly after the Bolsheviks unseated his cousin Czar Nicholas II, had lived long enough to become an object of fashionable nostalgia by a small coterie of Russian neo-Imperialists and intellectuals. The post-Soviet government had granted him a visa for a brief visit to St. Petersburg, and he was looking forward to another when he died in Miami while on a speaking tour. St. Petersburg, perhaps hoping for an event that could distract attention from the city's growing problems, granted permission for the the first royal funeral in Russia in nearly a century.

Not even the most fervent monarchist could have anticipated what happened next. Outside the old church that housed the Romanov crypt, specially restored for the occasion, the various strands of the Russian nationalist movement came together. Two rows of bearded men in Cossack uniforms lined the pathway into the chapel. Stern, black-robed Russian Orthodox prelates led the grand duke's grieving family —including his daughter Maria and her eleven-year-old son, Georgi Romanov, the new claimant to the throne—through the crowd with an air of proprietorship. On the fringes were dozens of black-shirted young men, some in heavy boots and thick leather belts, looking on enraptured. When the service ended and the dazed young Georgi Romanov was hustled into a waiting limousine, grown men knelt. Some had tears in their eyes. Romanov family members, who had flown in from their homes in Paris, Zurich, and New York, could not hide their astonishment at this display of atavistic reverence. "I really can't believe these people," one guest at the funeral told me as she boarded the chartered bus back to her hotel. "I don't mind telling you I'll be glad to get back to Paris."

For the Romanovs, the event was a briefly opened window on a past they had long since disavowed. But for their attending compatriots, it was proof of the triumph of Russian values. What democracy financed by Wall Street could match the splendor of a Russia blessed by God and czar?

"I think our country will return to a monarchy," Sterligov told me. "I can't tell you the date, but it will happen when all the democratic and revolutionary storms finally pass. No normal country would have put up with what we have been going through."

"But why do you need a czar?" I asked. "Can't you save the country yourselves?"

"A czar is brought up with the idea of service to the Orthodox world," he replied without hesitation. "No government alone, certainly not the present government, could protect us from outsiders buying our land and stealing our resources."

The Red-Browns attracted little serious Western attention in the euphoric aftermath of the Soviet Union's collapse. They seemed to be characters from a closed chapter of Russian history—from several closed chapters, in fact. Menacing KGB major-generals belonged on the rubbish heap of Soviet clichés, along with monarchists and neo-Stalinists. But Russians themselves were not quite as ready to dismiss what they had to say. As Sterligov carefully explained to me, a new czar did not have to be a hereditary monarch. Any strong figure could satisfy the overwhelming and undeniable need for order in Russian society.

This idea was hardly the property of the extreme right. "Even those who were once ardent supporters of perestroika are subscribing to reactionary slogans," Arkady Vaksberg, a liberal Russian journalist, warned in July, 1992. "People are demanding a strong hand at the top." Before the end of the following year, on December 12, 1993, Russia disgorged a bizarre imitation of just such a "strong hand." His name was Vladimir Zhirinovsky.

A pudgy fifty-year-old demagogue with murky connections to the KGB, Zhirinovsky captured the largest single bloc of votes during the

elections for the new State Duma (parliament). The platform of his mis-
leadingly titled "Liberal Democratic Party" included the restoration of
the czarist empire (including Alaska and Finland), the revival of Soviet-
era price controls, and the elimination of crime. It was an incoherent
package of bombastic populism, leavened with racist tirades against
Jews and other ethnic minorities who were allegedly getting rich on
Russia's tragedy. But nearly 23 percent of Russian voters—or about
thirteen million people—seemed to find it attractive.[7]

Zhirinovsky was no overnight phenomenon. Just two years earlier—
when the Soviet Union was intact—he collected six million votes and
a third-place finish during the presidential campaign that brought Boris
Yeltsin to power in the Russian Federation. Although he failed to turn
his impressive support into a political base, Zhirinovsky continued to
strut in the wings of Russian politics with his black-shirted bodyguards,
contributing to the angry babble of post-Communism.

The 1993 vote for Zhirinovsky stunned the outside world, which
until then had been congratulating itself on Russia's slow but sure movement toward democracy. Alarmed analysts in Washington, Bonn, and
London discovered frightening parallels between the German Weimar
republic, which collapsed when Hitler came to power, and the chaos of
Zhirinovsky's Russia. But Zhirinovsky was no more a fascist than Sterligov. Both men subscribed to a worldview that linked the "betrayal"
of Russia to crime and Western-imposed capitalism—a perception increasingly shared by millions of Russians with less extreme attitudes.

By the time Zhirinovsky mounted his campaign, public opinion was
already shifting to the right. In a survey taken in August, 1993, 52 percent of those polled put rising crime ahead of unemployment as the
country's gravest problem. The responses to other questions in the survey reflected the increasingly popular conviction that the transition to a
market economy benefited only criminals. When asked which government policies were needed to stabilize the economy, 59 percent favored
state control over "private business," which had become increasingly
associated in popular opinion with the black-market entrepreneurs and
speculators commonly believed to be stealing the country blind.[8]

Crime was the most salient issue of an election ostensibly about the
direction of economic reform. Even Yegor Gaidar, leader of the pro-
reform party "Russia's Choice," felt it necessary to promise an "all-
out campaign" against crime. But he sounded lukewarm next to the

ultranationalists. "Reform has meant nothing but bandits, beggars, and blood," said Aleksandr Nevzorov, a television journalist with inflammatory right-wing views who was chosen by voters in the most prosperous district of St. Petersburg after running on a harsh law-and-order platform. Zhirinovsky offered perhaps the most attractive anti-crime package of all when he promised to end in one stroke both inflation and street violence by sweeping Caucasians out of Russian cities. And he hinted at more draconian measures. In his last television appearance before the election, he promised to bring back laws last used in the 1920s to "set up field courts-martial and shoot the leaders of crime gangs on the spot."

Some foreign observers took comfort in the fact that Zhirinovsky's faction won fewer seats in the new parliament than Russia's Choice, the principal pro-reform party. All the same, the Communists and ultranationalists together made up the largest parliamentary bloc. Both Zyuganov's Communist Party and the Agrarian Party—a group sponsored by the old Soviet agricultural interests—have flirted with Zhirinovsky. Neither has so far been willing to enter into open alliance with him, and by late 1994 his influence had perceptibly diminished once again. Nevertheless, the Red-Browns have established themselves as a formidable political force.

Their supporters in state enterprises and the nomenklatura banking and financial establishment have already forced the government to abandon the rhetoric of so-called shock therapy and slow down the pace of economic decentralization. Whether this will actually reduce the patriots' appeal is the central question of Russian politics over the next few years. If prominent figures on the right like Aleksandr Rutskoi successfully establish their candidacies for the next presidential election (scheduled in 1996), they can expect to tap the same vein of disillusionment with crime and capitalism successfully mined by Zhirinovsky.

The law-and-order crisis has become intertwined with the economic debate. The Red-Browns have successfully argued that while the Russian frontier remains untamed, the country needs sheriffs more than economists. Few Russians seemed concerned about the extent to which the would-be sheriffs were contributing to the atmosphere of lawlessness.[9]

As Sterligov predicted in our chat, the "patriots" lost little time in taking justice into their own hands. The trend toward vigilantism began well before the 1993 election. In August, 1992, the St. Petersburg municipal police union announced an alliance with a local nationalist group to "fight the mafiya." Shortly afterward, attacks were reported on the city's large population of Azeri and Georgian traders. *Komsomolskaya Pravda,* which reported the story, predicted similar coalitions across Russia. "We are seeing the rise of questionable forces which present themselves as an efficient alternative to the supposedly corrupt and helpless democratic authorities," the newspaper said.

Examples of vigilante action came from all parts of the country. The city of Stavropol, in southern Russia, reintroduced *druzhniki,* the red-armband-wearing citizen police of the Soviet era. Cossacks in the southern Russian city of Rostov confiscated contraband on trains to Yerevan and "cleansed" the city of Caucasians. Cossack "regiments," often wearing the uniforms that had made their appearance at the grand duke's funeral, administered punishment to lawbreakers in the Krasnoyarsk region and acted as quasi-official border guards. Groups of young black-shirted toughs beat up prostitutes and homeless young men in railway stations. Many of these groups were financed and armed by the Red-Browns.[10]

Sterligov proudly revealed to me he had his own "intelligence" and "security" wings, and even a youth corps, and he admitted that some of the funds to support them came from "former state organizations"—which seemed to be a reference to the new commercial firms run by his former KGB comrades as well as to the nomenklatura-run enterprises. When I asked him to identify the supporters he claimed to have in various stock exchanges and Cossack councils in central and southern Russia, he refused.

"I cannot give you names," he insisted, "They will be attacked in the press, and this would hurt their business."

Hard-line groups seemed to have an inexhaustible supply of guns and money. The Russian Communist Labor Party (RCLP), led by a fanatically neo-Stalinist army general named Albert Makashov, who advocated confiscatory policies aimed at smashing the black market, put its arsenal of weapons at the service of the occupiers of the White House in October, 1993. The United Front of Working People, led by Viktor Anpilov, a former journalist and reputed KGB informer, was in the forefront of violent street demonstrations during 1992 and 1993, smashing foreign-language signs and taking over the television station.

Some participants in the rally later confided to Russian journalists that they had been given substantial cash payments.

The organizations of the New Right profited in turn from their ties with the old nomenklatura. When Vladimir Zhirinovsky ran for president in the spring of 1991, his running mate was Andrei Zavidia, a former bureaucrat who described himself as a private businessman. After the aborted coup, a search through Party archives revealed that Zavidia had been given a loan of four million rubles by the Communist Party Central Committee to help reestablish *Sovetskaya Rossiya,* the nationalist paper that published Bishop Ioann's anti-Semitic tirade and had been banned after the failed August, 1991, coup.[11]

This was not the only example of the odd coalitions forming around the anti-crime and anti-reform cause. One intriguing aspect of the ultra-nationalists' rhetoric was the extremely narrow focus of their crusade against the mafiya. They seemed most upset by the Caucasian gangs, non-Russian businessmen, and pro-reform ministers accused of corruption. These, as it happened, were the very enemies of the *vorovskoi mir*. The patriotic movement's hatred for corrupt Westernized bureaucrats and minorities was shared by many in organized-crime circles after 1991. Several months after my meeting with Sterligov, a reliable source told me that the Russian National Assembly was associated financially with the Lyubertsy gang in Moscow, which had a reputation for carrying out attacks against Caucasian gangs in the capital. It was impossible to find out if this was true—and Sterligov was not anxious to meet me a second time—but evidence pointing to an earlier connection between the KGB and the gangs surfaced in 1994 with the Moscow publication of a book called *Vor v zakonye,* whose authors were a former KGB security agent and a journalist. The book was largely an attempt to show how the agency was stymied by corrupt Kremlin politicians in its efforts to defeat organized crime in the 1980s. But it disclosed the existence of a secret 1988 memo outlining a strategy for dealing with the mob. The memo, signed by the first deputy chairman of the KGB at the time, suggested exploiting the quarrels between gang organizations "to attract the more patriotically minded criminal authorities to covert cooperation." [12]

The logic for such a move was certainly unimpeachable after 1991. In the looking-glass world of post-Communism, *vory* were patriots too. They submitted to no one in the defense of Russia's spiritual purity, and they at least could claim a credible anti-Communist lineage. Ted Kasyanov, the self-proclaimed mafiya hunter, former KGB instructor, and crime boss who was arrested in Kazan, freely acknowledged to me that he put his network of trained bodyguards and enforcers at the service of certain political groups such as Pamyat, a notorious anti-Semitic organization with branches in Moscow, St. Petersburg, and other cities. "I don't like politics, but Pamyat is the political organization closest to my way of thinking," he explained. He went on to describe this as the proper role for a patriotic criminal organization. "A true mafiya would defend Russia against the pollution of foreign money," he said. "Most of the American companies are run by Jews, and the Jewish mafiya here has close links with other foreign Jewish mafiyas." [13]

There was little doubt that mobsters were playing a role across the entire spectrum of Russian politics. During the early 1990s, many sided with the forces struggling against the old regime. This was a matter of self-interest. The *vory* knew that Kremlin conservatives were anxious to cut short the economic liberalization that had already produced such impressive black-market profits. But others took patriotic satisfaction in joining the campaign to weaken the system and the ideology they despised.

Gavriil Popov, who won election as Moscow mayor in the same campaign that took Yeltsin into the Moscow White House, has admitted that reformers obtained financial support from *teneviki* (shadow businessmen often connected to the underworld). "To the degree that we grew stronger politically, the amount of financial aid that we received from those quarters increased," he told the human-rights activist Lev Timofeyev in 1992. "During the election, they provided significant support to both me and Yeltsin. For example, we got money from them to print leaflets and handbills. Formerly, we had to prepare our literature by hand." [14]

But their support for the democrats eroded as gangsters decided that the reformers were, in the words of one of my underworld informants, "bad for business." In 1993, I met a wiry former boxer named Mark Melzer, who operated a Moscow gym and sauna that was a favorite hangout for crime bosses. "When he's in a sauna, a Russian man, even a gangster, will talk freely about anything," joked Melzer. "And you know what these guys are bothered by most? By politics. They can't stand the democrats in power now. They helped them, of course, during the coup. They sent guns and some of their men to the White House in August, 1991. But now they just blast the hell out of them. They say the financial reforms are pushing the country downhill. I agree with them myself, actually." [15]

Many provincial *avtoritety*, having financed the political campaigns of selected candidates during the December, 1993, elections, clearly expected to get something for their money, and they were prepared to take action when they were disappointed. At the beginning of May, 1994, Sergei Skorochkin, a parliamentary deputy, was attacked by a mafiya hitman on a central street of his home town of Zaraisk, one hundred miles southeast of Moscow. Skorochkin, a member of the centrist Union of December 12th Party, fired back in self-defense and killed his assailant. The deputy admitted that he had been close to a local gang which supported his business career and then his election campaign. He claimed to have paid the equivalent of sixteen thousand dollars to the gang in extortion money in 1993, but to have refused to make any more payments after his election. That, he said, turned him into a target for a revenge killing. [16]

It was not the first time mob violence had spilled over into parliament. On the evening of April 26, 1994, another parliamentary deputy, Andrei Aizderdzis, was shot to death in Moscow as he arrived home from an evening session of the Duma. Aizderdzis made a name for himself as an entrepreneur before entering politics. According to Moscow sources, he was tied to questionable interests in banking and metal exporting. He was also suddenly thrust into national attention that month as the publisher of the KGB security agent's book about organized crime, which had listed the names of 260 *vory v zakonye*. Ultranationalists in the Duma, led by Zhirinovsky, made his murder a political cause célèbre, suggesting that his opposition to the government had triggered a mob contract on his life. But other sources blamed his refusal to follow policies favored by some of his former "partners." [17]

A few months after the incidents, Mikhail Yegorov, head of the MVD's organized-crime division, charged that the connections between politicians and mobsters explained the Duma's resistance to the stiff measures proposed by the government against crime, such as giving police the right to seize financial records without warrants. "Checks on bank accounts will show what financial support politicians have," he said darkly. "It's only natural that they do not want such information made public." [18]

Pyotr Filipov, director of the Analytical Center for Social and Economic Policy, made a similar observation in his special report on crime to the Russian government. "It's clear that Russian crime bosses are collecting compromising materials about all high-ranking officials and politicians," he wrote in January, 1994. "In these conditions, the populist promise of Zhirinovsky to restore strict order might rally tens of millions of common people and, perhaps even more dangerously, hundreds of businessmen to the banner of National Liberalism." [19]

That report suggested another explanation for the links between the KGB, ultranationalists, and "patriotic" criminal organizations. The right-wingers' economic philosophy was strikingly similar to the *vorovskoi mir*'s. Both shared Russians' ancient fears of disorder and foreign influence. Although they were happy to see Russia's influence extend abroad, they considered it necessary to seal the borders against alien forces. "Our entrepreneurs right now are too weak and underequipped to stand up against Western capital," Sterligov told me. The general was careful to point out that he was not against business—he claimed to be a businessman himself. Since his retirement from active service, he worked as a consultant to a brokerage house that specialized in what he called "economic intelligence." Almost incidentally, he added that the brokerage was operated by "former and serving" members of the intelligence apparatus.

Sterligov has also publicly confessed to an admiration for the former Chilean leader Agosto Pinochet. The Russian general, whose professional past might have been expected to put him at the opposite pole from the rabidly anti-Communist Pinochet, perceived special virtue in the Chilean regime's corporatist economic policies. "The Pinochet dictatorship ensured stability and law and order," he said, in an interview with a Russian journalist. "I believe a [regime like Chile's] would be applicable to us . . . a rigid regime which provides optimal conditions for the development of a national economy." [20]

It would be perfectly consistent with the KGB memo (chap. 6) to expect Sterligov and his associates to support the activities of their "patriotic" underworld allies, whose destabilizing actions could push Russian society in the direction they wanted it to go. Even in the final years of Soviet power, I heard some senior Party members who opposed what they considered the "anarchic free-market capitalism" of pro-democracy activists praise the Pinochet regime as a model for the next phase of Soviet society. In the turmoil of post-Communism, Pinochet achieved near-cult status among certain businessmen, intellectuals, and politicians. "I myself would like to see a Pinochet, or a Franco, in Russia," admitted Father Mikhail Ardov, perhaps conscious of Pinochet's close alliance with the church. "We could finish off crime, pornography, and all the disgusting things which have swept into our society. We must get rid of crime by any means, even including repressive measures. Otherwise crime allows no reforms to take place." [21]

Several Russian observers have already warned of the long-term implications of the link between ultranationalists and the mob. "If the trend persists, we might get a situation similar to that existing in Latin America or Italy, where politics are made not by the government or parliament, but by organized crime," Pyotr Filipov wrote in his January, 1994, report.

In the Red-Browns' view, only an authoritarian state could achieve the order and discipline necessary to reign in domestic greed, prevent foreign exploitation, and eradicate crime. But even so-called moderates believed that the country's law-and-order problems could be solved by a return to the Imperial order of the immediate past. At parliamentary hearings in 1992, several speakers advocated a "Russian Monroe Doctrine," which treated the entire geopolitical space of the former Soviet Union as Russia's legitimate sphere of interest.[22]

If the philosophical home of Russia's *vory* was inside the ranks of the right wing, their rivals among the equally powerful *avtoritety* found a more congenial atmosphere among the former Party barons, state industrial chiefs, and directors of privatized companies, who were rising to increased power and influence at all levels of the Russian government. The violent competition inside the underworld was beginning to find its outlet in the quarrels of national politics. It was the ultimate irony: In reaction to the lawlessness he had fostered, the comrade criminal was becoming the dominant political figure of Russian life.

The Yeltsin government conceded intellectual ground to its critics in both camps, among the ultranationalists and the managerial elite. By 1994, all but one of the reform ministers who had joined the democracy crusade were out of power. Yeltsin chose a former Soviet energy bureaucrat, Viktor Chernomyrdin, as his prime minister, to replace Yegor Gaidar, the young economist who had been a favorite of the West.

In active "retirement" as leader of the powerful pro-reform Russia's Choice faction, Gaidar has felt free to lash out at the nomenklatura capitalists who engineered his downfall. In the process, he came up with a masterly profile of Russia's new comrade-criminal class. "The Russian bureaucrat," he wrote in the magazine *Ogonyok* in the spring of 1994, "has today been given ideal conditions for getting rich: the conversion of power into property. [He] has unlimited possibilities to take individual, uncontrolled decisions, handing out quotas to export produce, credits, and subsidies, support for individual banks, and so on. The conditions of our chaotic economy encourage him to open his own account in a Swiss bank. This is a very powerful force that controls . . . the heights of political and economic life . . . a force that requires an unstable economy. It does not need confiscatory policies, but at the same time it does not need real market relations, which would throw bureaucrats out of work and out of power." [23]

Gaidar was in effect explaining why Russia's post-Communist history has come full circle. The Yeltsin period was beginning to resemble the final disappointing years of Mikhail Gorbachev's administration. Like his predecessor, Yeltsin found himself resisting the kinds of measures which would have genuinely opened up the economy as he became convinced such measures would plunge Russia into even worse disorder and chaos. In the process, he was manifestly losing control over his senior bureaucracy. The popular backlash triggered by rising crime rates further narrowed his room for maneuver. After the election, he even borrowed the nationalists' anti-Western rhetoric. "We want to be equal in everything, as two great powers," he said, in reference to the United States. "Concessions on any matter humiliate our patriotic feelings." [24]

Not all of the nostalgia for the anti-materialist, spiritual values of "Holy Rus" was misdirected. A stable transition depended to a large extent on reinforcing those areas of cultural and social distinctiveness that would otherwise be swamped by Western commercialism. But it also required institutions that would provide the framework for legitimate business enterprise and a civil society: regulatory agencies for commerce and public finance, credible courts and police, a respected civil service—all the accoutrements, in short, of a state based on the rule of law.

The future of Russian democracy was tied to the government's ability to provide security to private business enterprises and to the people who owned them. But such security had long since come to appear an impossible dream. Gangsterism and official corruption were already pushing businessmen in increasing numbers out of the democratic camp.

19 The Chinatown Gang

For nearly five hundred years, Moscow traders and merchants congregated in a warren of back alleys near the Kremlin called "Chinatown," or *Kitaigorod*. Although *Kitai* means "China" in Russian, some historians believe that the name really comes from the baskets of earth (*kita*) used to construct the walls that once enclosed the area. But when I lived in Moscow, I heard a more poetic version of how the district got its name. To the God-fearing czars and patriarchs of Holy Russia, commerce was a necessary evil, corrupting all those who engaged in it, and the makers of wealth had to be segregated from the rest of the population behind a kind of Chinese wall to reduce the chance of their infecting the populace.[1]

I preferred this version because even if it isn't true, it should be. Russians have always been deeply ambivalent toward those who set themselves higher than their neighbors through the accumulation of profit, and the story of Kitaigorod over the centuries demonstrates this with special pathos. Long after the walls of Chinatown began to crumble, the district continued to be a mercantile ghetto. Furs, carpets, ikons, and European goods were sold there under the wary eyes of the czar's bureaucrats. By the mid-nineteenth century, Kitaigorod had evolved into the city's principal business center. The government still kept a close watch, but the area soon matched the business quarters of Paris and London in vibrant activity. The muddy streets were lined with banks, warehouses, shops, and restaurants, and even a stock exchange elbowed aside the gilded church domes and cupolas to become part of old Moscow's skyline.

But this uneasy coexistence of the sacred and the profane was not to last. The Bolsheviks, fired with visions of utopia, abolished the banks and exchanges of Chinatown after 1917. The country's other financial centers, such as St. Petersburg, received similar treatment, but Kitaigorod's proximity to the Kremlin made it a particularly obnoxious symbol of everything they detested about capitalism. In this, as in so many of their actions, Lenin's revolutionaries reflected the deep-set prejudices and fears of the thousand-year-old culture they claimed to be discarding. Within a decade of the revolution, Kitaigorod was a ghost town. The once-elegant commercial buildings were occupied by cold-eyed commissars, and works by Marx and Engels replaced the ledgers on the shelves. In order to leave no one in any doubt about the true balance of forces between commerce and ideology, the Communist Party Central Committee established its headquarters just at the perimeter of the old business district—roosting on Staraya Ploshchad (Old Square) like one of the formidable babushkas who guard the courtyards of Moscow apartment buildings against trespassers.

They were unsuccessful. With the fall of Communism, commerce returned to Kitaigorod. The streets once again filled with shops. Shopping arcades and banks reopened, and the clamor of trade revived in the timeworn streets near the Kremlin. Across Old Square from the Central Committee offices—now used by civil servants—stood the Moscow Raw Materials and Commodities Exchange, the nation's biggest trading house. But a visitor strolling through Chinatown today cannot escape a feeling of unease, as if the past might at any moment rise up to snuff out the present.

It was smart to be cautious. In March, 1994, a bomb destroyed a car owned by Konstantin Borovoi, founder and president of the commodities exchange and one of the richest men in Russia, just as he stepped out of it. A few days earlier, he had demanded that the government suspend trading on his exchange because of what he called "mafiya penetration." Instead, he was suspended as president. Borovoi survived the explosion, but he is proof that capitalism still lives behind fearful walls in modern Russia. More than a year before the attack, he told me that the post-Soviet prosperity of Kitaigorod was not quite what it seemed.

"There is dangerous money everywhere," Borovoi said as we sat in his office, tucked away from the pandemonium on the exchange floor. "So much loose, crazy money flying around that it's like something heavy—when it hits the ground it destroys everything else around it."[2]

Most of the money, he said, came from neither production nor industrial expansion, but from comrade criminals dealing in the suddenly liquid wealth of the old regime. The wealth had begun to flow before the regime had ended. A few months after Borovoi founded his exchange, in 1990, he was called to a meeting at the Soviet Ministry of Finance, where officials sought his help in sponsoring a "multinational" company that was to train civil-service personnel. "It was obvious what they wanted to do," he told me. "They planned to take money from several joint ventures they owned illegally, as well as hard currency they held in their accounts abroad, and launder it through this new company."

It was an offer Borovoi knew he was expected to accept. The finance ministry held the power of life and death over his exchange. In return for allowing private brokerage houses to operate without fear of intervention, the bureaucrats expected Kitaigorod to front for their own enrichment schemes. They may have carried attaché cases instead of machine guns, but their methods were no less thuggish than the extortion practiced by mobsters against shopkeepers and restaurant owners in every neighborhood in Moscow. There was a definite symmetry of goals: the nomenklatura intended to be the gang that ran Chinatown.

But in Borovoi's case at least, they misjudged their mark. The founder of Moscow's largest brokerage house was one of the few entrepreneurs wealthy enough and independent enough to stand up to the bureaucratic mafiya—or so he claimed. A stocky man with fair, thinning hair, Borovoi was a thirty-nine-year-old professor of mathematics when he started a small trade cooperative in 1987. "I didn't really intend to be a businessman," he said. "To tell you the truth, what motivated me was that I hated Communists so much. I wanted to prove that I could survive when everything was against me." He invested his profits from the cooperative in other service-oriented companies which were too small to attract the attention of either gangsters or greedy government inspectors. He soon had a small empire of over fifty firms, and a fortune large enough to allow him to experiment with some innovative ideas. His exchange brought together enterprises eager to barter surplus machinery for foodstuffs and other supplies for their employees. With the central administrative system increasingly snarled, it was an instant success. Borovoi felt confident that he could weather any attempt by the bureaucracy to disrupt his operations. He told the finance ministry to look somewhere else for help.

Yet even Borovoi's claim to be completely independent of the machinations of comrade criminals needed to be taken with a grain of salt. Several sources both inside and outside the Moscow business community suggested (without offering details) that the energetic commodities-exchange president enjoyed closer contacts with leading nomenklatura figures during the last years of Soviet power than he was willing to acknowledge.

Nevertheless, he was clearly strong enough to avoid the experiences of less fortunate businessmen who were unable to resist the bureaucracy's strong-arm tactics. According to Borovoi, demands for the transfer of enormous amounts of state monies to brokerage houses and banks by government ministries in the 1990s were often accompanied by visits from the KGB or gangsters. Borovoi's sources were unimpeachable. Following the lead of the Stolichny Bank's Aleksandr Smolensky, he hired former KGB agents as members of his exchange's security service. Paid well by their new employer, they felt under no obligation to conceal the operating methods of their former comrades. "They told me the KGB would often use criminal gangs during the Soviet era to extort money from cooperative businesses," said Borovoi. "Why should anything have changed? Organized crime would be nothing today if it weren't for KGB support." [3]

Borovoi's well-informed security staff also told him that officials of the old Soviet security organs continued to collaborate with nomenklatura who held high posts in the government. The bureaucrats who tried to enlist him in the money-laundering scheme were still in positions of authority. They never stopped trying to get at his business. He told me that there had been several attempts to infiltrate his exchange in the months before we met. His security service managed to deflect a few offers of "partnership" from companies they discovered were linked to criminal syndicates. In the most blatant attempt, one group even tried to gain access to his computer records by using the KGB's communications software.

The exchange president compared his enemies to the "dragon" featured in a famous 1940s satire on Stalinism written by the Russian playwright Yevgeni Shvarts. The dragon managed to intrude into the life of every character. "What we have now is a government mafiya, a bureaucratic mafiya, that acts just like the dragon in the play," he said. "It's not concentrated in one place, but it is present in different places at the same time. That's not an easy enemy to fight." [4]

There were other clues to the dragon's existence. In the summer of 1992, Galina Starovoitova, then President Boris Yeltsin's adviser on ethnic issues, discovered that the easy access she had enjoyed to the president had mysteriously disappeared. "I would sometimes call the president's office and ask for a meeting, and they would tell me it was 'impossible,' that he is 'very busy.' So I would ask them to tell me whom he was seeing that day, or with whom he was lunching, so that he could fit me in between meetings. They didn't like my questions, but they had to tell me—if they didn't, I would announce that I was coming in right away. And I would. I'd get in my car and arrive in his reception room. They would smile at me and let me in, but they were furious. If you want to influence the president, you have to be strong and not too sentimental." [5]

Starovoitova was one of Russia's most outspoken politicians. Her connection with Yeltsin went back to the perestroika era, when she had been a prominent democratic activist and a close ally of Andrei Sakharov, the nuclear scientist who had become one of Russia's most well-known dissidents. The conspirators of August, 1991, had placed her name eighth on the list of persons to be arrested—Yeltsin was first—once they secured power. She had been visiting family in London at the time of the coup and personally enlisted Margaret Thatcher's help in the defense of Yeltsin. "In Russia they called me the 'Iron Lady,' " smiled Starovoitova, who has used her large, imposing presence and sharp intelligence to carve out a rare place of respect in the predominantly male world of Russian politics. "But I didn't tell her that." She was also briefly mentioned as a possible defense minister during the early reform phase of the Yeltsin government.

Starovoitova's aggressive tactics toward the new crowd in Yeltsin's office worked for a while. But she soon found that her ideas and suggestions were getting "lost" on their way to Yeltsin. Memos relating to her portfolio, but written by others, were delivered to the president without her knowledge. "When I asked the person who had prepared the memo to send me the copy, he would tell me that 'someone' is not permitting him to do so," Starovoitova said. "It wasn't hard to figure out that this 'someone' comes from the old structures, the hard-liners who are linked to the military-industrial complex or to others in the old Party apparat. These are flexible, experienced *apparatchiki*. They know all about how to operate the mechanisms of government. Yeltsin brought a lot of them into his office just to protect himself, but they took over everything."

Starovoitova was also convinced that the bureaucrats who had secured a foothold inside the Yeltsin government were associated with the growing corruption around the country. As the comrade criminals took over the revolution, Starovoitova followed other pro-democracy activists out of government in 1993. She blamed President Yeltsin. "He has no illusions about these people," Starovoitova said sadly. "But the problem is, they know how to make his life easier."

Ironically, Mikhail Gorbachev had been ensnared in the same velvet trap. In the late Soviet era, a group called the Russian Union of Industrialists and Entrepreneurs—comprising managers of the military-industrial complex, the heads of state agricultural enterprises, and leaders of the government-owned mining, metallurgy, and petroleum complex—was launched, ostensibly to sponsor economic reform. The members, all middle-level nomenklatura, made no secret of their contempt for the ossified central administrative machinery of the Party. They prided themselves on their expertise, on their ability to get things done, and they welcomed the measures taken during the perestroika era that gave them power over decision-making in their plants and over the disposition of their profits. For the same reasons, they regarded the advocates of a competitive market economy as enemies who would usurp their new powers just when they were given the rights to exercise them. At best, these "radical" economists were inexperienced: what factories had they run? At worst, they were traitors who would destroy Russia's industrial might.

The new group of "Red managers" became a powerful force behind the scenes in the late 1980s. They worked successfully to defeat proposals made by Gorbachev's liberal economic advisers to reduce state subsidies and remove price controls. The Red industrialists even battled Gorbachev himself. In one meeting, held in December, 1990, they revealed the self-assurance that was to give them such a dominant position in the post-Soviet era.

Mark Masarsky, president of the pro-market Association of Russian Enterprises, remembered watching in shock from his seat on an upper balcony in the Kremlin Palace of Congresses as the industrial kingpins, their suits stiff with socialist labor medals, stalked to the microphone to denounce the country's political and economic course. They demanded that the president take harsh measures against the democrats. The speeches contained so much personal invective against Gorbachev that few could be printed in official accounts of the meeting.[6]

As Masarsky recalled in a conversation with me two years later, Gorbachev finally exploded in one of his well-known bursts of temper. He told his audience that they did not frighten him. "You think you can make a lot of noise and stamp your feet, and that your president will just sink his head into the sand," he shouted, and went on to borrow imagery from the Russian civil war of the 1920s. "It won't work—I'm not going to divide the population of this country into Reds and Whites." But he was drowned out by catcalls.

"I couldn't believe what I was seeing," Masarsky said. "The leader of our state was standing in front of them, but they were the ones who felt strong. Not a single one of them spoke in his favor."

It was no coincidence, Masarsky added, that some of the most outspoken critics of Gorbachev at that meeting, such as Vasili Starodubtsev, head of the powerful Association of State Agriculture Producers, later turned up as organizers and supporters of the August, 1991, coup. Gorbachev underestimated the danger they posed to his government; perhaps he thought he could still control them. In the final year of Soviet power, his tantrum apparently forgotten, Gorbachev swung toward the Union of Industrialists. He may have decided, as Yeltsin was to do later, that it was better to have the industrial and agricultural lobbies on his side.

The struggle between the Red managers and the entrepreneurs did not end with the collapse of the Soviet system; it intensified. The industrialists, now supreme in their regions and their factory fiefdoms, moved quickly to hobble the Yeltsin government. By 1992, they had their own political party—called the Civic Union—and there was no longer a reason to conceal their influence. "Power belongs to those who have property and money," said Arkadi Volsky, chairman of the Civic Union. "At present, it is not the government but the industrial managers who have both."[7]

If someone drew a composite portrait of the classic Soviet bureaucrat, it would look like Volsky. A poker-faced veteran of the state defense industries, he once worked as an aide to former Soviet leader Yuri Andropov, later serving as Gorbachev's trouble-shooter in the Karabakh dispute between Azerbaijan and Armenia, where he earned a reputation as an advocate of reforms. It was one measure of the new influence of industrialists that Volsky's name was widely mentioned as a possible prime minister in the Yeltsin government or even as a future president. But Volsky stayed in the back rooms of post-Soviet politics, where he could advance a subtle strategy for changing the course of Russian democracy. In September, 1992, he surfaced briefly to tell *Pravda* that the country needed to rid itself of politicians who "fool the people with fairy tales that freedom and independence will bring them prosperity."

The Civic Union managed to fool many observers in the West. Its gradualist rhetoric appealed to Westerners opposed to shock therapy. "They [Civic Union leaders] are intelligent, sincere, quality individuals, who are serious about improving their country," was one typical assessment, from an American who described himself as an "economic consultant" to the Russian defense industry. "They seem to have peaceful intentions." [8]

In fact, the Civic Union played a part in derailing Russia's hopes of developing a genuine free market. Although it did poorly during the December elections, it has continued to serve as a behind-the-scenes lobbying group for industrial managers opposed to rapid, large-scale privatization and the expansion of private property rights. This position happened to unite the Red-Brown coalition, the underworld crime lords, and all others who feared that the country was heading too far down the Western path. [9]

At the Civic Union's founding congress in Moscow in June, 1992, Aleksandr Vladislavlev, deputy chairman of the party, described the private entrepreneurs of Russia in terms calculated to win the sympathies of the disparate forces battling Russian capitalist democracy. "They make their money out of buying a planeload of umbrellas for thirty [American] cents wholesale and selling them for two hundred rubles," he sneered. "They increase their money tenfold via operations with computers; then they sell their goods abroad and become millionaires. Today the most profitable operation these people engage in is to buy a factory on the cheap and break it up with a bulldozer so they can sell the scrap metal, thereby destroying some director's life work. How can real producers have any kind of mutual understanding with people like this?" [10]

If entrepreneurs like Borovoi regarded themselves as being permanently surrounded by hostile forces, it was a reflection of the greater paranoia felt by their opponents. Borovoi himself was at the top of the list of enemies of the state wielded by ultranationalists like the former KGB officer-turned-financial consultant Gen. Aleksandr Sterligov. In one of his offhand remarks during our chat, the general informed me that if I wanted to understand the really "sinister" mafiya forces in the country, I should visit the president of the Moscow Commodities Exchange.

It was easy to see why Borovoi aroused hatred. His office at the exchange was connected by computer to branches across the country as well as to financial markets abroad. One of the three television sets installed on the wall opposite his desk displayed hourly stock quotations from the New York and London exchanges. Although this was normal anywhere else in the world, it challenged the walled culture of Kitaigorod, which perceived danger in the ability to make connections with the outside world free of the state's scrutiny.

Who knew what these emerging Russian capitalists were really up to? Wasn't it obvious that their computer lines and their contacts abroad enabled them to secretly plunder the country? These questions were not confined to technologically innocent factory workers or peasants in distant provinces. They were raised at the highest levels of government. The degree of misunderstanding and distrust of a modern capitalist economy was awesome.

"We keep saying we are poor—we are not poor," asserted then vice-president Aleksandr Rutskoi in early 1993. "We are fabulously rich, but we cannot manage our wealth in the interests of society while at the same time a handful of crooks are making fortunes.

"What's the use of talking all the time about democracy? We must not be humane to the degenerate who robs this country and makes it an impossible place to live in . . . look what we have done with this country! What romanticism! What democracy!"

Less than a year later, Rutskoi was fighting allegations that he had amassed a private fortune at public expense. But the attitudes he expressed were also shared by law enforcement agencies, a fact that considerably complicated Russia's approach to its law-and-order crisis. According to a memo obtained by Borovoi from a friendly police official, a 1992 meeting of senior division chiefs at the Ministry of Internal Affairs concluded that "millionaire capitalists" were one of the greatest dangers faced by law enforcement agencies. "The police considered money made by independent forces whom the state could not control as suspicious, wherever it came from," he said. "Industrialists and managers who earn profits from the state enterprises are acceptable, but rich people who have nothing to do with the state are dangerous. That's the mentality of the old Communist nomenklatura, and it is still part of our thinking."

Even a cursory glance back at Soviet history suggests that businessmen's fears of persecution are justified. Every entrepreneur I met in Russia called my attention to what had occurred after the New Economic Policy—or NEP, as it was known by its Russian initials—was introduced during the 1920s in an effort to rescue the young Soviet republic from economic disaster. The NEP allowed a limited form of private enterprise: peasants could sell their produce at whatever prices the market could bear, and small private retailing was encouraged. It was at first an extraordinary success. Food and consumer items not seen since before the revolution reappeared as if by magic, and streets in central Moscow such as Tverskaya Street (later renamed Gorky Street) blossomed with outdoor cafés and stores selling European goods. Foreigners commented on the resemblance between Moscow and the "civilized" cities of the West, just as they would do seventy years later.

But the resemblance then, as now, was only skin deep. The wheelers and dealers of the NEP economy, the so-called NEPmen, were ostracized and feared by their compatriots. They were accused of profiteering, of immoral behavior, and of promoting alien values. The average NEPman was caricatured as a gangsterish dandy strutting through town in a flashy Western suit, with a beautiful woman hanging on his arm. Eugene Lyons, an American correspondent assigned to Moscow at the time, called the NEPman a "burlesque on capitalism." In words that could describe the current situation in post-Communist Russia, he wrote that Soviet Russia's new class of entrepreneurs was a "class existing by sufferance, despised and insulted by the population and oppressed by the government. . . . [They] had money, comforts and other physical advantages, yet remained a pariah element, the butt of popular humor and the target of official discrimination." [11]

Although Lyons was then a sympathizer with the Bolshevik cause, he shrewdly observed that the behavior of the first Soviet capitalists was understandable. "Because [NEP] was young, born in chaos and in some measure outside the law, because it was at bottom uncertain of its tenure and therefore desperately eager to make the most of its advantage immediately, it was exceptionally vulgar, profiteering, crude and noisy," he concluded.

The NEPman never got the chance to outgrow his caricature. The Soviet leadership ended the experiment after six years, sensing correctly the NEP's long-term threat to the Marxist-Leninist agenda.[12]

Under perestroika, some NEP policies crept back into Soviet life. Private enterprise was given a limited rehabilitation, and Party history was stretched to readmit some of the architects of the NEP, such as Nikolai Bukharin, into the official canon. But the NEPman himself was never rehabilitated. As Russia emerged into the post-Soviet age, the "capitalist" remained an isolated and menacing figure. After seventy years of Marxism-Leninism, most Russians acted as if they believed that anyone who had the temerity to become rich must have done it illegally.

Since many of the wealthiest citizens of post-Soviet Russia were in fact corrupt bureaucrats or crime kingpins, this was largely true. But such attitudes made no allowance for the ordinary entrepreneur. According to an October, 1992, poll taken by the Russian Institute of Public Opinion, 58 percent of Russians agreed with the statement that private businessmen owed their success to "fraud, deception, and criminality."[13]

The inability to distinguish between criminal and legal profits scarred post-Communist society as deeply as it corrupted its predecessor. Borovoi, however, believed that he could make a difference. A week before we met, he launched Russia's first political party for businessmen, or, as he called it, a party for the "middle class." Grandly named the Economic Freedom Party, it was aimed at giving entrepreneurs a seat of their own in Russia's political theater. "If I don't take a high-profile role, the Internal Affairs Ministry will keep getting away with writing memos that call millionaires criminals," he joked. But then he added, with a frown, "There is no alternative—the way things are going now, we could have national socialism here."

From a pile of papers on his desk, he proudly handed me a mimeographed copy of the Economic Freedom Party's platform. It was a thick document, but the central plank was simple and, in the Russian context, radical: all state property was to be transferred to Russian citizens. The rest of the document was dedicated to constructing the framework of a democratic capitalist society—proposals that would have pleased any

Westerner concerned about Russia's future. They ranged from establishing an independent judiciary to securing legal protection for private corporations. "We see our task as promoting a new generation of politicians who can fight against the trade mafiyas that interrupt the normal flow of financial capital," the document said. "Only through economic freedom can our country escape from its dead end. . . . Economic freedoms need political protection now."

The Economic Freedom Party, however, seemed to have hit its own dead end. Only a few of its candidates during the December elections won seats. Borovoi himself lost embarrassingly to a prominent member of the Red-Brown coalition, the former Communist deputy and Olympic champion wrestler Yuri Vlasov. Three months later, the explosion that destroyed Borovoi's car and almost cost him his life made clear that even he no longer enjoyed immunity from the dragon.

Several of the Economic Freedom Party's principles—such as the right to private property and the freedom of commerce—were reproduced in the new Russian constitution, approved in the national referendum held concurrently with the December, 1993, elections. But without political or legal institutions to give those principles force, there was little reason to expect they would have any more impact than the "human rights" protections written into previous Soviet constitutions.[14]

When the time comes to write a history of Russian capitalism, Borovoi and businessmen like him will appear to their successors as post-Soviet versions of NEPmen—representatives of a species forced to accommodate to the narrow space allowed them by criminal entrepreneurs and the former Communist establishment. It would be pleasing to consider them also as pioneers of a Russian free-market economy, but like the NEPmen their history is likely to be written by their enemies. Daniel Yergin and Thane Gustafson, in their 1993 analysis of models for "Russia 2010," conclude that the state will play the preeminent role in the development of Russian capitalism. Whether that works to the benefit of Russian entrepreneurs and consumers, however, "will be determined to a great extent by the path Russia follows in getting there," they wrote.[15]

That path has already become clear. In early 1994, there were few people of any weight left inside the Russian government to mount a credible defense of the free market. By then, the Chinatown gang—like Borovoi's dragon—was everywhere. It led both the opposition and the government itself. Most of the reformers who entered government in

1992 were gone. Several had been hounded out of office; others simply handed in their resignations. The new cabinet around Yeltsin was dominated by former nomenklatura and their allies.

The senior minister responsible for agriculture, for instance, was Aleksandr Zaveryukha, a former collective-farm boss who ran in the December, 1993, campaign on the Agrarian Party ticket with the Russian Communist Party. (He was known to Western bankers as the "king of state credits.") [16] The new speaker of the Duma was an Agrarian Party deputy named Ivan Rybkin, whose photograph appeared in Moscow papers at the time in respectful audience with Anatoli Lukyanov, the former speaker of the Soviet parliament, who had been jailed for his part in the August, 1991, coup. (Lukyanov, freed from Matrosskaya Tishina prison under a general amnesty, was elected deputy in December, 1993). The ranks of deputy ministers and assistants were filled with former managers of the military-industrial complex and manufacturing enterprises.

Leading them all was the new prime minister, Viktor Chernomyrdin, a senior bureaucrat in the former Soviet oil-and-gas industry, who replaced the reformer Yegor Gaidar. From the beginning, Chernomyrdin revealed his biases toward state-supported industry. He warned that Russia would not become a "nation of shopkeepers." Although he promised to continue the anti-inflation policies of his predecessors, he made it clear that he had little sympathy for the small entrepreneurs struggling to survive in the Russian economy. His own background in the nomenklatura naturally inclined him toward the large resource and production industries who were in the process of negotiating as favorable terms as possible with the government's privatization strategists.

Reformers watched these events with impotent rage. "It is not acceptable that people who have done immense economic and political harm to the state, who are in principle open opponents of the policy of reform, should join the cabinet," fumed Boris Fyodorov, the thirty-five-year-old banker who quit as finance minister in January, 1994. "The domination in the cabinet of the lifeless and illiterate ideology of . . . Red economic managers . . . inevitably dooms the country to collapse and the people to a fall in living standards." [17]

No one—except concerned Westerners—was really listening. The New Russia had become entangled in the prejudices against private entrepreneurship inherited from the old Soviet Union—and from Russia's historic ambiguity toward business. As a result, Russians hardly had a chance to test free-enterprise democracy in practice before it was discredited. "One of the main reasons for popular disappointment is that most Russians sense that nothing much has changed," observed Galina Starovoitova in 1992. "I think our government does not feel the mood of the people."

This proved to be the most bittersweet result of the crime, corruption, and wheeling and dealing that engulfed the second Russian revolution. Less than a decade after a handful of Soviet reformers began their monumental struggle against Communist authoritarianism, the separation between the rulers and the ruled was as wide as it had been in the days of the czars and the commissars.

20 Who Lost Russia?

A winter afternoon in central Russia. Frost covered the windows of the commuter train moving toward Yekaterinburg. Inside one of the carriages, a man and a woman shared a bottle of beer. They appeared to be a couple, but the intimacy between them extended no further than wordlessly handing the bottle back and forth. Both were shabbily dressed. The man had tattoos on both hands, and when he raised the bottle to his lips, the inky whorls of long-faded designs were visible on his bare arms. A sullen, caged look marked him as a recent inmate of the prison *zona* near the city. He finished drinking, wiped his mouth, and tossed the bottle on the floor. It didn't break. The woman pulled another one from a voluminous bag and handed it to him. He grunted, then struck it several times against the window ledge with practiced skill until he had dislodged the cap. Silently, they began drinking again.

Sergei Molodtsov and I were the only other passengers in the car. He shook his head as he saw me staring at the couple, following my gaze to take in the pile of bottles and the food scraps and mangled newspapers on the floor beneath their feet.

"I travel every day on this train, and I never get used to this," he said. "If you weren't here, I would have been sitting as far away from them as possible. It's unsafe for a person traveling alone. Too many times, you see fights, or people pulling out knives. I've been robbed myself."

Sergei was one of the most remarkable people I met during my years in Russia. We had become friends after he helped me during an earlier trip to Yekaterinburg. A slender journalist in his late twenties, he had somehow escaped the post-Communist cynicism of his peers. Although there were times when he succumbed to the Russian inclination to melancholy, he had a cheering faith in his ability to survive the worst that life could throw at him. Nothing seemed to shake his composure. When a local mafiya figure once warned him about his newspaper articles, he laughed it off. Inflation cut his salary to a pittance, but he subsisted on bread and tinned sardines to take care of his children and pay an allowance to his wife, who had left him for another journalist.

He even supported his mother-in-law. He spent long hours shuttling between his office, his wife's new home, and his cramped flat, and often found himself on this commuter train at odd times of the day or night—which, as I could see from the grizzled inhabitants of the car we rode in, put his personal safety at risk.

The train ground to a halt at Yekaterinburg. We stepped onto the platform and descended a flight of stairs to a foul-smelling corridor, which led to the exits. Men lying in their own urine were slumped on the passageway.

"This," whispered Sergei, "is what I really wanted you to see. I get scared to death every time I come here."

As we walked down the corridor, people emerged from the gloom. Most were dressed in filthy clothes, their faces ravaged by disease or alcohol. They pushed against us without making a sound. An old woman silently held out her hands for change. I almost tripped over a man sleeping in a fetal position against the damp wall.

"Keep your hands close to your pockets," Sergei said.

Outside, in the street, he sighed with relief.

"Every time I go through that station," he said, "it seems as if I am at the bottom of the sea, cut off from the surface, and watching all the sea life swarming towards me. It makes me afraid I will never get back to the surface again."

A Russian patriot listening to Sergei's nightmare of drowning would have been moved to outrage. The scene of wretchedness at a provincial railway terminal demonstrated the ultranationalists' case. Could there be more damaging proof of the depths to which the collapse of the Soviet Union had brought its people?

Western complacency about the troubles of the shattered Soviet empire only added to Russian indignation. The complacency was understandable, to a point. For the first time in the memory of most people alive today, there was no longer a Soviet Union, nor a center of world Communism. The shadow of global nuclear war was gone, and the rest of us could enjoy the unfamiliar prospect of a world without a defined enemy. Meanwhile, our old antagonists became comic-strip versions of their former selves. The once-dreaded KGB collaborated with scholars and Hollywood scriptwriters. The former Soviet army hustled jet fighter rides for cash to wealthy American tourists. To Russians, however, history seemed a bit crueler.

Aleksandr Solzhenitsyn, Russia's most famous literary exile during the Cold War, captured the bittersweet feelings that accompanied the end of Communist rule in a speech to an American audience in early 1993. "Having lived through these seventy lethal years inside communism's iron shell, we are crawling out . . . barely alive," he said. "A new age has clearly begun, both for Russia and for the whole world. [But] Russia lies utterly ravaged and poisoned; its people are in a state of unprecedented humiliation, and are on the brink of perishing physically, perhaps even biologically." [1]

Solzhenitsyn may have taken literary license to stretch the point. But not by much. Russia's population declined in 1993 by 71,600 people, the first net decrease since World War II. Diseases of poverty, such as diphtheria, hepatitis, and dysentery, swept through many rural and urban areas after having been held in check by the Soviet medical system for decades. It was reasonable for many Russians to believe, as Solzhenitsyn hinted, that the second Russian revolution had done more for the world than it had done for them. [2]

Yet the fact of Russian misery was not new. Soviet men and women had suffered degrading homelessness, alcoholism, broken families, and dead-end lives long before the last Communist leader walked out of the Kremlin. Despite its military strength, the USSR was a failed state by most measures of social well-being. In 1985, the average life expectancy in the Soviet Union was sixty-three years—about the same level as Brazil—and forty-nine nations had lower infant-mortality rates. But even the poorest of Russians could take comfort from being a citizen of the world's second superpower. The sense of belonging to a great collective national enterprise made the Soviet state endurable to its citizens. That was now gone. [3]

In its place was an overwhelming sense of defeat, and crime rubbed the point in. The epidemic of lawlessness in the years following the fall of Communism underscored the humiliation and helplessness of life "at the bottom of the sea." It was not just the lack of any government control that appalled Russians, but the loss of a sense of community. In the summer of 1992—Russia's first post-Communist summer—a Moscow woman I knew was robbed as she returned from a shopping trip to her local market. Three youths roughly pinned her arms behind her back and took her groceries and some change. "There were dozens of people in the street," she told me afterward, with more hurt than anger in her voice. "But no one came over to help or shouted for the police. That never happened before. We used to look out for one another."

In post-Soviet Russia's predatory society, such neighborly help was available only for a price. Bodyguards and protection agencies offered a security that the state could not match. The growing number of kidnapping and hostage-taking incidents led one enterprising Moscow firm to offer "armed convoys" to foreigners and wealthy Russians, just as scouts hired themselves out to wagon trains in the American Wild West. The frontier was on everyone's doorstep. An army of unemployed workers, ex-convicts, petty thugs, and homeless people made streets in many large Russian cities unsafe. Every third crime was committed by an unemployed person during the first half of 1993, evidence that the connection between crime, poverty, and unemployment was now as fateful in the East as it was in the capitalist West. Urban disorder was also responsible for the drop in Russian standards of living. According to criminologists, racketeering and extortion added as much as 30 percent to the monthly inflation rate. But no figure could measure the way in which crime had changed how people lived and worked in post-Communist Russia.[4]

Igor Safaryan, a bespectacled former state defense worker, made a fortune in 1991 and 1992 after starting a brokerage firm. He lived like a man under siege. The windows of his modern, wood-paneled office were fitted with expensive security alarms, and there were no signs advertising his brokerage in the rickety building where he worked. Bodyguards followed him everywhere he went—"especially," he told me glumly, "when I am meeting someone new."[5]

Like Seran Akopyan, the embattled shopkeeper I met on Krasnoprudnaya Street, he was an Armenian hoping to take advantage of the capitalist dream in Moscow. And like Akopyan, he carried a gun. He pulled it out of his pocket to show me.

"They used to say that in America, the Colt made culture," he said, with a rueful smile. "That was two hundred years ago, when you had to watch what you said to a stranger because you didn't know whether he had a pistol in his pocket. Well, now I have a pistol in *my* pocket. The strange thing is, maybe that's a kind of progress for Russia. The state used to protect us from harm, but it also kept us under control. Now, we have the freedom to be insecure. There's a selection process going on. And only the strong will win, whether they are working for the state, for private finance, or even for the mafiya. It's survival of the fittest."

The lords of this jungle, however, were the mafiya. When the senior *vory* of the Thieves World met outside Moscow in December, 1991, to discuss the opportunities presented by the post-Soviet world, they recognized better than the reformers how deeply Russians yearned for a sense of purpose and order. One of the few national institutions un-touched by the Soviet catastrophe, they set about creating a new order of their own, and they were successful beyond anything they could have imagined. Post-Soviet society had become such a frightening place that certain segments of the mafiya emerged as self-appointed defenders of Russian traditions even though they were responsible for much of the chaos. Some of their clients certainly thought that the mob was more reliable than the government. "If you ask me, it's not such a bad thing if the mafiya takes control," said Borisovich, the drug dealer. "If you go out after midnight in Moscow, you take your life in your hands with all the drunks and hooligans, but the idiots in our government can't do a thing about it. The mafiya needs stability in society just as ordinary people do."

Following a path taken by organized crime in other countries, post-Soviet mobsters took advantage of the vacuum of power to create the only working system of authority in many parts of Russia. But unlike the Western mafia, Russian gangs and their counterparts around the former Soviet Union were able to exploit the institutions, structures, and civil servants of a state that was already criminalized by its previous rulers.

In the city of Tver, just north of Moscow, anyone who wanted to open up a sidewalk stand in 1994 was required to seek the permission of the local gang leader before getting a license from municipal authori-ties. Tver gangsters, like Konstantin Tsyganov of Yekaterinburg, rightly considered themselves the most dependable investment bankers in their city. They provided loans to young businessmen who would otherwise have found it impossible to obtain credit from government banks. The same system operated in the country at large. The principal pools of capital available for domestic investment following the Soviet collapse (other than foreign loans) were the coffers of the Communist Party and the *obshchaki,* the treasure chests of the Thieves World. The capital was channeled into commercial enterprises, banks, luxury shops, and hotels. It not only spurred the equivalent of Russia's first consumer boom but also merged bureaucrats and gangsters into a uniquely Russian form of crime boss—the comrade criminal.

"There's a big difference between the Russian mafiya and the Cosa Nostra," Safaryan explained. "In the West, criminal groups are involved in drugs or other kinds of illegal activities, but in our country the mafiya is involved in legal business. So most of my business friends can't avoid dealing with it."

By 1993, organized crime allegedly accounted for between 30 and 40 percent of the national turnover in goods and services, or about twenty billion dollars. Russian law enforcement agencies, who provided the estimate, did not explain how they arrived at the figure. This was not surprising, since no one could agree on an acceptable definition of criminal behavior.[6]

This was the heart of Russia's crime dilemma. The tension between "good crime" and "bad crime" recurs throughout this book. For people like Mikhail, the would-be dentist who turned to art smuggling to finance his clinic, crime was what one did to survive. "There are no laws protecting anyone, and the police are useless, so to tell you the truth, people are getting used to the mafiya," Mark Melzer, manager of the boxing club in Moscow, told me in 1992. "It's much clearer and easier to understand than anything else in our country. You know that if you pay, everything is all right. If you don't pay, then you are in shit." Such "clarity" at least offered comfort to the average Russian entrepreneur, who found it difficult to keep his hands clean. High taxes and red tape made it extraordinarily hard to conduct business without breaking the law. Nothing in the new Russian economy could be accomplished without a bribe. The only beneficiaries of the situation were corrupt bureaucrats and racketeers, who exploited the nation's legal chaos.[7]

As I pursued the trail of the mafiya through post-Communist society, I kept encountering officials who honestly felt that organized crime was a necessary evil in the transition to a market economy. Unable to perceive any satisfactory way of stopping it, short of the authoritarian measures used by the former regime, many even considered some forms of illegal behavior a productive means of eliminating the lingering monopolies of the Soviet system. It was an attractively unorthodox, but ultimately barren approach.

In the late spring of 1992, Konstantin Borovoi joined a group of wealthy private businessmen for an angry meeting with a senior minister in the Yeltsin government. The entrepreneurs had demanded the meeting to complain about government taxes on business earnings that reached as high as 60 percent. After hearing the complaints, the minister, a prominent young reformer, held up his hand and called for silence. He told them that the government knew what it was doing. The high taxes were designed to destroy the large Communist enterprises, and surely they recognized this to be in their interests too. "Look," he said, with a mischievous smile. "You are all supposed to be entrepreneurs. That means you are clever people. Surely you can figure out ways to get around the system."

The silence in the room dissolved into nervous laughter. "It was amazing to hear," recalled Borovoi. "A government official was telling us we had free rein to break the law. Nothing would happen to us if we were smart enough to avoid the taxes. In other words, the government would be our fellow conspirator." [8]

That surreal encounter encapsulated the frustration, the self-conceit, and the ineptness of Russia's post-Communist reformers. Possessing only an uncertain vision of what form capitalism might take in Russia, they were driven to treat entrepreneurs as a class of useful felons. Economic change had to be accomplished by subterfuge; reforms were implemented by winks and nods. Could it have been otherwise? Russian reformers never made a serious effort to find out. Instead of developing a legal and educational framework for the new market era, including guarantees of the enforcement of contracts and property rights—and other laws designed to provide a secure, equitable working environment for commerce—the government acquiesced in the frenzied profiteering that passed for Russian capitalism.

As a result, the entire country was enmeshed in a new black market. According to Moscow analysts, more than 3.5 billion dollars circulated inside Russia—a substantial amount of which represented illicit earnings—almost as much as the country's entire hard-currency reserve in 1994. The old black market had been a vast underground bazaar that turned millions of citizens into felons, from the cobbler who sold shoes privately to his neighbors in violation of laws against "profiteering" to the bureaucrat who bartered spare parts for oil. Russia's gangster capitalism demanded similarly furtive behavior from businessmen. The case of the real estate broker Viktor Kalinin, who kept his profits secret to hide his income from bureaucrats who might pass the information on to racketeers, was typical.

"The mob is the real KGB of today," wrote David Gurevich, a writer whose friend was murdered in February, 1994, in Moscow after refusing to turn over the assets of his company to racketeers. "[It purges] Russian society of people who should be directly benefiting from the long-debated infusion of Western money. . . . If this continues, no amount of Western money will prevent Russia from becoming a monster—a mob-run nuclear power." [9]

Gurevich was half-right. The Russian mafiya had not usurped the role of the KGB and other forces of the former Soviet establishment. Instead, it had joined them to create a new power structure.

To understand where Russia was heading, it is worth looking at the trauma of Italy, which discovered in 1994 that for more than three decades its prosperity had depended upon a secret alliance between organized crime, government, and industry. Russia, with a weaker and more unstable central government and a long tradition of official misbehavior under Communist rule, looked certain to surpass Italy. It would be even harder to root the comrade criminal out of his place at the center of Russian society.

Even before the Soviet collapse, the journalist Arkady Vaksberg warned that the mafiya could never be destroyed in Russia, because it would mean putting on trial the autocrats who benefited from it and encouraged it. "The [Russian] mafia is intact because it grew up with the system and has become an inseparable part of it," he wrote bitterly. "Which means that the mafia will only collapse when the whole edifice, i.e., the system itself, collapses." [10]

Despite appearances, the system never really collapsed after August, 1991. The most important item on Russia's political agenda was finding a way to break the connection between crime and government, and that meant neutralizing Borovoi's "dragon." But only a few Russians had any strategies to offer. "I think we should name a number of posts to which members of the old Party nomenklatura cannot be appointed for, say, three or five years," Galina Starovoitova suggested. "For instance, they should not serve as directors of large state enterprises, managers of the military-industrial complex, chairmen of state farms, or heads of local administrations. Let them do business, let them make money however they want to, as long as they don't run for office. Then, at least, we might have a situation in which the bureaucratic mafiya and the underworld mafiya will be competing with each other, and competition is good. If we can't distinguish any more between clean money and dirty money, we can at least hope that it will be available to the next generation once it is invested in the market economy."

That was easier to suggest than to accomplish. There was no trusted new "elite" to replace the old. A truly non-partisan civil service has always eluded Russian governments. Even the most tentative attempts to isolate bureaucrats from commercial interests were flawed. In July, 1993, parliament passed a long-awaited anti-corruption law, which prohibited bureaucrats, judges, and members of parliament from combining their jobs with work at foreign-controlled enterprises or joint ventures. The criminal code was amended to outlaw "the abuse, by persons authorized to perform state functions, of their status for illegal financial and other gain." [11]

But any effort to clean out corruption in the Russian government was doomed in advance, because it depended upon the nomenklatura in power to enforce it—and they certainly had no incentive to impoverish themselves. Anders Aslund, a respected Swedish economist who left his post as government adviser in 1994 after the reformers were pushed from power, observed that Russia's inflation rate was a reliable measure of the state of the struggle between free-marketeers and the bureaucracy. "The higher it is, the better the old . . . elite is doing." [12]

There were other ways of clamping down on crime. After three years of chaos, many Russians regarded with nostalgia not only the order imposed by the old regime, but also the methods it used. Faced with similar criminal anarchy after 1917, Lenin declared a "war on crime." He meant it literally. "Today is not the time to stroke people's heads," he remarked to the writer Maxim Gorky. "Today, hands descend to split skulls open." The police state that he established and Stalin later refined lasted for the next seven and a half decades. It remains attractive to large numbers of people.

On November 7, 1992—the day once celebrated in Soviet life as the anniversary of the Bolshevik revolution—*Pravda* published a mock report in which future Communist leaders triumphantly celebrated the centenary of the 1917 coup in 2017. "In the last quarter-century, our greatest achievement was that we managed to overcome the spiritual degradation that enveloped society in the period of Capitalist Restoration," the paper imagined a future manifesto as declaring. "The cult of petty commerce, speculation, [and] embezzlement, the demonstrative rejection of national culture, the Yankee-ization of spiritual values— these were the main bastions that the Soviet people had to overcome." [13]

It was, of course, sheer fantasy to imagine that the Communist regime would come back. Even the former nomenklatura—perhaps especially the nomenklatura—saw no virtue in returning to a centralized system that restricted their freedom to make profits. But the core of the message, which idealized an authoritarian society uncorrupted by latter-day NEPmen and Western-financed entrepreneurs, was increasingly popular.

Russia's post-Communist uncertainty has been duplicated in other countries of the former Soviet Union and Eastern Europe, where a reaction to falling living standards, government corruption, and organized crime has returned members of the former regimes to power. But again, far from signaling a return of Communism, these events suggest an increasing receptivity to authoritarian and nationalist appeals.

The newly liberated citizens of Communist societies form a dangerously unstable community in the post–Cold War world. One St. Petersburg engineer summed up the cynicism of his compatriots by cleverly turning around the old underground joke about Communism's secret pact in which the worker pretends to work and the government pretends to pay him. "We pretend to vote and the government pretends to govern," he said. "It's the mafiya which runs everything." Accustomed to living under rules that denied them individual choice, many former subjects of Communist regimes reacted with hostility and fear after the euphoria of freedom wore off—like inmates of an institution who are suddenly told to make their own way in the world. "Many find it difficult to cope," said Vaclav Havel, the Czech president, playwright, and former dissident. "They find themselves in a state of uncertainty in which they tend to look for pseudo-certainties. One of these might be submerging themselves in a crowd, a community, and defining themselves in contrast to other communities." [14]

Nationalism, xenophobia, and a carpetbagging morality are the legacies of Communism across Eastern Europe and the Eurasian continent. In its search for a solution to crime, Russia is moving toward a regime of state capitalism run by the former nomenklatura. Prime Minister Chernomyrdin, a likely candidate in the presidential elections scheduled for 1996, has successfully embodied the interests of state enterprise managers, resource industries, and privatized firms who want a continued dominant role for government in the economy. Former vice-president Rutskoi, the other prominent contender, offers a more nationalist version of the same, though he would probably push Russia further down the authoritarian path. Both would depend on the help of more activist police and security forces to control mafiya violence and street crime. But neither man is likely to be interested, for their different personal reasons, in tackling the roots of post-Soviet criminal influence inside the bureaucracy. They would neither cut off the sources of the comrade criminals' authority, by putting the country on a sound legal foundation, nor strengthen the independence of local governments and entrepreneurs, by widening access to money, property, and credit. With either of the two leaders, or others of similar background, the greater criminalization of the Russian economy is more certain, as is the further expansion of the post-Soviet mafiya overseas. Under this scenario, a half-joking comment from a Russian internal-affairs ministry official named Valeri Nikolayev takes on a more serious tone: "The West will [soon] have to protect itself against us by an armored shield rather than by an iron curtain." [15]

Although the reformers' inaction (and greed) are primarily responsible for the sabotage of their revolution by organized crime, the West must also shoulder some of the blame. Western advisers and specialists badly underestimated the impact that the collapse of Communist authority would have on a country as rigidly held together as the Soviet Union. The fact that the introduction of Western capitalist forms of behavior strengthened the worst elements of the last regime—the Party and underworld mafiyas—should have given the most ardent Western free-marketeer pause. But few knew, or at least few were willing to take seriously, how deeply criminality was embedded in the Soviet state.

The bureaucrats and managers of the former regime acquired new capital and political strength by exploiting the legal vacuum left by departing Communist authorities. Their only real rivals were the leaders of the old Russian underworld. But the *vory* who gathered outside Moscow in December, 1991, were overwhelmed by the forces of violence they unleashed. A post-Soviet mafiya emerged, incorporating the most entrepreneurial elements of the former nomenklatura and the gangster capitalism of the new. The comrade criminal—the personification of this new force—eclipsed all other political forces in Russia.

While this was going on, the West sat on the sidelines. Western leaders, quick to claim "victory" in the Cold War, never took a close look at the "losers." It was assumed that Russians would take to Western forms of economic and political development as eagerly as they had bought Western jeans and rock music tapes on the black market. The awkward questions were put on hold: what did we really want Russia to be? A junior partner? A friendly rival? A poor country that would never again be able to muster the resources and weaponry to threaten our homes? The failure to come to grips with those questions has come to haunt the post–Cold War order that once seemed so welcoming.

In the early 1950s, following Mao Ze-dung's triumph, a debate raged in the West over who had "lost" China. Closer study of the Chinese revolution made it clear that Western diplomats could not have prevented the Communist takeover. Russia's case, however, was different. The West was presented with a rare opportunity to shape the Russian transition to democracy. The old Communist bureaucratic establishment was initially in a state of shock. Russians were exhilarated at the prospect of change.

What could the West have done? Money was certainly not the answer. The loans and investments channeled into the post-Soviet states after December, 1991, were far less than the sums originally earmarked, but even larger amounts would have made little difference. There was a glaring absence of the kind of infrastructural reform which would have ensured that such aid was used productively.

The West's biggest mistake was to have expected more than Russia was able to become. We sensed, but did not fully understand, how sick Soviet society was. The so-called shock therapy, which has since been held responsible for everything from Russia's four-digit annual inflation rate to the revival of fascism, was a fiction—as those who hoped to carry it out admitted. "Many people in the West, it seems, prefer to close their eyes to the fact that there never was any shock therapy, ever, in Russia," wrote former finance minister Boris Fyodorov in April, 1994.[16]

All the measures taken—lifting price ceilings on subsidized goods, lowering barriers to private ownership, the privatization of state firms— merely continued the piecemeal approach that began under perestroika. They benefited only the criminals, swindlers, and Communist auto- crats who had long since staked their claims to Russia's riches. And they pushed the majority to what is now unremitting hostility and anger toward the idea of capitalism.

Similar delusions of instant change greeted the "thaw" that followed Stalin's death. The generation that came of age in those years—and which eventually went on to proclaim perestroika—was also bitterly disappointed by the slow pace of reform. Georgi Arbatov, who spent many years as an adviser to Soviet presidents and then as an apologist for perestroika abroad, was part of that generation. His fervent memo- ries of the post-Stalin period burst through in his book *The System*. It was impossible, he wrote, to expect a ruined field to become fertile overnight "after almost thirty years of being downtrodden by the power of government and Party authority and [by] the heavy steamrollers of arrogant, ignorant careerists and fanatical semi-literates indulging their base passions."[17]

It may have been equally misguided to expect post-Communist Rus- sia to abandon all the elements of its old system overnight. "To try to launch simultaneously a political revolution, an economic revolution and a social revolution, in a national culture that was not in fact ready for revolution at all, was to impose an intolerable burden on the Russian people," wrote Peter Reddaway, a veteran observer of Soviet society.[18] Reddaway's words explain the psychological and structural obstacles Russia faced after 1991, but they do not completely explain why the transition veered so quickly off course. And they ignore the possibility that some form of Western action might have made a difference.

The reformers, outgunned, outmaneuvered, and corrupted by the comrade criminals, were primarily responsible for the failure of their revolution. But an effort to establish a partnership of equals between the former Cold War rivals might have altered the odds. By emphasizing our willingness early on to help provide a climate of security for Rus- sians during the transition, by tying aid and economic assistance to the reform of legal institutions, by paying more attention to the flow of em- bezzled Soviet funds reaching the West—it might have been possible to contain Russia's plunge into criminal chaos, or at least to moderate its effects.

We are now in danger of losing the battle for the real stakes in Russian society, the country represented by the disillusioned, fearful streets of Yekaterinburg and dozens of other cities across Russia's wild frontier. The West's encounter with Russia's comrade criminals has produced a delayed reaction. Huge amounts of foreign captial are still pouring into Russia, but the bullish mood of Western businessmen is now tempered by crime, corruption, high taxes, onerous import duties, and government red tape. Meanwhile, Western governments—finally waking up to the danger presented by the Russian mafiya networks of drugs, weapons, and money-laundering—have begun to investigate ways to contain the threat.

Such cold-eyed realism needs to be accompanied by a recognition that the second Russian revolution is not over. One hopeful conclusion that can be drawn from the stories of Russian frontier capitalism I have presented here is that ingenuity and grit are very much alive behind the old Soviet borders. If any single factor proved that the second Russian revolution was as real as the first, it was the creation of thousands of small shops, exchanges, garages, and commodity houses in the face of some of the most ferocious and violent criminal organizations on earth.

This is the time, therefore, to sow the funds and advice that would have fallen on barren ground a few years earlier. The comrade criminal has not lost his grip on the new Russian economy, but, paradoxically, he has begun to feel confident enough to allow the beginnings of structural change, the expansion of private property rights and of privatization. He believes, of course, that he can now dominate the change. But the struggle has only begun. It is the moment to encourage those elements inside Russia who can offer him a run for his money. That means, for example, opening Western markets to Russian goods and establishing closer working relationships with Russia's law enforcement authorities. It is almost certain that such efforts will pay real dividends, as the West recognizes the full dimension of the historical change underway in Russia.

The struggle for survival in the post-Soviet empire has thrown up disturbing reminders of the past. But it has also revived a mentality that had been dormant for decades, perhaps even for centuries of czarist authoritarianism. Stronger, tougher, and more self-reliant citizens are visible everywhere one looks. Many of them are young, and for them what occurred between 1991 and 1993 was as much a rite of passage as a revolution.

"All my hopes, really the hopes of my generation, are on the youngsters I see now running up to wash car windshields at traffic lights," Igor Safaryan told me. "They are the ones who will live in a real economy. People like me are anomalies. I'm only thirty-eight, but I already feel like I come from a previous age."

"But some of those youngsters are already working for the mafiya," I said.

Safaryan smiled.

"They will simply be ordinary businessmen some day," he said. "That's what I mean by survival of the fittest."

There were an estimated forty-five million young Russians between the ages of sixteen and twenty-five in the early 1990s—almost one-third of the nation's population. To their parents, they already seemed like inhabitants of a foreign country. The older generation was appalled by statistics showing that large numbers of them were involved in criminal behavior, and by the fact that the slick stockbroker or the mafiya hitman had replaced the pantheon of Soviet heroes as role models for youth. "We are losing a whole generation of Russia," complained one writer in *Rossiiskaya Gazeta*.[19]

Young Russian capitalists were openly contemptuous of the standards of the older generation. "Older people have an ethics problem," Dmitri Zotov, the twenty-four-year-old manager of the foreign credit department at a private Moscow bank, told one Western reporter. "By that I mean they *have* ethics. To survive I can break a law if I need to, and the risks aren't too large. Older people wouldn't even think in such a way."[20]

This new, tougher generation crowded the striptease clubs, casinos, and discotheques of Russian cities, spent heavily in the car showrooms and perfume shops set up by Western firms, and took their holidays in London or Rome. They believed they had plenty of time before taking their rightful place as the heirs of the democracy revolution. "In a decade we'll be the heads of banks and big companies, and high up in government," said Slava Shikulov, whose export-import business already earned him enough to buy a dacha outside Moscow and a four-room apartment in the center of the city.

But would these young people survive the turmoil of the next decade and beyond to become the masters of a new Russia? Or were they doomed to the same fate as the NEPmen seventy years earlier?

Unlike the generation that preceded them, none appeared ready to influence the political direction of Russian society. Others, unfortunately, were willing enough to do it for them. The central question facing post-Communist Russia and its neighbors was whether fear would once again be allowed to close the windows that had opened in so many places. Those who played upon the prejudices and fears of an older Russia were in the ascendancy, and once again they offered seductively simple solutions. As long as young people were content to stay in their banks and discotheques, the outcome was inevitable.

But it does not have to be the only outcome. Shortly after the August, 1991, coup had failed, the journalist Sergei Molodtsov decided to take his first vacation in years. He spent ten days in the Siberian village of Oslyanka—so remote it did not appear on any map. To get there, Molodtsov had to travel by boat and then on foot. When he arrived, he discovered that there were no newspapers, and no one even owned a radio.

"The people of the village didn't know anything about the political situation," he recalled wistfully. "They hadn't heard of Yeltsin, and they didn't know there was a coup. They weren't even interested. No one had any money, but they lived well. They hunted and grew their own food, and there was more than enough to eat."

Molodtsov made a promise to himself when he returned home. "I decided that if the mafiya starts chasing me in Yekaterinburg, if things become completely intolerable there, I will go and live in Oslyanka," he said. "And no one will be able to find me."

It was a seductive dream. In my own travels across the former Soviet Union, I had seen several villages like the one he described. I once visited a remote hamlet in a beautiful mountain valley in the Altai region, on the border with Mongolia, where the descendants of Old Believers, who had broken from the main body of the Russian Orthodox Chuch three centuries ago, lived in sparse wooden houses and pursued their lives free of meddling apparatchiks in distant Moscow. At the time, it seemed a perfect refuge from the Soviet machine. But as I picture the village now, it represents an escape into the utopias that have deflected, seduced, and ultimately damaged Russians so many times before.

Sergei obviously thought so, too. He never returned to Oslyanka. Instead, he left Yekaterinburg for Moscow, where he obtained a new newspaper job. Like millions of others whose presence is hinted at in these pages, he was ready to live in the real world.

Notes

Introduction: Horse without a Bridle

Tass News Agency changed its name in 1992 to Itar-Tass. References to *Moscow News* are for both English and Russian editions unless otherwise noted.

Epigraph: Quoted in Michael Beschloss and Strobe Talbott, *At The Highest Levels: The Inside Story of the End of the Cold War* (Boston: Little, Brown, 1993), p. 463.

1. Vladimir Kalinichenko, interview with author, September 25, 1992. Kalinichenko, in fact, helped Martin Cruz Smith during his Moscow research for *Gorky Park*: "[Cruz Smith] wanted to get as close to a real-life [police] character as possible," Kalinichenko told one of my Moscow assistants. "And I provided much of this. In this sense I was a model."

2. Getting the money home still seems a forlorn hope. Most of it appears to be in untouchable Swiss bank accounts or on the expense accounts of foreign Communists. Russian investigators recovered only four million dollars from six countries by 1993. But during the Cold War, some 111 Communist parties and left-wing movements in more than eighty countries were financed by the Soviet party, with money siphoned from hard-currency accounts in the state budget. According to papers released from the Moscow Party Archives, twenty million dollars went to the U.S. Communist Party over the 1980s, and two million dollars to the Canadian party. See Tass dispatch of July 14, 1992, among many other accounts of the secret payoffs.

3. Crime statistics for 1992. Sources: *Moscow Tribune,* March 9, 1993; Itar-Tass, February 5, 1993. Police were disarming an average of five or six gunmen daily in the fall of 1992, according to a report in Tass, November 9, 1992. On the black market in September, 1992, you could buy a pistol or a revolver for eight thousand to twelve thousand rubles (between $17 and $26 at prevailing exchange rates); "Every 50th Person Is Armed," *Megapolis Continent,* no. 35, September 2, 1992. The 1993 statistics prepared by the Russian Internal Affairs Ministry were published in *Izvestiya* and reported in *The New York Times,* January 30, 1994. The number of 1993 murders was less than thirty thousand, and firearm offenses numbered just over twenty-two thousand—hardly a crime wave by Western standards for a nation of 150 million people, but compared to the level of crime in Soviet society, these were disturbing figures.

4. Aslambek Aslakhanov, interview with author, July 10, 1992.

5. Lenin robbery reported in George Leggett, *The Cheka: Lenin's Political Choice* (Oxford: Clarendon Press, 1981), p. 239.

6. Quoted in Tibor Szamuely, *The Russian Tradition* (London: Fontana Paperbacks, 1988; Secker and Warburg,1974), p. 43. Szamuely called Peresvetov Russia's "first political theorist." Ivan the Terrible died by poisoning in 1584. Unease in the country grew under his unassertive son Fyodor, whose death without an heir in 1598 sparked a succession crisis which many historians consider the beginning of the Time of Troubles. The end of Ivan's authoritarian regime left Russia largely rudderless until the first of

the Romanov czars, Mikhail, rallied the country to expel foreign invaders in 1613. The dynasty he established lasted until 1917.

7. Reuters dispatch from Moscow, February 12, 1993.

Chapter One: Thieves World

Epigraph: Quoted in Arkady Vaksberg, *The Soviet Mafia,* trans. John and Elizabeth Roberts (London: Weidenfeld and Nicolson, 1991), p. 10.

1. The Armenian was interviewed in Moscow by the author, March 31, 1993.

2. Quoted in *Moskovsky Komsomolets,* July 18, 1992.

3. Figures of organized-crime activities from *Tass,* October 30, 1992, and from MVD report for 1993, *The New York Times,* January 30, 1994. Accounts of other incidents in this chapter were widely reported in the Moscow press.

4. Col. Anatoli Zhoglo, interview with author, March 16, 1993.

5. Press briefing, June 9, 1992, at MVD headquarters, Moscow. Here, and throughout the book, I have elected to spell the word as *mafiya,* not only to accurately convey the Russian pronunciation, but also to emphasize that there are consequential differences between the Russian and foreign varieties of organized crime. Vaksberg believes that the first time the word was used in a Russian context was in the mid-1970s, by a senior official in the USSR Prosecutor's Office named Viktor Naidenov. Vaksberg, op. cit., p. 45.

6. Far East poll reported by Interfax, July 5, 1992. Yekaterinburg poll quoted by Tass, June 7, 1993.

7. New rules on exports reported by Reuters (Moscow), July 15, 1993.

8. The attack on the Crimean newspaper reported in *Megapolis Express,* April 28, 1993.

9. Tamara Lomakina, interview with author, September 25, 1992. See chapter 5 for the full story of Lomakina's beating.

10. Yevgeny Marchuk, chief of the Ukrainian Security Service (and former head of the Ukrainian KGB), spoke of the "increasing politicization" of crime. He noted that attacks on deputies, judges, and regional administrators had contributed to the rising crime levels across the republic. Quoted by Tass, November 19, 1992. Other reports on the rise of organized crime across the CIS come from Interfax, February 16, 1992, February 16, 1993 (Kyrgyztan), February 14, 1993 (Dushanbe), and July 17, 1993 (Kazakhstan).

11. Statistics on attacks on courts from MVD press release, October 26, 1993, and press conference in Moscow on the same date.

12. Quoted by Tass, July 2, 1993.

13. Zoya Korneyeva, interview with author, March 10, 1993.

14. Yevgeny Maksimov, interview with author, July 10, 1992.

15. Yeltsin quoted by Reuters, January 19, 1993. In the same speech, he said, "Everyone thinks political issues could lead to an explosion, but crime could as easily blow us asunder at the unbridled rate at which it is growing. . . . In growth of crime we are overtaking countries which have always been to the fore, such as for example, Italy."

16. Mafiya boyfriends quoted in Andrew Solomon, "Young Russia's Defiant Decadence," *The New York Times Magazine,* July 18, 1993.

17. Quoted in Matthew Campbell, "Murder Inc Makes a Killing in Moscow," *The Sunday Times* (London), August 10, 1992.

18. Reports on teen crime from Itar-Tass, January 15, 1993 (Surgut), Baltfax, March 7, 1993 (Tyumen). General statistics on youth crime reported by Itar-Tass, March 23, 1993.

19. Quoted by Reuters (Moscow), April 28, 1992.

Chapter Two: *Vor*

1. Vedentsovo assembly. Russian police sources have told me that they believe the meeting was held in the home of a crime boss known as Levon. Details are sparse. Police found out about the meeting only well after it had taken place. The dates given range from December 20 to December 25, 1991. (The 25th, ironically, was the day of Gorbachev's resignation).

2. Estimates of the black-market economy, naturally, vary widely. Experts on Vice-President Aleksandr Rutskoi's staff supplied the figure of 110 billion rubles in a 1993 "white paper" on corruption. General Aleksandr Gurov of the Russian Security Ministry, however, believes that it is closer to 250 billion rubles.

3. Colonel Anatoly Zhoglo, interview with author, op. cit.

4. Likhachev, quoted in Valery Chalidze, *Criminal Russia: Essays on Crime in the Soviet Union,* trans. P. S. Falla (New York: Random House, 1977), pp. 53–54.

5. Sometimes there was an extra cachet involved in larceny. In the province of Vologda, stolen seeds were said to take root more quickly than those obtained in the market. I am indebted to Valery Chalidze (op. cit.) for the analogy between the early peasant outlaws and modern criminals, for his analysis of nineteenth-century beggars guilds as well as some of the customs of twentieth-century bands that are covered in this section. According to Chalidze, in prerevolutionary St. Petersburg, gangs called themselves "choirs" in a mischievous attempt to flaunt their outlaw status in Czarist society. Richard Pipes has also written of the institutionalized lawlessness of early Russian society, in *Russia under the Old Regime* (1974; Penguin, 1984), pp. 45–49.

6. The Komsomol organization was usually added as a "collective" sponsor of the young would-be Party member. I owe much of this account of the customs of organized crime societies to Gen. Gurov.

7. Taken from an MVD videocassette screened by the author, March 16, 1993, at the Russian Organized Crime Unit in Moscow. The videocassette was picked up in a raid on one of Jam's headquarters at least six months earlier.

8. Chalidze, op. cit., p. 47.

9. Szamuely, op. cit., p. 342.

10. See Alan Bullock, *Hitler and Stalin: Parallel Lives* (New York: Knopf, 1992), p. 35. Several of Stalin's more conscientious colleagues demanded his expulsion from the Party because of his criminal connections. Later, Stalin himself tried to bury some of his more questionable connections. One of his closest associates in the Caucasian criminal underworld was an Armenian gangster named Semyon Ter-Petrosyan, believed to be a relative of the present Armenian president. Ter-Petrosyan, a convert to the Bolshevik cause who carried the nom de plume Kamo, put his singular talents to the services of Stalin with such success that he was later called the "presiding genius" of expropriations. Comrade Kamo, however, was killed—with suspicious timing, just as he was preparing to write his memoirs, in 1922. See Chalidze, op. cit., p. 22.

11. One well-known criminal and convicted murder who came to work for the KGB, named F. M. Kozyrev, was sentenced to be shot by the new regime for embezzlement. Felix Dzerzhinsky, founder of the Cheka, forerunner of the KGB, was a character witness at his trial. Leggett, op. cit., p. 142.

12. "Green" bands of brigands and army deserters, so called because they hid out in the forests, claimed thousands of members in Russia and Ukraine in the early 1920s. Although the Greens linked many of their activities to political opposition to the new regime, they bore a striking similarity to the Cossack raiders of the sixteenth century. Leggett, ibid., p. 245. After 1917, criminal groups adjusted quickly to the opportunities provided by revolution and disorder. Chalidze (op. cit., p. 76) reports that a "Central Committee of Vagabonds" flourished in northeastern Siberia and a "Hooligans' League" operated near Chita.

13. Yuri Nikishin, interview with author, September 22, 1992.

14. Seran Akopyan, interview with author. June 29, 1992.

15. Funeral of *Malina* reported in *Sovetskaya Rossiya,* September 5, 1992.

16. There are many sources for the Scabs War, both verbal and written. Both Gurov and Col. Zhoglo discussed it with me extensively. Several mafiya members relayed to me stories of the event handed down to them by their predecessors and confirmed its importance in Russian mafiya history. Chalidze also discusses it, op. cit., pp. 48–51.

17. For two accounts of Kvantrishvili's life and funeral, see Marcus Warren, "Moscow Mafia Takes Tip from Bureaucrats," *The Sunday Telegraph* (London), April 24, 1994; and Steven Erlanger, "A Slaying Puts Russian Underworld on Parade," *The New York Times,* April 14, 1994.

Chapter Three: Mozhaisky Embankment

1. Vitali Vitaliev, *Special Correspondent: Investigating in the Soviet Union* (London: Hutchinson, 1990), p. 107.

2. Some of Gurov's former colleagues have insisted to me that he was only relieved because of his lack of administrative abilities, but it was clear from the cool treatment he received from the senior Kremlin bureaucracy—and experienced as well by his boss, Vadim Bakatin—that he was still ahead of his time. Gurov's research paper is unavailable, but he elaborated on his ideas in a 1992 pamphlet, "Organizovannaya prestupnost—ne mif, a realnost" (Organized crime: Not myth, but reality), published by the Faculty of Law of the People's University (Moscow: Znanie, 1992). Gurov told me that the pamphlet contains the essentials of his early research as well as his newer ideas, and I have borrowed liberally from them in this chapter.

3. Colonel General N. V. Kallin, commander of the Moscow Military District, was appointed commandant of the city of Moscow on August 19, 1991, by Acting President Gennady Yanayev. His order no. 2, scheduled to be published August 22, would have divided Moscow into thirty-three separate police districts. Staff of the *Red Star* military newspaper provided the originals to *Kommersant,* which finally published them, on August 26, 1991, in a round-up of "what might have been" if the coup succeeded.

4. Car hijack figures from *Nezavisimaya Gazeta,* July 1, 1992.

5. Aleksandr Gurov, interview with author, July 13, 1992. Gurov was transferred in 1993 to become director of the Russian Institute of Security Problems in Moscow, but he is even further separated from his former crime-fighting role.

6. The saga of the star-crossed St. Petersburg mobster was covered at length by

Literaturnaya Gazeta, July 1, 1992, in an article entitled, "The Temptor of St. Petersburg." The author, Tatyana Putrenko, was one of many who enjoyed Vladimirov's generosity. "I was with actors and writers at the banquet in honor of the Petersburg festival," she wrote sheepishly. "We all drank and ate on his money."

Chapter Four: Comrade Criminal

1. In the first half of 1992, Moscow and St. Petersburg sold nearly half their shops to the "private sector." The privatization program was the biggest in Russian history to that point. But domestic trade was not fully liberalized. Shops were limited to markups of 25 percent. *Economist,* December 5, 1992.

2. Lev Timofeyev, *Russia's Secret Rulers,* trans. Catherine A. Fitzpatrick (New York: Knopf, 1992), pp. 98–99.

3. The connections between the black market and the rise of organized crime have been excellently traced in the work of Prof. Maria Los. See in particular "Internal Norms of the Second Economy," in Bruno Dallago, Gianmaria Ajani, and Bruno Grancelli, eds., *Privatization and Entrepreneurship in Post-Socialist Countries* (New York: St. Martin's, 1992), pp. 111–24.

4. For a detailed examination of the prevalence of bribery and corruption among the Soviet elite, see Maria Los, *Communist Ideology, Law and Crime: A Comparative View of the USSR and Poland* (London: Macmillan, 1988), pp. 155–61.

5. See Vaksberg, op. cit., for a fuller discussion of the fish mafiya, the cotton kings, and the trade mafiya. The story of Sokolov is on pp. 213–15.

6. Quoted in Timofeyev, op.cit., pp. 42–43. Shevardnadze recalled that he once summoned to his office about 150 senior officials, men who had "embezzled millions," and told them to stop. He warned that the authorities would catch them eventually, and that their children and families—and the Motherland—would suffer. He told them, "That's enough now. You've been accumulating all these years. Stop it!" As Shevardnadze put it, "They understood that there was a kind of humanism in this approach, and they did leave—they resigned and left their fields, so to say." One wonders whether he is telling the entire story.

7. Gorbachev speech to Communist Party plenum, June 15, 1987, author's notes. Unofficial estimates of the so-called unregulated consumer market ranged from five billion rubles to more than seventeen billion rubles. See Anders Aslund, *Gorbachev's Struggle for Economic Reform: The Soviet Reform Process, 1985–88* (Ithaca, N.Y.: Cornell University Press, 1989), pp. 150–51, for statistics of the black market in 1985.

8. Yeltsin discusses his battle against the Moscow trade mafiya in his autobiography, *Against the Grain,* trans. Michael Glenny (London: Jonathan Cape, 1990), pp. 88–107. The threats on his life were also reported by Itar-Tass, February 12, 1992. He has been quoted as saying that his biggest mistake as Moscow Party boss was to directly attack the "organized mafiya" (Vladimir Brovkin, "First Party Secretaries: An Endangered Soviet Species," *Problems of Communism,* vol. 39, January-February 1990, pp. 15–27).

9. Gregory Grossman, "The Second Economy of the USSR," *Problems of Communism,* vol. 26, September-October 1977, p. 40.

10. See Timofeyev, op. cit., p. 99. Timofeyev suggests that it might have saved the country a great deal of trouble later on, if the law had allowed this black-market wealth to expand production lines, build a factory, or increase labor productivity.

11. Gurov, interview with author, op. cit.

12. Vadim Bakatin, interview with author, March 31, 1993.

13. Colonel Zhoglo gave me the name of the man, but since there is no independent proof of his assertion, I have not identified him.

14. Quoted by Vice-President Aleksandr Rutskoi from White Paper and reported in *Nezavisimaya Gazeta,* February 12, 1993, among others. Similarly high percentages were given for other former Soviet republics: 3–5 percent in the Baltic republics, 10 percent in Belarus, 20 percent in Ukraine, 25 percent in Central Asia and Kazakhstan, and 40 percent in Transcaucasia.

Chapter Five: Life and Death on the Russian Frontier

1. Material on the Ternyak killing and Ternyak's background provided by Maj. Vladimir Koltsov, of the Criminal Investigations Department of the Ministry of Internal Affairs in Yekaterinburg, in a conversation with the author, September 30, 1992. Additional material from other private sources.

2. Uralmash has since been partially privatized, but in May, 1994, directors closed the factory "temporarily" for six months because of falling earnings. Workers feared that it would be permanent.

3. Chalidze, op. cit,. p. 17, introduces this interesting analogy between the quarreling boyars and the crime chieftains in connection with the early gang wars of the 1970s. I have extended it to what I think is the more appropriate period in light of the events of the post-Soviet era.

4. The story of Sochi's gang war is reported in *Literaturnaya Gazeta,* July 15, 1992.

5. Yeltsin was Communist Party leader of Yekaterinburg from 1976 to 1986, when he departed for Moscow to take a seat as candidate member of the Politburo and to become the capital's Party boss.

6. There has been much controversy over who gave the order for the czar's assassination, particularly over whether the local Yekaterinburg commissars acted on their own or under instructions from Moscow. The weight of evidence suggests that the order was approved by Lenin himself. The historian Eduard Radzinsky, quoted in a Reuters dispatch from Moscow, November 20, 1990, blames Lenin specifically. In 1935, Lev Trotsky recalled a conversation with Yakov Sverdlov, who said flatly, "We took the decision here [in Moscow]." See Marc Ferro, *Nicholas II: The Last of the Tsars,* trans. Brian Pearce (London: Viking, 1990), p. 255.

7. Leonid Zonov and Vladimir Koltsov were interviewed together by the author on September 27, 1992, and separately at various times between September 27 and 30, 1992.

8. Sergei Molodtsov, interview with author, Moscow, June 10, 1992.

9. Tamara Lomakina, interview with author, Yekaterinburg, September 25, 1992.

10. The quarrel between blues and whites is described by several sources, most authoritatively in *Trud,* July 28, 1992. Sergei Plotnikov, a local journalist and an expert in the city's mafiya history, expanded on the struggle in an interview with the author, September 27, 1992.

11. Details of Tsyganov's arrest reported in *Kommersant "B,"* May 5 and 12, 1993. Pampurin's press conference reported in *Kommersant "B,"* May 27, 1993.

Chapter Six: The Criminal State

1. This note was found by Sergei Aristov and the Russian team investigating the papers of the Central Committee in the fall of 1991. The story was reported in *Komsomolskaya Pravda,* December 7, 1991, and quoted in part in Timofeyev, op. cit., p. 119.

2. Evidence for the secret Party financing of post-Communist opposition newspapers has been widely published in Moscow, and I have also heard corroborative evidence from investigators. Party money, for instance, has been used to fund a strange assortment of anti-government newspapers, ranging from *Pravda* (on the left) to *Den* and *Sovetskaya Rossiya* on the right. In addition, the monies have gone to finance certain opposition groups. For more, see chapter 18.

3. Arkady Vaksberg provides a colorful account of the Sochi scandal in his book *The Soviet Mafiya,* p. 30. As a coda to the Sochi affair, all of the participants were reported to be living very comfortably and at liberty in the early 1990s (p. 72). For the Gelendzhik episode, see pp. 53–57. For the use of Party homes as brothels and narcotics trafficking centers, see pp. 158–61. For the story of the cotton affair, see pp. 111–23.

4. Yevgeny Myslovsky, interview with author, March 24, 1993.

5. Aslambek Aslakhanov, interview with author, July 10, 1992.

6. For an classic discussion of the nomenklatura, see Michael Voslensky, *Nomenklatura: Anatomy of the Soviet Ruling Class,* trans. Eric Mosbacher (London: Bodley Head, 1984).

7. See Timofeyev, op. cit., p. 8, for exchanges of "gifts." See Vaksberg, op. cit., pp 26–29, for discussion of Party mafiya wealth and costs of membership.

8. See Georgi Arbatov, *The System: An Insider's Life in Soviet Politics* (New York: Random House, 1992). The story of his mother's food shock is on p. 84. Arbatov estimated that bureaucrats spent less than 10 percent of their income on food, compared to 60–70 percent for normal families. It should be noted that Arbatov claims that he was often bitterly attacked by Party conservatives for the liberal views he espoused in private, and he defended his decision never to challenge the system publicly on the grounds that he felt his role was to work for reform inside it. "I do not think it is right to condemn everyone who did not follow the path of Sakharov . . . and other famous dissidents," he writes on pp. 242–43. "Had it not been for the many hundreds and thousands who worked inside the system, fought routine skirmishes, tried to stop the pressure of Stalinist conservativism . . . the process of revitalization would not have been possible at all."

9. Memo on Comrade Kulakov quoted by Aleksandr Kotenkov, at Moscow press conference, May 25, 1992.

10. See Vitaliev, op. cit., p. 130.

11. Arbatov, op. cit., p. 250.

12. Kotenkov press conference, op. cit. See also Introduction, n. 3, for cash supplied to foreign Communist parties.

13. Vaksberg, op. cit., p. 200.

14. Contemporary Russian analysts suggest that Andropov was less interested in righting injustices than in eliminating vulnerable opponents in his own drive to the top—acting much like a competitive mafiya lord.

15. Details of Shcholokov's suicide were provided to me by several Russian sources and published in many accounts.

16. Reported in *Rossiiskaya Gazeta*, August 8, 1992. V. Fetkulin, in charge of the Russian Criminal Investigation Department of the Russian Prosecutor's Office, told the same newspaper that a "significant number of top Russian Federation leaders and prominent political figures had been under constant KGB surveillance, and their phones were tapped." Material released from the archives after the coup show both Gorbachev and Yeltsin on the wiretap list.

17. Timofeyev, op. cit., pp. 15–16.

18. To say that the majority of Central Committee members at the February, 1990, plenum were reluctant to revoke Article Six is probably an understatement. A delegate named Mesyats, from Moscow, called the idea of relaxing the Party's grip on power an "unprecedented orgy." "This is not *glasnost* of 1985," he fumed. "Things have gone too far" (from author's notes).

19. Vadim Bakatin, interview with author, March 31, 1993. Party membership figures reported in *What The Papers Say* (Moscow), April 15, 1991. Membership dropped 14 percent in 1990, to 16.5 million. This was not calamitous for a party of eighteen million members, but it showed the start of a trend. Many others merely stopped paying their dues while keeping their Party membership cards. Despite their private anxieties, officials kept up a brave front. "The figures are not large enough to speak about a catastrophe or even an extraordinary situation," insisted Boris Pugo, then chairman of the Party's Central Control Committee. See also A. Craig Copetas, *Bear Hunting with the Politburo* (New York: Simon and Schuster, 1991), p. 20.

20. The information about the June, 1990, investment was contained in a September 27, 1990, letter from Boris Gidaspov, chief of the Leningrad Party committee and a prominent "conservative" before moving to Moscow, to Party Treasurer Nikolai Kruchina. Gidaspov's letter and the response from Kruchina were found in the Central Archives of the Communist Party in Moscow and published in the magazine *Ogonyok*, November 12, 1991.

21. Politburo memo reported in *Komsomolskaya Pravda*, December 7, 1991, and cited in Timofeyev, op. cit., pp. 119–21.

22. *Kriminalnaya Khronika*, no. 10, November 6, 1992. The paper also claims that Artyom Tarasov, a prominent member of the early cooperative movement, who fled to Europe, and the former Russian vice-premier Gennady Filshin were involved in the illicit exchanges.

23. Politburo resolution of June 11, 1991, *Ogonyok*, op. cit.

24. Reported in *What the Papers Say*, July 7, 1992.

25. From *Komsomolskaya Pravda*, July 5, 1991, cited in Timofeyev, op. cit., p. 114.

26. The Bashkiria bank affair was uncovered by the *Leninets* youth newspaper of Ufa and reported by Itar-TASS, September 18, 1992.

27. Timofeyev, op. cit., pp. 114–15.

28. Quoted by Timofeyev, ibid., p. 107.

29. See Yevgeniya Albats, *Mina zamedlennogo deistviya: Politichesky portret KGB* (Delayed-action mine: Political portrait of the KGB) (Moscow: Russlit, 1992).

30. Material relevant to the Santa operation was reported by Mark Deich in *Literaturnaya Gazeta*, June 25, 1992. Deich said that the papers were provided to him by officials of the Ministry of Defense.

31. *Literaturnaya Gazeta*, op. cit.

32. The situation along "East German lines" was a reference to the overthrow of Communist Party control in East Germany in 1989–90.

33. Shevardnadze said, among other things, "A dictatorship is advancing. No one knows what kind of dictatorship it will be."

34. The other candidates in the race, aside from Yeltsin, were Prime Minister Nikolai Ryzhkov, Aman Tuleyev, a union leader from Bakatin's home region of Kemerovo, and right-wingers Vladimir Zhirinovsky and Gen. Albert Makashov. Bakatin came in last behind Makashov, with 3.4 percent of the vote.

35. Pavel Voshchanov, "Who Will Live Well in a Banana Russia?" *Komsomolskaya Pravda,* June 12, 1992. Voshchanov names a number of former Party and KGB officials, whom he says were responsible for secreting funds abroad and who are now prominent members of the post-Soviet power structure. "The corrupt nomenklatura clan," he wrote, "is already rearing a new political elite."

36. Aleksandr Muzikantsky, press conference, Moscow, August 30, 1991.

37. *The Independent on Sunday Magazine* (London), March 7, 1993.

38. See *Moskovskie Novosti,* March 26, 1993.

39. Mikhail Gurtovoi, head of the short-lived Russian Anti-Corruption Commission, told me in March, 1993, that his group had recovered 1.5 billion rubles from banks and businesses set up by the Central Committee. Andrei Makarov, one of the lawyers prosecuting the case against the Communist Party, told *Vechernyaya Moskva* on March 24, 1993, that he believed the missing funds inside the country came to twelve billion. Aleksandr Smolensky, the well-connected chairman of the Stolichny Bank, one of Russia's richest private banks, gave me the estimate of fifty billion rubles during an interview in July, 1992. I am inclined to believe that Smolensky is correct. The government estimate of Party wealth was quoted by Interfax, July 3, 1992. As an example of how the Party tried to hide its fortune, in 1990 it officially reported that the total value of its buildings, printing presses, summer camps for workers, and other assets was 4.9 billion rubles, of which 2.3 billion belonged to local Party organizations.

40. Kalinichenko and Nikolai Emelyanov, conversation with author, July 20, 1992.

41. Timofeyev, op. cit., p. 74.

42. Yeltsin on bribery quoted in the Moscow magazine *Delovye Lyudi* (Business People), December 1992. Warning of the bureaucracy's political ambitions is from Yeltsin's television address to the Russian people, reported by Reuters, March 22, 1993.

43. Poltaranin quoted in *Rossiya,* no. 43, 1992.

44. Number of regional violations cited by Peter Reddaway, in *The New York Review of Books,* January 28, 1993. Regional bureaucrats want the "privatization process to be as uncompetitive for themselves as possible," noted Philip Hanson, a student of post-Soviet affairs. "The danger is of 78 Albanias." See Philip Hanson, "Russia: Economic Reform and Local Politics" *The World Today* (Journal of the Royal Institute of International Affairs, London), vol. 49, no. 4, April 1993. His prediction was borne out several months later. In July, 1993, after the debate on a new Russian constitution, the Yekaterinburg region declared itself the new "Republic of the Urals." Several other regions followed similar paths.

45. The drive of local nomenklatura to take control began at the republican level when the Soviet Union still existed. Zhores Medvedev, a well-known analyst of Soviet and Russian affairs, has written that the "declarations of sovereignty" by republics in 1990 and 1991 were a reaction to the central government's plan to distribute shares in central industries according to the size of each republic. Russia, the biggest republic,

naturally supported the plan, but Ukraine, the Baltic republics, and the Transcaucasian republics wanted full control over state enterprises on their territories. After the coup, all fifteen republics immediately passed laws granting themselves full ownership of Union property within their borders, depriving the central government of the means to administer the Soviet economy. This nomenklatura-sponsored act, more than anything else, may have led to the final breakup, according to Medvedev. See "Who Will Own Russia?" *Moscow Times*, March 25, 1993.

46. The Melnik case reported in *Moskovskiye Novosti*, February 18, 1993. Bakatin was not implicated in any way.

47. Timofeyev, op. cit., p. 143.

Chapter Seven: Post-Soviet Man

1. Mark Rudinshtein, interview with author, Moscow, July 7, 1992.

2. An August, 1994, survey published by *Argumenty i Fakty* suggested that about fifty million people—between 25 and 30 percent of Russia's population—could be defined as middle class. They earned up to 500,000 rubles (about 250 dollars) a month. Another 5 percent, or nine million citizens, were classified as upper middle class, and some 3.5 percent (or 2.5 million people) were ruble millionaires. Reported in "Radio Advertisers Tune In to Russia's Evolving Middle Class," *The New York Times*, August 15, 1994. Moscow financier Konstantin Borovoi estimated that forty million people were involved in the non-state economy, in an interview with *Nezavisimaya Gazeta*, May 15, 1992. These do not seem unrealistic figures. By midsummer of 1993, according to Richard Layard, a professor at the London School of Economics and an adviser to Yeltsin, an estimated 20 percent of all Russian industrial workers were employed in private industries. Cited in "Russia Opens Up Market But Few Have Money, *The New York Times*, November 18, 1993.

3. For an upbeat view of the Russian economy in 1994, see Steven Erlanger, "End of Russia's Economic Slide Brings Eerie Calm," *The New York Times*, August 22, 1994.

4. "IMF Approves Loan for Russia with Conditions," *The New York Times*, March 23, 1994.

5. See "St. Petersburg's Sour Taste of Capitalism," *Moscow Times*, March 10, 1993. *Izvestiya* quote from Celestine Bohlen, "A New Russia: Now Thrive the Swindlers," *The New York Times*, March 17, 1994. The MMM scandal was reported by several news outlets, including Reuters, July 28, 1994.

6. Vladimir Kalinichenko, interview with author, op. cit., July 20, 1992. For a wider discussion of the Zapalsky case, see the interview with Mikhail Gurtovoi, Kalinichenko's boss and head of the anti-corruption commission, in *Megapolis Express*, August 26, 1992.

7. Quoted in "Russia, Wolf at the Door," *Barron's*, October 19, 1992.

8. The facts about Russian government officials' connections with business were widely reported in many Moscow newspapers. The Belarussian case was reported in *Rossiiskaya Gazeta*, January 10, 1992.

9. Sergei Skorokhodov, "Deputy vs. Looter," *Rossiiskaya Gazeta*, December 26, 1992, p. 7.

10. The Kishinev investigation was reported in *Izvestiya*, September 16, 1992. The Armenian corruption was reported by Interfax, September 8, 1992, and by Itar-Tass, September 13, 1992.

11. The unveiling of the Azerbaijan crime syndicate was reported by *Nezavisimaya Gazeta*, September 16, 1992.

12. For details of the Kyrgyztan case, see *Izvestiya*, March 12, 1993.

13. For the Ukraine oil swindle, see *Izvestiya*, October 28, 1992.

14. For the report of oil selling at below-market prices, see *Ekonomika i Zhizn*, no. 38, 1993. For Cobalt smuggling, see *Den*, no. 6, 1993. Bunich quoted in *Business World Weekly* (Moscow), March 26, 1993.

15. Tyumen oil scam reported in *Moscow Times*, December 22, 1992.

16. Gurtovoi quoted in *Trud*, October 3, 1992.

17. Russian oil turning up in Hungary reported by *Rossiiskaya Gazeta*, March 12, 1993.

18. M. Sarafanov and N. Lirov, "Flight of Capital from Russia," *Ekonomika i Zhizn*, no. 38, 1993. The authors list a number of ingenious techniques used by Russians to smuggle capital abroad. Most involve collusion with foreign partners. They include understating final contract prices on export deals, so that the difference paid by foreign buyers is deposited in foreign banks; arranging for payments of bogus shipments of goods; and providing revocable "letters of collection," in which an exporter agrees to deliver goods if a foreign partner will certify that the goods never arrived and pay the difference into his foreign bank account. In 1993, the official MVD estimate for capital sent abroad rose to 25 billion dollars. See chapter 16, n. 31.

19. Aslambek Aslakhanov, interview with author, March 25, 1993.

20. Yuri Lebedev, interview with author, July 8, 1992.

21. For a sarcastic treatment of Soviet Man, see Aleksandr Zinoviev, *Homo Sovieticus* (London: Victor Gollancz, 1985).

22. Figure reported in *Rossiiskaya Gazeta*, March 5, 1993.

23. Aslakhanov quoted by Itar-Tass, February 12, 1993.

Chapter Eight: How to Steal a Billion Rubles

1. This incident and its consequences were reported in *Trud*, July 14, 1992; *Rabochaya Tribuna*, June 12, 1992; and *Vek*, September 4, 1992.

2. The promissory note was a standard feature of banking during the Soviet era. Under the old system, banks compensated for the long delays in transferring money by writing credit vouchers for their clients, which could be used in place of cash. Since they did not have to settle their accounts until the end of the year, no one worried about the occasional shortfall in funds.

3. The sources for this story come from the criminal underworld and police, and were confirmed to the author by an acquaintance of the late banker Petrov.

4. Report of arrests of Central Bank officials by Interfax, June 19, 1993.

5. See "One Billion Rubles Lost in Scam," *Moscow Times*, January 28, 1993. The three-hundred-billion-ruble fraud was reported by Itar-Tass, July 9, 1993.

6. Sergei Yegorov, interview with author, July 3, 1992. Aslambek Aslakhanov also maintained that the Chechen affair was a "criminal conspiracy of banking structures." In an interview with *Nezavisimaya Gazeta*, published August 8, 1992, he said that the Central Bankers were behind the promissory notes. "There are very good camouflage experts among financiers of the top echelon," he said.

7. See "A Fig in a Safe," *Kuranty*, October 6, 1992.

8. Konstantin Borovoi, interview with author, July 9, 1992.

9. Garegin Tosunyan, interview with author, April 8, 1992.

10. See *Komsomolskaya Pravda,* September 26, 1992.

11. Aleksandr Smolensky, interview with author, July 8, 1992.

12. The banker had provoked questions about his unusual operating methods before. In 1989, Smolensky was interviewed by the American journalist Hedrick Smith for his book *The New Russians.* The young, leather-jacketed entrepreneur had just opened his first bank with the profits of his successful cooperative. In the two years since he had left his job in the state construction industry, Smolensky proved so skillful at exploiting the slender opportunities of perestroika that, as he boasted to Smith, he already earned twice as much as Gorbachev. His new bank specialized in short-term loans, for six months or less, at interest that, according to Smith, worked out to an annual rate of 130 percent. To the fascinated Smith, Smolensky sooner resembled a loan shark than a banker. See Hedrick Smith, *The New Russians* (London, Hutchinson, 1990), pp. 272–76.

13. Yegorov's open letter reported by Reuters, Moscow, July 16, 1993. The killings continued, and private bankers finally went to the extreme of declaring a one-day strike in late 1993.

14. See *Komsomolskaya Pravda,* July 4, 1992.

15. Savings banks, or *sberegatelnye banky,* popularly called *sberbanky,* still existed in 1994. In Soviet times, interest on private accounts varied from 2 to 5 percent, depending on how long an account was left untouched. Interest rates were raised on September 20, 1993, to correct for inflation. Foreign residents were obliged by law to deposit their hard currency in the official Foreign Trade Bank; but once deposited, their money seemed to sink out of sight. A simple withdrawal of funds required complicated paperwork and hours of standing in line. High commissions were charged for every transaction. Statements of account were often undecipherable, and bank clerks rarely bothered to answer their phones. Sometimes, a hapless teller would have to ask a customer to return the next day, because of the lack of foreign currency. When the economic situation worsened during the final years of the regime, foreigners lost access to their accounts for months at a time.

16. Agapov interview reported in *Stolitsa,* no. 38, 1992.

Chapter Nine: Masters of Moscow

1. Figures on privatized apartments come from the *Moscow Tribune,* March 12, 1993.

2. Moscow residents have told me that a two-room apartment in the central districts of the capital sold for between $55,000 and $120,000 in 1993. Flats in suburbs went for a quarter or half that, depending upon how far they were from the center of the city.

3. See "Old Ladies Are Casualties of Housing Shortage," *Moscow Tribune,* March 12, 1993. According to a report from Moscow broadcast by National Public Radio on March 30, 1994, Moscow police identified at least fourteen people murdered for their apartments. Many of the one thousand unidentified corpses in the city morgue were suspected to have been victims of apartment privatization schemes.

4. See *Literaturnaya Gazeta,* June 10, 1992.

5. Yuri Shchekochikhin, interview with author, July 2, 1992.

6. Aleksandr Tsopov, interview with author, March 24, 1993. The Moscow city documents referring to real estate deals mentioned in this chapter are in my possession.

7. See *The Wall Street Journal*, January 24, 1992; *Kommersant*, June 2, 1992.

8. Andrei Stroyev, interview with author, July 6, 1992.

9. *Kommersant*, May 19, 1993; more material on Stroyev's activities was published in a *Literaturnaya Gazeta* report of May 5, 1993. There were reasons even then to doubt Stroyev's insistence that his bureaucratic past had nothing to do with his business success. A former American employee of Perestroika told me, on condition of anonymity, that nearly all the American "advisers" had quit because of their suspicions about the relationship between senior government officials and the firm. The employee, in fact, passed on to me rumors of threats made to at least one American who raised questions. Interview with author, July 6, 1992.

10. Documents from party archives reproduced in *Ogonyok*, November 12, 1991.

11. Russian reporters who tried to contact Stroyev in 1993 were told that he was "ill" in America and unable to return. I also tried, unsuccessfully, to contact him in 1994.

12. My first interview with Viktor Kalinin took place on March 14, 1993. A second interview, to expand on some of the earlier points, was conducted on March 26, 1993.

13. The report of the Analytical Center for Social and Economic Policies, prepared by chairman Pyotr Filipov, was presented to the government on January 17, 1994. See "Graft and Gangsterism in Russia Blight the Entrepreneurial Spirit," *The New York Times*, January 30, 1994.

Chapter Ten: "They Can Shoot, They Can Kill"

1. An article on Volodya Mironov appeared in *Kommersant*, September 8, 1992.

2. Report by the Analytical Center for Social and Economic Policies, op. cit.

3. The story of Ted Kasyanov emerged in a series of interviews with the author. The first occurred on June 12, 1992, at his karate school. I next met him at his home, on June 30, 1992. After his arrests, Elena discussed some aspects of his case with my researcher, Toby Latta, on September 12, 1992, and I returned to his apartment for interviews with Elena and the family lawyer, Nina Sukhova, on September 30, 1992.

4. See *Sobesednik*, no. 35, 1992.

Chapter Eleven: The Smugglers

1. Even Sheremetievo employees joined the game of miracle-making. Thefts of freight, luggage, and mail at the airport increased by more than 200 percent between 1991 and 1992. One noteworthy day, a million dollars' worth of diamonds and seven hundred thousand dollars in platinum ingots went missing from the cargo bays of two Aeroflot planes. The suspected culprits were security guards. A few conscientious airport workers actually quit to protest rising crime. *Izvestiya*, however, took a more sarcastic view of their decision. "They realized how easy it was to become stained in this 'field of wonders,' " commented the newspaper. See *Izvestiya*, December 30, 1992.

2. For more specific examples of how the Baltic states in particular benefited from the contraband trade, see chapter 15.

3. These were some of the practices widely reported in Russian newspapers throughout 1992 and 1993. They led to increased restrictions on the borders marking the new Commonwealth of Independent States. The CIS was created in December, 1991, by Russia, Ukraine, and Belarus. Seven other former Soviet republics joined soon

afterward: Moldova, Kazakhstan, Armenia, Uzbekistan, Turkmenistan, Tajikistan, and Kyrgyztan. Georgia agreed to apply in 1994.

4. Edgar Aaro, interview with author, Tallinn, March 22, 1993.

5. During the 1980s, 50 percent of shoe repairs and 40 percent of car repairs were obtained from illicit private businesses, which were often workers operating secretly in their own factory or enterprise. For other statistics of the black market in 1985, see Aslund, op. cit., pp. 150–51. Some estimates of the extent of the black economy ran as high as 83 percent of the Soviet population. See William A. Clark, *Crime and Punishment in Soviet Officialdom: Combatting Corruption in the Political Elite, 1965–1990* (Armonk, N.Y.: M. E. Sharpe, 1993), p. 73.

6. See Gregory Grossman, *Second Economy: Boon or Bane?* Berkeley-Duke Occasional Papers on the Second Economy of the USSR, vol. 11, no 2. (Berkeley and Los Angeles: University of California Press, December, 1987). Grossman, a professor of economics at the University of California, Berkeley, has contributed many pioneering studies of the black market and its negative impact on Soviet society. In his article in *Problems of Communism,* op. cit., he observed, "The [Soviet] public seems to accept petty illegalities as a normal and even inevitable part of making one's way in a refractory and shortage-ridden environment."

7. Chalidze, op. cit., p. 168.

8. Details of the "average smuggler" profiled by Itar-Tass, October 15, 1992.

9. "Mikhail," interview with author, March 10, 1993, Moscow.

10. *Kommersant,* August 17, 1992.

11. Vaksberg, op. cit, pp. 245–46.

12. Fr. Mikhail Ardov, interview with author, March 15, 1993.

13. They also found ten aircraft, an MI-8 helicopter, dozens of military armored vehicles and tractors, eighty tons of gunpowder, one hundred thousand ammunition cartridges, and a "significant" amount of foodstuffs, medicine, and consumer goods. The total value of the items confiscated in the operation, called "Trawl," was estimated at thirty-seven billion rubles. The figures were reported by Interfax, February 3, 1993.

14. Sergei Selyutin, "Landslide Theft of Antiques," *Megapolis Express,* April 26, 1993. In 1992, the Russian Ministry of Culture and Tourism drafted regulations for a new federal customs agency to combat the smuggling of objets d'art. According to most reports, it was a dismal failure. See *Kommersant,* August 17, 1992.

15. I am indebted to Igor Baranovsky, of *Moscow News,* for information about the international art-smuggling network.

16. "Borisovich," interview with author, March 12, 1993, Moscow.

17. The curious non-response of Russian youth—with some notable exceptions—to perestroika would repay further study. One revealing "youth movement" of the time was called "Black Rose." Its adherents were people in their teens and twenties, all heavy-metal fans who dressed in black and espoused with deadpan irony the virtues of Stalinism and Communism.

18. Belarus security chief Eduard Shirovsky reported in 1993 that thirteen-year-old boys and girls in the city of Svetlogorsk were drug addicts. See *Rossiiskaya Gazeta,* January 10, 1993.

19. Figures on drug crime were provided by the drug squad of the Moscow Police. Additional statistics come from Itar-Tass, dispatches of January 16, 1993, and October 27, 1992.

Chapter Twelve: *Narco-Bizness*

1. The Vyborg bust was reported in *Izvestiya*, February 26, 1993, and by Interfax, February 24, 1993. There have been some larger hauls of cocaine reported elsewhere in the world. Five tons were picked up in Turin in 1992; and what remains so far the world's largest haul, police intercepted twenty-one tons in Los Angeles in 1989. For this information, I am thankful to Juan Gonzalez, a columnist for *The New York Daily News*, who has reported on the activities of Colombian drug cartels in the United States.

2. Itar-Tass, February 15, 1993, provided the figures about narcotics passing through Central Asia and Russia. A report on the Czech operation, "Operation Green Ice," was published in *The Toronto Star*, January 10, 1993. For the views of academics and foreign police on Russia's narcotics trade, see, among others, Rensselaer W. Lee III and Scott MacDonald, "Drugs in the East," *Foreign Policy*, no. 90, Spring 1993, and Nancy Rubin, of the International Peace and Security Program at Carnegie-Mellon University, "Central Asia's Drug Bazaar," *The New York Times*, op-ed page, November 16, 1992.

3. Valentin Roshchin, interview with author, March 10, 1993.

4. Vladimir Kalinichenko, interview with author, July 20, 1992.

5. The ideal money-laundering conditions included the lack of monitoring of currency movements inside and outside the country; easy evasion of exchange controls; weak banking regulations; no requirement for reporting suspicious transactions; and a significant trade in gems (which offered an easy way to invest hard cash). For other conditions that Russia fit, see the complete list in *International Narcotics Control Strategy Report*, April 1994, published by the U.S. Department of State, Bureau of International Narcotics Matters, p. 477.

6. The figure of 1.5 million drug users was announced at a Russian Ministry of Internal Affairs press conference in Moscow, October 1, 1992. Soviet statistics appeared in a Tass dispatch of June 21, 1990. The figure of 7.5 million was provided by Dr. Natalia Shubanova at Moscow's Addiction Clinic No. 17. See n. 7.

7. Dr. Igor Chenikh and Dr. Natalia Shubanova, interview with author, March 12, 1993. Shubanova said that her information showed that more than 11 percent of the nation's addicts were children aged ten to twelve years in 1992.

8. From the transcript of a press conference delivered by Gen. Aleksandr Sergeyev, Moscow, May 11, 1993, in author's possession.

9. In April, 1993, a draft law was prepared that would have restricted the legal protection for drug use to medical purposes, but it was lost in the rubble of the Russian parliament building, which collapsed in October, 1993.

10. Narcotics profit figures were reported in *Moscow News*, November 11, 1992, and at the MVD press conference of May 11, 1993.

11. See Itar-Tass, February 9, 1993. For an interesting report on the "new" Far East drug industry, see *Moscow News*, June 25, 1993.

12. The story of the Uzbek farmers was recounted by Jordi Bordas, Eduardo Martin de Pozuelo, and Santiago Tarin, "El narcotráfico que nace del caos" (Narcotics traffic born of chaos), *La Vanguardia/Revista*, February 5, 1993.

13. Col. Vladimir Khairedinov, interview with author, March 17, 1993. The information on the Globus letter and the struggle inside the Russian underworld came from police and gangworld sources.

14. Lynnley Browning, in a dispatch by Reuters, St. Petersburg, July 12, 1993.

15. I owe the story of the Kazan chemistry students, and the subsequent anecdote

about the gangland wake, to Olivia Ward and Toby Latta, of *The Toronto Star*'s Moscow bureau, who heard it, in turn, from Col. Arkadi Kuznetsov in 1993.

16. Author's interview with Armenian ganglord, March 31, 1993.

17. Russian police were the main sources of information about the activities of foreign drug businessmen in Russia, but some information has appeared in Russian publications. Itar-Tass reported, on March 4, 1993, an MVD statement that thirty separate international drug-smuggling groups had been identified in Russia.

18. Vladimir Kalinichenko, interview with author, September 25, 1992. Casein is separated from the whey proteins of milk by a high-speed centrifuge. The process was used in the making of paper, glue, paint, and plastics but has since been supplanted by petroleum products. I am indebted to Jack Simpson, of Burlington, Ontario, for information on the process.

19. See *Rossiiskaya Gazeta,* January 21, 1993. This has often been advanced as one of the factors behind the Armenian-Azeri dispute over Karabakh. *Moskovskaya Pravda,* October 28, 1992, reported that drug revenues were used to purchase weapons for the Armenian paramilitary force fighting in Karabakh.

Chapter Thirteen: The Guns of Grozny

1. See "Professional Killers," *Moscow News,* December 31, 1993.

2. Summary of homicides by Russian internal affairs minister Viktor Yerin, at a Moscow press conference in February, 1994.

3. The figure of thirty million unregistered weapons in the CIS appeared widely in Russian news reports quoting police sources in 1993. Some believe it is even higher.

4. According to one observer, more people were killed in Tajikistan's civil war between October, 1992, and March, 1993, than in any other conflict in the former Soviet Union. The official casualty toll in the war was twenty-five thousand dead but some estimates place it as high as eighty thousand. For an excellent account of the Tajik conflict, see Shahrbanou Tadjbaksh, "The Bloody Path of Change," *Harriman Institute Forum,* Columbia University, New York, July, 1993. Gun dealers certainly reaped enormous profits. The army newspaper *Krasnaya Zvezda* reported in late 1992 that a submachine gun purchased for five thousand rubles in Afghanistan sold for one hundred thousand rubles in Tajikistan. See *Krasnaya Zvezda,* September 24, 1992. In one incident, in October, 1992, an army helicopter traveled from Tajikistan to Afghanistan with a load of carpets that dealers hoped to trade for guns. When they were intercepted, the helicopter passengers claimed that they worked for the Badoshkan National Front.

5. Yuri Yudin, interview with author, March 15, 1993.

6. Caucasus officer and Western analyst quoted by Reuters, March 9, 1993. The figure of 70 percent was given by Russian internal affairs minister Viktor Yerin in a statement published by *Krasnaya Zvezda,* October 24, 1992.

7. The jointly signed article by the two customs officials appeared in *Rossiiskaya Gazeta,* October 30, 1992. The information on Baltic gun dealers was provided to me by journalists from *Respublika* of Vilnius, Lithuania, during a conference on crime in Russia and Eastern Europe sponsored by the Freedom Forum in Zurich, Switzerland, January 20–21, 1994.

8. Aslambek Aslakhanov, interview with author, March 25, 1993.

9. A report on the hostage incident and Rutskoi's involvement in the gun smug-

gling (including photographs of the permits issued to top officials) appeared in Igor Baranovsky, "A Colt for the Vice-President," *Moscow News*, no. 48, 1992.

10. For a good account of the troubles in the Caucasus, see *East European News*, vol. 5, no. 22, November 4, 1991; also Aleksandr Ignatenko, "What Is a Caucasian . . . without a Kalashnikov Automatic Rifle?" *Rossiya*, December 30, 1992.

11. Gen. Dzokhar Dudayev's interview took place in Grozny, November 23, 1991.

12. One of the dissidents was Dudayev's former personal secretary. The criticism was reported in L. Krutakov, "The King Is Made by His Retinue," *Komsomolskaya Pravda*, December 5, 1992. The *Moscow News* report appeared on February 18, 1993.

13. By August, 1994, the quarrel between Dudayev and his opponents had exploded into open war. Russia was accused of sending troops and weapons to Chechen dissidents to overthrow the president. This adds an interesting dimension to the clandestine cooperation between Soviet army officers and Chechen arms dealers.

14. Details on Chechen gangs are from *Komsomolskaya Pravda*, April 25, 1992. The membership of the Chechen gangs in Moscow was then estimated at 1,500. To get a sense of proportion about this figure, during the trial of mafia boss John Gotti in New York, prosecutors claimed that the membership of all the "five families" in charge of the city's mafia came to no more than one thousand. Ivan, a Chechen gangster who refused to tell his real name, bragged to my research assistant Toby Latta, in an interview on July 6, 1992, "We can control Moscow with an iron fist."

15. Mark Masarsky, president of the Association of Russian Enterprises, made this remark in an interview with the author on July 9, 1992, but refused to provide details. He would only say, "We've been taking our own precautions."

16. Igor Baranovsky, interview with author, September 30, 1992.

17. Reported in *Nezavisimaya Gazeta*, February 20, 1993.

18. Reported by Itar-Tass, July 24, 1992.

19. See *Vek*, August 21, 1992.

20. Details of this case were reported in several places. See "Marshals Squabble over Army's Future, Colonels Are Arming Mafiya," *Komsomolskaya Pravda*, June 23, 1993; "Arms Race," *Kommersant*, June 26, 1993; *Moscow News*, June 25, 1993.

Chapter Fourteen: Soviet Army Bazaar

1. The Arzamas-16 story is reported by Kirill Belyaninov, "A Leak," *Literaturnaya Gazeta*, January 20, 1993.

2. The precise number of Russian nuclear weapons is impossible to obtain. The figure of thirty thousand comes from a Central Intelligence Agency estimate of mid-1992, with a margin of error of five thousand warheads. It is quoted by Seymour M. Hersh, "The Wild East," *The Atlantic Monthly*, June, 1994. One U.S. expert told Hersh that no one knew how many warheads had been destroyed in accordance with the START I Treaty, in which Russia and the United States agreed to reduce each side's strategic and tactical warheads to fifteen thousand by the year 2000. "In fact, we don't know within thousands how many warheads they had," he added. The problem is compounded by the difficulty of monitoring the disposition of nuclear arsenals in the other Soviet successor states.

3. For example, Kenneth R. Timmerman, in "It's Time to Stop Russia's Nuclear Mafia," *The Wall Street Journal*, November 27–28, 1992, reported that Kazakhstan

police broke up a ring attempting to market tactical nuclear weapons to Iran. In June, 1994, the Russian justice minister Yuri Kalmykov admitted at a conference in Valletta that "spare parts" from Russian nuclear technology "are in the hands of organized crime in Europe via Russia." He gave no further details. Reuter's, Valletta, June 14, 1994.

4. "U.S. Agrees to Purchase Russian Uranium," Policy Update No. 3, published by Business Executives for National Security, Washington, D.C., September, 1992. Number of nuclear sites from *Literaturnaya Gazeta*, op. cit.

5. Cases reported by *Literaturnaya Gazeta*, ibid. Many cases of purported nuclear smuggling appeared in the press around the Soviet Union during 1992 and 1993. Most are impossible to confirm. In October, 1993, Ukrainian police seized nine containers of radioactive strontium-90, a rare metal with number of defense applications, bound for Poland. In November, 1992, authorities in Belarus seized three kilograms of uranium (its grade was not identified) and arrested a Russian trying to smuggle the load into Poland. Two Polish farmers were arrested after trying to market radioactive cesium they claimed to have obtained from Russian soldiers.

6. The estimate of three hundred seizures was given by Bernd Schmidbauer, co-ordinator of Germany's federal intelligence service, reported by Reuters, August 18, 1994.

7. Sources for the German plutonium seizure come from Craig R. Whitney, "Germans Seize 3rd Atom Sample, Smuggled by Plane from Russia," *The New York Times*, August 14, 1994; Craig R. Whitney, "Germans Suspect Russian Military in Plutonium Sale," *The New York Times*, August 16, 1994; "Germans Seize More Weapons Material," *The New York Times*, August 16, 1994; and Reuters, August 18, 1994.

8. See George Perkovich, "The Plutonium Genie," *Foreign Affairs*, vol. 72, no. 3, Summer 1993, p. 153. The material smuggled in from Moscow was found to be mox, a mixture of plutonium and uranium oxides used in reactors in Western Europe and Japan and under experimental use in Russia. According to official U.S. estimates, an atomic weapon can be made from 8 kilograms (17.6 pounds) of plutonium, 8 kilograms of uranium-233, or 25 kilograms (55.1 pounds) of uranium enriched to contain 20 percent or more of uranium-235. Some experts say that these estimates are way out of date and that primitive bombs can be made with three kilograms or less. A 1994 proposal by the U.S. Natural Resources Defense Council, a private group, would lower "threshold" amounts for safeguards to one kilogram of plutonium-239 or uranium-233, and to three kilograms of enriched uranium. See William J. Broad, "A Smuggling Boom Brings Calls for Tighter Nuclear Safeguards," *The New York Times*, August 21, 1994.

9. Figure of uranium ore comes from *Literaturnaya Gazeta*, op. cit. Stockpile statistics from Policy Update No. 3, op. cit.

10. *Literaturnaya Gazeta*, op. cit.

11. See Timmerman, op. cit., November 27–28, 1992. See also Hersh, op. cit.

12. See William J. Broad, "Experts in U.S. Call Plutonium Not Arms-Level, *The New York Times*, August 17, 1994.

13. Reported in *The Toronto Star*, February 24, 1993; Reuters, Moscow, February 23, 1993.

14. The scandal of the Baltic Air Fleet was reported by *Krasnaya Zvezda*, November 6, 1992. Details on the Pacific coast affair were published in the *Moscow News*, January 21, 1993. Public outrage over the Pacific taxi service increased when a report, a month after Grachev's speech, disclosed that hundreds of young navy conscripts

assigned to the Far East nearly died from exposure, for lack of proper clothing and rations, during a training exercise on a remote Pacific island.

15. *Krasnaya Zvezda,* op. cit.

16. Reuters, March 9, 1993.

17. *Moscow News,* op. cit.

18. The commercial activities of the Soviet army are paralleled by the People's Liberation Army of China. The Chinese military was described as a "vast business organization, trading in arms and a wide variety of other products and services," in an article by George Melloan, "From Communism to Crime Is a Short Journey," *The Wall Street Journal,* March 7, 1994.

19. Report on St. Petersburg military-commercial enterprises from *Nezavisimaya Gazeta,* June 6, 1992. Anatoli Zhilin quoted in the *Toronto Star,* op. cit.

20. Yuri Yudin, interview with author, March 15, 1993.

21. The accusations against Grachev and other high officials in connection with the Western Army Group in Germany were taken from Special Prosecutor Nikolai Makarov's report to the Supreme Soviet on corruption, June 26, 1993; copy in author's possession.

22. *Financial Times,* April 29, 1992.

23. From a report of the Stockholm International Peace Research Institute, cited in the *Moscow Tribune,* March 13, 1993.

24. Sergei Plotnikov, interview with author, September 27, 1992.

25. See *Problems of Communism,* January-February 1990, p. 89, fig. 1, a chart showing the general organization of Soviet defense production. Among sources listed are the U.S. Central Intelligence Agency.

26. *Moscow News* (in English), March 26, 1993.

27. Aslambek Aslakhanov, interview with author, March 25, 1993.

28. Charge against the vice-premier were made in Makarov's report, op. cit. The Ukraine missile deal was reported by Itar-Tass, July 2, 1993.

29. The *Observer* obtained a list of Soviet armaments being offered to European brokers along with their prices. The list included a used T-72 battle tank going for fifty thousand dollars, a MIG-29 going for twenty-five million dollars, and an aircraft carrier being offered at four billion dollars. See the *Observer,* June 21, 1992.

30. Aleksandr Mokhov, quoted in "Uranovye Nesuny" (Uranium Leaks), *Atompressa* (official publication of MINATOM), February, 1993. "No Western police agency has been able to come up with any evidence of buyers, despite our requests," he declared. In 1993, three Russian reporters tried to penetrate the underground nuclear trade. In a report published in *The Bulletin of Atomic Scientists,* March/April 1994, they maintained that much of the material offered for sale was bogus. European police reports as well as Russian police sources contradict this. But it does raise questions about who is cheating whom. Excerpts from the article were published in "The Players in This Shell Game Need Plutonium, Lead and Moxie," *The New York Times,* "The Week in Review," February 27, 1994.

31. See *Literaturnaya Gazeta,* op. cit.

32. The best sources for the complicated story of red mercury are an investigative report by A. Craig Coppetas in the *Moscow Times* weekend review of January 16–17, 1993; and *Komsomolskaya Pravda,* April 30, 1993. The critics' case was summed up in the report by Special Prosecutor Nikolai Makarov, op. cit.

33. *Sovetskaya Rossiya,* July 1, 1993; another source for this story is *Kommersant "B,"* April 27, 1993.

34. Estimate of 110,000 atomic-industry workers cited by Arkadi Volsky, president of the Russian Union of Industrial Managers and Entrepreneurs, in *Krasnaya Zvezda,* no. 158, 1992. Volsky, whose organization is the main lobbying group for defense managers, also provided the estimate of the total size of the military-industrial complex used earlier in this chapter.

35. St. Petersburg isotopes reported by Yevgeni Solomenko, "Smuggling Death," *Izvestiya,* November 19, 1992. Mercury discovery reported by Interfax, March 23, 1993.

36. See *Izvestiya,* November 19, 1992. Also, Michael R. Gordon with Matthew L. Wald, "Russian Controls on Bomb Material Are Leaky," *The New York Times,* August 18, 1994.

37. The argument that commercial interests played a part in the Black Sea dispute was made to me by several unofficial sources, including both Russian and Ukrainian naval officers, during a visit to Sevastopol in the spring of 1992. All Russian troops were withdrawn from Lithuania in August, 1993. The remaining thirteen thousand troops in Latvia and three thousand troops in Estonia were withdrawn on August 31, 1994. Total Soviet forces in the Baltics once amounted to nearly two hundred thousand. For two interesting accounts of the strengthening of military influence on Yeltsin, see Stephen Foye, "Updating Russian Civil-Military Relations," *RFE/Radio Liberty Research Report,* November 13, 1993; and Susan L. Clark, "Security Issues and the Eastern Slavic States," *The World Today,* October, 1993. A broader look at the trend was provided by the Strengthening Democratic Institutions Project at Harvard University's John F. Kennedy School in a special January, 1994, report, entitled "Back in the USSR."

Chapter Fifteen: The Baltic Connection

1. Estonia declared independence on August 20, 1991; Latvia did so the next day. Lithuania had formally declared independence more than a year earlier, on March 11, 1990. All three nations were recognized by Western countries in August and September, 1991. Russia followed soon after.

2. Estonia's chief industries are listed in the 1993 *World Almanac* as agricultural machinery and electric motors. Mikhail Yegorov, head of the Russian MVD's organized-crime division, provided the sixth-place figure for non-ferrous metal exports at a Moscow press conference, October 8, 1992.

3. Statistics on metal smuggling as well as other illicit activities, such as the smuggling of refugees, were supplied by Juri Pihl, Director of the Estonian security service, in an interview with the author on March 22, 1993. The Estonian currency, the kroon, is pegged to the deutschmark, at one deutschmark to eight kroons. Estonia's gold and foreign currency reserves were about 2.2 billion kroons (170 million dollars) by the end of 1992, and the number of kroons in circulation increased from about 600 million to 970 million as of November, 1992. Figures published in *Estonia Magazine,* Winter 1993.

4. Oil statistics provided at MVD press conference, Moscow, September 25, 1992.

5. *Estonia Magazine,* op. cit.

6. Information about the Tiit Madisson commission was supplied by the helpful staff of the Estonian Press Service, Tallinn; and newspaper files.

7. I am indebted to Alan Martinson, director of the Estonian Press Service, and Juri Pihl, of the Estonian security service, for information about Tiu Silvas.

8. Sandis Metuzans, interview with author, March 19, 1993.

9. Egar Aaro, interview with author, March 22, 1993. Elvo Priks, an adviser to the Estonian Ministry of Defense, was also present at the interview and supplied additional information used in this chapter.

10. The difference between currency rules in Russia and the Baltic countries, particularly Estonia and Latvia, is dramatic. In Russia, conversion from rubles to dollars is only permitted through a currency auction, and the client is required to show proof of a Russian bank account. In Estonia, no proof of identity is required at any of the auctions or currency windows provided by banks and special brokerages. In return, fees and commissions can be high. Alan Martinson was a helpful guide through the intricacies of Baltic finance.

11. Conclusions of Russian task force on smuggling published in *Sovetskaya Rossiya,* February 13, 1993.

12. Baturin quoted in *Komsomolskaya Pravda,* July 4, 1992.

13. Latvia's bank crisis began in November, 1992, when three of the major banks—Union Baltic, Tartu Commercial, and North Estonian—closed on the grounds that they no longer had cash for depositers. They claimed that the government had not helped them recover money owed them from Moscow. But authorities responded that the banks, in particular Tartu Commercial, were engaged in illegal banking practices. The problem was lack of regulation. Any bank can establish itself with a minimum capital base of ten thousand dollars, and there is no government scrutiny. One banking insider called it a Wild West atmosphere and suggested that businessmen might feel more secure for the moment putting their money in foreign accounts. *Estonia Magazine,* op. cit.

14. Juri Pihl, interview with author, March 22, 1993.

15. The Estonian division of the KGB disbanded its operations after August, 1991, on the condition that the pension rights of its employees be honored and the names of informers be kept secret. The government agreed, but the KGB officials took all their records with them when they left. Informed local observers believe that the KGB network continues to operate in the country, with close ties to the Russian security service.

16. *Estonia Magazine,* op. cit.

17. See Pelle Neroth, "Gun Law Rules in Wild, Wild East," *The European,* October 1–4, 1992. According to *USSR Yearbook 1990* (Novosti Press), the population of Tallinn is 482,000.

18. Col. Laimonis Liepinch, interview with author, March 19, 1993. Lt. Col. Sergei Chornyuk, head of the Riga organized-crime squad, also provided the author with helpful information about the Baltic gang world.

19. Yuris Blaumans, interview with author, March 19, 1993.

20. A popular and controversial film of the perestroika years, entitled *Interdevochka* (Intergirl) brought the phenomenon to public attention. It came to be a scornful phrase applicable to any Soviet woman who married in order to emigrate.

21. Information on Lithuanian crime figures reported by Interfax, March, 1993 (undated), and *Izvestiya,* September 23, 1993.

Chapter Sixteen: The Evil Empire Revisited

1. For the story of Chechens in London, see "Prostitute Found at Shooting Penthouse," *London Evening Standard*, March 3, 1993. Other details reported by the *Sun*, March 3, 1993, and Interfax, March 22, 1993. See also n. 10.

2. Figures of Russian criminal activities in Eastern Europe come from a multitude of sources. Mikhail Yegorov, head of the Russian MVD's organized-crime division, provided details at a Moscow press conference, October 8, 1992. See also Alan Cowell, "East Europe Is a Land of Opportunity to the Mafia," *The New York Times*, September 2, 1993. Antti Turkama, of the Finnish National Bureau of Investigation, said in an interview with the *Sunday Telegraph*, published June 7, 1992, that Russians were able to exploit the lack of organized-crime syndicates in Finland: "Russian criminals . . . see us as a lucrative market."

3. Quoted in *Moscow News*, May 14, 1993.

4. MVD press conference, op. cit.

5. Reuters, March 2, 1993.

6. Metals-industry experts acknowledge that the glut of cheap aluminum and nickel from the Commonwealth of Independent States forced a sharp drop in world prices and caused major losses (in the case of aluminum, about seven billion dollars in 1992). Russian government officials say that much of this "overproduction" represented unlicensed exports, that is, metal shipped by industrial managers via unofficial channels—in other words, with the assistance of a complex network of corruption and organized smuggling. Stocks of nickel available through the London Metals Exchange rose from 3,462 metric tons in January, 1991, to 78,804 in February, 1993. See Celestine Bohlen, "Billions Bleed out of Russia As Its Wealth Is Sent Abroad," *The New York Times*, February 1, 1993. Aluminum-industry officials blamed the quadrupling of Russian aluminum exports since 1991 for lowering prices to about fifty cents a pound, less than one-third of their peak in 1988. See "Eight Losing Quarters Don't Tarnish Alcan," *The Toronto Globe and Mail*, May 10, 1993. Prices continued to drop in 1994. See Ann Imse, "Russia's Wild Capitalists Take Aluminum for a Ride," *The New York Times*, February 13, 1994; and "Pros Mull Effects of Russian Upheaval," *The Wall Street Journal*, March 3, 1994. For additional signs of industry concern, see *JOM (Journal of Minerals, Metals, and Materials)*, September, 1993, p. 4, and January, 1993, p. 16.

7. The Prague summit of mafiya chieftains was reported by Itar-Tass, November 5, 1992, and again in Birna Helgadottir, Vitali Vitaliev, and Roberta Bonometti, "A Beast Emerges from the Wreck: Moscow Mob Widens Its Net," *The European*, April 1, 1993.

8. Details on the Yerevan funeral of Rafik were reported in *Vechernyaya Moskva*, July 2, 1993. Information about his life and achievements—as well as other activities not otherwise noted in this chapter—come from Russian police and gangland sources.

9. Reuters, October 13, 1992.

10. The surviving Armenian, Gagic Ter-Ogrannisyan, was married to a British Broadcasting Corporation producer. His sister-in-law, also a British citizen, was murdered in May, 1994, in what was considered a revenge killing. The professional assassin used hollowed-out bullets tipped with wax and filled with mercury explosive to inflict horrific wounds, a standard gangland touch. See "Chechen's Justice Hits Willow Way," *Sunday Times* (London), May 8, 1994.

11. *The Times* of London report was cited in an Itar-Tass dispatch from London, March 15, 1993. Chechen vice-premier Yaragi Mamodayev was accused by the Chech-

nya security ministry in 1993 of manipulating oil sales abroad. Some heavily discounted Chechen oil was said to have been sent to Serbia in violation of the United Nations blockade imposed on portions of the former Yugoslavia. See *Komsomolskaya Pravda,* March 20, 1993.

12. "13 Indicted In Oil Scheme Laid to Mob," *The New York Times,* May 6, 1993.

13. Col. Anatoli Zhoglo, interview with author, March 16, 1993. An FBI official privately told me in New York that information from Russian police was usually discounted, "because it always seems too vague for us to act on." By mid-1993, however, American police officials insist that they were alert to Yaponets's presence.

14. See chapter 2 for an account of the Vedentsovo meeting.

15. "Crime As an Export: Only the Highest Quality," *Novoye Russkoye Slovo,* October 26, 1992.

16. See Brian Duffy and Jeff Trimble, "The Wise Guys of Russia," *U.S. News and World Report,* March 7, 1994. The Kuznetsov murder and its ramifications were reported in *Literaturnaya Gazeta,* July 15, 1992, in a joint investigation with *The Los Angeles Times.* For a fascinating treatment of Soviet-emigre crime activities, see Robert I. Friedman, "Brighton Beach Goodfellas," *Vanity Fair,* January, 1993; also Anne McElvoy, "Russia's Violent Export," *Times* (London), March 4, 1993. Additional information about Russian crime in America was provided to me by Bill Doran and other agents of the New York FBI office.

17. Quoted by Reuters, May 24, 1993.

18. The story of the Miami summit comes from a senior source in the U.S. Drug Enforcement Agency who did not wish to be named. For accounts of Russian mob activities in London, see Dean Nelson and Peter Beaumont, "Businesses Bow to Rule of Moscow Mafia Gangs," *Observer* (London), May 8, 1994; for mob pressure on hockey players, see Joe Lapointe, "Russian Crime Groups Harassing Expatriates," *The New York Times,* December 24, 1993. A good recent overview of Russian gangland operations in the United States can be found in Selwyn Raab, "Influx of Russian Gangsters Troubles FBI in Brooklyn," *The New York Times,* August 23, 1994.

19. Reported by Steve Goldstein, "Sounding a Warning on Russia's Mafia," *The Philadelphia Inquirer,* May 26, 1994.

20. Ian Burrell, "Russian Mafia Told Briton: Sell Arms to the IRA or Die," *The Sunday Times* (London), May 1, 1994. Greed as well as ideology encouraged the Kremlin to network beyond Soviet borders. According to Moscow officials who examined archive documents after the 1991 coup, the Politburo transferred crude oil to Italian companies for windfall profits in 1983. Soviet diamonds were also secretly sold on the international market to fund clandestine operations in Afghanistan and Southeast Asia. The archive documents confirmed that Soviet Communists provided aid to terrorist groups, including those in Italy, Northern Ireland, and Libya. Documents seen by the author in Moscow confirmed that KGB agents carrying briefcases stuffed with cash delivered annual subsidies to Communist parties in Italy, France, the United States, and dozens of other countries.

21. Crime profit estimate provided by Hans-Ludwig Zachert, president of the German Federal Police Agency, quoted by Reuters, June 23, 1994.

22. Cal Millar and Jack Lakey, "Metro Russian Registers Arsenal," *Toronto Star,* August 27, 1993.

23. I met Boris Birshtein in Moscow in 1988. At the time, he was operating a small textile imports firm. Birshtein spoke openly of his close connections with the Commu-

nist establishment. "You just need to get in the saunas, and that's where you really do business," he boasted. He was then beginning a close association with leading Canadian politicians and academics. According to unverified reports in the Russian press, Gorbachev commissioned Birshtein to funnel Communist Party money out of the country before the coup. A former KGB resident in Zurich, Col. Leonid Veselovsky, was identified as the key bagman in the transfer and was closely associated with Seabeco. See Mark Almond, "Introducing Kgb Plc," *The Spectator,* July 10, 1993.

24. For research on Yakubovsky's background, I am indebted to Jennifer Gould, who interviewed him in Toronto and uncovered his history in Moscow in a series of articles for *The Toronto Star,* in September and October, 1993. Additional information was published by Celestine Bohlen, "The Kremlin's Latest Intrigue Shows How Real Life Imitates James Bond," *The New York Times,* November 23, 1993.

25. See Jack Lakey, Cal Millar, and Jennifer Gould, "Russian Scandal Becomes As Wild As Any Spy Novel," *The Toronto Star,* October 3, 1993. In September, 1993, the staff at the Toronto offices of Seabeco denied that Birshtein had anything to do with them. But the company kept huge stocks of cash on hand in its safe to smooth the passage of visiting Commonwealth delegates.

26. Russian justice minister Yuri Kalmykov, press conference, August 18, 1993, Moscow. Transcript in author's possession.

27. See *International Narcotics Control Strategy Report,* April 1994, op. cit., p. 498.

28. Even Yakubovsky's Russian allies made it clear that they took a jaundiced view of their informant. At his press conference, Justice Minister Kalmykov compared Yakubovsky to Ostap Bender, the popular fictional character created by the Odessa satirists Ilya Ilf and Yevgeni Petrov. According to *The Handbook of Russian Literature,* ed. Victor Terras (New Haven: Yale University Press, 1985), p. 198, Bender was a "crafty, cynical and witty rogue who meets a world of honest plodders, dull bureaucrats and greedy philistines with sovereign nonchalance and supercilious irony."

29. In February, 1994, sources in Moscow informed me of plans to revive the case against Rutskoi.

30. See *Moscow News,* June 25, 1993.

31. Quoted in *Global Finance Magazine,* September, 1993.

32. Vladimir Kalinichenko, interview with author, September 29, 1992.

Chapter Seventeen: Cops and Commissars

Epigraphs: The first is spoken by Michael, the revolutionary, in *Vera, or The Nihilists,* a play written by Oscar Wilde in 1880, at a time when London was beginning to fill with exiled reformers and radicals from Russia. The date of the letter to Gorky is unknown, but Lenin went on to insist that "opposition to violence is our ultimate ideal." Quoted in James H. Billington, *The Icon and the Axe* (New York: Vintage, 1970), pp. 476–477.

1. Igor Voloshin and Lev Simkin, "The Judicial System in the USSR," pamphlet (Moscow: Novosti, 1989). The authors were both described as Soviet lawyers.

2. Vadim Bakatin, interview with author, op. cit.

3. For an examination of law enforcement in the twilight years of the Soviet state, see Louise Shelley, "Second Economy in the Soviet Union," in *The Second Economy in Marxist States,* ed. Maria Los (New York: Macmillan, 1990).

4. Even before the Communist era, law was considered an instrument for imposing order rather than a vehicle for applying the vague concept of justice. Count Benck-

endorff, chief of the secret police under Czar Nicholas I, once declared, "Laws are written for subordinates, not for authorities." Pipes, op. cit., p. 290. Not surprisingly, Russians reacted with the same cynicism. A Ukrainian legal scholar, B. Kistiakowskii, commented in 1909 that "the total lack of equality before courts killed respect for law. A Russian by whatever name he goes will get around or violate the law anywhere he can with impunity; and the government will do the same." Quoted from the booklet "Human Rights and Legal Reform in the Russian Federation," published in March 1993 by the Lawyers Committee for Human Rights, p. 17.

5. Stanislava Gorodenskaya, interview in *Izvestiya,* January 28, 1992.

6. John Hazard, "Soviet Law Takes a Fresh Breath," *Harriman Institute Forum,* vol. 5, no. 6, February 1992. See also Hazard's later analyses of the evolution of law-making in "Prospects for a Rule of Law State," *Harriman Institute Forum,* vol. 7, no. 1–2, September-October 1993.

7. I am indebted for much of this chapter's discussion of the shortcomings of Russian criminal law and judicial institutions, as well as the ambitious early concepts of post-Soviet reformers, to "Human Rights and Legal Reform in the Russian Federation," published in March 1993 by the Lawyers Committee for Human Rights, available from the Lawyers Committee for Human Rights, 330 Seventh Ave., New York, N.Y. 10001. In a trenchant overview of the Soviet system, the booklet argues that "the Soviet state created law, but was not bound by it" (p. 17).

8. Jury trials were not actually introduced until January, 1993, after long and bitter opposition from right-wing and Communist parliamentarians. Itar-Tass, January 5, 1993.

9. Lawyers Committee, op. cit., pp. 71–73.

10. Ibid., pp. 16–17.

11. Korneyeva, interview with author, op. cit.

12. See Korneyeva's comments in chapter 1.

13. *Megapolis Express,* April 28, 1993. The police arrest and conviction record continued at the same pace through 1993. According to MVD figures presented in Moscow in October, 1993, nearly 5,000 gang members were arrested in 1993, but only 1,175 cases were brought to court, and convictions were won in 800 of them. But the successful convictions included 144 "crime leaders," the MVD said. In 1994, MVD organized-crime division chief Mikhail Yegorov complained that only 19 percent of the 18,000 persons found guilty of possessing firearms were sent to jail.

14. *Trud,* December 5, 1992.

15. MVD press conference, Moscow, October 26, 1993.

16. Lawyers Committee, op cit., pp. 95–96.

17. Police salaries reported by Reuters, Moscow, May 31, 1993.

18. The unofficial figure of two million MVD officers was obtained from sources inside the ministry. Other figures were reported in MVD year-end statistics published in January, 1994. I am also obliged to Col. Vladimir Roshailo, head of the Moscow Police organized-crime squad, for information concerning police structures. He was interviewed by me on March 17, 1993.

19. Figures on police casualties from Interfax, October, 1992, January 21, 1993, June 16, 1993. By comparison, in the United States 72 policemen were killed by gunfire in 1993, and a total of 139 killed in line of duty. The highest casualty rate since the United States began recording the figures was 95 policemen killed by firearms in 1974. See *The New York Times,* January 1, 1994 (Associated Press report from Washington).

20. Col. Anatoli Zhoglo, interview with author, March 16, 1993.

21. MVD officials at the October 26, 1993, press conference, op. cit., complained that they had been able to bring to court only eight "banditism" cases in 1993 against major gangs, because they could not persuade local procurators to apply the article more forcefully. I use the pronoun "he" throughout my description of post-Soviet criminals because, according to the MVD, only 11.3 percent of the 1.1 million Russians convicted of crimes in 1992 were women.

22. Stepankov's proposals were published in *Trud* and reported by Reuters, March 23, 1993. In May, 1994, a draft law on organized crime was finally completed by the Russian parliament. It was expected to be passed later in the year.

23. *Rossiiskiye Vesti*, May 11, 1994.

24. Mark Masarsky, interview with author, July 9, 1992. For a view of an earlier Masarsky, see Hedrick Smith, *The New Russians*, op. cit., pp. 276–85. Smith wrote, after meeting him in 1989, "If Gorbachev's gamble on private enterprise is going to pay off it will hinge on entrepreneurs like Masarsky." "Lazy people" quotation from *Komsomolskaya Pravda*, December 23, 1992.

25. Figures on police corruption quoted in a report of the Analytical Center for Social and Economic Policies, prepared by chairman Pyotr Filipov, presented to the government on January 17, 1994. Nikolai Ryzhkov quoted in *Komsomolskaya Pravda*, December 9, 1992.

26. Aleksei Kochetov, interview with author, September 22, 1992.

27. One prominent example of police *bizness* activity involved P. Bogdanov, the former Moscow police chief, who received regular payments from a joint venture called Sov-Kuwait Engineering. Documents of the company's finances showed that the venture paid for overseas trips by Bogdanov and his deputy when he was still chief. The venture, as it turned out, was chaired by Boris Bershtein, president of Seabeco, who was often escorted by a flashing police motorcade when he visited Moscow. See *Literaturnaya Gazeta*, June 10, 1992. In 1992, the Moscow Foreign Correspondents Association, of which I was vice-president, prepared a "white book" listing requests for bribes and payoffs from government and police officials and compiled from experiences of foreign journalists. It was a sobering list. It should be added here that no money was given to anyone interviewed in the course of research for this book. I did have to pay a fee, however, to "middlemen" who arranged meetings with several of the mobsters.

28. See *Rossiiskiye Vesti*, February 26, 1993. Police extortion reported in *Moskovsky Komsomolets*, July 7, 1993. Other information about police, unless otherwise noted, comes from the MVD report for 1993, presented at a March 11, 1994, press conference in Moscow by Internal Affairs Minister Viktor Yerin.

29. MVD ring reported in *Izvestiya*, May 6, 1994. Figure of senior policemen collaborating with gangsters from *Rossiiskaya Gazeta*, May 3, 1993. In a 1993 interview with Olivia Ward of *The Toronto Star*, MVD colonel Arkadi Kuznetsov admitted, "People are leaving the MVD and security ministry and handing over their experience to criminal groups. This is a big problem."

30. I was present at a meeting between Stepankov and the Moscow Foreign Correspondents Association in 1992, during which the procurator-general calmly defended his interview charges as a method of raising money for the department.

31. See, among other sources, Steven Erlanger, "Yeltsin Urges Forces to Join in New Amity," *The New York Times*, February 25, 1994.

32. For a fuller account of the parliamentary corruption scandals of 1993, involving Rutskoi and his rivals, see chapter 16.

33. After the events of October 3–4, 1993, the main medical administration of the Russian government reported the toll at 144 people dead, including 76 civilians, and 878 wounded. Police later found two thousand assault rifles, more than two thousand pistols, eighteen machine guns, twelve grenade launchers, and a Strelka surface-to-air missile in the White House. They also found 170 million rubles in cash, believed part of a secret payment of 348 million rubles provided by the Russian Central Bank just before the rebellion. For other data, see Foreign Broadcast Information Service (FBIS), Sov-93–201, October 20, 1993.

34. Accounts of the war on crime following the White House assault come from eyewitness reports provided to me as well as "Moscow Police Wage War on Crime," *The New York Times,* October 13, 1993.

35. Ibid.

36. Col. Dmitri Medvedev, interview with author, March 30, 1993.

37. MVD plan reported in Foreign Broadcast Information Service (FBIS), Sov 93–198, October 15, 1993

38. *The New York Times,* "Anti-Crime Decree Sets Off a Storm of Outrage," June 19, 1994.

39. Reuters, June 10, 1994.

40. *The New York Times,* op. cit., June 19, 1994.

41. *Lawyers Committee,* op. cit., pp. 98–103.

42. See Georgi Podlesskikh and Andrei Tereshonok, *Vory v zakonye: Brosok k vlasti (Vory v zakonye:* A leap toward power) (Moscow: Khudozhestvennaya Literatura, 1994).

43. *Komsomolskaya Pravda,* June 4, 1992.

44. Quoted in *The Times* (London), September 18, 1992. For stories of commercial activities of former KGB personnel see also *New Times* (Moscow), January 8, 1992.

45. See chapter 6 for an account of the Kryuchkov plan.

46. *Rossiiskaya Gazeta,* July 18, 1992.

47. Speculation on the reasons for Golushko's dismissal was reported by Steven Erlanger, "Amnesty of Foes Brings Disarray to Yeltsin Team," *The New York Times,* March 1, 1994.

Chapter Eighteen: General Sterligov and His Friends

1. Gen. Aleksandr Sterligov, interview with author, July 16, 1992. Sterligov seems to be referring here to the KGB rather than to ordinary policemen, who were generally kept in the dark about organized-crime structures and were not trained to deal with them. But it is debatable how much even the KGB knew in the years leading up to the Soviet collapse, despite the contentions of the 1994 book by Podlesskikh and Tereshonok (see chap. 17, n. 42).

2. Survey quoted in *Moskovskaya Pravda,* July 20, 1992.

3. For a useful overview of Russian nationalism from the czars to the modern day, see Walter Laqueur, *Black Hundred: The Rise of the Extreme Right in Russia* (New York: HarperCollins, 1993).

4. See "Bitva za Rossiyu" (Struggle for Russia), *Sovetskaya Rossiya,* February 20,

1993. The "Protocols" were forged by the Czarist secret police, the Okhrana, in 1903, using material plagiarized from an anti-Semitic tract already published in France. On November 27, 1993, a Moscow district court formally ruled the "Protocols" a forgery—the first time they had ever been so acknowledged in Russia. A suit had been brought by the Pamyat organization against the *Jewish Gazette* of Moscow, claiming that references to it as anti-Semitic were libelous. The *Gazette* in its defense brought up the Pamyat newspaper's reprinting of sections of the "Protocols." After the judgment, Pamyat leader Dmitri Vasiliev complained, "They have no decency left to say the 'Protocols' are a fake when the entire history of Russia after 1917 is solid proof that they are genuine."

5. Fr. Mikhail Ardov, interview with author, March 15, 1993.

6. See, *Laqueur,* op. cit., pp. 17n3 and 48n4.

7. According to final figures supplied by the Russian Central Election Commission, Zhirinovsky's Liberal Democrats won 22.79 percent of the vote, which gave them 59 of the 225 seats earmarked in the Duma for preferential-party votes. The closest runner-up was the reformist Russia's Choice, with 15.38 percent and 40 seats. The Russian Communist Party won more than 12 percent and the Agrarian Party nearly 8 percent of the popular vote. Allied with Zhirinovsky's bloc, they would control about 112 seats. For a post-election analysis, see "The Russian Elections and After," *The World Today* (Royal Institute of International Affairs, London), vol. 50, no. 3, March 1994.

8. Surveys quoted in *The New York Times,* "The Week in Review," April 18, 1993.

9. By 1994, there were indications that Zhirinovsky's appeal was eroding, but only because Russians were turning to more "solid" candidates on the right. See Alexander J. Motyl, "Vladimir Zhirinovsky: A Man of His Times," *The Harriman Review,* vol. 7, nos. 7–9, March–May 1994; also Michael Specter, "The Great Russia Will Live Again," *The New York Times Magazine,* June 19, 1994.

10. According to Walter Laqueur, the Cossack revival reflected "in microcosm the renaissance of national bolshevism." See Laqueur, op. cit., pp. 193–202. This was an ironic switch. Long before their emergence in the eighteenth century as the famous cavalry farmers who defended the czar's frontiers against Asia and Europe, the Cossacks had been mounted highwaymen themselves. The so-called frontier knights of the steppes were originally bands of escaped thieves and outlaws. Even after they had cloaked themselves in the mantle of defenders of the Orthodox faith, many of their raids were aimed at plunder and brigandage. Much of their income came from robbing trade convoys. During the Time of Troubles, they frequently switched sides. For a good account of the Cossack revival, see Andrew Wilson and Nina Bachkatov, "Russia: The Cossack Revival," *The World Today,* vol. 49, no. 1, January 1993.

11. The loan to Zavidia has been documented in, among other places, Laqueur, op. cit., p. 257.

12. Podlesskikh and Tereshonok, op. cit., pp. 69–71.

13. Kasyanov, interview with author, June 30, 1992.

14. Quoted in Timofeyev, op. cit., pp. 21–22. During the coup, several criminal-business "cooperatives" unabashedly put their weapons and strong-arm connections at the service of Russia's beleaguered democracy. "It was as much a matter of life or death for those entrepreneurs if the coup succeeded as it was for the Yeltsin people," Vladimir Kalinichenko told me.

15. Mark Melzer, interview with author, June 9, 1992.

16. Alessandra Stanley, 'Where Politicians Sometimes Tote Assault Rifles, *The New York Times,* May 10, 1994.

17. I am indebted to Toby Latta, my assistant in Moscow, for speculation and circumstances surrounding the April 26, 1994, shooting of Andrei Aizerdzis.

18. See *The New York Times,* op. cit., June 19, 1994, and Reuters, June 24, 1994.

19. The report compiled by the Analytical Center for Social and Economic Policy in Moscow, headed by Pyotr Filipov, was called "Organized Crime and the Probability of National Socialists' Coming to Power in Russia." It was published in *Izvestiya,* January 26, 1994.

20. Sterligov interview by Interfax, July 8, 1992.

21. Fr. Mikhail Ardov, interview with author, op. cit.

22. See Roman Solchanyk, "Back to the USSR?" *The Harriman Institute Forum* (Columbia University, New York), vol. 6, no. 3, November 1992.

23. *Ogonyok,* March 1994 (date unavailable).

24. *The New York Times,* December 26, 1993. Gennady Burbulis, the former Marxist-Leninist professor who had been President Yeltsin's virtual second-in-command until 1992, confessed in October, 1993, that the government had slowed down economic reforms in hopes of finding a compromise with the former establishment. See, Foreign Broadcast Information Service (FBIS), Sov-93–201, October 20, 1993.

Chapter Nineteen: The Chinatown Gang

1. For a brief description of Kitaigorod and its history, see Helen Boldyreff Semler, *Discovering Moscow* (New York: Hippocrene Books, 1989). pp. 71–72. Interestingly, the first foreign embassy to Muscovy (from Britain), the Angliskoye Podvorye, was established in the district in the mid-sixteenth century. Russia's leaders believed that their people needed as much protection from foreigners as from commerce. See Kathleen Berton, *Moscow: An Architectural History* (New York: Macmillan, 1977), in particular p. 45.

2. Konstantin Borovoi, interview with author, July 9, 1992. Borovoi's car was blown up in Kostroma, about 150 miles east of Moscow, while he was campaigning there for local elections.

3. Borovoi is not the only one to have discovered the involvement of the KGB in illegal businesses and extortions. Author's interviews with sources such as Vladimir Kalinichenko and Aslambek Aslakhanov supplied other examples. "The nomenklatura knew years ago that the system would come tumbling down, and prepared themselves," Aslakhanov told me. "They had plenty of money ready to continue their activities. As far as I am concerned, it doesn't matter how high they were in positions of power. They are worse criminals than the *vory* because they put their own interests above the interests of the state."

4. *The Dragon,* based on a fairy tale, was one of the most popular plays written by Yevgeni Shvarts (1896–1958). Written in 1944, it was canceled by Stalinist censors after its first performances.

5. Galina Starovoitova, interview with author, May 27, 1992.

6. Mark Masarsky, interview with author, op. cit.

7. Volsky quoted in the *Financial Times,* November 2, 1992.

8. Paul F. Murray, letter to the editor, New York Times, November 5, 1992.

9. The Swedish economist Anders Aslund was one Westerner who saw through the Civic Union. He called it simply an "alliance of the vested interests of the old system." Aslund, who served as economic adviser to the Yeltsin government, was understandably biased; but he pointed out that the Volsky group's full-employment policies would turn Russia toward a corporatist economy dominated by heavily subsidized industries, and that instead of protecting Russian citizens they would lead to further impoverishment. See Aslund, "Go Faster on Russian Reform," *The New York Times*, op-ed page, December 7, 1992.

10. Quoted in *Nezavisimaya Gazeta*, June 2, 1992.

11. Eugene Lyons, *Assignment in Utopia* (New York: Harcourt, Brace, 1937), pp. 84–85.

12. The NEP is usually regarded as having run from 1921 to 1927.

13. Survey reported by Itar-Tass, November 1992 (date unavailable).

14. Of 106.1 million Russian voters, 54.8 percent took part in the referendum/election; 58.4 percent of those voted in favor of the constitution, 41.6 percent against. Figures reported by *The New York Times*, December 21, 1993.

15. See pp. 180–85, Daniel Yergin and Thane Gustafson, *Russia 2010 and What It Means for the World* (New York: Random House,The Cera Report/Cambridge Energy Resource Associates, 1993).

16. Zaveryukha announced in January, 1994, that the cabinet would spend about nine billion dollars on agricultural subsidies for the year, an estimated rise of 7 percent over 1993. A month later, he said he needed an additional 34 trillion rubles (21.2 billion dollars) in subsidies for state farms.

17. Fyodorov's remarks taken from transcript of statement published in *The New York Times*, January 27, 1994.

Chapter Twenty: Who Lost Russia?

1. Solzhenitsyn speech reprinted in *The New York Times Book Review*, February 7, 1993.

2. The Russian population in 1993 was estimated at 148.6 million. See *Business World Weekly* (Moscow), March 26, 1993. There were seventy thousand registered cases of viral hepatitis, forty-five thousand cases of bacterial dysentery, and forty thousand cases of salmonella poisoning before the end of 1993. St. Petersburg reported a sharp rise in deaths from tuberculosis and other infectious diseases. Only two out of every three infants were properly immunized; the rate of tuberculosis among teenagers and children had doubled in the previous year. Dr. Gennadi Kolesnikov, the city's chief health officer, said, "The figures can be compared only to a national disaster." See "St. Petersburg Death Rate Skyrockets," *Moscow Tribune*, March 17, 1993.

3. See Aslund, *Gorbachev's Stuggle*, p. 19.

4. Figure on extortion and inflation rate cited by Filipov report, op. cit.

5. Igor Safaryan, interview with author, June 30, 1992.

6. Figures about criminal turnover published by Interfax, May 25, 1993.

7. In 1994, Yakov Gilinsky, deputy director of the Institute of Sociology in St. Petersburg, drew up a (non-exhaustive) list of the situations in which a businessman was required to pay money under the table: ". . . when registering enterprises, when taking lease of premises from state bodies, when acquiring licenses for the [commercial] use of those premises, when obtaining low-rate bank credit, when reporting to the tax in-

spection, when [going through] customs formalities." Compiled in "Black Market and Organized Crime in Russia," a paper presented at the Conference on International Perspectives on Crime, Drugs, and Public Order, held at the John Jay College of Criminal Justice, New York City, June 12–17, 1994.

8. The government was merely making its powerlessness sound like a strategy. Commercial firms avoided paying the equivalent of nearly ten billion dollars in taxes in 1992—a sum which, according to Vladimir Gusev, head of Russia's tax collection service, represented about 15 percent of potential state revenues.

9. David Gurevich, "The Mob—Today's KGB," *The New York Times,* op-ed page, February 19, 1994.

10. Vaksberg, op. cit., p. 255.

11. A resolution accompanying the amendment quixotically called on the government to give officials a "decent standard of living" so that they would not be tempted to receive kickbacks. It also required civil servants to make public their monthly incomes.

12. Julie Corwin, Douglas Stanglin, Suzanne Possehl, and Jeff Trimble, "The Looting of Russia," *U.S. News and World Report,* March 7, 1994.

13. Serge Schmemann, "A Bit Wryly Moscow Summons the Masses," *The New York Times,* November 8, 1992.

14. The St. Petersburg engineer's comment was reported by Anatol Lieven, "Mafia and Muggings Battle St. Petersburg's Image," *The Times* (London), May 9, 1994. Havel's words were quoted in "Havel Calls the Gypsies Litmus Tests," *The New York Times,* December 9, 1993. See also Vaclav Havel's speech, April 22, 1993, at George Washington University, Washington, D.C., reprinted in *The New York Review of Books,* May 27, 1993.

15. Quoted by Interfax, April 20, 1993.

16. Boris Fyodorov, "Moscow without Mirrors," *The New York Times,* op-ed page, April 1, 1994.

17. See Arbatov, op. cit., p. 49.

18. *The New York Review of Books,* January 28, 1993.

19. *Rossiiskaya Gazeta,* June 1, 1992.

20. Adi Ignatius, "In Capitalist Moscow Young Business Grads Reap Money and Envy," *The Wall Street Journal,* August 2, 1993.

Glossary

anasha. Hashish.

apparat. The name denoting the entire civil service during the Soviet era. The elite membership of the apparat was known as the *nomenklatura* (see below).

apparatchik. Civil servant, often used indiscriminately to cover the *nomenklatura* officials as well.

avtoritet. Authority. Leader of one of the new commercial-oriented mafiya groups.

baklany. Punks.

bandity. Hoodlums, as referred to commonly by the police.

bespredel. Disorder, lit. "without limits."

blat. Old Soviet term for contacts in the right places. When someone manages to use contacts to get a favor or a job, it is done *po blatu*, through contacts.

blatnye. A catch-all term used by hoodlums to refer to themselves and their way of life. The gangs' answer to the police's description of them as *bandity*.

brat na pont. To bluff, to take someone by storm.

bratsky krug. Circle of brothers, said to be the main inner structure of the *vorovskoi mir*. Also called *bratskaya semyorka* (brotherhood of seven).

brodyagi. Vagabonds, leaders-in-training. A criminal caste below *vory*.

byki. Bodyguards, lit. "bulls."

chainik. Prison bully, lit. "cheap teapot," like the ones used in prisons.

chornye smorodiny. Nickname for the Caucasian *vory,* lit. "black currants." Also called simply *chornye, "*blacks."

dan. Taxes or tribute collected by racketeers.

fartsovshchik. Black-market dealer, usually young, working the street corners. Appeared in the 1980s.

gastrolyor. Guest criminal from other cities, lit. "guest artist."

grokhnut. To shoot, lit. "to bang." One of several slang words for killing.

kaif. A high from drugs. To be *v kaifu* is to be on a high.

kit. Big fish, lit. "whale"; a crime target.

klichka. A gang member's nickname or handle.

kolol. Drug injection.

lovit kaif. To get high on drugs.

lovrushniki. Another name for *chornye smorodiny,* the Caucasian *vory.*

limon. A "lemon," or one million rubles.

loshadka. Methadone, lit. "little horse" or "hobbyhorse."

lunakhod. Police van, lit. "moonwalker."

mafiya. Generic term used across the Soviet Union since the 1970s to denote

Party barons accused of corruption, black-market speculators, or some-times just sections of society the speaker does not happen to like. By 1992 it carried an additional meaning, describing the groups of criminal entre-preneurs and corrupt officials who came to prominence in the post-Soviet era.

makler. Apartment broker or fixer.

maslichny mak. Oily poppy, generally used to refer to opium production.

ment. Cop.

moshchenniki. Swindlers.

musor. Cop, lit. "garbage."

MVD. Ministry of Internal Affairs.

na narakh. Behind bars, in prison.

na svobodye. Out of prison, on the loose, lit. "free."

nayekhat. To raid, to apply gang pressure, to extort, to collect *dan,* lit. "to run over."

nomenklatura. The elite membership of the Soviet governing system, so called because their names appeared on the list of names (Lat. *nomencla-tura*) of the most loyal Party officials eligible for senior posts at home and abroad.

obshchak. Criminal treasury.

OMON. Elite counterterrorist unit of the Ministry of Internal Affairs (MVD).

opushchiny. Persons who have been raped in prison. From *opuskat*, "to lower."

organizatsiya. Organization. Another word for gang or syndicate, most often used abroad.

pakhan. Crime boss.

panama. Dummy company, usually set up by bureaucrats as a tax dodge in the 1990s.

patsani. Young lads—the warriors who make up criminal gangs.

perekupshchiki. Brokers or middlemen involved in smuggling arrangements.

pika. Knife, lit. "lance" or "pike."

po ponyatiyam. Lit. "by agreement," referring to a gentlemen's agreement reached among gangs or between a gang and its extortion targets.

podkhod. Coronation of a *vor,* lit. "approach."

posadit na piku. To stab to death, to cut up with a knife, lit. "to put on a pike."

prishit. To kill, lit. "to sew up."

prishli mne kapustu. Lit. "send me a cabbage," a way of saying you are owed money or a favor.

razboiniki. Gang warriors.

razborka. Settling of accounts, judgment (often achieved by violence).

sborshchiki. Collectors of taxes from traders at markets.

sdelat kozyol. Lit. "to turn into a goat," to make lower-class. Prison slang for making someone a homosexual slave.

shalit. To make mischief.

skhodka. Criminal assembly, council of *vory*.

shpana. Groups of common hoodlums or toughs.

sidet. To be in prison, lit. "to sit."

sportsmeny. Lit. "sportsmen," young former athletes or boxers who act as enforcers and bodyguards. Identified by the Western tracksuits they usually wear.

stakan. Lit. "a glass," a unit measurement used by drug dealers.

strelka. Council meeting or appointment, lit. "little arrow," as in the small hand of a watch.

suki. Turncoats, scabs, traitors, lit. "bitches."

tat. Thief.

telet chefir. Prison expression for making strong tea. Also means to have nothing left.

tolkach. Fixer, hustler. Used mostly during the Soviet era to identify black marketeers operating out of state enterprises.

torpedo. Contract killer.

tsekhovik. Owner of a black-market factory.

tusovka. A slice, as in the slice of society occupied by golden youth (*zolotaya molodyozh*) and young mafiosi.

ubrat. To kill, to waste, to rub out, lit. "to tidy up."

uryt. To kill, lit. "to bury."

vor. Crime lord, lit. "thief."

vor v zakonye. Godfather of a Russian gang, lit. "thief within the law or code."

vorovskoe blago. Criminal welfare. What every *vor* must defend.

vorovskoi mir. Thieves World, Thieves Society.

vzyat. To harass, to rob, lit. "to take," as in *vzyat laryok,* "to rob a kiosk." Also slang for taking bribes.

zamochit. To beat to death, lit. "to piss on."

zapodlo. Shady business; underground commerce.

A Note on Currency Rates

The massive, accelerating inflation during the final years of the Soviet Union and the first years of post-Communist power has made it difficult to provide constant, dependable equivalents for the ruble sums used in this book. Where possible, I have converted sums from rubles to dollars according to the rates prevailing at the time. But the following table can be used as a rough guide to values of the ruble. Through 1991 I used the official bank rate rather than the commercial rate. Because the ruble has fluctuated wildly, all rates are approximations.

November, 1990: 1 ruble = $1.75.
    $1 = 0.57 rubles
July, 1991: 1 ruble = $0.55.
    $1 = 1.81 rubles
September, 1992: 1 ruble = $0.005.
    $1 = 200 rubles
December, 1992: 1 ruble = $0.002.
    $1 = 500 rubles
March, 1993: 1 ruble = $0.001.
    $1 = 1,000 rubles
December, 1993: 1 ruble = $0.0008.
    $1 = 1,250 rubles
December, 1994: 1 ruble = $0.0003
    $1 = 3,306 rubles

Bibliography

Albats, Yevgeniya. *Mina Zamedlennogo Deistviya: Politichesky Portret KGB* (Delayed-Action Mine: Political Portrait of the KGB). Moscow: Russlit, 1992.

Arbatov, Georgi. *The System: An Insider's Life in Soviet Politics*. New York: Random House, 1992.

Aslund, Anders. *Gorbachev's Struggle for Economic Reform: The Soviet Reform Process, 1985–88*. Ithaca, N.Y.: Cornell University Press, 1989.

Berlin, Isaiah. *Russian Thinkers*. London: Penguin, 1979.

Berton, Kathleen. *Moscow: An Architectural History*. New York: Macmillan, 1977.

Beschloss, Michael, and Strobe Talbott. *At The Highest Levels: The Inside Story of the End of the Cold War*. Boston: Little, Brown, 1993.

Billington, James H. *The Icon and the Axe: An Interpretive History of Russian Culture*. New York: Vintage, 1970.

Bukovsky, Vladimir. *To Build a Castle: My Life as a Dissenter*. New York; Viking, 1978.

Bullock, Alan. *Hitler and Stalin: Parallel Lives*. New York: Knopf, 1992.

Buss, Gerald. *The Bear's Hug: Religious Belief and the Soviet State*. London: Hodder and Stoughton, 1987.

Chalidze, Valery. *Criminal Russia: Essays on Crime in the Soviet Union*. Translated from Russian by P. S. Falla. New York: Random House, 1977.

Clark, William A. *Crime and Punishment in Soviet Officialdom: Combatting Corruption in the Political Elite, 1965–1990*. Armonk, N.Y.: M. E. Sharpe, 1993.

Colton, Timothy J., and Thane Gustafson, eds. *Soldiers and the Soviet State*. Princeton, N.J.: Princeton University Press, 1990.

Conradi, Peter. *The Red Ripper*. New York: Dell, 1992.

Copetas, A. Craig. *Bear Hunting with the Politburo*. New York: Simon & Schuster, 1991.

Dallago, Bruno, Gianmaria Ajani, and Bruno Grancelli, eds. *Privatization and Entrepreneurship in Post-Socialist Countries*. New York: St. Martin's Press, 1992.

Deutscher, Isaac. *Stalin*. Harmondsworth: Penguin, 1986.

Ferro, Marc. *Nicholas II: The Last of the Tsars*. Translated by Brian Pearce. London: Viking, 1991.

Grossman, Gregory. *The Second Economy: Boon or Bane for the Reform of the First Economy?* Berkeley-Duke Occasional Papers on the Second Economy in the USSR, vol. 11, no. 2, December 1987.

Grossman, Gregory, with Keith Bush. *From the Command Economy to the Market*. Dartmouth: Dartmouth Publishing Co.,1991.

Grossman, Gregory. "A Note," in Karl C. Thalheim, *Stagnation or Change in Communist Economies?* London: Center for Research into Communist Economics, 1986.

Fishlock, Trevor. *Out of Red Darkness: Reports from the Collapsing Soviet Empire*. London: John Murray, 1992.

Herzen, Alexander. *From the Other Shore*. Oxford: Oxford University Press, 1979.

Laqueur, Walter Laqueur. *Black Hundred: The Rise of the Extreme Right in Russia*. New York: HarperCollins, 1993.

Leebaert, Derek, ed. *Soviet Military Thinking*. London: George Allen & Unwin, 1981.

Leggett, George. *The Cheka: Lenin's Political Choice*. Oxford: Clarendon Press, 1981.

Los, Maria. *Communist Ideology, Law and Crime: A Comparative View of the USSR and Poland*. London: Macmillan Press, 1988.

———. *The Second Economy in Marxist States*. London: Macmillan, 1990.

Lyons, Eugene. *Assignment in Utopia*. New York: Harcourt, Brace, 1937.

Maclean, Fitzroy. *To Caucasus: The End of All the Earth*. London: Jonathan Cape, 1976.

Martin, Lawrence. *Breaking with History*. Toronto: Doubleday, 1989.

Medvedev, Zhores. *Gorbachev*. London: Basil Blackwell, 1987.

Motyl, Alexander J., et al. *The Post-Soviet Nations: Perspectives on the Demise of the USSR*. New York: Columbia University Press, 1992.

Nahaylo, Bohdan, and Victor Swoboda. *Soviet Disunion: A History of the Nationalities Problem in the USSR*. New York: Free Press, 1990.

Pipes, Richard. *Russia under the Old Regime*. London: Weidenfeld and Nicolson, 1974. Middlesex: Penguin, 1984.

———. *The Russian Revolution*. New York: Vintage, 1991.

Podlesskikh, Georgi, and Andrei Tereshonok. *Vory v zakonye: Brosok k vlasti* (Thieves-in-Law: A Leap toward Power). Moscow: Khudozhestvennaya Literatura, 1994.

Remnick, David. *Lenin's Tomb: The Last Days of the Soviet Empire*. New York: Random House, 1993.

Rosner, Lydia. *The Soviet Way of Crime: Beating the System in the Soviet Union and the USA*. South Hadley, Mass: Bergin and Garvey, 1986.

Roxburgh, Angus. *The Second Russian Revolution*. London: BBC Books, 1991.

Schapiro, Leonard. *The Communist Party of the Soviet Union*. New York: Vintage, 1964.

Smith, Hedrick. *The New Russians*. London: Hutchinson, 1990.

Solzhenitsyn, Alexander. *The Gulag Archipelago*. London: Fontana, 1974.

Szamuely, Tibor. *The Russian Tradition*. London: Secker & Warburg, 1974. London: Fontana, 1988.

Timofeyev, Lev. *Russia's Secret Rulers*. Translated by Catherine A. Fitzpatrick. New York: Knopf, 1992.

Vaksberg, Arkady. *The Soviet Mafia*. Translated by John and Elizabeth Roberts. London: Weidenfeld and Nicolson, 1991.

Vitaliev, Vitali. *Special Correspondent: Investigating in the Soviet Union*. London: Hutchinson, 1990.

Voslensky, Michael. *Nomenklatura: Anatomy of the Soviet Ruling Class*. Translated by Eric Mosbacher. London: Bodley Head, 1984.

Yeltsin, Boris. *Against the Grain*. Translated by Michael Glenny. London: Jonathan Cape, 1990.

———. *The Struggle For Russia*. Translated by Catherine A. Fitzpatrick. New York: Times Books, 1994.

Yergin, Daniel, and Thane Gustafson. *Russia 2010 and What It Means for the World*. The Cera Report/Cambridge Energy Resource Associates. New York: Random House, 1993.

Zinoviev, Alexander. *Homo Sovieticus*. London: Victor Gollancz, 1985.

Index

eign activities of, 25, 56, 256–71; and
"gangster-bureaucrats," 70–71; and
"gangster-capitalists," 40, 43, 54–58;
in Grozny, 221–23; and gun smuggling, 209–14; history of, 9, 30–32,
34–36, 40–42, 99; and KGB, 293–
94, 310–11, 313, 320, 338; and lack
of respect for outsiders, 17; and law
and order, 17–18, 20, 26, 29–30, 38,
40–43, 87–88; leadership of, 28–43;
in legitimate business activity, 40, 54–
58, 159–60, 335–36; in Lithuania,
252–53; *mafiya* as term for, 21–22; and
military-industrial complex, 234–36;
and New Right organizations, 310–
15; new-style crime bosses in, 42–43,
56–57, 76–78, 80–81; nomenklatura and government bureaucrats as
allies of, 110–14, 130, 253, 335–42;
police's weaknesses against, 282–84;
political power of, 21–27, 36–40, 42,
55–56, 88–89, 221–23, 311–15, 335–
42; Prague summit of, 257; in prisons,
19–20, 33–34, 39, 40, 42, 85–86,
258, 260; on Russian frontier, 73–92;
shopkeeper's relationship with, 59–
62; silence surrounding, 47–48; social
events of, 161–67; structure of, 30–32,
39–40; Vedentsovo meeting of, 28–30,
335, 341; violence committed by, 15–
17, 24, 29–30, 39–40, 42, 60, 75–76,
79–85, 92, 132–33, 141, 174, 176, 178,
249–53, 258–60, 262, 291–92, 312,
338; wealth of new crime bosses, 40,
43, 57–58; youth's interest in, 26–27.
See also *Avtoritet* (authority); Chechen
gangs; Drug trafficking; Smuggling;
Vor
Ossetians, 216, 217

Pampurin, Andrei, 91–92
Panamas (dummy corporations), 129
Panichev, Valentin, 229
Perestroika, 4, 7, 42, 48, 57, 67–70, 107,
130, 233, 242, 253, 306, 321, 322,
327, 343
Perestroika (real estate firm), 149–54
Peresvetov, Ivan, 5

Peso, 38
Petroleum and oil, 126–27, 241, 243–44
Petrov, Aleksandr, 133
Pihl, Juri, 250
Pinochet, Agosto, 313–14
Plotnikov, Sergei, 89, 234
Plutonium, 224–27, 228
Podolski, 16–17
Polecat, 83
Police, 36, 44–54, 195, 199, 210–13,
281–84, 286–93, 325–26. *See also*
Crime
Poltaranin, Mikhail, 111
Popov, Gavriil, 147, 300–301, 311
"Post-Soviet Man," 117–30, 149–54,
178–79
Prisons, 19–20, 33–34, 39–42, 85–87,
117–20, 201, 258, 260, 281, 331
Privatization and private ownership: in
Baltics, 250; of banks, 101–6, 131–
43; and consumer boom, 120–28;
and Economic Freedom Party, 327–
28; entrepreneurs, 318–20, 324–30,
337; and KGB, 104–6, 112; lowering
barriers to, 342; and nomenklatura,
101–14; and organized crime, 22–23,
59–72, 344; outside of Russia, 124–
26; private monopolies, 22–23, 123;
property ownership debates, 121–24,
144, 155; public opinion on private
businessmen, 327; pun on, 104; real
estate speculation, 144–60; shopkeepers, 59–72, 120–21; and youth,
345–47
Procuracy system, 275, 280–82
Prokofiev, Yuri, 153
Property ownership, debates on, 121–24,
144, 155
Prostitution, 252, 253, 255, 256
Protection and security services, 59–72,
137–38, 161–79, 211, 287, 320, 334
Pugo, Boris, 51–52, 100

Radioactive materials. *See* Nuclear smug-
gling
Rashidov, Sharaf, 95
Raspberry, 38–39, 42

Rock Valley College

DEMCO